Researching on the Internet

Other Prima Computer Books

Available Now!

Access for Windows 95: The Visual Learning Guide
ACT! 2.0 for Windows: The Visual Learning Guide
Build a Web Site: The Programmer's Guide to Creating, Building, and Maintaining a Web Presence
CompuServe Information Manager for Windows: The Complete Membership Kit & Handbook
    (with two 3½-inch disks)
Create Wealth with Quicken, Second Edition
Cruising America Online: The Visual Learning Guide
Data Security
Excel for Windows 95: The Visual Learning Guide
IBM Smalltalk Programming for Windows & OS/2 (with 3½-inch disk)
Interactive Internet: The Insider's Guide to MUDs, MOOs, and IRC
Internet After Hours
Internet for Windows: America Online 2.5 Edition
The Internet Warp Book: Your Complete Guide to Getting Online with OS/2
Introduction to Internet Security—From Basics to Beyond
Microsoft Office in Concert, Professional Edition
Migrating to Windows 95
OS/2 Warp: Easy Installation Guide
PageMaker 5.0 for Windows: Everything You Need to Know
PowerPoint for Windows 95: The Visual Learning Guide
PROCOMM PLUS for Windows: The Visual Learning Guide
Sound Blaster: Making WAVes with Multimedia
Stacker Multimedia
UnInstaller 3: Uncluttering Your PC
The USENET Navigator Kit (with 3½-inch disk)
The Warp Book: Your Definitive Guide to Installing and Using OS/2 v3
Web Browsing with America Online
Web Browsing with Netscape Navigator 1.1
Web Browsing with NETCOM NetCruiser
Web Browsing with Prodigy
Web Browsing with The Microsoft Network
WinComm PRO: The Visual Learning Guide
Windows 3.1: The Visual Learning Guide
Windows 95: The Visual Learning Guide
Windows 95: A to Z
Windows 95: Easy Installation Guide
The Windows 95 Book: Your Definitive Guide to Installing and Using Windows 95
WinFax PRO 4: The Visual Learning Guide
Word 6 for the Mac: The Visual Learning Guide
Word for Windows 95: The Visual Learning Guide
WordPerfect 6.1 for Windows: The Visual Learning Guide

How to Order:
For information on quantity discounts contact the publisher: Prima Publishing, P.O. Box 1260BK, Rocklin, CA 95677-1260; (916) 632-4400. On your letterhead include information concerning the intended use of the books and the number of books you wish to purchase.

Researching on the Internet

The Complete Guide to Finding, Evaluating, and Organizing Information Effectively

Robin Rowland
Dave Kinnaman

PRIMA PUBLISHING

P is a trademark of Prima Publishing, a division of Prima Communications, Inc.

Prima Publishing is a trademark of Prima Communications, Inc.

Prima Online is a trademark of Prima Publishing.

Prima Computer Books is an imprint of Prima Publishing, Rocklin, California 95677.

Project Editors: Stefan Grünwedel and Dan Foster

Editorial Assistant: Kelli Crump

ISBN: 0-7615-0063-4

Library of Congress Catalog Card Number: 94-74105

Printed in the United States of America

96 97 98 AA 10 9 8 7 6 5 4 3

Contents

Acknowledgments . . . . *ix*
Introduction . . . . *xi*

1 Getting Started **1**
A Brief Internet Primer 1
Basic Hardware and Software 5
Connecting with Software 9
Internet Messenger: Target E-mail 13
Internet-a-Phobia 16

2 Choosing a Service Provider **25**
The Client-Server Model 26
Direct Internet Access 27
Indirect Internet Access 28
Commercial Online Services 31
In-House Connections 32
Internet Hardware and Software 33
Possible Internet Access Problems 36
Internet Access Checklist 39
Further Resources 42

3 Getting Ready for Research **45**
What Areas Are the Best on the Internet for Research? 47
What Areas Are Not the Best on the Internet for Research? 47
Getting Ready for Research 48
The Tao of Good Research 49
The Who, What, When, Where, Why, and How of Research 50
Technical Skills 53
The Advantages of Computers and the Internet 55
Online or Offline? 65
Evaluation 66
The Ethics of Research 72

4   Internet Research Tools **73**
E-mail and Mailing Lists 73
Usenet Newsgroups 81
Gopher, Veronica, and Jughead 83
World Wide Web Browsers 84
File Transfer Protocol (FTP) and Archie 86
Hytelnet and Telnet/Remote Log-in Resource Listings 90
Internet Relay Chat (IRC) 93
News Scanning Services 93
Evaluating the Internet at the Washington Post 95

5   Keeping Up with the Internet with FTP **99**
An FTP Shopping List 100
The Net Changes Daily 101
Net Awareness 101
FTP Basics 103
Three Methods of FTP 104
FTP Command Line Examples 110
What's SimTel? 122
Summary of Basic FTP Commands Used in Examples 124
Credit Where Credit Is Due 125
FTP Examples with WS_FTP 126
Key FTP Sites for the Changing Internet 130
Massachusetts Institute of Technology—Usenet FAQs 138
SimTel Software Mirrors 139
Using FTP Without Direct Internet Access 142
MIT Treasure House 148
Filenames Can Be Misleading 150
John Iliff and His Window on the Internet FTP File 153

6   What Is the Internet? **157**
Present at Creation: Len Kleinrock, UCLA 157
Putting on the Net: Michael Hart, Project Gutenberg 162
Remembering the Holocaust: William Connelly, U.S. 172
Tracking Alzheimer's on the Internet: Dr. J. Edward Jackson, UCSD 176
Network Cyberspace: George Lewis, NBC News 177
The Evolving Internet: Dan Tinker, University of Toronto 178
Sunrise on the Internet: William Graves, UNC 180
More Tips for Researchers 182
The Internet Is Only a Tool 183

7 Netiquette **185**
Be Nice to Other People 186
Be a Lifelong Learner 193
Give Back to the Net 196
Communicate Clearly 199
Conserve Network Resources 201
Behave Lawfully and Humanely 204

8 Focusing Your Aims **209**
Outline Before You Start 210
Working Offline 220
Online Temptation: Don't Be an Information Pack Rat 235

9 Libraries on the Internet **237**
The University of Michigan 238
National Libraries 244
Other Library Resources on the Internet 255
Research Library Organizations 259
Library Mailing Lists 259

10 Stop Signs on the Infobahn **261**
Whose Law Applies? 263
Whose law applies? 264
The Long Arm of the Law 265
Copyright 266
Citing Online References 272
Moral Rights 273
Neighboring Rights 275
Patent Law 275
Trade Secrets 276
Defamation 276
Identity Hacking 282
Censoring the Internet 284
The Future of Law on the Internet 287
Finding It on the Internet 288

11 The E-mail Interview **293**
Lurk and Research 295
Networking on the Net 299
Finding Family, Finding Friends 301
ProfNet 303

Why Conduct an E-mail Interview? 304
E-mail Success Stories 311
The Delphi Study: Academic E-mail 312

12   Finding the Right Information with Gopher **315**
Gopher Basics 316
Gopher Client Software 318
WSGopher Toolbar Buttons 319
Gopher Bookmarks 321
Saving and Printing Files with Gopher 324
A Beginning Inventory of Gopher Bookmarks 325
Gopher Searches with Veronica 329
Gopher Searches with Jughead 333
UNIX Gopher Client Instructions 333
More Gopher Information 339
From Here 340

13   Researching on the World Wide Web **341**
The Web is Easy to Use 342
Searching Indexes on the Web 344
Web Resources Organized by Subject 353
From Here 355

14   Government Resources on the Net **357**
The U.S. Federal Government 357
U.S. State Government on the Net 361
Canada 361
International Government Sources 367

15   The Net for Everyone **369**
The Internet and Scholars 369
Finding Electronic Journals Online 372
The Business of the Internet 372
Software Agents 374

Index *377*

Acknowledgments

We both gratefully acknowledge the inventiveness, creativity, generosity and diversity of the multitudes of people who every day contribute time, effort, and vitality to the Internet, without whom this book would have been impossible.

We appreciate the many ways that our agent, Margot Maley of Waterside Productions, has guided and improved this project. Also Matt Wagner of Waterside for his early support and advice.

We also thank Sherri Morningstar at Prima Publishing, who originally commissioned the book, and our editor, Stefan Grünwedel—as well as Dan Foster and Kelli Crump, who kept the project together to the end.

—*Robin Rowland and Dave Kinnaman*

Thanks first to my collaborator on this project, Dave Kinnaman, who joined me in a project that was both demanding and exhilarating. He was supportive and, when necessary, critical.

A number of others also need special thanks. Larry Rose, Josh Hodgson, Brian Alton, and other special friends who gave encouragement and support throughout the project. I want to thank my colleagues and friends, first at CTV National News and, later, at CBC National News for their support. Also thanks to my colleagues and students at Ryerson Polytechnic University School of Journalism for their advice and understanding.

Thanks to Christa Weber and Dan O'Brien who transcribed the interview tapes.

I interviewed 200 people in person—by phone and by e-mail—for this book and many (not all, of course) are quoted in the pages. Thanks to all. About 100 more answered e-mail questions for certain aspects of the book. Special thanks to Chin Huang, Larry Spero, Dean Tudor, Nora Paul, Margot Williams, Tom Johnson, and Vivienne Monty for their special advice and help.

In the software industry, special thanks to Bea McKinney at AskSam, Donna Loughlin at NetManage, Neil Lubin at Micro Logic, and Dave Carter and Chris Brockbank at Microsoft.

—Robin Rowland

I especially want to say "thank you" and "bless you" to two people who gave me hope and quick encouragement when I needed it most—Jill Ellsworth and Jerry MyCue. I also offer my deepest appreciation to LouAnn, Jerry, Richard, and Jill for their gracious and timeless comfort, support, and trust.

—Dave Kinnaman

Introduction

The Internet: it's the Net, the Web, the matrix. It's chaotic, anarchistic, organized, and authoritative. The Internet is "in." It's hot. It's the place to be in the '90s.

Thousands of virtual communities populate the Internet—some small, some large—stretching from Bangor to Barcelona. The Internet is the research tool for the 21st century.

As a researcher (student, librarian, journalist, business leader, or scholar), you can meet people on the Internet from Moscow, Montreal, and Milwaukee, the rich and famous, experts from every field of human endeavor, and thousands of ordinary folks. You can visit those people—electronically. The electronic doors on many (but not all) of those virtual communities are wide open. As for the others, you can ring the (electronic) bell, and often you'll find the doors swinging open.

On the Internet you'll find megabytes of data: the latest financial figures, government reports from to A to Z and back again, as well as some of the greatest literature created by human beings. If you want to find out about tattoos, the Internet can tell you about designs and how people can get a "tat" and get it safely. If you want the latest information from scientists mapping genes in the human body, you can find it on the Net. If you're in fourth grade and you're assigned to design a stadium for a National Basketball Association franchise, you'll find help for that project on the Net too.

Welcome to the world's greatest public library. More than you can imagine is at your fingertips on the Internet. Checking out information is easy. It'll be on your computer's hard drive in seconds.

Who Should Read This Book?

If you want to do research on the Internet, this book is for you. You may be:

» A student who has just received an Internet account at a public school, high school, or university

» A reporter, editor, or research librarian for a newspaper or television network and the company is about to get Net access

» Working in a one-person public library with a dial-up account

» A corporate librarian who has to get the latest information for a dozen executives with widely different demands

» An experienced hand at a major research university

» A small business person working from your home office, miles from anywhere, connected by a single phone line

» A company employee working in a glass and steel tower at the crossroads of the world's communications networks in New York, Los Angeles, Toronto, London, or Hong Kong

» Someone who is curious about the Internet and wants to learn how to find information to meet personal needs

You all have one thing in common. You are on the Internet for a purpose—to do research. You may have heard news stories about the Internet and want to try it out. You may feel you have to get on the Internet to stay competitive. You may be a scientist finding that scholarly journals published on paper just can't keep up with your field. Or you're a reporter on deadline, you need the key piece of information for your story, and you need it *fast*.

This book is about the Internet, the computer, and research. It combines all three. If you're new to the Net, if you've just bought your first computer, *Researching on the Internet* will help you through those first steps. If you've been on the Net for years but can't find that crucial file you downloaded six months ago, read on. If you've done paper research for 20 years and know libraries like the back of your hand but you're just merging onto the information superhighway, this book will boost you up the ramp (and help you avoid all those clichés in the future).

Research Is *Not* Net Surfing

Are you ready to be a hero? That's what you'll be if you do research on the Internet. Why a hero? Because, in mythology, a hero is a man, woman, or child who sets out on a journey through a strange and magical land with a *purpose*.

The world wide spider web of the Internet is a strange and magical land. The holy grail is the object of your research.If you're going to do research on the Internet you will have a goal: an essay to write for school, a report to produce for your news organization, a key piece of data to find for your business or for a library client. Keep that goal in mind while we look at Net surfing.

Millions of people surf the Net; you may even do it yourself. Think of surfing. Ocean surfing. It's a sun-screen afternoon in Southern California. Waves crash onto a sandy beach. You inhale the salt spray. The hot sun sparkles high above the blue-green ocean in a cloudless blue sky. The surfers, in wet suits, look like tiny black insects as they float on their boards waiting for the right wave.

Come closer, get in the water. It's cool, but you're soon used to it. You can see the waves coming from the west. The first one is small and you let it pass. The wave gently picks you up as it goes by, then it bumps you back down. The next one builds far out. It's a good one and you ride it in. As you near the beach, the white sea foam dances around you. Then you're on the beach, grasping the wet sand with your toes.

Now you're Net surfing, sitting at your desk, watching your computer monitor. You're on the Net because you enjoy it. It's fascinating to virtually leap—in just seconds—from your chair to a World Wide Web site in Melbourne, Australia. You've heard about a piece of interesting software stored at a Net site in Norway, so you're off there with a click of your mouse. You find that software and moments later a copy is safe on your hard drive. You're searching for a site on the World Wide Web, one a friend has told you about, and you're looking for the right pointer. On your way, something else catches your eye and you're off on another road, another journey. You follow that trail and you find yourself climbing the volcanoes of Mars. That's Net surfing.

Now to research. You have a goal. You have to go on the Internet, find what you need, and bring it back alive. That's why you're a hero. Joseph Campbell, in his classic book, *The Hero with a Thousand Faces*, writes of the typical hero who "ventures forth from the world of common day into a region of supernatural wonder; fabulous forces are there encountered and a decisive victory is won: the hero comes back from his mysterious adventure with the power to bestow boons on his fellow man."

On the road, the hero meets the first challenge, the guardian of the threshold. You too will have to meet the challenge of finding an Internet service provider and setting up your system before you can journey into a new wondrous world.

"Beyond the threshold," Campbell writes, "the hero journeys through a world of unfamiliar yet strangely intimate forces, some of which severely threaten him (tests), some of which give magical aid (helpers). When he arrives at the nadir of the mythological round, he undergoes a supreme ordeal and gains his reward."

That's a good description of research on the Internet.

As you can see in Figure I-1, a whole world is just a mouse click away on the Internet.

The Research Process

As a journalist, I've been doing research for 20 years, in libraries, in archives, by snail mail (that means letters on old-fashioned paper, with envelopes and stamps), on the phone, and now on the Internet.

What I've been doing instinctively for years, librarians give a simple name. They call it the *process* of research. To a librarian, the process of research is as important as the "button pushing" of hardware and software.

It's the aim of this book to help you do research on the Internet, no matter what kind of service provider you use, or what software you choose. Once you know the process, once you know the basics of research, then you can keep up

Figure I-1.
The University of Buffalo's clickable map of the World Wide Web is a gateway for research on the Internet.

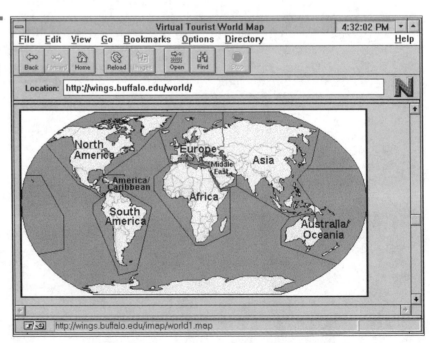

with the Internet as it grows, as it changes daily, as more and more information becomes available, and as Net browsing software evolves.

The focus will be on the *process* of doing research on the Internet. To do the research, you do have to know how to push some software buttons. I'll show you how I do research on the Internet. You can learn to push the same buttons.

To work on the Net, I use a variety of Microsoft Windows compatible software. Specifically, I use a commercial application, Netmanage's Chameleon (version 4.1) suite for the Internet, plus many of the popular freeware or shareware programs created for Internet access, such as Hgopher, WSGopher, and Eudora Pro.

The Internet is built around the UNIX operating system, so I sometimes find it convenient to use UNIX applications for specific tasks. You can easily use Macintosh computers too. Almost all computer platforms have Internet (TCP/IP) software access.

Evaluating Data

A key problem facing any researcher is evaluating the material you find on the Net. *Researching on the Internet* won't just tell you how you can find material on the Internet; it will describe how information gets on the Net. It will also be a "people" book with information and advice from researchers, software designers, and list moderators who work on the Net.

The examples will help make it easier for you to judge material once you find it.

By knowing how the information gets on the Internet, you will be able to decide the value—and validity—of the research material you find. And if you find what you are looking for, you may be a hero after all.

How This Book Is Organized

Researching on the Internet is a project-based book. It will tell you:

- » How to choose a service provider
- » Hardware and software basics
- » How to get ready for research
- » The research tools on the Internet
- » What the Internet is and explain its customs
- » About the value of working offline

» How to handle material once you've found it

» The legal problems facing Internet researchers

Researching on the Internet has an international perspective. The Web knows no boundaries. The material you want may be stored in Australia or Hong Kong. The person with the answer to your question may be in Johannesburg or Bangkok, or may live right around the corner. The software on the Net comes from around the world. Canadians developed Archie and Hytelnet. Mosaic and its descendants hail from the United States. From Australia comes Trumpet Winsock, which allows PCs a "live" SLIP connection to the Net. HGopher comes from Great Britain and WSGopher comes from Idaho. Easyview, a free form text retrieval database for the Macintosh, was developed in Turkey. The world beckons!

Ready to sign on? Let's get started.

1
Getting Started

You're a researcher. You've worked in libraries and archives. You've used the phone and old-fashioned shoe leather. Now you're about to get on the Internet—or, if you're already on, to use the Internet to its full potential.

In the summer of 1994, an estimated 3,212,000 hosts supported the Internet. In the Spring of 1995, *Time* magazine estimated that there were 4.8 million Internet hosts. That means there is a lot of information out there. You're joining approximately 30 to 40 million people around the world, exploring something that is almost alive, growing daily, evolving.

This book aims to be researcher-friendly, to eliminate technical barriers whenever possible, and to enable you to concentrate on doing research on the Internet. If you're looking for a service provider, the next chapter will tell you how to find one that will fit your budget, and your technical and research needs. This chapter is for those of you are who are just starting. It briefly tells you what technical information is important, regardless of whether you access the Internet from your home office, in a company or university.

A Brief Internet Primer

So, what is the Internet? Put simply, it's a data web, a network of information and ideas, a worldwide conduit connecting people. The words "information superhighway" are already a cliché (some people are now calling it the Infobahn or I-way), but like all clichés, the "information superhighway" has a bit of truth in it. Highways have always joined people and communities. The Nile was the highway for ancient Egypt. Modern American superhighways follow forest tracks first made by natives. Along with trade and travelers, ideas followed those ancient highways, technical ideas for art, science, and engineering, for peace and war. Those travelers recounted myths, legends, tall tales, and factual history. Often it would take years, or even decades, for ideas to travel from one end of a continent to another. Now everything moves at the speed of light.

In the 1990s, information travels through an extensive network of computers, joined by local area networks, telephone lines, fiber optic lines, and communications satellites. One of those networks is the Internet (there are others). The Internet is often called a network of networks.

The Internet is also a method of linking computers so they can talk to each other. It's that simple. The computers use a "protocol" to talk to one another. A protocol is defined either as a language or a rule book that lets the communication take place. On the Internet, two protocols help each other out. Together they are known as TCP/IP, or Transmission Control Protocol/Internet Protocol. With TCP/IP, a home PC can talk to a VAX mainframe on another continent; a Macintosh can communicate with a supercomputer in the next block.

If you're sending an electronic mail message, the Transmission Control Protocol breaks up the message into small *packets*. The Internet Protocol sends the packets on their way, just like the post office or a private courier with paper mail (also called "snail mail"). Then, at the destination, TCP puts the packets back together in the proper order and the recipient reads your e-mail message.

The Internet uses a system called *packet switching*. Each one of the packets created by the TCP has information about its origin and destination. Various computers read the destination code and send the packet along to the next closer computer, until it reaches its destination.

Some other networks connected to the Internet don't use TCP/IP. The large academic network known as *Bitnet* has its own protocol. Information from Bitnet enters the Internet through what's known as a gateway. Mailing lists are prime tools for the researcher and the most popular mailing list sofware program, LISTSERV, began on Bitnet. Many private bulletin board systems that exchange information with the Internet by telephone use a protocol known as UUCP, or UNIX to UNIX Copy Program, to talk to the Internet. The popular Usenet, which has thousands of newsgroups, started using UUCP to send its information among computers.

To be strictly technical, the Internet is defined by the TCP/IP protocol, not the Bitnet or UUCP or OSI (Open Systems Interconnection) protocols. But with the recent explosion of public and media interest in the Internet, anyone connected to the Net by any protocol speaks of being "on the Internet."

Now we come to UNIX. UNIX is an operating system, not unlike DOS or Windows or System 7. It's a question of evolution. The first computers on the first version of the Internet, the United States Department of Defense Advanced Research Projects Agency (DARPA), used UNIX. Bell Labs developed UNIX in the early 1960s for big mainframe computers and a multitasking, multiuser environment. UNIX allowed many people in a university, research lab, or office to use the computer at the same time.

When UNIX began, computers were at a relatively early stage of their evolution. The computer language and its commands were created by computer people for computer people. That means that many UNIX commands are even more obscure than the ones in DOS. If you have only used a graphical user interface (GUI) such as Microsoft Windows and the Macintosh, UNIX can seem mysterious and frustrating.

UNIX works like DOS, with command line prompts. Instead of the C prompt one sees with DOS, a UNIX prompt is often a dollar sign ($) or a percent sign (%). The UNIX system has many languages and dialects, and it has also developed its own version of the English language. A command line system for UNIX is called a *shell*; a standard UNIX Internet account that returns a command line prompt is called a *shell account*. You can have a shell account through dial-up access or through a network or both.

As more and more people join the Internet, the free market (and the free market has a special meaning on the Internet) is providing ways around the need to know a lot about UNIX. For some users, it's the only way to survive on the Net. The easier it is use the tools on the Net, the easier it is to do research.

In the past year or so, a live telephone link to the Internet using TCP/IP has become popular. There are two TCP/IP protocols. One is SLIP, which stands for Serial Line Internet Protocol, and a second is PPP; Point to Point Protocol. A SLIP/PPP account is often difficult to set up if you are using a dial-up service provider. (If you're using a Local Area Network, the network administrator will save you the headache.) Once it is running, however, a SLIP/PPP allows Windows or Macintosh software to do most of the work for you. We'll take a longer look at SLIP and PPP later in this book.

Internet Tools

The Internet is an information system. That means you need tools to find and retrieve that information. In brief, the most common Internet tools are:

» **E-mail**: Electronic mail.

» **Usenet Newsgroups**: At present there are approximately 13,000 newsgroups, in many languages, on the Internet. These forums range from groups for cat lovers, haiku writers, and gardeners through technical discussions of various aspects of the computer world to frank discussions of human sexuality.

» **Telnet**: A system for signing into remote Internet computers.

» **FTP**: File Transfer Protocol. A system for downloading files from a remote site to your own computer or uploading from your computer to a remote site.

» **Archie**: A keyword and name search system for finding files at FTP sites.

» **Gopher**: A menu-based system for finding information on the Internet. Once a researcher finds a document's title, it can be retrieved by using arrow keys on a command line Gopher menu or by clicking the mouse using Gopher software on a PC. A collection of documents is called a *Gopher site*.

» **Veronica**: A indexing and keyword retrieval system for finding *titles* or *file references* of documents at many Gopher sites.

» **Jughead**: An information retrieval system for Gopher using a search defined by the user.

» **IRC**: A system for live conversations on the Internet with talk among people from all over the world connected by the Net to discuss a topic of interest.

» **WAIS**: Wide-Area Information System. WAIS is another search system. It finds information by searching for keywords across databases, file directories and lists, documents, newsgroups, and other Internet resources.

» **World Wide Web:**. The World Wide Web is an Internet browsing and information retrieval system. It uses a system called *hypertext* to link one document to many others. A hypertext link allows you to click on a reference and jump to another document. For example, if you are reading a Web page of medical news, and you want to find the original article from a medical journal, a hypertext link could lead either to a reference to that journal or to the text of the journal itself, in another computer a thousand miles from the first.

The launch of the World Wide Web coincided with increased government, business, and personal interest in the information superhighway. The addition of easy, graphical *Web browsers*, such as Mosaic and Netscape, made it easy for more people to *surf* (browse) the Internet and brought us today's explosion of interest in exploring the Net.

All the Internet tools and their advantages and disadvantages for research will be discussed in later chapters.

Basic Hardware and Software

The Internet was originally designed so a variety of computers could talk to one another. That means you can get on the Internet, no matter what kind of computer you have.

The people contacted in researching this book use a variety of methods to get on the Internet, ranging from sophisticated to simple. Here's a sampling of the hardware and software (don't worry about the technical terms):

The Pompidou Centre in Paris, France:

We are connected to the Internet through a 64K line which is hooked to a CISCO 4000. This router is our Internet gateway. Our LAN consists of interconnected Ethernet and Phonenet networks. The software depends on the type of machine we're on. On UNIX platforms, there is a set of "standard" TCP/IP tools, such as Berkeley Sendmail and NNTP, Telnet, FTP, and CNEWS. On the Macintosh's, we use MacTCP, and on PCs, Chameleon.

A reporter in Arizona:

Dell Pentium (P60) PC, U.S. Robotics Sportster 14.4 fax/modem, and Delrina WinComm Pro through a university Net account.

A professor at Washington University in St. Louis, Missouri:

We connect via about 80 CISCO routers, 7500 nodes with various hardware. I use a Mac.

A professor at the University of Wisconsin:

A desktop PC with Ethernet card connected to a mainframe using Elm (an electronic mail program in UNIX).

A professor at the University of California at San Diego:

A 386/387 20 MHz IBM-PC clone (no name) with Xircom Ethernet card to Novell Network to campus mainframe via fiber optic cable; a 486/66 laptop with either ATT KIT 14.4 PCMCIA modem or Xircom 10bT network card via same network or via mainframe with modem; ccmail for MS DOS; PCplus (DOS or Windows); Mosaic for Windows.

A librarian in Washington, D.C.:

Networked NCSA Mosaic (Windows-based Web browser), Archie, FTP, Telnet, etc. (Since our server is still largely under construction, I have also used a private service called Delphi just to "get my feet wet." I also have an additional private access to e-mail and some other oddities through a local BBS.)

A public school system in Michigan:

We have a direct connect to the Internet by way of a CISCO router and 56K baud modem, which serves our nine school buildings, all connected by fiber. We are currently using LanWorkplace for DOS, Telnet, FTP, Gopher, and WAIS, which can run on our lowest 8088 workstations. We will soon be using Netscape, which requires more power and memory, on our 386 and 486 workstations.

A major U.S. television network's news division:

The news service is hooked up to the Internet for e-mail purposes through a DEC VAX system. Additionally, a small number of us have PCs of various sorts connected to Netcom, CompuServe, and America Online.

What do I use? At home, I use a 486/66 Ampaq PC clone and a Zoom 14.4K voice fax modem to connect to two Internet services: Internex Online, a dial-up commercial service in Toronto, and a second at Ryerson Polytechnic University where I teach part time. In an office I share at Ryerson, a 486/25 connects to the university computer system called Matrix. Matrix consists of several powerful computers linked by a campus communications backbone. The computers work together and appear to the user almost as a single machine. Users can access Matrix from PCs and terminals throughout the campus, and from a home computer via modem.

It's traditional on the Internet to give computers and software unique and sometimes unusual names. The Internet searching tools are named for the comic book characters Archie, Jughead, and Veronica. At Ryerson, the three computers (or servers) are called Malthus, Turing, and Hopper. Malthus and Turing are IBM RS/6000 machines running the AIX operating system, one of the many dialects of UNIX. Hopper is a Sun SPARC server 1000 dedicated to processing electronic mail traffic within the campus and across the Internet. Hopper runs Solaris, another dialect of UNIX similar to AIX. Matrix also is tied into the university library's online system.I also use my IBM 486/25 subnotebook and an external modem when I'm not at either location.

The beauty of the Internet is its connectivity. Almost any computer will open this world to you. But what is the best kind of computer to do research on the Internet? That topic is next.

The Computer

The computer is often provided for you by your school, university, or employer. If you have a choice—or if you're working from home—get the most powerful computer you can, with the fastest modem and the largest hard drive you can afford. The more powerful the computer and modem, the fewer the barriers to your search on the Internet, especially if you're using the new Windows Internet applications.

With more and more Internet tools available for Microsoft Windows, the best choice is a 486 or higher IBM-compatible PC. Although a 25 MHz 486 will work, higher speeds work best with today's software, so, if possible, get a 33 MHz or 66 MHz CPU—better yet, if you can afford it, get a high-speed 90 or 100 MHz Pentium.

Get the most memory you can afford. For Windows 95, 4MB is barely adequate, and you could run into trouble if you are using a Web browser (more about that later) and access an especially large file. If you can afford it, 8MB is a good choice and 12 or 16 will enhance your work. You can never have too much RAM. Windows 95 really wants 16MB of RAM.

A large hard drive is essential. If you're doing research, or accessing a large number of mailing lists and newsgroups, the files on your disk can grow rapidly. Thus a 250 to 500MB hard drive is required at least for a beginning researcher. It can handle all the software you'll need, plus raw data downloaded from the Internet, and organized data you've already analyzed. One gigabyte (1,000 MB) hard drives are common among more experienced researchers.

Similarly, get the best monitor you can afford. While most people are still using 14-inch monitors, a 17-inch high-resolution color monitor is easier on the eyes during a long online session.

A Modem

If you're not connected to a business or university LAN (local area network), you'll need a modem to connect to the Internet. Again, if research is your aim, get the fastest possible modem.

The 14.4 (14,400) baud modem has quickly become the standard as of 1995. Older 2400 and 9600 baud modems are too slow to handle traffic for Windows-driven World Wide Web browsers such as Netscape, Mosaic, or Cello. The older modems can, however, handle basic text-based Internet functions.

The demand for data is increasing the popularity of the 28.8 baud modem. Internal modems are cheaper by about $20 to $50 than external modems. An external modem has the advantage of portability. You can always use a high-speed external modem with an older, backup computer, if your main unit has a major problem. For high-speed communications (such as 14.4 and 28.8 baud) with an external modem, you will need an UART (Universal Asynchronous Receiver/Transmitter) serial card or port if your PC doesn't have one. The 16550 UART chip takes over some of the modem control from your computer's CPU, handling flow control and buffering the information you're sending back and forth to make sure none is lost.

Caution

A high speed internal modem usually has the 16650 UART chip as part of the board. Its external equivalent modem from the same manufacturer won't. Always check the specifications before you buy to see if you also should purchase a new serial card with a better UART chip.

Notebooks and subnotebooks can use either a mini external modem or connect to a PCMCIA slot on the notebook. Again, don't choose anything less than a 14.4K modem and double-check the specifications for both the notebooks and the PCMCIA modem to make sure they are compatible.

Other Hardware

You're doing a lot of research. Your data is irreplaceable. Consider purchasing a tape backup system and back up frequently. If you're going to be online a lot, or have a live connection to the Internet (at a large company or institution) an Uninterruptable Power Supply (UPS) may also be a consideration. (A UPS also protects your PC from power surges.)

Tip

You can connect to the Internet even if you are on a bare-bones budget. I still keep an 8 MHz IBM-compatible XT with a 30MB hard drive and an old 2400 baud modem as an ultimate backup. On the XT, and with the old modem, I use the menu system created by my service provider and UNIX commands to find what I need on the Internet. While an older computer and a slow modem limit the Internet tools available to you on UNIX, the old equipment won't stop you from exploring the Web. If you have an older computer, but can upgrade the modem, invest in the fastest modem you can. It's the speed of the modem, not the computer, that counts. Later, when you can afford it, you can upgrade the computer system.

Phone and Other Communication Lines

Your home telephone line is usually fine for dialing into the Internet. If you're going to be online for hours, however, and you can afford it, invest in a second phone line. That line could handle both modem and fax traffic, leaving your primary phone number free for voice calls and messages.

Phone lines come in three basic types. First is the good old-fashioned twisted pair copper phone line invented by Alexander Graham Bell. It's sometimes called POTS (Plain Old Telephone Service) by phone company techs when they're speaking English, and known as an "asynchronous switched analog line" in tech talk. Second, there is an enhanced phone line usually called a *data capable circuit* and, third, a fully digital *ISDN* (Integrated Service Digital Network) line.

If you have the best modem you can afford, one with both the latest error detection and compression capability, POTS should work well for your needs. A data capable circuit is much more expensive. If a phone company does offer this kind of circuit, they will bill you at business line rates. Generally, a data capable circuit is the same POTS line that comes into your home, but the company tests the line and adds equipment such as amplifiers and filters at the customer's location and the phone company switching station. The phone company usually guarantees a higher level of service with a minimum of line noise.

An ISDN line can provide a digital line to a service provider, the phone company, or both. The ISDN signal is all digital, from one end to the other, but, in most cases, is still switched through the public telephone network. The ISDN usually has three lines or channels. Generally, two 64K "B" channels carry voice and data, and the third 16K "D" channel controls the signal. The ISDN ends with a NT1 or Network Terminator box.

An ISDN line does not use a modem. It uses equipment called a Terminal Adapter (TA) that has a similar function to a traditional modem. The TA sends the digital signal from your computer down the line to the service provider. A terminal adapter is available either as an external unit or an internal board.

There are also three types of Point to Point leased lines used by Internet service providers and large businesses that have a lot of net traffic. Many Internet service providers receive their signal with a 56K Fairly High Compressible Bandwith leased line. You'll hear a lot about the most powerful Internet lines. A T1 line can handle data at 1.5MBs per second. A T3 line, the top of the Internet communications heap, handles data at 44.7MBs a second. The cost of T1 and T3 is too expensive for individual users but may be part of a corporate or university communications system.

Connecting with Software

You have several ways to connect to the Internet. The first is by using traditional communications software with a freeware, shareware, or commercial program. There are also specific communications programs geared for accessing Internet electronic mail and newsgroups. A third type of communications software creates a live connection between the Internet and your computer using the TCP/IP protocol over a SLIP or PPP connection.

Communications Software

You'll find some form of communications software sold with your modem. That software will work well for most purposes. Robust shareware is also available if you're on a student or low budget. If you're connecting to the Internet with a communications package, it is probably best to invest in high-end communications software such as Wincomm PRO, PROCOMM, or Crosstalk, which have features to make your life on the Internet a little easier.Windows 95 has a new feature called HyperTerminal that has many of the features of other commercial communications programs. It's an upgrade of the limited Terminal program packed with Windows 3.1.

Almost all communications programs have some form of scripting that automates your access to the Internet. It's convenient to get up in the morning and have the computer run a script to retrieve your e-mail and newsgroups while you're taking a shower or making breakfast.

Terminal Emulation

Many of the computers you once saw in offices before PCs became a standard (and you may see them even today in some offices) were not really computers. They are called "dumb terminals" because with little memory and processing power, they are pretty stupid. A dumb terminal usually has a simple, monochrome video terminal that displays just text, a keyboard and a line connecting it with a powerful minicomputer or mainframe elsewhere in the building.

If you're on the Internet, you're going to be talking to many different computers. To do this, you're going to need a communications program that will pretend to be a dumb terminal. That part of the communications program is called *terminal emulation*.

The most popular form of terminal emulation is VT100 or VT102, which was originally used with Digital Equipment Corporation computers. DEC computers successfully took on IBM in the mainframe and minicomputer market in 1980. VT100 became an accepted standard on the Net. Unless you're told otherwise by your service provider, set your communications software to VT100 emulation (see Figure 1-1).

Transfer Protocol

The other important feature of a communications program is the transfer protocol—the language you use to download files to your computer and upload material to your account on the Internet.

The most popular transfer protocol today is Zmodem (see Figure 1-2), which has evolved from earlier systems known as Xmodem and Ymodem. Xmodem was a simple transfer protocol that sent a 128-byte packet to the receiving

Figure 1-1.

Setting VT100 terminal emulation in WinComm PRO

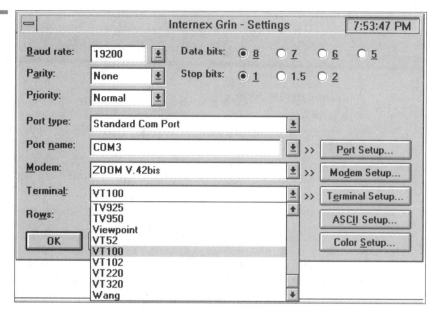

computer, checked it for errors, and then sent another packet. Zmodem is faster, has better error-correcting capability, and uses a 1024-byte packet. Zmodem is the standard on most Internet service providers and bulletin board services.

A second transfer protocol commonly used on the Internet is Kermit. Kermit is mainly used for communication among mainframe computers—and thus it has a role on the Internet. Kermit has error-correcting capability but is much slower than Zmodem. Kermit is commonly used on many university Internet systems to transfer files between hosts, and between hosts and remote computers, usually in a professor's office or at a student's work station.

Figure 1-2.

Setting the transfer protocol in Wincomm PRO

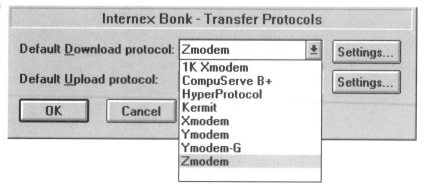

Offline Readers

A key tool for handling the flood of information on the Internet is an offline reader that can handle e-mail or both e-mail and newsgroups.

Internet Messenger

A new approach to reading files offline is Delrina's Internet remote/offline mail reader, Internet Messenger, an enhanced feature of Wincomm PRO (version 1.1). Delrina designed Internet Messenger to work with dial-up Internet service providers that use a UNIX shell account. The software dials into your service and downloads (or uploads) electronic mail. It works on a majority of UNIX accounts—but not all—simply because there are so many different service providers and varieties of UNIX in the growing Internet universe.

Internet Messenger comes with preconfigured accounts and scripts for at least 30 different service providers across North America. Delrina also says it will work with customers and service providers to set up mail retrieval scripts for individual systems.

Despite the popularity of such Internet search systems as the World Wide Web or Gopher, e-mail is perhaps the most important tool for Internet research. If your aim on the Internet is to concentrate on e-mail and to save money on access charges, Internet Messenger is an option you should consider. A second use for Internet Messenger is for offsite handling of e-mail. As a part-time instructor at Ryerson, I am only on campus two days a week. I use Internet Messenger to dial in to my campus account once or twice a day and retrieve my e-mail. Internet Messenger also gives the user the option of logging off or returning to the UNIX shell and using traditional UNIX commands to search the Net for information or files.

QWK SOUP Offline Readers

Many freeware and shareware offline mail readers are based on a different approach to accessing the Internet. The most popular are Yarn for DOS, Win Yarn (a Windows front end for Yarn), and MacSOUP for the Macintosh. All three use a system called QWK SOUP to gain access to mail and newsgroups. Even if you do have more sophisticated access to the Internet through a TCP/IP connection, and use a TCP/IP mail reader such as Eudora, it's worth considering using a QWK SOUP offline reader if you deal with a large volume of e-mail and news.

QWK SOUP evolved from QWK, a software program developed to handle mail on simple dial-up bulletin boards. QWK, however, did not migrate well to the Internet. For example, many QWK readers had trouble handling long Internet addresses. So QWK SOUP (SOUP stands for Simple Offline Usenet Packet) was developed specifically for the Internet.

Internet Messenger: Target E-mail

When Delrina designed Wincomm PRO 1.1, Marc Camm, the company's Director of Communications Products, and his team wanted a product that would both be easy for novices to use but have enough power to satisfy advanced users. "Two of the main focuses are feature rich and usability," Camm says.

So why did Delrina decide to create software that concentrated on e-mail rather than full Internet Access?

"If you look at our customer base," Camm says, "the people who use Delrina products, who use WinFax PRO, those people want to communicate. On the Internet, the easiest thing, the friendliest thing for the user, is to do mail. You can't get lost doing mail. The same people who want to send and receive faxes, want to send and receive e-mail. It's another form of messaging. So we looked at all of the levels of functions on the Internet, mail, news, FTP, chat, and then information surfing or browsing. We said which one of these can we deliver in a very simple fashion, to give the user a very positive experience on the Internet? And that was mail.

"Part of using an Internet application and the complexity of it is setting up a TCP/IP stack. Internet Messenger uses an Internet shell account. We developed technology to exchange mail over shells and that removed the complexity of TCP/IP setup and installation. TCP/IP is basically overkill to do Internet mail.

"You don't really need to have a knowledge of the Net at all," Camm says, "all you need to do is have someone's address you can mail to, or have them mail to yours. So Internet Messenger provides and facilities communication the way WinFax PRO does. It allows you send, receive, and manage e-mail on the Internet."

To work with a QWK SOUP reader, your service provider must install QWK SOUP on the UNIX system and write a script that integrates the service with the offline readers on your PC or Mac. You use your communications software to go online and start the QWK SOUP script on your service provider menu or UNIX shell. You then download a compressed packet (for example, using PKZIP on a PC) containing your mail and newsgroups. Once the packet lands on your hard drive, you uncompress it, import the news and mail into the offline reader, and read the material.

TCP/IP-Based Software

The fastest-growing segment of the Internet market is software that gives a home- or office-based personal computer "live" access to the Internet through a TCP/IP connection.

A few years ago, there was little or no user-friendly software available for a TCP/IP connection. The development of software called the Winsock TCP/IP communications stack (Winsock means *Windows Socket*) for Microsoft Windows has created a variety of software called Winsock clients. A Winsock client (also known as Winsock compliant) is software that uses the Winsock TCP/IP communications stack to do something on the Internet, such as searching for material using a World Wide Web browser or Gopher or reading Usenet news or writing e-mail messages. Once a TCP/IP connection is set up, Winsock complaint Windows software takes over and you can point and click to reach your destination.

Operating Systems

One factor working to hasten the acceptance of TCP/IP applications for personal computing is the integration of TCP/IP protocols into computer operating systems, notably Windows 95, Windows NT 3.5, and IBM's OS/2 Warp.

Windows 95 comes with a built-in 32-bit Windows Socket TCP/IP that works with both a local area network and the SLIP and PPP dial-up protocols. Windows 95 also comes with its own Internet e-mail system and two of the most popular Internet tools, FTP and Telnet. Windows 95 TCP/IP should also work with existing freeware, shareware, and commercial Winsock clients such as Netscape.

Like Windows 95, IBM's OS/2 Warp, includes its own version of TCP/IP software as well as Internet tools such as e-mail, a newsreader, Gopher, FTP, Telnet, and a World Wide Web browser called WebExplorer.

Commercial Software Suites

A number of companies have jumped on the to provide Internet commercial TCP/IP software suites. This software includes Netmanage's Chameleon, Frontier Technologies' SuperTCP Windows, and Spry's Internet in a Box. Each program has its advantages and disadvantages. Fierce competition and Net feedback are forcing quick bug fixes and upgrades.

Netmanage's Chameleon 4.1 comes with a number of preconfigured account sign-up and configuration protocols for major Internet suppliers. Among the tools offered by Chameleon are WebSurfer (a World Wide Web browser), an e-mail reader, a news reader, Archie, FTP, Telnet, and other tools called Ping, Whois, and Finger (see Figure 1-3). Other freeware and shareware Winsock clients will also work with Chameleon's Newt TCP/IP stack.

Figure 1-3.
Chameleon's suite of
Internet tools

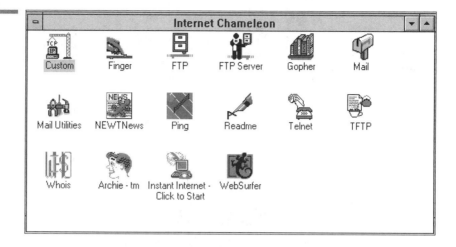

Freeware and Shareware

The "free market," as mentioned earlier, has a special meaning on the Internet. A great variety of Winsock-compliant freeware and shareware is available on the Net. Often an author creates the software as a challenge and for the love of the Internet. Or a team of people who have never met before form a virtual community to create a piece of software. The authors get immediate feedback on the Net from users around the world; bugs are fixed, new features added. Other Winsock software comes from the academic world, created to solve a research or software need at a university.

This software is still protected by copyright, either in the name of the author or the institution. Files can often be copied and distributed freely, but it is both illegal and unethical to rip off the author by either selling the software for profit without a license from the author or by re-engineering or plagiarizing it. Commercial TCP/IP software is driven not by love, but by the marketplace and the desire to make a profit. The result is often a more integrated system such as the suites of tools we've discussed, as opposed to the more individual items created by freeware or shareware authors.

Sometimes the two systems, commercial and freeware, combine. Eudora is a Winsock-compliant e-mail reader available in two forms on the Internet: a free "postcardware" version and a commercial version. The first graphical Web browser, Mosaic, was developed in an academic environment at the U.S. National Center for Supercomputing Applications in Urbana-Champagne, Illinois. Mosaic is freeware, but a number of commercial software companies have licensed it to create their own versions. Part of the original Mosaic team now works for Netscape Communications Corp. in Mountain View, California. They have created Netscape, currently the Net's most popular Web browser. Netscape is not a Mosaic clone. It was created from the first line of code up.

Figure 1-4.
Some of the shareware
and freeware tools
available for the Internet

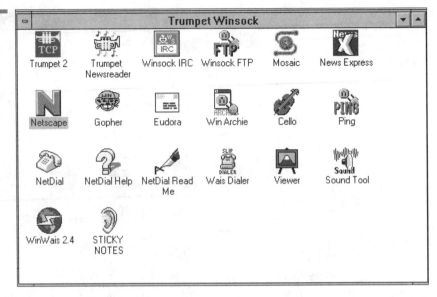

If you do not have a commercial suite or an operating system that supplies a Winsock stack, then use Trumpet Winsock, Version 2.0, shareware Windows TCP/IP software that can connect to the Internet either by using a telephone or through a local area network.

Popular freeware or shareware software (see Figure 1-4) for Windows includes the Eudora e-mail reader already mentioned, WSFTP, WSArchie, Winsock IRC, HGopher, WSGopher, the Cello and Mosaic Web browsers, the Trumpet NewsReader, News Express, and Free Agent. We'll discuss how to retrieve those files later in the chapter that explores FTP.

Internet-a-Phobia

The first computer I used had the intelligence of an amoeba. To say the computer had the brain of an insect would be an insult to an insect.

It was 1977 and I was a copy clerk at the Canadian Broadcasting Corporation's network radio newsroom. The CBC had an internal wire service that sent news each morning to affiliated stations across the country. I wrote news copy on a primitive word processor and then dumped the words on the monitor screen to a machine that punched paper tape and then sent the tape to a teletype transmitter.

Four years later I was working in the videotex industry, an ill-fated attempt to create online services in the early 1980s. The main computer system I used was driven by a Digital Equipment Corporation minicomputer. Only one option was available: typing commands at a prompt. Even those commands were obscure. No one, it appears, had yet thought of the word "copy." To copy a file from one eight-inch floppy disk to a second eight-inch floppy in a second drive, you had to use the command "PIP" which stood for "peripheral interchange program."

Things were a little better when I bought my first personal computer, an Osborne, in 1983. The CP/M operating system, at least, was based (mostly) on the English language, not obscure technical talk.

All through those years I've taken to computers; they like me for some reason, and, for some reason, I've liked them. That's not true of most people. Let's take a look at a widely reported poll taken by Gallup for MCI. In the fall of 1994, Gallup surveyed 600 American white-collar workers. Here's what they discovered:

» Forty-nine percent said they were cyberphobic or resistant to new technology. More women (39 percent) feared new technology than men (27 percent).

» About 65 percent use a computer either at work or at home.

» Sixty-six percent don't use e-mail at work.

» About 60 percent said they hadn't heard of the Internet despite all the recent publicity. (That, of course, doesn't include you, otherwise you wouldn't be reading this book!) Only 10 percent of those white collar workers knew how to access the Internet.

Why are people afraid of computers? According to Gallup and MCI:

» Fifty-six percent feared losing privacy.

» Thirty-eight percent feared information overload.

» Thirty-eight percent said they were afraid of losing personal contact with colleagues.

» Thirty-five percent were worried about having to constantly upgrade their skills.

» Nineteen percent were afraid of being passed over for a promotion.

I'm part of the 12 percent who Gallup classified as "early adopters" of new technology. (Fifty-nine percent say they won't use technology until it's been proven.) Through all those years, I've been drafted as an office "computer guru," I've helped many colleagues get started with computers, and helped with software or hardware problems (usually without calling tech support).

So, why are people afraid of computers? I've found three basic reasons.

First, a new user can feel overwhelmed by what he or she may perceive as the complexity of computer software, difficult and obscure software commands, and often confusing and incomprehensible software features.

Second, once a problem arises, and a new user can't find a way out, he or she feels helpless, and then decides, "I'm just not a computer person." The user gives up and never goes beyond basic word processing and spreadsheets.

Third, the secret language of tech talk intimidates the user. Faced with the arrogance of some of the self-appointed threshold guardians of cyberspace (who I call *tech lords*), the user again feels helpless and gives up.

You will confront all of those problems as you access the Internet. UNIX, the Net's main operating system, is often obscure and difficult to learn. Some users, even with years on the Net, don't venture beyond e-mail and newsgroups. Then there is what I call *matrix machismo*, the belief among some old regulars on the Internet that it should belong just to them. They revel in the most obscure UNIX commands and flame (attack) Net newbies with the feeding frenzy of sharks or piranhas.

Don't worry. Some simple tricks can help you overcome computerphobia. I'm not a psychologist, but I've found that borrowing some ideas from modern cognitive therapy will help you. When a newbie approaches a computer (or the Internet), it's often that person's own feeling of helplessness when they face a computer, rather than their actual computer skills, that defeat them.

Dr. Martin Seligman is a professor of psychology at the University of Pennsylvania, the author of the best-selling book *Learned Optimism: How to Change Your Mind and Your Life* (Pocket Books, 1990), and the moderator of a scholarly Internet mailing list on "learned helplessness." To be brief, Dr. Seligman has found through years of clinical and field research that people who are pessimistic, who have learned through life to feel helpless about a situation, don't succeed as much as optimists. The optimists, on the other hand, believe that problems are temporary, and can be overcome.

In a telephone interview, I asked Martin Seligman about learned helplessness and computers.

"Part of the reason my generation of scholars isn't as active [on the Internet] is because of a feeling of helplessness about computers," Seligman says.

He believes recent interactive, graphical software has not been successful with many people of the older generation, even though young people find it easy.

Seligman is president of the division of Clinical Psychology at the American Psychological Association. He advocates what he calls "electronic clinical psychology" and wants to bring all six thousand members of the American Psychological Association onto the Net. "I notice that some of the younger and more computer-literate types are on, but none of the great old clinicians. I'm afraid this learned helplessness of people who sort of grew up with quill pens."

In years of helping people with computer problems, I've found that many people do feel helpless when confronted by a computer, or by a difficult hardware or software problem. That's when they give up.

So here are my hints for overcoming computerphobia or Internet-a-Phobia

You're Smarter than the Computer

You're not a dummy. Computers were once mysterious objects locked away in a secret room somewhere in an office building and guarded by a special priesthood of technicians and programmers. They were expensive, costing hundreds of thousands, if not millions, of dollars. The big mainframes needed those special refrigerated rooms, free of dust and dirt and grubby users, just to keep working.

Now there's a personal computer on everyone's desk, but for many people this computer priesthood still exists. You'll find some of them on the Internet.

Remember it's the computers that are dummies. I wasn't intimidated by computers because the first computers I used were so stupid. In the early days, a user quite often had to figure out on his or her own how to get something to work. There was no help. You just had to do it. Quite often I'd find that a problem wasn't my fault, that the programmer had forgotten something or hadn't foreseen a new situation.

Computers only do what you tell them to do. Programmers are (gasp!) fallible. They make mistakes. Sometimes they don't realize how their software works in the real world, despite their own tests and feedback, whether from beta testers or later from users.

In the 1990s, there's an additional problem. When the personal computer first hit the market place in the mid-1980s, there were many small programming companies with new ideas, eager to sell those ideas to the computer-using public. Some of those programmers may have been tech lords but, more often than not, they listened to feedback from their customers.

The marketplace has matured at warp speed. Now it's often corporate considerations, which have little to do with the end-user, that may govern how software is created, designed, and released.

So, don't be intimidated by the computer, and don't be intimidated by a software manual that weighs more than the computer itself. Don't let yourself be intimidated by someone who considers himself a tech lord.

If you chose the right service provider and the software that's right for you, and if you learn from this book a little about how the Internet works, then you'll be fine. Don't let matrix machismo intimidate you either.

There's no reason to feel helpless when you sit down in front of computer. By breaking down a task and setting a goal, you can quickly find yourself making progress.

Break Down the Task

I'm a whiz at computers because I've worked with hunks of dumb silicon since 1977. Too often a new user feels that he or she should be an expert on the first try. That's a self-defeating thought. You're minimizing the task ahead and maximizing the difficulty of learning.

You wouldn't expect to drive a car on a superhighway after just one lesson, or climb a remote granite cliff after just one session at an indoor climbing gym. So take the computer (and the Internet) at your own pace. Choose the task you'll be doing the most and learn it bit by bit. If the software has self-tutorials, practice them until *you are comfortable* with the computer and the software.

If you're using a word processor, transfer your basic typing skills—something you already know—before trying something fancier like using fonts to create a special layout. On the Internet, start with the simple basics, e-mail, newsgroups, and FTP, before moving on, when you feel you are ready, to Gopher, Telnet, and the World Wide Web. With today's software, that transition will be easier than you think.

Set a Goal

Set a goal for yourself, a goal that's just a bit beyond your expectations. Then write down your goal so you will remember it. Like football or hockey, aim for that goal no matter what. If you're nervous about research on the Internet, a starting goal could be to do a successful search for some information on the World Wide Web. Then, once you found material on the Web, you could also try to find more information by a Gopher or WAIS search. If you're no longer intimidated by the thought of the Net and the challenge of the computer, keep going—try something new. Set a new and tougher goal.

Be Prepared for Setbacks

In the world of computers, things can go wrong. And they will. It's been said many times. Save Your Work. Back up your hard drive. If you're new and just starting out, save that file frequently; back up often. That way you won't lose your work. (That person at the next desk who types for hours without saving or backing up is probably a jerk. What if there's a power failure? Your work will be intact to the last save and his last save will be three hours old. Don't be intimidated.)

Remember, it's hard to break a computer unless you drop it or smash it. You can't break the Internet. It was designed to survive a nuclear war. You can always reinstall the software if you accidentally delete an operational file.

In the early 1980s, when I worked in the videotex and teletext industry, backing up was drilled into every employee. Those old eight-inch floppy disks would often die overnight. You'd back up before you left work and find the next morning that one of the disks had gone bad. So you were glad to have the second one around. For me saving frequently and backing up my work has become (almost) second nature.

Learn from Your Mistakes

If something goes wrong, analyze it. Try to figure out what went wrong. Did you push the wrong button? Were you making finger errors and typing in the wrong command?

Make a note of the mistake. Find out where in the sequence of events something went wrong. Check with the manual again. Have you broken the task down into steps? Were you trying to rush through something? Take the time to find the correct way of doing a task. Do it at your own speed.

Could it be the software? Perhaps. There's a good chance there is a fault somewhere in those thousands of lines of code. Try to find a way of working around the problem before calling tech support. Keep notes of what you did.

Often tech support will ask you to try to duplicate the error so they can find out how to solve the problem. If you're online you can often e-mail tech support and get an answer without paying for long-distance charges while you're on hold (listening to third-rate elevator music and golden-toned announcers with sales pitches).

Reach Out for Support

Don't be afraid to ask for help. Your office or class or dorm probably has a computer guru who is willing to help you. There's a difference between a guru and a tech lord. A guru is friendly, and knows that he or she has made horrendous computer blunders in the past. A guru knows that computers are dumb, that programmers are human beings like everyone else, and that corporate computer services three floors up often has no idea what's going on in the real world of work. A tech lord is someone who is a self-anointed part of the computer priesthood and thinks he or she knows it all and likes to demonstrate their superiority. Don't let tech lords intimidate you.

On the Internet, you have a world of helpful gurus at your fingertips. You can usually post a message on the appropriate mailing list or newsgroup and get an answer to your problem quite quickly. One word of warning, however: each mailing list and newsgroup has its own customs. Those customs are usually outlined in an FAQ (frequently asked questions) file. We'll tell you ways of getting an FAQ a little later.

Take Risks

You're going to feel uncertain at times. That's natural when you're trying something new. But if you've backed up your data, you can feel a little more confident about trying something more difficult.

Don't be afraid to experiment, to try something new. One of the wonders of computer software is the sudden discovery of a feature you didn't know existed—a feature that helps you solve a vexing problem.

Once you have an Internet service provider, budget some time for experimenting. Consider the money you spend on those experiments your Internet tuition fee. Fool around. Subscribe to a newsgroup. If you don't like it, unsubscribe. When you feel ready, Telnet to a computer on another continent. Explore it. If you don't get in, try again later. Perhaps all the gateways are busy. If you find nothing interesting, back out and Telnet somewhere else. Enjoy yourself.

Talk Back to Your Thoughts

"I'm no good at computers."

Wrong. You just don't know enough about them at this moment. Don't let what the cognitive therapists call "automatic thoughts" defeat you. Talk back to your automatic thoughts, to self-defeating attitudes. What's an answer to "I'm no good at computers?" You have no problem doing basic word processing and spreadsheets. You've played a game with your children. So that does mean you're no good at computers? No.

You are good at computers. To use the analogy of the computer game, you start at level one. So lets move on to level two and then to level three. When a kid plays a computer game and finishes level one, he or she is eager to try the second level and to see what new challenges there are at level three. So don't let your adult thoughts stop you from going to the next level of word processing or spreadsheets or exploring the Internet.

Be optimistic. See yourself using software like an old pro. Imagine yourself having a stimulating electronic conversation with a fascinating person you've never met before. Know that you will be able to mine the Internet for the information you need. Remember, if you're optimistic about your work on a computer, about your research on the Internet, you'll keep going, reach a goal, take risks and have fun.

If you're pessimistic, if you let your own thought that I'm no good at computers defeat you, you'll stay in that country road beside the information superhighway. You'll miss all the excitement on the I-way.

Reward Yourself

When you've completed a difficult assignment using the computer, when you've found the information you need on the Internet, acknowledge your success to yourself.

Give yourself a reward. You've earned it. Get out from in front of that monitor, go to a movie, treat a friend to a night out, enjoy yourself. Get ready to go for another computer or Internet challenge.

Further Reading

If you're interested in reading more about cognitive therapy, I'd recommend three books:

Martin Seligman. Learned Optimism: How to Change Your Mind and Your Life. New York: Pocket Books, 1990.

David D. Burns. *The Feeling Good Handbook*. New York: Plume Books 1990.

Rick Hansen and Dr. Joan Laub. *Going the Distance: Seven Steps to Personal Change*. Vancouver: Douglas and McIntyre, 1994.

Both Martin Seligman and David Burns are psychologists. For a slightly different approach read *Going the Distance: Seven Steps to Personal Change*. Joan Laub is a psychologist from Englewood, Colorado. Rick Hansen is a Canadian wheelchair athlete who pushed his wheelchair 25,000 miles around the world through 34 countries to raise money and awareness for spinal cord research, wheelchair sports, and the potential of people who have disabilities.

2

Choosing a Service Provider

This chapter gives you a brief overview of the advantages, disadvantages, and attributes of several kinds of Internet access for research. A checklist section near the end of the chapter will help you decide what kind of *Internet Service Provider* (ISP) you need and to help you contact and evaluate the ISPs available to you. The goal here is to get you connected to the Net, so you can begin to pursue your research while you read the rest of this book.

Note *The term Internet Service Provider is abbreviated as ISP throughout this chapter. Some people also call them Internet Access Providers or Internet Account Providers (IAPs), or simply Internet Providers (IPs). They mean the same thing.*

Before we talk about choosing an ISP, a discussion of a few basic concepts will help you see where your current or anticipated Internet service fits into the range of options available. Once you know about the client-server relationship between Internet computers, then we'll explain direct and indirect access to the Net, and provide you with the details of what a good old-fashioned UNIX-shell Internet account will give you.

Then we'll explore commercial Internet accounts, and talk about Internet access that is related to your education or employment. We'll explore how you can learn more about your hardware and software needs, and where to seek help when things aren't working as they should. Finally, the checklist that ends this chapter helps you shop for the Internet services you need, as will a brief review of other sources of help and information about Internet service providers.

The Client-Server Model

One of the most basic features of the Internet is its distributed architecture. The Internet doesn't rely on one single, central computer to do any particular job. Instead, it relies on many computers doing parts of the overall task. A simple way to think of this task-sharing is in terms of a pair of computers forming (and reforming) partnerships in a client-server relationship.

Of course, out on the Internet it is rarely just a single pair of computers, one client and one server going into business together. Usually many clients and even many servers join the fray, and the relationships between the client and server can be quite fleeting and transient. But the moment any pair of computers are working together may be easiest to understand by thinking of the connection between them as a client-server relationship.

So, what's a client and what's a server? Imagine the two computers involved to be people. For a moment, pretend your computer is your multilingual research assistant, and the remote, Internet resource host computer you want information from is the wealthy foreign owner of the research data you need. The wealthy owner of the information you need, however, does not speak your particular language. Enter your research assistant (the client computer), who does speak the needed language, and knows exactly how to phrase your questions so that the owner (the server or *host* computer) will understand the question and try to answer it.

Most of the work done on the Internet is based on client-server relationships like that just described. Your access to the main resources of the Internet is through client software programs that interact with host or server programs and the data that they have at their disposal. Technically, things get *much* more complicated than this description, but the principle of client-server relationships is the point here.

So, knowing how to use client software is the key to finding the data you need. You need to know how to find and gain access to the software client, how to open it, and how to tell the software client what you want it to do. You also need to know which server or host computer might have your desired information. Or at least you need to know *how to find out* which host computer might have your desired information, so you can point your client towards the right server. Sometimes you actually have to fill in the blanks to tell the software client what you want, and sometimes you just point and click to indicate your choices—it depends on the software clients you use.

Direct Internet Access

If you have direct Internet access and the client software is on your own computer's hard drive, right near your screen and keyboard, you have the most control and choice possible. You can configure the software just as you please, and you can use it whenever you access the Internet. You may have a suite of TCP/IP software that includes clients for most or all of the Internet tools, or you might have a different unrelated TCP/IP client software program for each: e-mail, Usenet news, Telnet, File Transfer Protocol (FTP), Gopher, WAIS, World Wide Web, Internet Relay Chat, Ping, Finger, and so on. All of your TCP/IP client software uses up storage space on your own PC's hard drive, and the research trophies you bring home are stored directly to your hard drive, too.

Note   *As we explained earlier, TCP/IP means Transmission Control Protocol/Internet Protocol, and it's the set of engineering and software rules that work together on the Internet to interconnect the many networks and to allow the various Internet tools to work. The most fundamental TCP/IP services are remote login (Telnet), file transfer, and e-mail. TCP/IP can work with any kind of computer and any operating system, and it can continue to work even when parts of the network are broken or disconnected.*

The two most common ways to have direct TCP/IP Internet access are to purchase a SLIP/PPP account and to have direct TCP/IP access supplied by your employer or your educational organization. Within the educational community, colleges and universities lead the way in providing direct Internet access to staff and students, but more recently many high schools and grade schools have begun to offer direct Internet access for educational research.

The most obvious hardware that allows you to connect *directly* to the Internet includes the wiring and connecting devices. The two most common connections are:

1. Telephone line connected to a fast modem connected to your PC running SLIP/PPP software.

2. Local Area Network (LAN) cable connected to an Ethernet card connected to (or inside) your PC.

If your computer runs Microsoft Windows 3.1 or OS/2 and has a 9600-baud modem (or faster), you can probably use SLIP/PPP to connect to the Internet. If you've made modem phone calls with your Macintosh (color LC or faster recommended), you can use inexpensive or shareware software such as MacSlip, MacPPP, or InterSLIP to connect *directly* to the Internet via your modem, telephone line, and an Internet Service Provider.

If your school or business has a computer network that is connected to the Internet, you probably have a way to get access to a computer directly connected to the Internet, or to get your own computer directly connected to the Net though a network in your building or over a telephone line. Start asking around, and once you've found who already has access, you can ask them how they got it.

Indirect Internet Access

If you don't have direct Internet access, the next best thing is to have remote access to a computer that is directly connected to the Internet. This is also common on college and university campuses, and some commercial services operate this way. With indirect Internet access you treat your personal computer as if it didn't have a brain. Your PC becomes just a "dumb" terminal—nothing more than a keyboard and monitor passing messages to and from a remote computer connected to the Internet where the client software does your bidding.

Your computer is considered dumb because it doesn't need much of what you bought it for to fulfill the terminal function. Terminals don't need floppy drives or hard drives. Terminals don't have a 486 CPU, a mouse, or onboard memory. All they need is a keyboard, a screen, and wires to connect them to the remote Internet computer that is running client software for you. To fool the remote Internet computer into thinking your personal computer is dumb, you tell your communication software to *emulate* a terminal.

If you've ever used a modem to connect to local computer bulletin boards (BBSs), you've probably already learned to set your communication software terminal emulation. While most BBSs use ANSI-BBS terminal emulation to display colors and graphics, the Internet standard terminal emulation to use is DEC VT-100 (VT-102 is close enough, too). One disadvantage of terminal emulation is that most of your mouse functions will be lost, because terminals don't even have a mouse.

UNIX Shell Accounts

The predominant, old-fashioned, but still common way to have indirect access to the Internet is through a UNIX shell account. When you use a UNIX shell account, you use client software on a computer that is connected to the Internet, and your computer acts as a terminal—it's used only to communicate with the Internet connected UNIX computer.

When you use the UNIX FTP client, UNIX Gopher client, or UNIX World Wide Web client to retrieve a file from a distant computer, the file lands in your "home" directory in your account space on the Internet client UNIX computer, *not on your PC's hard drive*. To get the file all the way home, you have to *download* it from your Internet account UNIX space to your hard drive—another software procedure to learn and remember. Likewise, if you've written a document you want to put up on the Internet, you'll have to *upload* it to your Internet shell account space first, before it's available to send out on the Net with a UNIX e-mail client.

Note

Many shell accounts allow you to use the Zmodem file download protocol from the UNIX command line. If your modem communication software includes this as an option, the software may recognize the incoming Zmodem download and switch on a Zmodem transfer automatically. To try this, type the following at the UNIX prompt:

```
sz filename.ext
```

The file you want to download should be substituted for "filename.ext." Chances are that the file will be on your hard drive right away.

A UNIX shell account provides command-line access to:

» Online text-based e-mail-reader(s) such as PINE, Elm, vi, or EMACS

» Online text-based Usenet newsreaders such as tin, Tass, or PINE v3.91

» Daily Usenet newsfeeds of several thousand groups

» Text-based UNIX Gopher client (a nongraphical interface)

» Text-based World Wide Web browser Lynx (a nongraphical interface)

» Personal file and e-mail storage space (1 to 10 megabytes, or more)

» E-mail delivery, sending, and storage service

» Command-line FTP, Telnet, IRC, Talk, Finger, Whois

Some shell accounts offer a menu system for novice users. The nice thing about the best of these menus is that all available options are displayed at any choice point. Even expert users may not remember all of the options and their syntax, and the menu makes remembering unnecessary!

The advantages of the old-fashioned UNIX shell account are:

» Shell accounts are flexible and usually provide rapid response times

» No menus are needed, but menus are often available

» Shell accounts are usually the least expensive

» Shell accounts are active and accessible 24 hours a day

» Shell accounts are easy to automate by writing UNIX scripts

The disadvantages of the old-fashioned UNIX shell account are:

» Shell accounts have a text-based nongraphical interface

» Shell account users are dependent on available software clients

» Shell accounts are more difficult for novice users

» Shell accounts are not simple, intuitive, or easy to use without study

» Learning command syntax is often a trial-and-error proposition

» Shell accounts have many of their abilities hidden in technical manuals

» Shell accounts are limited by the speed and capacity of the host system

» Shell accounts don't have a mouse; they are text-based only

» After you retrieve files from the Internet, you still have to download them from your shell account to your hard drive

Many ISPs offer modem users a possible upgrade to SLIP/PPP service for a *graphical* Gopher client, Web browser, and other TCP/IP clients to run on their own hard drive, rather than on the ISP computer. Changing to SLIP/PPP moves you from indirect Internet access to direct access, and allows you to send and receive files directly from your PC hard drive.

Tip   *SLIP/PPP service is explained later in this chapter, in the section entitled "TCP/IP, SLIP, and PPP."*

Some commercial ISPs are smooth enough to take advantage of your PC's abilities, even while treating your PC as a dumb terminal. They do this by using your PC to automate file downloading. That way the remote client computer doesn't have to store your files any longer than you are connected to the service. Because it saves the commercial service provider storage space, this file downloading function was cost-effective for them to automate first!

In addition, America Online, Netcom, and the New York City ISP Pipeline have brought out Windows- and Macintosh-compatible graphical software interfaces that allow you to use your mouse to navigate the Net.

If you already know a lot about basic Internet tools, and you are already devoted to the Windows/Macintosh Graphical User Interface (GUI), you may find indirect Internet access to be a step backwards and unsatisfactory. But if you are comfortable with the DOS command line, and mainly use text-based rather than graphical interfaces, indirect access may suit you just fine. Direct access usually costs more.

Commercial Online Services

As the name implies, commercial online services are not free. You pay not just for the computer, modem, telephone line, and (possibly) long-distance toll charges, but you also pay a monthly fee and other charges based on what services you use and how much you use them.

Several commercial services are now available all the way across North America. These include the major providers CompuServe (CIS), America Online (AOL), Delphi, GEnie, Netcom, Prodigy, and several smaller, more specialized or regional service providers. Some of these provide access to their own searchable databases or other research services in addition to sometimes limited Internet access.

CompuServe, America Online, GEnie, and Delphi provide so many additional services (such as stock quotes and trading, travel services, news wires, special interest groups and forums, catalog-like shopping, reference books, and more) that their customers sometimes consider e-mail and other Internet research tools as inessential frills. These commercial online services have developed into online communities of their own, and are sometimes characterized as providing "one-stop shopping," which is quite the opposite of the way many people use the Internet to find information from all over the world.

There are also many fine ISPs that sell you a part of their connection to the Internet, but provide no research databases other than Usenet newsgroups, or only one or two databases. These ISPs have much lower monthly prices, but you are *on your own* and have to find and use research data out on the Net itself, rather than on the dedicated machine of the ISP.

Tip   *Rural Internet Access*

A Kansas Internet Service Provider called Databank offers SLIP/PPP direct Internet access for $19.95 per month plus $5.00 per hour through a toll-free telephone *number. This includes access to over 9,000 Usenet newsgroups, plus e-mail, Telnet, FTP, Archie, Gopher, WWW, WAIS, and other services. If you live away from urban Internet Service Providers, and would pay toll charges to use the nearest ISP, this may be an attractive flat-fee alternative. Call Databank at 913-842-6699, fax at 913-842-8518, or e-mail: support@databank.com to find out more about this rural Internet solution.*

E-mail ISP Pricing

To obtain free information about services available and prices from Internet Service Providers, send an e-mail message with the subject "info" and the message body "info" to their *info* e-mail address. Here are some examples:

» `info@aol.com`

» `info@compuserve.com`

» `info@databank.com`

» `info@delphi.com`

» `info@io.com`

» `info@netcom.com`

» `info@psi.com`

» `info@well.com`

» `info@world.std.com`

The "info" message that is automatically mailed back may not be the complete fee schedule, so you might want to follow up with a request for the "detailed fee schedule."

Many of these ISPs have arrangements with public data networks so that if you live in an urban area you can call a local telephone number and then be connected to their service at a discount long distance rate from throughout North America. The biggest public data networks are the CompuServe Packet Net, SprintNet, BT Tymnet, and PSI Net.

In-House Connections

Universities, colleges, large government departments, and large businesses may already have computer networks with Internet access in the areas where you work or study. How do you obtain access?

Company Internet Access

If some of your coworkers already have Internet access, there is a good chance you can too. Find out which departments and which workers are allowed Internet access. See if staff development is offered for additional workers to learn Internet skills, and if so, who in your department has taken those courses. Check to see if there are any network cables physically close to your workstation, and who is the closest person on the network who already has Internet access.

Sometimes you may find that your computer is presently capable of Internet access, and only a few minor settings must be changed to open the Net to you. Other times it may be necessary to upgrade your computer or its network connection with new software and/or hardware.

Tip

If your coworkers use modems to access the Internet, rather than an installed (in the wall) network cable, then you should consider a second telephone line for your workstation. If your computer is using the phone for data, you can't use the phone for voice!

Educational Internet Access

As mentioned previously, most universities, colleges, and many other schools are making Internet access part of their educational curriculum. College students typically may open an account simply because they are enrolled, rather than because they associated with a particular course of study. More grade schools and high schools are offering similar access every day. Student accounts are often available by telephone, so that off-campus students may access the educational opportunities of the Net from home.

To find out how to open your own account, check with the computer center help desk or the library help desk.

Internet Hardware and Software

Almost any computer can be hooked to the Internet. However, the closer your computer and operating system software are to the mainstream, the more support and application software will be available to you. This section reviews how you can learn more about your computer hardware and software so your Internet research will be smooth and trouble-free.

Learning About Local Hardware

Most educational organizations that provide Internet access also offer education and training in how to use the Net effectively. If you get Internet access through a school, college, or university, there are probably several course offerings, ranging from beginning to advanced, to teach you all about the Internet. Just visiting your local computer center or computer laboratory and asking a few questions will often be enough to alert you to formal and informal Internet learning activities.

If your employer provides Internet access for some or all employees, there are bound to be orientation classes, and advanced user training may also be available. Again, check at the staff development office and the computer center to see what's available.

One of the most educational things you can do is to label every wire going into the back of your computer. Find out the name of each of those little ports and connectors. If some ports are not in use, find out what they could do if you were to use them. You may have capabilities you don't even know about.

Local Dial-up Internet Service Providers

Many urban areas in North America have abundant ISP offerings to choose from. Each offers a local telephone number and each wants you to open your account with them. See if they have an introductory or "money back" offer for you to become acquainted with their services. Sometimes a few hours online will convince you that you need an easier interface or a menu to start with, or more hours of support available. If you can pay more for these services, and they are available from another ISP, then the cheapest ISP may not be the best one for you.

Use the checklist at the end of this chapter to remind you of the important topics you should discuss with your prospective ISPs. Choosing an ISP is a little like planning a vacation or buying a computer. You'll need to study and explore all the options available, make some choices based on your wants, needs, and funds available, and then enjoy the results!

LANs and Other Direct Internet Links

Some employers provide Internet access for many of their workers. Most colleges and universities provide inexpensive Internet access to interested students and staff. When an employer or educational organization makes a major investment to providing Internet access, one of the cheapest and most effective ways is to link many computers together into Local Area Networks (LANs) so that many computers can efficiently share a major connection to the Internet.

If many computers in the same building need Internet access, linking them together with an Ethernet network LAN is a standard, inexpensive solution. Each computer is equipped with an Ethernet (or similar type of network) adapter card and networking software. If your computer has access to the Internet but you don't have a modem or the communication software to dial a modem telephone call, then you probably are part of an Ethernet LAN or similar computer network.

When many computers are networked and sharing an Internet connection, ideally the workload is spread out during the work day and no bottlenecks occur when too many computers want to use the Internet connection at the same time. Network administrators often try to manage and rearrange the demands on the Internet connection, and on the network in general, in order to reduce overall costs and improve service. Sometimes budgets are too limited to supply ideal Internet service for everyone, so compromises are made.

If you get your Internet access on a network, you should know who to contact when the network is out-of-service. Ask how you can tell if a problem is in your computer, or in the network. Find out how to call for each type of potential problem, and always treat the service technicians nicely. They often can help you a little *more*—if they're inclined to. If network orientation and security classes are offered, sign up!

TCP/IP, SLIP, and PPP

As more Internet users have demanded direct connections to the Net and TCP/IP client software on their own personal computers, the prices for direct connections have decreased remarkably. Most urban areas have SLIP/PPP access available for around $20.00 per month or less. In some very competitive online access markets, such as Austin, Texas, SLIP/PPP access can be had for as little as $12.50 per month (paid one year in advance).

Tip

Don't try using SLIP/PPP for the World Wide Web with less than a 9,600-baud modem. It will work too slowly. And, if you haven't yet bought a modem, be sure to get one that complies with the V.34 engineering standard. Buying a V.34 modem will ensure that you can communicate with most other modems for years to come, and your new modem is likely to run at a snappy 28,800 baud.

Windows 95

Windows 95 simplifies life for many Internet researchers because it has TCP/IP built right into the operating system. It has lots of other advanced features, too. It enables the more powerful 32-bit version of Mosaic and Netscape, and is compatible with other 32-bit TCP/IP software such as WS_FTP32 and WS_Watch.

Tip

A growing number of Internet assets are related to Microsoft's Windows 95 product. The following Windows 95 Info Page links many Windows 95 related items and has a dozen 32-bit software programs available for downloading:

`http://www.pcix.com/win95/win95home.html`

Possible Internet Access Problems

Computer networks are somewhat newer than personal computers, and plenty of kinks still need to be ironed out in making all the networks behave acceptably and play nicely together. As mentioned in Chapter 1, your local Tech Lords may stand in your way, rather than encouraging and facilitating your Internet access. This next section reviews several "everyday" problems you may encounter and suggests solutions for these problems.

The problems covered range from those at the ISP end to problems that can only be on your own personal computer.

System Capacity Overloads

Every ISP has problems occasionally, but the good ones anticipate problems before they occur and make plans to minimize the impact of inevitable problems on their users. When an Internet Service Provider has more user accounts than it can accommodate, users notice that the system slows down and becomes erratic, sometimes stopping altogether. System failures and outages of various kinds become more frequent and last longer. Excuses get overused and evaporate when you consider what they mean.

After you've signed up for an Internet account that costs money each month, you expect to be able to use your account. What if you just get busy signals half the time when you try to get on the Net?

Your satisfaction depends on the other providers available to you. If there are more reliable providers in your local area, it might be worth a higher monthly fee to be assured access at the times you need access. Shop around, and try to speak with satisfied and unsatisfied customers—especially customers with needs similar to yours—before you sign up.

Telephone Problems

When you begin to use your new modem to do research on the Internet, you're probably using the public telephone system to connect. Anything that could disturb a voice telephone conversation can also disrupt a computer telephone connection. If your modem connection to your ISP keeps dying, for instance, it can be because of a recent rain or flood that can cause audible noise in the telephone connection.

Note

If you report "noise in the line" to your telephone company, emphasize that you can hear noise in the line and it makes it hard to talk, and don't mention that it's your computer that is really having the trouble. Telephone repair service seems to be more sensitive to human problems than computer "malfunctions."

If you have advanced calling features such as call waiting turned on for the phone line your computer is using, you'll need to carefully study your communication software's setup codes. Before you place a computer telephone call with your modem you should turn off call waiting (or any other service that could interrupt the call unnecessarily). Check with your telephone company for the exact sequence to activate and deactivate your advanced calling features. And be sure to incorporate the deactivation sequence into your communication program's modem setup sequence.

Tip

*To turn off call waiting, so an incoming call won't interrupt your Internet research, you usually add the keystrokes *70, (including the comma) before the phone number you want the modem to dial. Study your modem manual and check with your telephone company to be sure.*

In some areas "local" telephone calls are billed by the length of the calls. This is particularly prevalent for business accounts. If you intend to use a telephone line for Internet access, try to have it billed as *unmeasured service*, so you won't have to worry about the length of your Internet phone calls.

Problems with Your PC

When your computer won't do right, what do you do? The most extreme problems can sometimes be solved by simply turning off the power to the computer, waiting five minutes for all internal charges to dissipate, and then rebooting from scratch. This allows the computer to re-establish its internal setup and boundaries, and sometimes this is all that is needed.

Microsoft Windows 3.1 allows some application programs—Excel, for example—to usurp system resources and not give them back when the application program is closed. This eventually drains resources below 40 percent and programs begin to misbehave and act unpredictably. Windows users quickly learn to exit Windows and re-enter Windows in order to regain those "lost or stolen" system resources. To check on the available resources, pull down the Program Manager's Help menu and click on About. Free resources will be shown (as a percentage) at the bottom of the popup box.

If you're having trouble with your PC, one of the most likely causes is the last (most recent) change you made in your setup—perhaps you installed some new software last night? Try reversing that last change, and see if the problem goes away. Experts are careful to only make one change at a time in a computer setup. Each change is tested, to see if problems develop with the everyday software, before a second change is made.

Of course, it's always a good idea to make a backup copy of your most important files. Here are some crucial files that should be backed up onto a disk *before* you install new hardware, software, or make any big changes in any DOS or Windows computer:

Back up before you experiment! Back up before you install!

» `C:\autoexec.bat`

» `C:\config.sys`

» `C:\windows\win.ini`

» `C:\windows\system.ini`

» `C:\windows\winsock.ini`

» `C:\windows\mosaic.ini`

» `C:\windows\quicken.ini`

» `C:\wsgopher\wsgopher.ini`

Something else the experts do is—*gasp*—read the manuals that came with the software and hardware. The "problems" and "frequent questions" sections in the booklets and papers that came with your hardware and software are designed to help you solve the usual problems that might arise. Experts save those booklets and papers, and consult them when problems don't go away easily.

Sometimes software becomes corrupted and needs to be reinstalled from scratch. If you've had times when the computer just stopped working and you had to reboot, or if you've had power outages, chances are that, whatever your computer was trying to do when things went wrong, it probably didn't finish the job, and may have left some messes here and there on your hard drive. This is one way that software becomes corrupted.

It's no fun, but sometimes it's necessary to reinstall Windows, DOS, word-processors, Web browsers, and other software because it isn't working right anymore. Reinstalling is a lot of work, and resetting everything so it's just how you like it can take weeks, but it's better than malfunctioning software.

Provider Reliability

An Internet Service Provider can disappoint you in many ways. Some are within the provider's control; others are not. You can be very unhappy, for example, that the Net is unavailable for your research at a time when you face a deadline, but if your entire region has lost its Internet connection due to a construction accident, it's unlikely that your ISP can do much about it.

One of the best ways to find out about an ISP's service is to talk candidly with current subscribers to that service. Are they satisfied with the technical support and responsiveness they have experienced? Do they get busy signals every day, or every night when they try to connect? Has the system ever slowed down noticeably, so that they became bored while waiting for the computers to do their jobs?

Ask the ISP for the help desk telephone number and hours. Are they available five days a week or seven? Are they open when you will be using the service? Give them a call. Are they alert and attentive to your questions? Even Internet gurus need technical support when trying new software and services, and it's important to have someone to listen and make helpful suggestions when you get into trouble.

Are there scheduled times when service will be unavailable, or is the service available 24 hours a day, 365 days a year?

Ask how many users the ISP can reliably handle at one time, and how often they reach or exceed the system's capacity. Ask them what happens on Friday night at 8:00 P.M., when crowds of users want to be on the Net simultaneously.

Find out how many of the ISP's users have needs similar to yours, and find out if there are any groups or types of users that are larger than yours. Most ISPs respond first to their biggest customer's demands.

Internet Access Checklist

What Equipment and Software Do You Already Have?

Is my computer ready for the Internet?

What Internet services do I need?

☐ Personal Computer

☐ Monitor

☐ Keyboard
☐ Mouse
☐ Megabytes of onboard RAM memory
☐ Megabytes of *available, empty* hard drive space
☐ Modem

Modem baud rate:
☐ 9,600
☐ 14,400
☐ 28,800
☐ Modem telephone wire and wall connection
☐ Fast (16550 UART) serial port for external modem
☐ Communications (modem) software

E-Mail

Is e-mail batched (delayed) or sent and received instantaneously?

Are charges based on the number or size of messages sent or received?

Can e-mail be read and composed offline?

File Transfer and Storage

Are you charged based on the size of your file transfers?

Are there maximum limits to the size of file transfers allowed?

How much storage are you allowed with your account?

Is additional storage available for temporary holding?

Is additional storage space available for an additional fee?

Telnet

Is Telnet client access available at the UNIX prompt?

Is Telnet only available through a menu of sites?

Are there Telnet sites that are forbidden or discouraged?

Usenet

Is a "full" Usenet newsfeed (thousands of newsgroups) available?

Are some newsgroups censored or not carried based on content?

Are major wire services and ClariNet newsgroups available?

Can the Usenet news-server be accessed via SLIP/PPP?

Can Usenet newsgroups be read offline?

Gopher

Is Gopher client access available at the UNIX prompt?

World Wide Web

Is there a World Wide Web (WWW) client available at the UNIX prompt?

Archie

Is Archie client access available at the UNIX prompt?

WAIS

Is a Wide Area Information Server (WAIS) client available at the UNIX prompt?

Internet Relay Chat

Is Internet Relay Chat (IRC) client access available at the UNIX prompt?

Is IRC restricted or is access controlled?

Service, Support, and Costs

Are "man" (help manual) pages available?

Are there online tutorials?

Is user training available?

Is human help available during the hours you intend to use the service?

Are support questions answered in real time, or after a delay?

Do current users feel that the support is acceptable?

Are rates based on the time of day you access the service?

What should you expect to pay for total annual service costs?

Access and Activity Restrictions

Can you set up your own World Wide Web home page?

Are MultiUser Simulated Environments (MUSEs) available or discouraged?

Are multiuser games allowed? Are a variety of games available?

Are there limits to how long you may remain connected per day?

Can you arrange to have a permanent numerical Internet (IP) address?

Security and Privacy

Under what circumstances will someone read your e-mail?

Do they log your Internet service activities?

How long are activity logs preserved?

Who has access to the activity logs? Why?

Is any sort of encryption available or supported?

Are other security services available?

Personal Convenience

Will you be able to continue to use your communication package?

Will you need to learn a new proprietary menu/interface?

Is SLIP/PPP available if you choose to upgrade?

Will you need to obtain and install a suite of TCP/IP client software?

Will they forward and/or store your e-mail for you?

Further Resources

This chapter was meant to help you through the sometimes challenging process of getting yourself connected to the Internet. For further help there are several sources you can consult.

The following Usenet newsgroups regularly discuss and post information about Internet Service Providers:

» **alt.internet.access.wanted**

» **alt.bbs.lists**

» **ba.internet**

» **news.answers**

» **alt.internet services**

In addition, several magazines carry information about Internet Service Providers, including *Boardwatch, CONNECT*, and *Online Access*.

To understand your hardware and software better, the first step is to read the manuals and help files that came with them. So, try looking in the index of your computer hardware and software manuals and in other computer books looking for words such as "troubleshooting," "error messages," or whatever seems to be preventing your successful Internet access. If you are a Windows user, you can press the F1 key or click on Help and search for advice from your Windows software.

If you've chosen to subscribe to America Online (AOL) for your Internet research, consider reading *The Official America Online for Windows Tour Guide*, by Tom Lichty (1994, Ventana Press, 543 pages). Lichty explains in detail how to use AOL for e-mail, how to work offline (off the meter) with flashsessions, how to upload and download files and information, how to access and search the many research databases available through AOL, and how to use the AOL Internet interface.

Or, if you've decided to use CompuServe for research, check out *Using CompuServe*, by Jill H. Ellsworth and Matthew V. Ellsworth (1994, Que Corporation, 460 pages). The Ellsworths' demonstrate, in clear, graphic steps, how to access the extensive information resources available to CompuServe subscribers (with over 100 pages of detailed reviews of the data sources available and their usefulness), including how to work offline to reduce charges, how to use e-mail, how to upload and download, how to use CompuServe's available financial services, and how to get the most out of all these services.

Or, check with the computer gurus at your school or workplace. Computer hardware and software stores as well as computer repair shops often know of experts who are also willing to assist you in getting on the Internet.

If you are shopping for an Internet Service Provider, here are several links to lists of ISPs and other resources:

Ameriway: Internet Access While Traveling

```
http://fohnix.metronet.com/HomePages/chuckoh/htm/access.
    html
```

Colossus: The List

```
http://thelist.com/
```

Contacts for Connectivity Around the World

```
gopher://rain.psg.com:70/11/networks/connect/
```

Network-USA Internet Service Providers Catalog

```
http://www.netusa.net/ISP/
```

POCIA: Providers of Commercial Internet Access

```
http://www.isp.net/pocia/
```

alt.internet.access.wanted FAQs

```
ftp://rtfm.mit.edu/pub/usenet/alt.internet.access.wanted
```

NixPub—Public Access UNIX Sites

```
ftp://vfl.paramax.com/pub/pubnet
```

PDIAL—Public Dial-up Internet Access List
by Peter Kaminski (kaminski@best.com)

```
ftp://rtfm.mit.edu/pub/usenet-by-group/news.answers/pdial
ftp://ftp.best.com:/pub/kaminski/
gopher://cscns.com/00/News%20and%20Information/pdial
http://www.cis.ohio-state.edu:80/hypertext/faq/usenet/pdial
    /faq.html
```

3

Getting Ready for Research

How does a researcher find material? Asking questions is one way. Wondering through the stacks of a library is another. Filling in forms at an archive so you can shuffle through boxes of long-forgotten government documents is yet another. Using the Internet is the latest way of finding information. The basics of research are centuries old, and most of its age-old principles apply to work on the Internet, whether you're a student, a business person, a journalist, or a scholar.

There's one difference. Once most researchers worked in great halls. Five thousand years ago, the archivists of ancient Mesopotamia gathered clay tablets written in cuneiform. Two thousand years later, philosophers and scholars from around the Mediterranean came to Alexandria, to study at that city's magnificent library with its half million scrolls. Students at Alexandria's schools of astronomy, medicine, and mathematics used the great library for research, searching through all the materials they could find, much as many of us do today.

A man named Ts'ai Lun is said to have invented paper in China about 105 A.D. Printing began in the seventh century. China created books and libraries of philosophy, astronomy and alchemy. Emperors supported eminent scholars in their work.

Back in Europe, medieval monks used parchment to copy ancient manuscripts and preserve them in libraries safe from the ignorance of the Dark Ages. The great universities grew out of the bosom of the church and flourished in the Renaissance. The founding of the universities created a new form of scholarship and new libraries. Gutenberg invented movable type and printing spread new knowledge across Europe.

New national governments founded great national libraries. One was the British Library, with its circular Reading Room and walls of old leather-bound books reaching up to the building's dome. Researchers, with the privilege of a Reader's Ticket, worked at the same tables as generations before them. The Library of Congress in Washington and La Bibliothèque Nationale in Paris offer the same sorts of treasures. In the nineteenth century, public free lending libraries were born, some bankrolled by the steel baron Andrew Carnegie.

For all those centuries, people had to go to the library. It may have been a perilous journey through dangerous times to a far-off monastery or just a gentle spring walk around the corner from home. For those who research, it has always been a joy to wander through those great libraries where one still has access to the stacks. The late historian and author Barbara Tuchman loved research so much she wrote a book about it: *Practicing History*. She says ambling through the stacks at Harvard's Widener Library was "my Archimedes bathtub, my burning bush, my dish of mold where I found my personal penicillin." It is only in the stacks that you can find that book you had never heard of before, the one with the key gem of information, sitting beside the one you were seeking. Card or computer catalogs, while helpful guides, are not always as favorable for serendipity.

Today's generation of students, the Net-veterans from the old ARPANET days, and those of you who are just venturing online can all find the same joys in searching the Net. On the Internet you can click the wrong Web pointer and end up browsing through a totally unrelated subject. Or click the right pointer, and serendipity strikes and you discover something you never thought of.

So, now, how do you prepare to do research online?

First, you must remember that the Internet is only one tool among many. You cannot ignore traditional libraries and archives—and you will find that even those libraries and archives are going online. You cannot—yet—read their hard copy holdings from the comfort of your home. But you cannot ignore the advice of experts or the testimony of witnesses—and you may find some of them on the Internet too.

At this early stage, the Internet seems to be best for volatile information—fast changing data. E-mail is a new tool for the researcher. The e-mail explosion has created a new form of communication. Making contact around the world is cheap and easy with the Net, saving long distance and travel costs. (Chapter 12 takes a look at the do's and don'ts of the e-mail interview.)

What Areas Are the Best on the Internet for Research?

The Net keeps you current. You can find out what topics people are discussing. The Net can help you with your research in the following ways:

» You can identify experts or interesting angles in your subject.

» You are alerted to what's new in the field.

» You're alerted to breaking news and information.

» It can help you narrow down a broad topic.

» It can help you widen a limited topic.

» The Net broadens horizons. It's international.

» It exposes you to a wide range of voices on all topics.

» It enables you to use e-mail to verify information.

» Through e-mail it gives you a means to pre-interview or follow up with sources.

» The Net helps you find links to paper sources in libraries and archives.

» It helps you find illustrations and graphics or links to illustrations in hard copy.

The Internet is open 24 hours a day, 365 days a year, despite rain, shine, sleet, snow, and sometimes even hurricanes and earthquakes (and depending on your service provider).

What Areas Are Not the Best on the Internet for Research?

The Internet isn't a panacea—it won't be good for everything. Sometimes it suffers from what is called the "noise to signal ratio." There's a lot of nonsense posted out there. Never forget: "garbage in, garbage out." Here are some of the problems you will probably encounter while researching on the Net:

» It's difficult to evaluate the material on the Net.

» Confirming information can be difficult if there's no "paper trail."

» Books and magazines are still the best method for storing most information in an easily accessible form. After all, the word magazine comes from the Arabic word *makzan*, which means storehouse.

» It's often difficult to collect, store, and collate all the material on one topic from a Web or Gopher site.

» Much of the information on the Internet comes to you in e-mail and newsgroups. It's easy to be swamped, and sorting out what is relevant takes time.

» The Internet is growing so quickly that it's almost impossible to keep up with the changes. The whole spectrum of information available by e-mail, Usenet, Gopher, and the World Wide Web can overwhelm a researcher.

» Key sites are often busy and hard to access.

Despite the difficulties you'll encounter online, the Internet nevertheless offers research opportunities that are more than worthwhile for most topics. A spirit of adventure will go a long way toward making your online safaris rewarding.

Getting Ready for Research

So now you're about to do some research on the Internet. Let us take some first steps:

1. Write a goal or focus statement. It's your first step on the Internet road map.

2. Decide what research you can do on the Internet and what you should do in traditional ways in a library. Ask if you can (and can afford to) also use a commercial information database such as Dialog or Lexis/Nexis.

3. Create a game plan for your research. Are you going to cruise using the World Wide Web or Gopher or make the most of a focused keyword search using Archie, Veronica, Jughead, or WAIS?

4. Prepare an outline of what you already know, what you need to know, and what would be nice to know. (The value of outlines will be discussed in Chapter 8, "Focusing Your Aims.")

5. Remember what end product you want, whether it's a term paper, a news report, an internal memo for your boss, or an article in a

scholarly journal. Whatever it is, the document should be clear to the reader. When starting out on a research project a researcher should *always* keep the reader in mind (your ultimate "end-user," to use computer jargon). See that reader, visualize that reader, whether it's your professor, your boss, or your mother.

The Tao of Good Research

By Dean Tudor

There are no secrets to doing research.

There are many secrets to misguided research.

Research is simple; cultivating it is difficult.

Hard work develops discipline,

Discipline develops intent,

Intent develops patience,

Patience develops faith.

Therefore,

Trying to research without hard work, you lack skill.

Trying to research without discipline, you lack consistency.

Trying to research without intent, you lack focus.

Trying to research without patience, you lack timing.

Trying to research without faith, you lack energy.

Likewise,

Skill develops consistency,

Consistency develops focus,

Focus develops timing,

Timing develops energy.

This is the essence of good research.

(Reproduced with permission)

The Who, What, When, Where, Why, and How of Research

Journalists have always used the five W's—who, what, when, where, and why (plus how)—as a way of focusing their stories. It's a good standard to follow whenever you are doing research. Ask yourself the six questions about your goals whenever you embark on a project.

Nora Paul, of the Poynter Institute for Media Studies in St. Petersburg, Florida, also recommends that researchers ask the same questions when embarking on a database search, whether it's a commercial database or the Internet. By asking those questions before going online in a commercial database such as Dialog or Lexis/Nexis, the researcher saves much money. Those systems often add access charges and downloading charges to their online charges. By asking the same set of questions, a researcher using the Internet can also save time and money. The authors have adapted Nora Paul's outline to focus on all kinds of research on the Internet.

Deciding What You Need

Your first step in research is to develop a guideline for the kind of information you are seeking. Research for a term paper is different from research for a news story or an internal business memo.

Who?

Who is your project about? A politician, a Broadway star, a little-known historical figure, a criminal, a competitor, or a customer?

Who have you already talked to? Who is your project for? A reader of some kind, a teacher, an editor, or a supervisor, and beyond that newspaper buyers, academic colleagues, or members of a business team?

What?

What is the information you need about? A person, a place, a country, a company, or a report on a scientific research project?

What kind of information do you need? Interviews from around the world, statistics or data, new sources of information, or confirmation of material from other sources?

What kind of story/report are you writing? A news report, a business report, or a term paper?

What type of information will be most useful?

What information do you already have?

When?

When is the information needed? In minutes on a breaking news story, in a hurry for an important client, or in a couple of months on a major project?

When did the event you are researching take place? The older it is, the less likely you will find it on the Internet.

When does the information change? Every few minutes for stock quotes, every few hours for weather forecasts, or never for an archived document?

Where?

Where did the event you are researching take place?

Where have you already looked for information?

Why?

Why are you looking for the information? Checking information you have, looking for a source, fishing for a story or research idea, looking for new customers or new data to give you a competitive edge?

How?

How much information do you need?

How are you going to use the information? In a story or report, in charts or graphics, or will you input the data into some type of program for further number crunching?

How would you prefer the information to be delivered? ASCII data you will keep on a disk, or material you will want to print to hard copy?

Finding the Right Internet Source

Once you've determined what you already have and what you want, the next step is to choose where you're going to find it on the Internet. Again, you should ask yourself some questions.

Who?

Who might have the kind of information you're seeking? Should you seek out individuals on a mailing list or Usenet newsgroup, or the help person at a Gopher or World Wide Web site?

Who would have the most current/most retrospective data?

Who has done this type of research before so you can get advice?

Who was responsible for collecting the information you have found online? This is a good question to ask in the appropriate mailing list or newsgroup if you don't know.

What?

What kind of search should you perform? A Veronica, Jughead, Archie, or WAIS search using key words? A check of subject-oriented Gopher sites? A check of World Wide Web pointers from Lycos, or Yahoo or similar sites?

What are the possible sources of error in the data? Check for bias, problems of methodology, and outdated material.

What do you do if you don't find any information or find too much?

When?

When do you do the search?

What are the peak and off-peak hours for your service provider? Will you be able to dial in?

What are the appropriate hours for the site you are going to search? Would it breach netiquette or local rules to use a site during these hours?

Would it be easier to use a site on the other side of the world that might not be busy during business hours in your own time zone?

Where?

Where should you do your search? Which Web, Gopher, or FTP sites are most appropriate and most reliable?

Why?

Why are you doing the search? Are you looking for essential information, for material you need to know, or for something that would just be neat to have?

Why was the information originally collected and posted? Is it a government database, a commercial Web site created by a marketing department, or, as is still common on the Internet, someone's labor of love, either in an academic or a private setting?

How?

How are you going to put your research strategy together?

How much is this going to cost?

How much are you willing to spend?

How might you find the same information offline?

How can you get help if you run into trouble?

How will you use the information in the story or report?

How will you attribute. footnote, or reference your research?

How consistent is this information with material from other sources, whether on or off the Net?

Technical Skills

If you want to do research quickly and efficiently, you must learn and practice the technical skills in this book. Nothing can be more frustrating on a research project, especially one with a tight deadline, than fumbling with your keyboard late at night trying to figure out what you've done wrong. It's a good idea to start small, to try to retrieve small files or small amounts of data, just to get the practice. When the time comes to do a major project, you'll be able to do it. It's no different from practicing for a tennis match.

Divide and Distill

The biggest problem any researcher will find on the Internet is the overwhelming amount of material that's available on the Net. Here, old-fashioned research skills are paramount. There's little difference between being overwhelmed by boxes of files stuffed full of papers and being overwhelmed by subdirectories stuffed with 300-kilobyte files. You always have to keep your reader in mind as you research. As much as you might want to show off all the research you've done, your reader doesn't want to be overwhelmed any more than you do. So you may have to be ruthless in excising anything that isn't essential.

In his book *Writing Well*, William Zinsser has good advice:

Most nonfiction writers have a definitiveness complex. They feel that they are under some obligation—to the subject, to their honor, to the gods of writing—to make their article the last word. It's a commendable impulse, but there is no last word. What you think is definitive today will turn undefinitive by tomorrow, and writers who doggedly pursue every last fact will find themselves pursuing the rainbow and never settling down to write. Nobody can write a book or an article "about" something. Even Tolstoy couldn't write a book about war and peace or Melville write a book about whaling. They made certain reductive decisions about time and place and about individual characters in that time and place. Every writing project must be reduced before you start to write it.

Therefore, think small. Decide what corner of your subject you're going to bite off, and be content to cover it well and stop. Often you'll find that along the way you've managed to say almost everything you wanted to say about the entire subject. This is also a matter of energy and morale. An unwieldy writing project is a drain on your enthusiasm. Enthusiasm is the force that keeps you going; it also conveys itself to the reader. When your zest begins to ebb, the reader is the first person to know it.

Barbara Tuchman, a solid historian and best-selling author, said in *Practicing History*, that a researcher needs to keep the subject as narrow as possible:

The writer of history, I believe, has a number of duties vis-à-vis the reader, if he wants to keep him reading. The first is to distill. He must do the preliminary work for the reader, assemble the information, make sense of it, select the essential, discard the irrelevant—above all, discard the irrelevant—and put the rest together so that it forms a developing dramatic narrative. . . . To offer a mass of undigested facts, of names not identified and places not located, is of no use to the reader and is simply laziness on the part of the author, or pedantry to show how much he has read. To discard the unnecessary requires courage and also extra work. . . . The historian is continually being beguiled down fascinating byways and sidetracks. But the art of writing—the test of the artist—is to resist the beguilement and cleave to the subject.

Tuchman's warning, written in 1963, six years before the first experiments with what would grow into the Internet, is even more relevant today. It's easy on the Internet to be beguiled by the fascinating byways and sidetracks of the World Wide Web, available at the click of a mouse.

There's also more information these days—a lot more—and not just on the Net. Ingram Olkin, a professor of statistics at Stanford University, reports that in 1940 there were 2,300 biomedical journals. By 1994 there were close to 25,000. In 1951 there were just 91 papers reviewing other papers in psychology. By 1992, there were 1,195. There were 3,379 academic papers about mathematics published in 1940. In 1992, there were 58,208. With new electronic journals on the Internet, with specialized newsgroups and mailing lists, the amount of data is growing dramatically. Every researcher must divide and distill.

In *On Writing Well*, William Zinsser recommends picking the two best examples out of all your research. Two examples, or at the most three, will usually tell all a reader needs to know. "Always start with too much material. Then give your reader just enough," Zinsser advised.

Knowing When to Stop

You have to know when to stop your research, but it's tough to know when. At some point you must write what you've found, to let your readers know what you have discovered. But there's always that extra file to look for, that last letter to the last contact to write, that last phone call to the last source. On the Net there's always another 10 or 15 or 50 new e-mail messages in your mail box every morning.

Barbara Tuchman advised: "One must stop *before* one has finished; otherwise, one will never stop and never finish. . . . I too feel compelled to follow every lead and learn everything about a subject, but fortunately I have an even more overwhelming compulsion to see my work in print. This is the only thing that saves me."

For a journalist, a deadline that is minutes away "concentrates his mind wonderfully" (as Samuel Johnson observed about the prospect of a hanging). A deadline is the end of the road, the goal you're shooting for, so always keep in it mind. A term paper, as we all know, is often written in an all-night session the morning before it is due. That deadline, set by the professor, has concentrated the student's mind (surprise, surprise). The boss in business wants that report on his desk Monday morning, so it had better be there. The problem for the academic, and for the author without a deadline, is that studies, of any sort, can go on indefinitely. One must finish, eventually, if only so one can be free to move on to the next project. Set a deadline for research long before the deadline for writing or delivery. End the bulk of research on that day no matter what. Journalists are always told that the time comes when "you go with what you've got." You can tie up loose ends, or check facts a second time, ask a few follow-up questions or complete a long-postponed interview. Just don't do anything new. Ask yourself how much such work is actually going to add to your project.

If something major happens—something that does change the focus, or the results, or your thesis—then reopen your research and ask for a deadline extension, if possible. If not, write what journalists call the "second-day story." Ask yourself if late material can be added in an appendix or afterward, or published in a follow-up article or paper. Such alternatives may keep your from ripping out chapters already written and starting over.

"What it requires," Barbara Tuchman wrote, "is simply the courage and self-confidence to make choices and, above all, to leave things out."

The Advantages of Computers and the Internet

There are special advantages to using a computer for research, advantages that have been obvious, but expensive, for years on commercial online databases such as Dialog and Lexis/Nexis.

When everything works well with your dial-up or network connection and the Internet connections themselves, computers are fast and information is readily accessible. As the Internet grows, it becomes more comprehensive, but at present, it can be hit and miss. One site can have substantial amounts of information on the subject you're interested in. On the other hand, you can search the Net and come up empty on another subject. That will change as more libraries, government agencies, commercial sites, organizations, and individuals join the World Wide Web or create Gopher or FTP sites. Computers have changed the way research is carried out for one special reason—the computer's ability to manipulate data. You can use keyword searches to sort and find the material you want.

The other advantage to using the computer is the ease of handling the information once you've retrieved it. You've got your data on your hard drive. Now you can use the computer to combine the information in new ways or find a new idea from it. Freeform or text-retrieval databases are best for this act.

Creating your own database from all the information you've retrieved has been likened to putting together the pieces of a puzzle. Academics call this approach *mosaic theory*. It is based on the idea that if a mosaic is a picture made out of hundreds of small colored tiles, a mosaic of information can be pieced together using data from many sources until a new picture is formed. Without a computer, it may have been impossible to do all that searching, and without search engines and keyword-search software, it may have been impossible (or would have taken years) to put it all together.

If you've put part of your puzzle together, and think you see a pattern, then it's time to go back to the Net to fill out the pattern. Don't stop there. Go to the library, read books (including all the footnotes, the acknowledgments—often a valuable guide to new sources—and bibliographies), newspapers, magazines, and papers, whether in hard copy or microfilm. Then pump at least a précis of that print information into the free form database. *Et voilà*, behold, you have yet more connections when you do a new search.

Tree Structure or Hypertext

The most common way data is presented on the Internet, whether on a Gopher site or a World Wide Web site, is by using what's been known for years in the computer world as *tree structure*. It's the same structure as the directory of files on your computer. There is an initial or *root* directory, and then branches leading to directories and subdirectories, like the trunk and branches of a tree.

Most likely you will follow a series of tree-structured menus to find what you want online, whether it's a file at an FTP site or information at a Gopher or World Wide Web site.

The World Wide Web adds one more advantage: *hypertext links*. Hypertext is an information-retrieval system that lets you jump directly to a related subject—but you don't choose the links, a programmer does. You would likely begin by going down through a tree structure until you find a page that interests you. On that page will be a series of highlighted words or perhaps graphics. Click on one of those items and you jump to a new page, perhaps half way around the world, that may or may not have the information you are seeking. That Web page may have yet more links to other pages—such Net surfing can be great fun, and can also lead to exactly what you want, but sometimes it leads to dull dead ends.

Search engines

Computers can cut your search time to minutes by using keywords to search for information. On many commercial databases, a researcher can pick a word from a title or subject listing, a word in the text itself, the author's name, the source publication or book, an accession number, a date, or an index number from the Dewey Decimal or Library of Congress systems. These words are often called keywords. To adhere to a strict definition, however, a keyword is also called a descriptor, a word that describes the content of the article.

For researchers, a keyword is a key that unlocks the electronic world. On the Internet, Veronica, Jughead, and Archie are search engines that use keywords, as are a growing number of World Wide Web sites including one of the most popular, Lycos, shown in Figure 3-1 (http://lycos.cs.cmu.edu), and Britain's Jump Station II, shown in Figure 3-2 (http:www.stir.ac.uk/jsbin/jsii).

WAIS—Wide Area Information Servers—also uses keywords to search a series of specialized databases or servers that allow text searching on a specific subject. WAIS then *weights* the search results, which tells how well that search engine thinks the results match your original request. The search results you get are thus given in priority order, which can be very helpful if you don't have time to prioritize the results yourself.

Another system that uses keywords to search for material in Usenet files is Stanford University's Netnews filtering service. It does keyword searching among the thousands of Usenet newsgroups. It uses a system similar to WAIS, searching for terms using plain English. You e-mail the keywords to the server netnews@db.stanford.edu. The server does the search for you overnight and, based on the statistical distribution of the keywords, returns a score to evaluate how relevant the search may be for you. A list is generated and then you can retrieve the articles you want using a *get* command. We'll look at these Internet tools in greater detail later in the book.

WAIS, Netnews, and some Web browsers allow you to narrow your search using what's known as *relevance feedback*. Once you have your initial list of

Figure 3-1.

The Lycos search engine

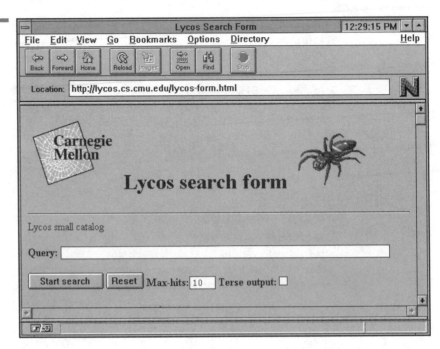

Figure 3-2.

The Jump Station II
search engine

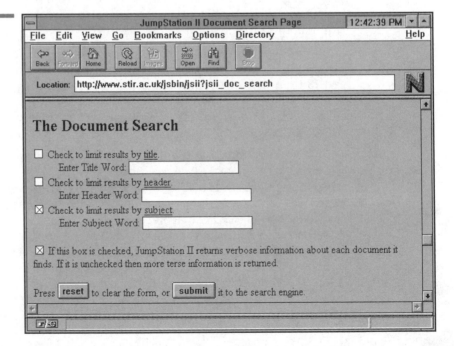

responses to a search, you narrow down the list by telling the search engine which ones you like. The computer then conducts the search again.

Let's take an example. A student in Toronto asked for information about the *San Francisco Examiner*. We used a Lycos search to try to find the *Examiner's* home page. Lycos added up the matches to the keywords, noting in its FAQ that "order of terms is unimportant." It adds, "The searcher will prefer documents that match more of your search terms, that match your term more closely (*glow* matches *glows* better than *glowworm*), that have more occurrences of any one term, and occurrences earlier in the document."

At first we tried the word "examiner" but it was quickly apparent that searching for this word resulted in too many documents. The same result came from using "San Francisco." So we tried "San Francisco Examiner," which Lycos used as "San+Francisco+Examiner," as seen in Figure 3-3. On March 25, 1995, Lycos returned 7,701 documents matching at least one of the terms. (Six days later on March 31, the same search found 8,349—the Net grows every day.) Using the weight sum of the all the matches, Lycos printed out the first ten matches.

Scrolling down, the *San Francisco Examiner* home page is the fourth choice that Lycos found, shown in Figure 3-4, with the URL address of this San Francisco Examiner and a clickable pointer.

Figure 3-3.
A Lycos search for the
San Francisco Examiner

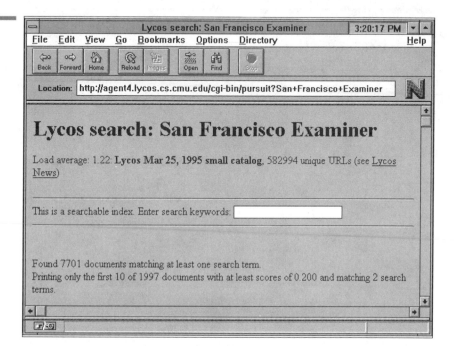

Figure 3-4.
A Lycos pointer to the
San Francisco Examiner

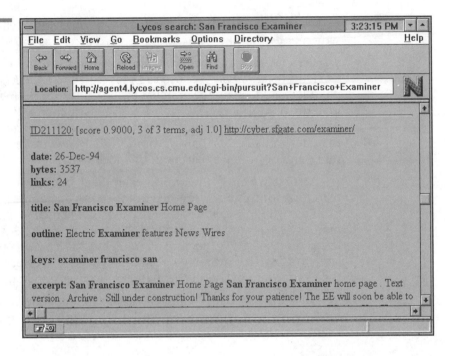

Figure 3-5.
The electronic version of
the *San Francisco Examiner*

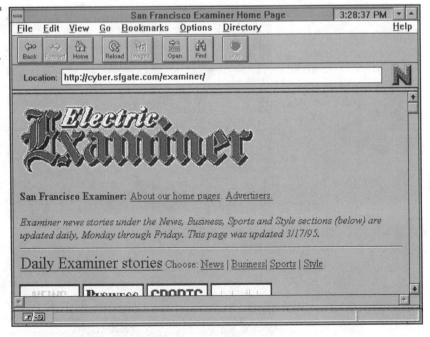

Clicking on the pointer leads to the *Electronic Examiner* as seen in Figure 3-5.

In these searches, you have to use your own judgment. The Lycos weighting system thought the best match, with a score of 1.000, was a medical journal on colposcopic examinations. A general San Francisco page was second with a score of .9477, and next was the combined San Francisco and *San Francisco Examiner* electronic pages, called The Gate, with a score of .9308.

There's also another method of searching databases, called *Boolean searches*. In these search you use *Boolean operators*; the words OR, AND, and NOT are the most common. Other Boolean operators are the words LIKE, EXACTLY LIKE, EQUAL TO, LESS THAN, and MORE THAN. Boolean searches can be used to ferret out numbers and dates as well as text on commercial information databases such as Dialog or Lexis/Nexis. Boolean searches are also used in relational and flat file databases (the kind that is used for mailing lists), and in free form or text-retrieval databases such as AskSam as well.

Boolean searches are relatively simple. For example, let's say you are looking at a commercial information database for information on laws affecting the Internet. It's a huge topic. So you could do a Boolean search for *Internet AND law*. If you wanted to look at all the laws except those on pornography you could look for *Internet AND law NOT pornography*.

Let's make the search a little narrower by confining ourselves to North America:

Internet AND law NOT pornography

United States OR Canada

The OR command lets the computer search include both terms. However, things are changing so fast, so let's narrow the dates. Here's what we are searching for now:

Internet AND law NOT pornography

United States OR Canada

MORE THAN 1993*

This means the computer is looking for information about the Internet and the law in the United States and Canada, excluding pornography, that was posted after the end of 1993.

You should note that this is a very simple example and each software application or search engine has its own syntax for actually writing out a Boolean search.

Yet another form of searching a text database is a *proximity search*. Proximity searches look for two words within a certain distance of each other. Proximity searches are most common on full text information databases, the kind that include newspaper, magazine, or journal articles. Again, it's worth noting that every one of these databases has its own software and search syntax.

To go back to the previous example you might, for example, ask for information about law on the Internet this way (using the Lexis/Nexis syntax for this example):

Internet w/5 law

This means you're instructing the computer to look for the word "law" within five words of the word "Internet." You could then combine the proximity search with a Boolean search to do something like this:

Internet w/5 law w/15 (United States OR Canada) AND date aft 12/93 AND NOT pornography

We're looking for text with the word "Internet," with the word "law" within five words of "Internet," the words "United States" or "Canada," within fifteen words of the word "Internet," published after December 1993, but also eliminating anything including the word "pornography."

A Lexis/Nexis search, using just the Current News database, carried on out April 7, 1995, got four hits using that Boolean operator, listing stories in the *Washington Post*, *New York Times*, *The Nation*, and the *Connecticut Law Review*.

So now you're asking "What about the Internet?" At this point, we're going to use the same example to show that the Internet isn't as powerful as a commercial information database, at least not *yet*. If you're using Veronica you can only use the AND, OR, and NOT operators. Parentheses also help narrow the search—but only on some Veronica servers; a few reject parentheses. (We'll talk more about Veronica in the next chapter.) So, let's try using Veronica's syntax:

Law AND Internet (United States OR Canada) NOT pornography

If we type in the preceding Boolean search phrase using Chameleon's Gopher, it is accepted by Veronica, as shown here in Figure 3-6:

Figure 3-6.

A Veronica search using
Chameleon Gopher

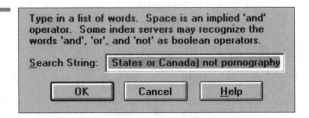

This search comes up with nothing. So we expand it, first dropping the reference to "pornography." Still nothing, so let's drop one more condition—"(United States OR Canada)"—and we're left with "law" and "Internet" and behold, we get a large list of returns, as shown in Figure 3-7.

Veronica is a limited search tool. It only searches the Gopher *titles* of articles, not the full text. So while a Boolean search eventually turns up an answer, it also shows that the Internet is still developing into a full-fledged research tool. You still have to do a lot of searching on your own.

There's one other approach for searches, called *structured query language* or *SQL*. SQL is most often used with relational databases, where data is stored in a number of different tables. Common relational databases are FoxPro, Paradox, and Access. The SQL language is a way of using simple English (or any other real language) to ask questions and get information from the database using Boolean operators and then, in addition, sorting the information with commands such as *order by* and *group by*. SQL is currently most useful in databases with distinct fields, but as more information becomes available on the Internet, SQL will also probably find its place in future search engines.

There's a debate at the moment about whether the Net will eventually go with relevance feedback or Boolean searches. It's likely both approaches will develop as the Net grows. Already some of the World Wide Web search systems are developing Boolean search capability.

Figure 3-7.

A Veronica search using the terms "law" and "Internet"

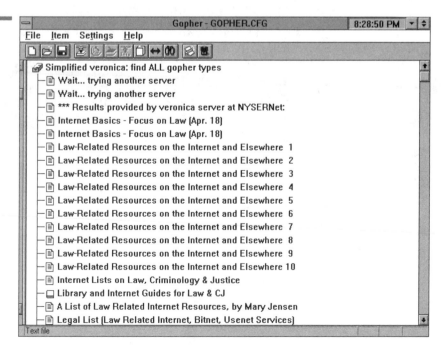

One Weird Word

So how do you choose which word to search for? Again, the high cost of the commercial databases provides a clue. Each search on Dialog or Lexis/Nexis costs money, so librarians, over the years, have found ways to make the most efficient word searches. Ruth Von Fuchs, who teaches online search techniques at the University of Toronto's Faculty of Information Science, calls it the "one weird word" approach.

She recommends starting off with the rarest word or phrase in a search. If you're not sure, she advises that you look for those words that are "at the heart of the matter" for your topic. One example she uses in her course is "ozone layer." "Ozone" is a better choice than "layer." Layer could, of course, bring up recipes for three layer cakes.

At this point, on the Internet, most search engines use only one field. If you have a multiple choice of fields, such as "author," "title," or "subject," again chose the field best suited to your search. If you're doing a search on Ernest Hemingway, do you want books by Hemingway? The obvious choice is in the author field. Books about Hemingway? The obvious choice is the subject field.

In choosing the one weird word to start off your Internet search, go back to the five W's and the check list at the beginning of this chapter. Ask yourself who the story is about, who it's for, and what you're looking for. This will help you narrow down the focus to that one weird word. A student, a journalist, and a business person will each have a different focus and, as he or she narrows the focus, may choose a different keyword.

If you can't find the word or phrase you want, begin by writing a question to yourself. Von Fuchs advises that a researcher should imagine writing a telegram, where every word costs extra.

One word can often eliminate a second. In most cases, someone searching "malpractice" would not need to add the word "doctor." On the other hand, lawyers and even journalists have been accused of malpractice. So someone searching for malpractice by lawyers may need to narrow the search by adding the word "lawyer."

One suggestion is to write the search terms underneath each other—and then eliminate the unnecessary words. The academic term for this is *concept analysis* but librarians might say they are "listifying" it. Lets go back to our original example.

Law

On the Internet

In the United States

or Canada

after 1993

As it turned out, if we were using a Veronica search, which can only look at Gopher menus and titles, we would have eliminated the bottom lines until we reached the answer of just two words "law" and "Internet."

On the other hand, if you're searching using tree structure, it's still a good idea to have your "one weird word" in mind as you go down those branches. On the World Wide Web, all those weird words are chosen for you by whoever designed the page. If you find that your weird word matches their weird words, you may have found what you're looking for.

Online or Offline?

A few years ago, most people doing research on the Internet were stuck with access to the big computers and the hard-to-learn concepts of UNIX. For many people the awkwardness of UNIX was a barrier to handling research material (on the other hand a minority loved it and still do).

In the past, those who could spend hours working with an awkward UNIX system weren't usually paying for it. Their access was through a university, the government, or the military. They often had unlimited access and never saw a bill. Now many people are working at their desks, in their offices or homes, at a personal computer. You get to pay the bills, so you might want to consider what research or preparation work you can do offline. Whether you have a dial-up or network connection, working offline gives you many advantages.

As we mentioned in the first chapter, tools for the Net are growing in number. These tools work both online and offline—and they make the life of a researcher much easier.

The first advantage to working offline is cost. If you have to store, and find, and manipulate material on your home directory on your service provider's system, the clock and the online charges are ticking. Whether it's a commercial text database system such as Dialog or Lexis/Nexis, a commercial service provider such as CompuServe, or your local Internet service provider, it's always a good idea to get what you want and then get off—fast.

Second, if you are using either a QWK SOUP or a SLIP/PPP offline mail or newsreader, then you have greater freedom. You can download your mail, read it at your leisure, and store it in the appropriate folders or as part of your own text-retrieval system. If you subscribe to a large number of newsgroups, working offline gives you more time to filter through the junk and noise and find the material you need.

Caution

Web browsers such as Netscape and Mosaic are now offering access to newsgroups, but you should remember that, using the present versions, those sessions are live and thus can drive up costs and are not always easy to store as text on a hard drive.

Third, working on your own PC allows you to create your own filing system to handle the material you find online. We'll have some suggestions later on ways to handle research material on your PC. No matter what system you chose, it's *your* system and you've created it. Often, if you're working online, you're working with a system someone else has designed, and quite often that person was a tech lord, a programmer or a systems analyst who may not know all that much about the demands of the research you are doing.

Evaluation

Once you've prepared your search strategy and found some material on the Internet, you now have to evaluate it. The ancient Greeks were first to record their evaluation of data. Earlier people may have done it—they may have looked at the claims of some ancient pharaoh or king sculpted into the wall of a palace or temple and scoffed. They didn't do it publicly and they didn't leave their writings for future generations. New pharaohs and new kings simply chiseled out the claims of their predecessors.

A man named Hacataeus of Miletus, part of Ionia, a city whose ruins are found in what is today Turkey, is considered one of the founders of both history and geography. He traveled throughout Greece, the Persian Empire, and Egypt in the sixth century B.C. Hacataeus wrote two books, *A Map of the World*, which was probably the first geography or travel book, and an epic history called *Genealogies*. His opening sentences in *Genealogies* are significant: "What I write here," Hacataeus said, "is the account I considered to be true. For the stories of the Greeks are numerous, and my opinion, ridiculous." Hacataeus was perhaps the first person we know of who evaluated his data and then stood by that evaluation. He had gone to Egypt and realized that the time line of history was longer than his fellow Greeks had assumed. Egypt, he discovered, was ruled by men when Greece was supposedly still ruled by the gods.

Herodotus of Halicarnassus (another Ionian city, also in modern Turkey), lived about a century later and is called the "Father of History." Herodotus is best known for his account of how the Greeks defeated the Persian invasion. His nine-volume history contains much more—accounts of his travels to the Black Sea region that the Greeks called Euxine, and to Babylon, Phoenicia, and Egypt.

Herodotus was a man of his time; he stood between the time of epic poetry and factual history. His stories contain a mixture of myth, tall stories, and fact. Herodotus evaluated the stories he was told—not all modern scholars agree with his conclusions—but he took the first steps toward evaluation. Herodotus would often qualify his stories with "as I am informed" and in one famous passage, "I am bound to state what is said, but I am not bound to believe." He allows himself an out that any modern journalist would use, the quotation: "The Athenians say that a great snake lives in the Sanctuary as guardian of the citadel, and they present a honeycake every month as to a creature existing." He hedges his bets when addressing the gods: "Please do not be angry with me—supposing you do exist. But at this time of day, you know, one must really draw the line somewhere."

Herodotus traveled by foot and by ship. The Net researcher stays home and (to mix metaphors) trawls the Infobahn. The modern researcher, like Herodotus, must decide where and when to draw the line on research. The danger on the Net is that much of the information is just the same as Herodotus gathered—anecdotal accounts that must be checked and double-checked. Let's suppose for a moment there was a Net back then.

```
Newsgroup: alt.travel.trireme
From:      Alexis@Parthenon.edu
Subject:   Inscriptions on Pyramids
Does anyone know what's inscribed on the pyramids?
Thanks in advance.
Alexis


To:        Alexis@Parthenon.edu
From:      Herodotus@thurii.org
Subject:   Inscriptions on Pyramids
The inscriptions tell the amount of money spent on onions
and leeks for the workers who built the Pyramids. I know, I
was there myself.
Herodotus
```

There's one problem with the story. Most modern scholars believe that the inscriptions, which probably disappeared in the Middle Ages, were religious. Herodotus was fooled by his tour guide.

Beware the honestly posted but inaccurate message, whether in a newsgroup or by e-mail. No matter what's been posted, the researcher should check the source. Is the source authoritative, unbiased (or can the bias be identified and qualified?), reputable, up to date? One good thing about the Net is that usually someone jumps into a debate and says, "no, this information is wrong."

So what should one watch for in evaluating information on the Net? One factor to realize is how information gets *on* the Net. The interviews in this book tell you how some successful group moderators, list owners, and librarians evaluate the information they post. We've also talked to people about the information they get *off* the Net and how they evaluate material. Use your own judgment, and check online information against paper sources if you have a chance. Remember the old adage, "If in doubt, leave it out."

Perhaps the best way of evaluating the data you find on the Internet is to use a traditional twelve point check list.

Evaluation Check List

1. **Recency.** Do the data appear to be the most current on the subject or the most appropriate for an historical time period?

2. **Relevancy.** Is there a direct correlation to the subject? Is the tone of the source popular, scholarly, or technical?

3. **Authority.** What is the reputation of the data? What is the reliability of the source (history, context, viewpoint)?

4. **Completeness.** At what point has the researcher gathered sufficient data to produce a relatively unslanted report? Can the subject be understood by the researcher and the intended audience?

5. **Accuracy.** Does the source furnish background data and/or in-depth data? Are the complex issues oversimplified? Are the terms adequately defined?

6. **Clarity.** Can bias be recognized? Are there any logical fallacies? Are all assumptions (hidden or otherwise) identified?

7. **Verifiability.** Can subjective materials be verified? If not, why not?

8. **Statistical validity.** Can the conclusive data be supported by standard statistical testing? Was statistical inference is needed? Are there clear explanations for using "averages" or "percentages?"

9. **Internal consistency.** Do the data contain internal contradictions?

10. **External consistency.** Do the data reflect any contradictions among the source documents?

11. **Context.** Do the data reflect some sort of common sense or experience of the world within the context of information demand? Can fact be distinguished from opinion? Are sources taken out of context? Can the document be placed within the circumstances of the era that produced it?

12. **Comparative quality.** Are some data clearly inferior to other data? Which are the "best" data in context of the above eleven tests (i.e.,

most recent, most relevant, the most authoritative, the most complete, the most accurate and so forth).

—From *Finding Answers: The Essential Guide to Gathering Information in Canada* by Dean Tudor, McClelland & Stewart, 1993. (Reprinted with permission of the author.)

You should always be evaluating the information as you browse the Net. Check the little things that journalists watch for. A misspelled name, for example, could be a warning sign, even in an academic paper, that the author was careless in other areas as well. Do any statements seem exaggerated? If so, why has the author exaggerated? Is it a spur-of-the-moment statement by e-mail, or is that exaggeration more deliberate? Are you reading instant analysis, quick off the mark, or the results of a carefully crafted study, or a meta-analysis, which is a study of all previous studies on a subject? What do you think has been left out of the report? What an author omits may be just as important to a researcher as what an author includes. What's left out could reveal much about the bias of the information you are reading.

Don't ignore bias as a valuable source of information, as well: Even an untrustworthy source is valuable for what it reveals about the personality of an author, especially if he or she is an actor in the events. Barbara Tuchman writes: "Bias in a primary source is to be expected. One allows for it and corrects it by reading another version. . . . Even if an event is not controversial, it will have been seen and remembered from different angles of view by different observers. If the event *is* in dispute, one has an extra obligation to examine both sides. As the lion in Aesop said to the Man, 'There are many statues of men slaying lions, but if only the lions were sculptors there might be a quite a different set of statues.'"

Barbara Tuchman also says the researcher should be on the lookout for *corroborative detail*. She notes that whenever an author makes a generalization, she was "instantly on guard," and her immediate reaction was, "Show me." What is the proof offered for any statement? In one way corroborative detail is proof of what the writer is trying to prove. In another, it is the anecdote that enlarges and enlightens. Corroborative detail adds the human dimension to a story, whether it is Tuchman's description of Russian headquarters in her book *The Guns of August* or a few lines describing and humanizing a patient in an otherwise technical report in a medical journal. Consider one example, in a paper titled "Statistical and Theoretical Considerations in Meta-Analysis," published in the *Journal of Clinical Epidemiology*. In this paper, Stanford University's Ingram Olkin discusses the subject of uncertainty, both in general terms and as it applies to the study of statistics. He uses corroborative detail, two popular reports on drug trials that appeared in the *New York Times* on March 2, 1994, to support a technical discussion of statistical formulae.

There's another problem, growing in the 1990s, called by some the *Crossfire Syndrome*, after *Crossfire*, the CNN public affairs show and its tabloid television imitators. The Crossfire Syndrome drowns out the moderate voices in favor of polarization and polemics. Confrontation between polar opposites may make for good television, but it often paints a distorted view of reality. On the Net, the Crossfire Syndrome is acute. In flame wars, the shouters on both sides are left to use up bandwidth while the moderate voices back off. Political correctness of any sort, right or left, religious or secular, also distorts material. The researcher, if he or she is honest, must seek out the facts behind the bias.

It's been said many times that there is no such thing as objectivity. The honest researcher tries to be *fair*. The best researcher is both prosecutor and defense attorney, searching out the facts on all sides (there are often more than two).

Finally, you should note that there are many kinds of research. Scientific research comes to mind first when one considers the varieties of research, so we've included a list of hints for evaluating scientific studies prepared by the American Statistical Association. But, to choose another example, what are the rules for political research? It's one area of research that is unabashedly partisan, yet still should be scrupulously accurate. Political researchers are active on the Internet. It's not their job to be objective. Yet, at the same time, the rules for political research are valuable and relevant to other players in the field, so we've also included the "Ten Rules for Political Research," to stand alongside the scientific rules.

So now, if you're ready for research, in the next chapter we'll take a closer look at the tools you can use on the Internet.

Some Questions To Ask to Evaluate Studies

1. Was this a well-planned and executed study?

» Was the study clearly identified in advance?

» Was the study population clearly identified?

» Was the design appropriate for answering the study question?

» In comparative studies, was an appropriate control (unexposed or untreated) population used?

» Was the study large enough to provide a convincing study (good statistical "power")?

» Were efforts made to reduce nonresponse to surveys and other causes of missing data?

» Were efforts made to assure accurate collection and coding of data?

» Were the data analyzed by an experienced data analyst?

2. Was the report well written?

» Were the goals of the study clearly specified?

» Were the results presented in enough detail that a knowledgeable reader could draw his or her own conclusions?

» Is there an adequate assessment of the strength of evidence? Namely, are confidence intervals and p [probability] values provided to give readers an understanding of the possible role of chance in producing the observed result? Are potential systematic sources of error discussed, such as a hidden factor that explains an association between two variables?

» Is there adequate discussion of the previous literature, including a review of relevant positive and negative studies?

3. Was the study published in a peer-reviewed journal?

4. Are definitions being used consistently?

» Many apparent statistical anomalies arise because the definition of a term such as "AIDS" may change. Problems of definition also afflict "meta-analyses," which are designed to combine information from various studies, because the quantities being measured may not be the same in all studies.

5. Does the study claim to prove a causal relationship?

» If so, was the study a designed experiment with random allocation of treatments to subjects (the strongest type of study to establish causality)? If the study was observational (not randomized), was there a diligent effort to rule out possible hidden factors than explain a statistical association?

—From a handout distributed at the Science and Journalism session at the convention of the American Statistical Association, Toronto, August 16, 1994. No author.

Ten Rules for Political Research

1. It's great to be first, but first you have to be right.

2. Know the people who know. Find the rabbi.

3. Everyone has an agenda.

4. Sometimes there is no one on the grassy knoll. Know when to cut your losses.

5. Never imagine your facts, but use your facts imaginatively.

6. If you can't run with the big dogs, stay on the porch. Know your limits.

7. Make sure it's going to hurt them more than it hurts you.

8. Know the system.

9. The game moves as you play.

10. The other guy is never as dumb as you hope and you're never as smart as you think you are.

—courtesy of Mac Penny

The Ethics of Research

The U.S. National Academy of Sciences publishes a guide "On Being A Scientist: Responsible Conduct in Research." It is available on the World Wide Web at:

`http://www.nas.edu/pub/reports/on_being_a_scientist/`

4

Internet Research Tools

This chapter introduces and profiles several Internet services. Each service has its own software clients, although some commercial products are integrating several different software client services into a single product. The Internet research services mentioned in this chapter include e-mail mailing lists (and how to find them), Usenet newsgroups, Gopher, World Wide Web, File Transfer Protocol (FTP), Archie, Telnet (remote log-in), Hytelnet, Internet Relay Chat (IRC), and news scanning research services.

E-mail and Mailing Lists

To use Internet mailing lists for research, you'll need *at least* these three things:

1. Internet access with e-mail
2. An Internet e-mail reading/composing software client
3. Ways to find mailing lists of interest

Chapter 2 showed you how to get Internet access. Here we'll need to talk more about e-mail software clients, and how subscribers control their own Internet mailing list subscriptions. Then we'll show you how to find Internet mailing lists on almost any topic.

The most important thing for researchers to remember about Internet mailing lists and Usenet newsgroups is netiquette. It would be a good idea to read Chapter 7, on netiquette, *before* using either newsgroups or mailing lists for research. To get the most out of a mailing list you must understand the peculiar, singular habits of one mailing list at a time, and you should also be recognized as a contributor to that mailing list or newsgroup. Many groups will entertain inquiries from outsiders, but their best in-depth responses are often reserved for familiars.

E-mail Software Clients

The three most advanced Internet e-mail software clients on the Net today are PINE, Eudora, and Chameleon. These e-mail programs include all the basic e-mail functions, and also include advanced functions such as the ability to attach digital files to e-mail messages.

Whatever e-mail program you use, be aware that you alone are responsible for the appearance of the messages you send when they are received by your correspondents. Some *newbies* try to pretend that confusing messages with broken words, disorganized paragraphs, and uneven lines can be blamed on their software or hardware. Silly newbies—their messy messages reflect on themselves and show their inattention to detail, not their allegedly alien software!

So, there is no excuse or alternative: All users must learn how to do the best they can with the software they are using. This usually entails the most dreaded requirement in our technological age—reading the "fine" manual (or *RTFM*, as they say on the Internet). Learning to use your e-mail program also requires some dry-run e-mail messages to yourself, to a few trusted friends and *yourself*, and then later single messages to individuals on the Net, all *before* posting a message to a newsgroup or a mailing list. The idea is to send things out and see what your messages look like when they are sent back to you.

If you are shopping for an e-mail program, be sure to get one that can handle MIME. MIME stands for Multipurpose Internet Mail Extensions, and MIME allows regular Internet e-mail messages to carry graphics, audio, video, and other kinds of digital files. The MIME portions of your e-mail messages travel as *attachments* to the text e-mail messages and arrive at the same time as the e-mail messages. If your e-mail program *cannot* handle MIME, you may sometimes receive files of indecipherable nonsense in your e-mail mailbox instead of getting a useful MIME-attached file.

Elm

Elm is a free set of UNIX e-mail software programs that are copyrighted by the Usenet Community Trust. Many UNIX shell account providers make it available as one of their basic e-mail reading, composing, and handling programs. Elm is revised from time to time, and the following Web page has links to relevant FAQs and all available free software:

`http://www.myxa.com/myxa/elm.html`

PINE

If you have a UNIX shell account, one of the most powerful and versatile e-mail programs available to you is PINE, from the University of Washington. PINE upgrades its features regularly and has several advanced features unavailable in competing UNIX e-mail products.

Because its appearance is monochrome and text-based rather than offering a color, graphically displayed interface, PINE looks a lot like DOS or UNIX. You can use PINE to read, reply to, delete, and compose e-mail. It will also allow you to forward e-mail. It can also hold your outgoing e-mail compositions as pending drafts while you double-check a few details.

PINE also allows you to grab addresses right off your incoming e-mail to put them into your electronic address book, so you don't have to type in and proofread the e-mail addresses of your friends and associates.

For further information about PINE, you can read the Usenet newsgroup comp.mail.pine or send e-mail to pine@cac.washington.edu, or you can visit this URL with your Web browser:

`http://www.cac.washington.edu:1180/pine/index.html`

Chameleon

Chameleon is a Windows compatible Internet client suite that includes an e-mail program with the ability to handle MIME attachments and to UUENCODE and UUDECODE e-mailed items for you. It handles all the required e-mail functions and has some features not found in the freeware version of Eudora.

Like WSArchie and WS_FTP, the Chameleon Archie and Chameleon FTP clients are linked so that after Archie finds a file on a remote FTP server all you have to do is click to initiate the FTP client and begin the file transfer.

Installation of Chameleon is smooth and straightforward, especially compared to installation for the shareware version of Trumpet WinSock.

To find out about the current version of Chameleon, including FAQs and free samples available, visit this Web page:

`http://www.netmanage.com/netmanage/nm3.html`

Eudora

Eudora, along with the maker's newest product called Eudora Pro, has been actively improved and upgraded for several years in response to user requests and Internet developments. You can use Eudora to read, reply to, delete, and compose e-mail. Eudora deals effectively with UUENCODED files, and has the capacity to send and receive MIME attachments. One of the features that has made Eudora popular is its ability to filter incoming and outgoing messages into appropriate mailboxes. Their newest product includes built-in WinSock and SLIP/PPP software to simplify the user's life.

To find out more about Eudora Pro, telephone 1-800-238-3672, write e-mail to quest-rep@qualcomm.com, or visit this Web page:

`http://www.qualcomm.com/quest/`

Pegasus

Pegasus, also called *Pmail,* is another internationally popular e-mail program that operates across several platforms. To find further information, FAQs, and background information about Pegasus e-mail software, or to download a copy, use a Gopher or Web browser to visit this URL:

`gopher://risc.ua.edu/11/network/pegasus`

Internet Subscribers Control Their Own Subscriptions

In contrast to some magazine and newspaper subscriptions, subscribers on the Internet have complete control over their own mailing list subscriptions. Almost all Internet mailing lists are free, and the subscriber decides when to turn each subscription on or off, and when to put the mail on hold for a while. This shifts the responsibility for starting and stopping mail from the sender to the recipient, and this shift in responsibility is confusing to some Net newbies.

Magazine and newspaper publishers won't keep sending you their new issues if you stop paying for the product. The magazine or newspaper (the *sender*) controls when you start and stop receiving a subscription to their product, even if they do start or stop your subscription based on your payment. But on the Internet, payment is not usually part of a subscription, and the computer that handles your subscription couldn't care less whether you get a copy of the next message or not—your subscription is completely up to you, to start, change, or cancel at any time.

Some mailing lists have restrictions that prevent people outside a certain geographic region, or not enrolled in a certain college class, for instance, from being allowed to subscribe. Even if an automated mailing list has a restricted screening process before you can subscribe to the list, the subscriber is often expected to put his or her own mail on *hold* when they go on vacation, or to cancel the subscription when they want to exit from the mailing list altogether.

Note

There are a few publicly available manually operated mailing lists that are not computerized. Manually operated lists still require the assistance of the moderator and necessitate some delays for human processing. But manually operated mailing lists are not common. Today the great majority of Internet mailing list subscriptions are automated and under subscriber control.

Because you are in control of your own Internet mailing list subscriptions, it is a sign of rudeness or ingenuousness to ask the people on a mailing list for help in subscribing, unsubscribing, or putting your mail on hold. Everyone does this clerical work for themselves, and everyone has the same instructions to work from—the subscription instructions are e-mailed to every new subscriber (don't lose it)!

If you have any doubt about the correct e-mail address for sending clerical instructions to the subscription robot or for sending on-topic messages to the people on a mailing list, there is an easy, standardized way to send a request for help to the human mailing list *moderator* or *owner*. Address your e-mail *SOS* to the name of the mailing list followed by a hyphen and the word *request*.

For example, the e-mail address to write to the moderator of the health related Internet mailing list *Allergy* is Allergy request@tamvm1.tamu.edu. The general form of the address, which works for all known e-mail mailing list subscription software, is listname-request@node.domain.

Tip

If for some reason the listname-request address fails and you still have no help after a few days, write to the postmaster at the node where you thought the mailing list should be. The general form of the postmaster address is postmaster@node.domain. Postmasters are generally very busy and may handle hundreds of e-mail messages a day, so give them a break. If they can help, they usually will. Mostly, postmasters try to forward your message to someone who might be able to help you.

Mailing List Software Instructions

Although there are over two dozen different kinds of Internet mailing list management software programs now in use, the three most popular, LISTSERV, listproc, and majordomo, account for well over half of the traffic. If you can use only these three kinds of subscriptions, most of the thousands of Internet mailing lists are available to you with no more study needed. Finding LISTSERV lists is pretty easy, and finding the right listproc and majordomo lists is getting easier as new indexing tools come online.

Caution

Older versions of listproc are often confused with LISTSERV, and new users sometimes assume they are dealing with the familiar LISTSERV, when they are actually dealing with an older version of the listproc software that once was called listserv or listserver.

To learn more about the Internet mailing list software programs LISTSERV, listproc, and majordomo, send e-mail to each of the following addresses with the subject line *help*, and the message body *help*:

» `listserv@listserv.net`

» `listproc@inet.ed.gov`

» `majordomo@greatcircle.com`

Tip

With these three help files permanently saved on diskette and printed on paper, you will have the rules and commands for the majority of Internet mailing lists at your disposal at all times. When you are about to go on vacation and want to set your subscriptions on hold, or when an unexpected priority emerges, it's nice to already have copies of these mailing list rules ready for immediate use.

Finding Internet Mailing Lists

Stephanie and Peter da Silva at arielle@bonkers.taronga.com keep a list of publicly available mailing lists. The da Silvas' document is commonly referred to as PAML, but you should remember that the PAML list does *not* contain entries for all Internet mailing lists—PAML only contains mailing lists that are available to the public *if* the list owner or moderator has asked Stephanie to include the list in PAML.

Here are two ways to access the PAML list of mailing lists using either FTP or a WWW browser:

`ftp://rtfm.mit.edu/pub/usenet/news.answers/mail/mailing-lists/`
`http://www.neosoft.com/internet/paml/`

Or, to get a list of global LISTSERV mailing lists, you may either use Gopher or FTP:

```
gopher://hearn.nic.surfnet.nl/
ftp://ftp.nic.surfnet.nl/surfnet/net-
    management/earn/services/listserv.lists
```

An e-mail alternative also exists. To get instructions on finding more mailing lists, send exactly this e-mail message: *get lists of lists* to Nodak at LISTSERV@vm1.nodak.edu.

Private Mailing Lists

Some mailing lists are strictly private and not publicly available. Private lists often do not announce or advertise their existence in any way. (It's not easy to find private mailing lists, although spammers keep trying.)

Tip

For all practical purposes, private lists cannot be found and are unavailable for research purposes unless a list member or the list owner/manager is willing to divulge its existence during your research. If you don't ask, you surely won't find private lists.

InfoMagnet

There are over 6,000 publicly available LISTSERV mailing lists on the Internet today. Using InfoMagnet you can find LISTSERV Internet mailing lists on almost any topic, and once you find them InfoMagnet will actually *subscribe* to or *unsubscribe* from the mailing list for you. InfoMagnet is a Windows-compatible mailing list subscription handling program. InfoMagnet also will put your mailing list subscriptions *on hold* for you when you go on vacation, and generally keeps track of your subscriptions for you. InfoMagnet requires you to have Windows and at least a SLIP/PPP connection to the Internet.

InfoMagnet will help you select mailing lists based on keywords. And InfoMagnet will send the subscription request to any or all of these mailing lists for you. And that's not all. InfoMagnet can also keyword-search the archives of each mailing list for you (if it's possible), and will get you a sample of the recent messages on the mailing lists you're interested in.

Note

To find out more about InfoMagnet, contact John Buckman at jbuckman@shelby.com, or write to the Walter Shelby Group at 4618 Maple Avenue, Bethesda, MD 20814, or call 301-718-7840.

Tile

Another search tool, brought to you by the same people who make InfoMagnet, allows you to use the Web to keyword-search for Usenet newsgroups, LISTSERV mailing lists, and FTP sites. It is associated with the software product named *Tile*. You can find it at:

`http://www.tile.net/tile/`

LWGate

Yet another, similar Web interface is also available to search the global list of over 6,000 LISTSERV mailing lists. Its URL is:

`http://www.netspace.org/cgi-bin/lwgate/search-other.htm`

LWGate also has a growing collection of LISTSERV, listproc, majordomo, and smartlist mailing lists that you can search and *subscribe to* using a Web browser. Its URL is:

`http://www.netspace.org/cgi-bin/lwgate/`

Caution   *The global LISTSERV list is a very big file containing thousands of mailing list descriptions. Please be sure to carefully read the Help message on that page and specify a search keyword before you try the global search at LWGate/Search-Other. Otherwise, you could end up getting a very large piece of e-mail from yourself!*

LISTSERV Database Search

One of the valuable features of the LISTSERV mailing list program is that it can easily create and allow you to search archives of the topical discussions on thousands of mailing lists. One of the most notable LISTSERV sites is in North Dakota. Its address is listserv@vm1.nodak.edu, so we call it "Nodak."

You send Nodak the following search commands to find mailing lists on any new research topic. You should notice that the *keywords* could be changed to *any* other words you are interested in. The commands say, in effect, search the mailing list databases New-list, Intgroup, and Lists, then send me a single line that describes each instance of the keywords I specify ever occurring in any of these three mailing lists' databases.

```
//DBlook JOB Echo=No
Database Search DD=Rules
//Rules DD *
```

```
Select keyword keywords in lists
index
Select keyword keywords in intgroup
index
Select keyword keywords in new-list
index
```

When Nodak responds, you get a set of all the instances of the search words in these databases of mailing lists. The ones that seem the most interesting can then be requested in full-text form, rather than index form.

To request the items that are most interesting, you carefully choose the number of that item from the leftmost column of the output from your first search, and send the next request to Nodak in the style given below, using the item numbers you want in the places where the template has #####. Don't forget to fill in your keywords again, too.

```
//DBlook JOB Echo=No
Database Search DD=Rules
//Rules DD *
Select keyword keywords in lists
print ##### #####
Select keyword keywords in intgroup
print ##### #####
Select keyword keywords in new-list
print ##### #####
```

The ability to create and search mailing list archives makes LISTSERV a very popular product, as proven by the fact that over 20,000 LISTSERV mailing lists are publicly available.

Usenet Newsgroups

There are around 13,000 Usenet newsgroups at this writing. There is no firm number, because newsgroups are always being formed, and others become extinct. Some newsgroups are local or regional in content, and might not be interesting to people around the world. So any one news-server may, or may not, carry the local newsgroups from another region or country, or all the newsgroups that any one researcher might want to read.

Usenet is organized hierarchically. The top levels of Usenet newsgroup hierarchy names are the leftmost parts of the dotted name. Table 4-1 lists some of the most well-known Usenet hierarchies.

Table 4-1.

Usenet Hierarchies

Hierarchy	Discussion Topic
alt.	Vast range of topics
bionet.	Biological sciences
bit.	Bitnet and LISTSERV groups
biz.	Business
clari.	News services through ClariNet
comp.	Computer science
ddn.	Defense Data Network
gnu.	Free Software Foundation GNU project
ieee.	Institute of Electrical and Electronic Engineers
k12.	Kindergarten through high school
misc.	Topics not covered elsewhere
news.	Usenet news and news software
rec.	Recreation and entertainment
sci.	Science
soc.	Social issues
talk.	Discussions and debates

Tip

If you've seen references to newsgroups that are not showing up on the news service you're using, ask for them. I once wanted to keep up with some newsgroups from the San Francisco Bay Area (they start with ba.) which were not usually available on the news-servers in Austin, Texas. But in just hours they were available—all I had to do was ask. Likewise, if, for your research, you want to read the local newsgroups for a remote location, ask your Internet Service Provider for information about newsgroups currently available from that geographical area. The Internet makes great distances insignificant, rendering research data more available than ever.

Some newsgroups, such as the ClariNet, *"clari,"* groups, are only available from profit-making entities. A news-server can only supply these commercial groups by a contractual arrangement, usually where money changes hands. Because these groups are not free, as the remainder of Usenet is, commercial groups are slightly less available. Depending on the value that media network newsfeeds and wire service stories might have for your research, you might consider paying a premium for an Internet Service Provider that makes these commercial newsgroups available.

To read Usenet news, you'll need to learn to use newsreading software. UNIX users commonly read Usenet news with programs named *nn*, *rn*, *xrn*, *trn*, *gnus*, and *tin*. Windows users use one of the Windows Internet client suites such as Internet in a Box, or a free-standing newsreader such as Forté Free Agent, Netscape Navigator, Nuntius, or Trumpet. Or anyone can use most any Gopher to access Usenet. WSGopher, highlighted in Chapter 12, comes with built-in bookmarks for reading Usenet newsgroups.

A large set of resources for Usenet readers, including beginners, has been collected at Indiana University, and is available at the following URL:

`http://scwww.ucs.indiana.edu/NetRsc/usenet.html`

This site has several primers and FAQs about Usenet, links to the chapters of many newsgroups, information about how to read newsgroups, post messages, how to cancel your posts, how to create new newsgroups, how to use the various newsreading software, and general background information about Usenet.

The Forté Free Agent newsreader for Windows is available free either by FTP or by Web browser:

`ftp://ftp.forteinc.com/pub/forte/free_agent/fagent10.zip`
`http://www.forteinc.com/forte/`

NetNews Filter Service

The NetNews Filter Service at Stanford University can perform keyword scans through much of Usenet every day for you. This free service throws a very wide net and catches lots of dross, but if you're willing to *manually* throw out the near misses, you can also find some excellent leads from throughout Usenet with the NetNews Filter Service.

To find out more about this service, send the e-mail message *help* to the address netnews@db.stanford.edu or point your Web browser to the following URL:

`http://woodstock.stanford.edu:2000/`

Gopher, Veronica, and Jughead

Gopher is a powerful, advanced use of the Internet's distributed processing nature. Gopher is popular because it is easy to use and powerful enough to organize, index, search, and deliver vast amounts of useful information.

Gopher is a kind of TCP/IP service on the Internet. It's a kind of Internet server-client software, too. Thousands of Gopher servers are now available on the Net. These Gopher servers, taken together, present an abundance of information, offering digital files on almost any topic under the sun.

Veronica and Jughead provide ways to search for information on Gopher servers. They rely on indexes of the names of documents and files, and on indexes of the names of folders or directories on the many Gopher servers. Chapter 12 is devoted to explaining and demonstrating the research uses of Gopher, Veronica, and Jughead.

World Wide Web Browsers

The World Wide Web is a rapidly growing source of Internet research material. Many new Internet users who were previously inhibited from venturing out onto the Net are willing and able to explore using a user-friendly Web browser. And several easy-to-use browsers have become available in the last few years.

This section gives you leads to four Web browsers—Lynx, Cello, Mosaic, and Netscape. There are several more commercially available Web browser products that won't be mentioned. Perhaps you could use the Net research skills you're learning here to seek out some of the others, or perhaps you'll find that one of these four browsers meets your needs.

Lynx

This nongraphical Web browser (also know as a *text-based* browser) is very similar to the UNIX Gopher, except that it can handle WWW hypertext in ways that Gopher cannot. Most users access Lynx either because they are in a hurry—Lynx is fast because it ignores the graphics that can slow down Mosaic and Netscape—or they use Lynx because they do not have access to a graphical Web browser.

Figure 4-1 shows what Lynx looks like. Lynx is the Web browser you should expect to have available if you have a UNIX shell account without SLIP/PPP, as mentioned previously in Chapter 2. (With Lynx, you can browse the Web even without SLIP/PPP access.) If for any reason your UNIX shell account does not have Lynx, ask your ISP support people to get it free from the University of Kansas by FTP or Web browser:

`ftp://ftp2.cc.ukans.edu/pub/lynx/`

Cello

Cello offers many basic features for Web browsing, but it is no longer being actively developed. Figure 4-2 shows you the Cello home page. Cello's primary

Figure 4-1.

Lynx looks like text on a monitor

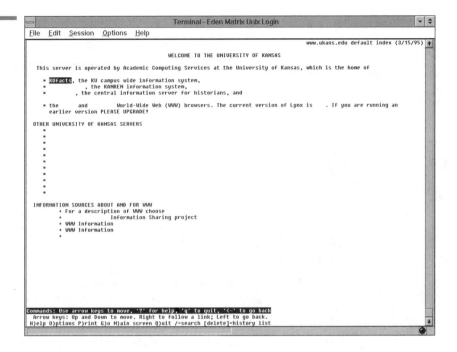

Figure 4-2.

The Cello home page at Cornell University

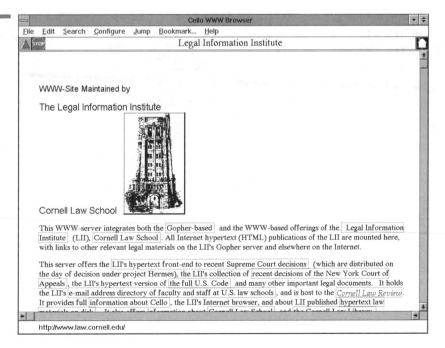

attraction is that it works for Web browsing, and that the software Web client is available at no cost by FTP:

`ftp://ftp.law.cornell.edu/pub/LII/Cello/Cello.zip`

A useful FAQ file is also available at this URL:

`http://www.law.cornell.edu/cello/cellofaq.html`

Mosaic

Mosaic was the first Windows-compatible Web browser to become enormously popular. Mosaic's phenomenal popularity can be traced to the fact that it was the first free, easy-to-use, mouseable graphical Internet browsing tool with clickable hypertext links. Mosaic uses HTML coding language and makes it easy to create documents on the WWW.

To learn more about Mosaic you can send e-mail to mosaic@ncsa.uiuc.edu. To get a copy of the latest version of Mosaic, visit the University of Illinois at Champaign-Urbana at this URL:

`http://www.ncsa.uiuc.edu/SDG/Software/Mosaic/`

Figure 4-3.

The Mosaic home page at Indiana University

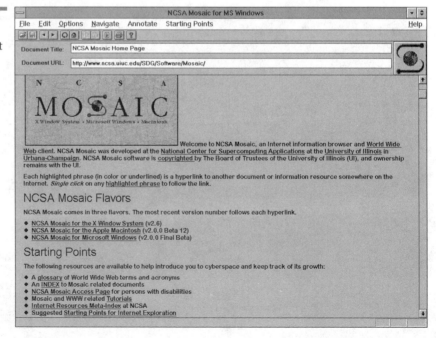

Netscape Navigator

Netscape was written by many of the same software engineers who originally designed Mosaic. Netscape is available in 32-bit versions that work with Windows 95, and Netscape is leading the way in Web software development at this writing. Other teams are scrambling to catch up, but Netscape has a lead that will be difficult to match.

To get a copy of the latest version of Netscape by FTP or WWW, here is the URL for Netscape Navigator's mirror sites:

`http://home.mcom.com/comprod/mirror/index.html`

Figure 4-4.
The Netscape home page

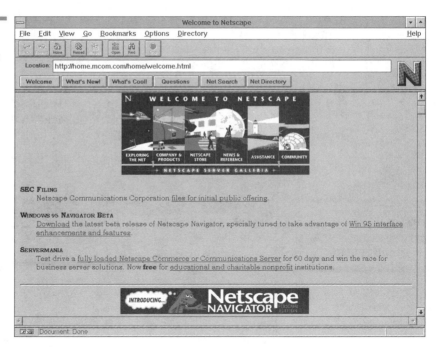

File Transfer Protocol (FTP) and Archie

FTP will be discussed and explained in detail in Chapter 5. FTP is one of the three most basic Internet services, along with Telnet (or remote log-in), which is covered in the next section, and e-mail, which we discussed at the beginning of this chapter. FTP allows the Internet researcher to make a copy of a distant document, software program, or other digital file. The newly copied file usually ends up in your UNIX account space or home directory. on your ISP's computer or on your hard drive, depending on whether you have an indirect or a direct Internet connection.

FTP can also be used in reverse to copy a file you have in one place onto a distant computer. And FTP can be used to nose around remote FTP servers that may have interesting files on them. But Archie can tell you *which* FTP servers have the files you want, so let's talk about Archie now.

Archie

Archie is a service that keeps track of the contents of most of the FTP servers on the Internet. The Archie servers have inventories of the files and directories on hundreds of FTP servers. When you perform an Archie search, you specify a *word* or *root word* that must be in the title of the file or name of the directory you're seeking. The Archie server responds by telling you the Internet address for the "hits" found on FTP servers throughout the Internet, along with the directory and filename of the matched items.

For example, if you are looking for Internet software clients that run with the Windows operating system, you might want to search an Archie server for the words *clients* or *winsock*. What you'll get back is a list of FTP locations (sites) where directory names and/or filenames match your search word.

Figure 4-5.
WSArchie found these directories and filenames with the word *winsock*

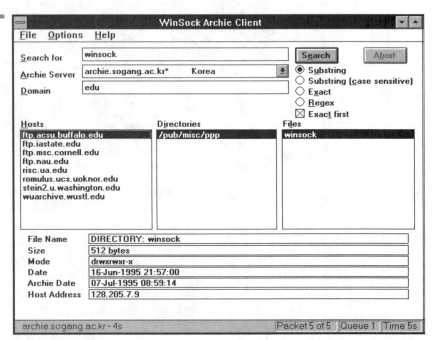

WSArchie searches are based on your keywords. The search shown in Figure 4-5 was based on the word winsock, and turned up several directories with the name *winsock*. You can tell they are directories—even though they are showing up in the "files" list box on the right side of the screen—because down below in the file detail area it says whether the highlighted item is a file or directory. And when you double-click on *winsock* in the "files" list box, WSArchie goes to that site and searches the directory for all filenames, and displays the filenames in the file list box, as shown in Figure 4-6.

Figure 4-6.
WSArchie found these filenames in the directory *winsock*

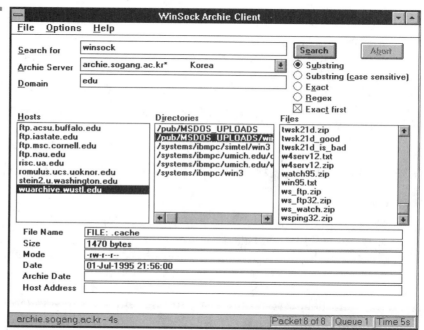

The operation of checking for all the filenames in a directory is called *expanding* the directory. WSArchie also makes the Expand option available as an entry in the File menu. Other options included on the File menu are Save, Retrieve, and Exit, as shown in Figure 4-7.

The Save option allows you to create a text file of your search results. This makes a record of your work, and allows you to return to that research later. The

Figure 4-7.
The WSArchie File menu includes Save, Retrieve, Expand, and Exit

Retrieve option allows you to immediately invoke an FTP transfer of the item highlighted. And the Exit option closes the WSArchie software client.

Most UNIX shell accounts have an Archie client available to you. You can read the manual pages by typing *man archie* at the UNIX prompt.

You can obtain the WSArchie client free at these FTP addresses:

```
ftp://ftp.demon.co.uk/pub/ibmpc/winsock/apps/wsarchie/
ftp://ail.telecom.uqam.ca/etc/canelle/pc/win31/winapps2
ftp://ftp.txdirect.net/pub/windows/
ftp://ftp.sunet.se/pub/pc/windows/wsarchie
```

Or you can browse the many WinSock client applications available at these WinSock repositories to find WSArchie and other WinSock clients:

```
http://uts.cc.utexas.edu/~neuroses/cwsapps.html
http://homepage.eznet.net/~rwilloug/ewa.html
```

Hytelnet and Telnet/Remote Log-in Resource Listings

The Internet protocol and service called Telnet is also known as *remote log-in*. As mentioned before, Telnet is one of the three most basic Internet services; if you don't have Telnet, you don't have complete Internet access. Telnet allows you to connect to a remote computer and use resources and services on that remote server. If you've ever used your modem to dial up a local computer bulletin board, you'll understand that Telnet is very similar, except the connection is over the Internet rather than a telephone line, and the remote computer is likely to be halfway around the world, instead of just across town.

Hytelnet is an eclectic Internet resource that comes in many shapes, sizes, and modalities. Hytelnet contains the information necessary to log in remotely and enter Telnet sites all over the Internet. Hytelnet can be used as a hypertext document or executable on some computers. Sometimes Hytelnet is printed as a paper document, and Hytelnet is used as a database of Internet resources on many systems. Several versions are available for various computers and setups (Macintosh, DOS, UNIX, Gopher, HTML, and more).

Many people use Hytelnet over the Internet as an online searchable index. For example, this URL connects to a search tool at EINet that includes Hytelnet:

```
http://galaxy.einet.net/howto.html
```

Although Hytelnet information can be delivered in many different ways, users tend to think and speak of *everyone* using the same Hytelnet they do. Some versions of Hytelnet are built so that users can connect to the remote Telnet site they are reading about by just clicking a mouse or pressing an Arrow key. But the several manifestations of Hytelnet are different. Some are more comprehensive, and some versions will only work on certain computers. Because several versions of Hytelnet can be edited locally, one Hytelnet site might be more up to date, or more obsolete, than another site.

The University of Waterloo has several Hytelnet links in its Gopher, so you can use the following Gopher address to check out the Hytelnet sites at El Paso Community College, Oxford University, University of North Texas, University of California at Irvine, University of Adelaide, and Washington & Lee University:

`gopher://watserv2.uwaterloo.ca:70/11/servers/guides/hytelnet`

And Hytelnet can be yours free by FTP. Be sure to choose the filename with the highest version number, where *xx* in the filename is the highest version number:

`ftp://ftp.usask.ca/pub/hytelnet/pc/latest/hytelnxx.zip`

A DOS version of Hytelnet is usually available at:

`ftp://oak.oakland.edu/pub/msdos/hypertxt/hytelnxx.zip`

Learning about Hytelnet

Hytelnet and its database of Internet-accessible Telnet sites were developed by Peter Scott at the Systems Department of the University of Saskatchewan Libraries. He can be contacted at aa375@freenet.carleton.ca or by postal mail at 324 8th Street East, Saskatoon, Saskatchewan, Canada S7H 0P5. Peter's article, "Using Hytelnet to Access Internet Resources," can be obtained from the University of Houston by sending an e-mail message to LISTSERV@uhupvm1.uh.edu. The message body should say:

`get scott prv3n4 f=mail`

The UNIX version of Hytelnet was developed by Earl Fogel at fogel@herald.usask.ca of the University of Saskatchewan. The Macintosh version was written by Charles Burchill at burchil@ccu.umanitoba.ca of the University of Manitoba. And Lou Montulli at montulli@stat1.cc.ukans.edu at the University of Kansas answers questions about the HTML version.

You can also join the mailing list HYTEL-L, which announces new versions of Hytelnet and new, updated, or deleted files. To subscribe to HYTEL-L, send e-mail to LISTSERV@kentvm.kent.edu. The message body should say:

```
subscribe hytel-l Your Name
```

Caution

Some older copies of Hytelnet may contain links (and log-ins and passwords) that no longer work. Try to check the file date and version number when you use Hytelnet. Please report bad addresses and the version number of the Hytelnet you used to contact the people mentioned above.

Other Telnet Resources Lists

The Missouri Research and Education Network (MOREnet) Gopher has a set of over 20 Telnet links at this URL:

```
gopher://services.more.net:70/11/other_resources/tools/telnet/all
```

The Michigan State University Gopher has over 75 Telnet links arranged alphabetically at:

```
gopher://burrow.cl.msu.edu:70/11/internet/type/misc
```

The Princeton University Libraries' Gopher has several more Telnet sites listed at this URL:

```
gopher://library.Princeton.EDU:70/00/.gopher-files/guide_internet_
        res/telnet_sites
```

Scott Yanoff's Internet Services List

Since 1991 Scott Yanoff at yanoff@alpha2.csd.uwm.edu has produced many popular indexes and resources lists, and his "Special Internet Connections and Internet Services List" is found in repositories throughout the Net. Several of his early lists are largely Telnet site collections. The latest Web version contains over 20 Telnet sites.

Yanoff makes his list available by posting it regularly to the Usenet newsgroup alt.internet.services and by an auto-reply e-mail service at inetlist@aug3.augsburg.edu. Or you can get Yanoff's list by FTP or Web browser:

```
ftp://ftp.csd.uwm.edu/pub/inet.services.txt
http://www.uwm.edu/Mirror/inet.services.html
```

Internet Relay Chat (IRC)

Creative researchers may find more than they expect out on the Internet in the IRC channels. IRC is one of the most unrestricted and free parts of the Net, if you have access to it at all. Because IRC is a heavy resource user and is difficult to control once the door is open, some Internet Service Providers do not allow the IRC Internet protocol to be used from their node(s).

Caution

Some educational ISPs, such as the Texas statewide educational network TENET, have limited or eliminated access to IRC. Tenet simply does not offer school teachers (or students) in Texas the IRC Internet protocol. This arbitrary choice simplifies system administration, but also prevents users from experiencing for themselves the advantages and/or disadvantages of IRC.

With the standard Internet *Talk* and *Ytalk* protocols, you can communicate with one person or more at once, in real-time over the Internet. IRC is like talking with *many* people at once, all in real-time. There are many IRC servers throughout the Net, and they can allow thousands of people to be in communication on IRC all at the same time. People select an IRC channel when they sign on, and then participate in the activity on that channel.

Some IRC conversations are worthwhile; some are considerably less so. IRC can be very confusing. It depends on which channel(s) you are involved in, and the activity of the day.

Research uses of IRC are just beginning to be explored, and we do not delve deeply into IRC usage here. However, we do acknowledge that IRC has fine research potential in areas of human social behavior and human communication, and has very practical group communication applications that can be immediately useful to researchers.

To learn more about IRC, get the IRC Primer (the file is called IRCprimer1.1.txt) by FTP:

```
ftp://nic.funet.fi/pub/unix/irc/docs/IRCprimer1.1.txt
ftp://cs-ftp.bu.edu/irc/support/IRCprimer1.1.txt
ftp://coombs.anu.edu.au/pub/irc/docs/IRCprimer1.1.txt
```

News Scanning Services

Newshound and HeadsUp look through the Internet and in other proprietary information sources all day each day and look for news stories for you. Depending on the quality of their source material, and on the ability of the software to identify items that will be especially interesting to you, they may send you research material you can use or lots of e-mail for you to scan and delete.

Mercury Center Newshound—*San Jose Mercury News*

For $10 per month Newshound will keyword-scan a wide range of newspaper and wire service stories for you, e-mailing the relevant items directly to you. They hope to get news to you before it appears in your local paper. Here are some questions you can have answered by asking Newshound to scan keywords for you:

» What's your competition up to?

» What's going on in your home town?

» How is the out-of-town press treating your company?

» What's the latest news in your hobby?

» Is your neighborhood in the news?

» Did anyone pick up your press release?

» Have you or anyone you know been mentioned in the press?

» How are the companies in your investment portfolio performing?

For more information about Newshound send e-mail to:

`newshound-support@sjmercury.com`

or call toll free: 1-800-818-6397

HeadsUp Individual, Inc.

HeadsUp lets you choose from a large list of around 1,000 topics that they collect articles about, and they send you new two-sentence briefs of new articles every day. They use about 500 different sources for the 15,000 or so fresh articles they handle each day. If you find any of the two sentence briefs to be interesting, you then ask for the whole article and it is e-mailed to you.

HeadsUp has a free 30-day trial period, and then costs $29.95 per month plus $2.97 per full text article (via e-mail) if you ask for more than five articles per month. For more information about this service, send e-mail to heads-up@enews.com or telephone 617-273-6000; fax 1-800-417-1000 or 1-800-414-1000.

Another interface to this same service is available. This is a free categorized headline reading service, unless you choose to buy a copy of the whole story. All the details are at this URL:

```
http://www.newspage.com/
```

Evaluating the Internet at the *Washington Post*

Margot Williams is a research librarian and an Internet columnist for the *Washington Post*. Part of her job is to evaluate the material the *Post's* librarians search out and find on the Internet. We asked her advice on how to find and evaluate material on the Net.

"It depends on what their research is for—there's a lot of fun things that you can do," Williams says. "If you're using your research for things that go into publications and they're going to be printed, you've got to be particularly careful of the sources of your information, and also be aware that the materials could be copyrighted information that's posted up there, or people could claim that it's copyrighted.

"My basic concern as a news researcher is that I'm taking information from a reliable source . . . and that I'm not giving large amounts of copyrighted information to people without the understanding that they can't include it except under fair use.

"So what I tend to do when I'm looking for Web sites or Gopher menus, the important thing to me is finding out which ones are the best as far as authoritativeness is concerned, so I tend to stay mostly with government sources of information. There are more and more of them now available. It's really quite exciting to see the Commerce Department, the State Department of the United States, to see the World Bank and European community and Japan Transportation Department [on the Internet].

"My eye just tends to go towards government sources of information, which is what we do in our regular research as well," Williams says. "I don't tend to look at it as any different from doing research the way we've always done it."

The Internet is not usually a high priority for the *Washington Post* research staff to go to look for material. The *Post*, of course, has a budget to pay for major commercial database services such as Lexis/Nexis.

"I have a staff of researchers who have the whole world at their fingertips and we search every kind of database imaginable," Williams says, "and since Internet is the most difficult one to use, it's not the first place to go."

"At the *Washington Post*, where we cover the whole country and the whole world, we've got a . . . I guess it's called 'surfing' now, but we don't call it surfing. . . . It's research into publications and sources that may be someplace where we don't have a bureau or we don't have a reporter, Williams says. We're looking for background and we've got to go everywhere to get it. So that's also where the Internet is good, because there is stuff there from all over the world. You don't have to be there to do the research in a remote location."

"I just got Mosaic recently," Williams says. "Now that we've all seen Mosaic, we're all very excited about that, but we are not about to get SLIP connections for everybody in the newsroom or even in my department right now. I'm just hoping we will, but since it's not working all that well yet, I'm waiting to see. I think in a year or two it's going to really take off, or probably [quicker] than that, but I'm waiting until the best stuff is out there before buying software and buying phone lines.

"I love Gopher. I like the U.S. Department of Congress. I like Fedworld, but Fedworld's a local phone number so we just dial into Fedworld directly from Washington. I like all of those virtual reference places . . . the virtual libraries that have all the reference books on them.

"I really like to go to all the geography servers, [especially] the geography server at the Peabody Museum at Yale where you can put a place in and get its latitude and longitude, so that if you really were mapping you could locate the place and get some of the geographical information. And there's also the Martini Geography server, all those geography servers really fascinate me. You put the name of the place in, and how many places named 'Clinton' there are in the United States, or how many 'Paris' there are in the United States. It's a lot of fun. But it's also kind of useful."

When the *Washington Post* was preparing to cover the possible invasion of Haiti, the research staff found valuable material in the National Trade Databank. "It has a name that sounds morbid," Williams says. "It's on the U.S. Department of Commerce bulletin board, and in there is so much other stuff that I don't know how they're going to publicize it so that people will use it that way, but the State Department background notes are on there, the Human Rights reports for all the countries in the world, all the Army Area Handbooks that are available are on there. Unfortunately, the Haiti area handbook was not there. We had to run out to the store and buy it. The Haiti background notes were not in there, but the most recent Human Rights report was in there, and I guess we had it in another format. This way, when it was in electronic format, we could send it to the reporter that was preparing to go to Haiti, and I could send it to him [by] e-mail. I guess he just printed it out, but he could have kept it on his PC and taken it with him if he wanted to get some of the facts out of that.

"There's so much other stuff in there. . . . It's also a CD-ROM, and we have a subscription to that CD-ROM. It's an inexpensive CD-ROM, [but] it's a really good source of information."

She also warns reporters and others to be aware of potential problems. "There's a Whitewater home page on the World Wide Web; it's up in Dartmouth. It really looks nice. I have it on my hot list, but when you click on it, it has all kinds of strange information from the point of view of the person who put it together, this Whitewater home page and all the files lying behind it. For example, one of the words you can click on is the word *murders*, and it tells you how many murders have taken place during the Whitewater question, so the 'murder' of Vince Foster is one of the topics, and you click on the word *murder*, then it takes you to some articles from the *New York Post* that describe how Vince Foster was murdered."

The *New York Post*'s stories on the alleged murder were later discredited, but, Williams says, "This thing doesn't discredit them, it just puts them out there as if this is actually information, and without an idea of who it's coming from. I can imagine that some people might just find their way there somehow, and then be there using that information for purposes for which it shouldn't be used."

So remember, it's researcher beware.

This chapter told you about the tools of the Internet worker's trade. The next step for Internet researchers is to begin learning the in-depth use of some of these tools. The next chapter, Chapter 5, tells you what you'll need to get started with research using File Transfer Protocol (FTP).

Later, Chapter 12 covers how to use Gopher, Veronica, and Jughead, and Chapter 13 gives you an overview of the World Wide Web. These tools, Gopher and the World Wide Web in particular, are growing rapidly in usefulness and popularity, so studying them closely is likely to pay off in research dividends.

5

Keeping Up with the Internet with FTP

One of the easiest—and most useful—Internet tools is File Transfer Protocol (FTP). It's valuable both for retrieving software tools for all kinds of research and, in many cases, finding research files themselves.

Some of you reading this book will already have some form of FTP software on your hard drive, especially if you've purchased a suite of Internet software such as Chameleon or Internet in a Box or if your software came from a service provider such as Netcom's NetCruiser. Yet you will find that some of the files we recommend are useful for your research needs.

We'll first cover the old-fashioned command line method for FTP, and then the slick new Windows version. We'll also give you a hand-picked collection of FTP sites arranged by sample research topics to begin your work. We'll also point you to a service that sends newly archived software automatically to you. Finally, we'll tell you about a slower but effective way to use Internet e-mail to do all your FTP transfers.

In showing you how to use the old command line FTP method, we'll actually *use* FTP to retrieve several related files. The files we're after are software programs used to uncompress and decode your trophies when you get them home. They'll enable you to read or use retrieved files after you use FTP to copy files into your own space from a remote computer. We'll also get detailed FAQ documents you may want on several topics related to FTP.

Note *FAQ means Frequently Asked Questions. Thousands of FAQs and similar documents exist on the Internet. They contain the questions most frequently asked in that neck of the woods, as well as the most frequent answers! If you're new to an area of the Internet, it's worth reading that neighborhood's FAQ so you don't pester the locals with basic questions. That's why it's there.*

An FTP Shopping List

Here is your first FTP shopping list:

» **WS_FTP**, the Windows FTP program that we recommend you use.

» **Trumpet WinSock version 2.0b**, a shareware program you may need to run the WS_FTP program (or any other TCP/IP program) with Windows 3.1. Windows 95 has its own TCP/IP connection.

» **PKUnzip**, a widely used shareware program you will need to uncompress the files you get when you FTP.

» **The Compression FAQ**, which is about compression software, platforms each program is used on, and where you can FTP current copies of each compression program.

» **The FTP FAQ**, which has more technical detail than this chapter and contains further information on compression.

» **WINcode**, a UUENCODE coding-decoding program used to allow the transfer of software programs, graphics, compressed files and other *non-text* files as though they were text. UUENCODE allows people to transfer these complex files over older networks and network connections that were designed to handle only ASCII text.

Note *ASCII means American Standard Code for Information Interchange, which is a lowest common denominator for text files. Almost all text processing and word processing programs will accept (or import) ASCII text. So ASCII files, often given the extension .txt, are quite prevalent on the Internet. Almost all README and 00INDEX files (more about these "marker" files shortly) are stored in ASCII for this reason.*

Before we actually go FTP "shopping," let's discuss how this fundamental Internet tool is useful for research, and cover some of the basics you'll need to harness its power.

The Net Changes Daily

Even as this book was being written the Internet was growing, with new domains, Web sites, and files added every day. This chapter's title is "Keeping Up with the Internet with FTP," but we don't mean keeping up in the sense of knowing what the current events are throughout the worldwide Internet. That would be a pretty big full-time job all by itself.

What we mean, instead, is that you can use the Internet to stay ahead of the printed page—keeping up with the most current versions of research software and the most current knowledge on thousands of topics, by relying on FAQs that you get free from FAQ repositories and other archives, available by FTP from the Internet seven days a week, 24 hours a day.

New user-friendly software is coming out daily—especially Windows-compatible Internet software, with built-in TCP/IP. Software that is ready for Windows 95 has preceded it to market. After you use the old, command-line version of FTP, and then use the new Windows version of FTP, you'll see the great leaps forward that software developers have made in developing Internet tools that are truly user-friendly.

Net Awareness

To try to keep up with current events on the Internet, one would have to subscribe to, read, visit, and follow-up daily on at least these mailing lists, Usenet newsgroups, and Gopher/WWW sites:

E-mail Mailing Lists

Carr-l: Computer Assisted Reporting and Research

Edupage: Weekly education and technology developments

Net-Happenings: A deluge of events and developments

Net-Train: Discussion of how people learn about the Net

Newlist: New and changed mailing lists announcements

Scout reports:

NEWSLTR Digest: G. Sackman's digest of Electronic Newsletters

WWW-Announce: Announcements of new Web sites and events

Usenet Newsgroups

```
alt.best.of.internet
alt.internet.services
comp.answers
comp.archives
comp.dcom.telecom
comp.infosystems.www.announce
comp.internet.net-happenings
comp.os.ms-windows.announce
comp.society
comp.society.futures
misc.int-property
news.announce
news.announce.important
news.announce.newgroups
news.announce.newusers
news.answers
news.lists
```

Gopher and World Wide Web Sites

CERN What's New:
`http://info.cern.ch/CERN/HotNews.html`

EINet Galaxy:
`http://andromeda.einet.net/galaxy/CommunityNews.html`

GNN Whole Internet Catalog:
`http://nearnet.gnn.com/wic/nunu.toc.html`

NCSA What's New:
`http://www.ncsa.uiuc.edu/SDG/Software/Mosaic/Docs/whatsn`
`    ew.html`

Netscape What's New:
`http://home.mcom.com/home/whats-new.html`

Peripatetic Eclectic Gopher:
`gopher://peg.cwis.uci.edu:70`

Washington & Lee—Web:
`http://netlink.wlu.edu:1020/`

Washington & Lee—Gopher: `gopher://liberty.uc.wlu.edu:70`

Yahoo—What's New:
`http://www.yahoo.com/new.html`

Subscription and access information for each of these noteworthy resources (and many more) is given in Chapter 4, "Internet Research Tools."

FTP Basics

FTP means *File Transfer Protocol*. File Transfer Protocol is one of the central, core tools of the Internet, part of the TCP/IP suite of protocols. FTP allows you to make a copy of a file and move it from a remote computer to your computer (or to your space on your service provider's computer). Once you find an FTP site that contains material important to your research, File Transfer Protocol is how you'll "bring home the bacon." A file you retrieve using FTP may be a news release, a full-text legal document, brand new software, a sound or picture file, an index of odor sources used in perfumes, or just about anything else that can be digitally represented.

FTP is primarily used as an anonymous Internet service, accessible without a password or an account. There are literally millions of files freely available by *Anonymous FTP* on the Internet. These remote FTP servers don't care (too much) who you are. They will give their files to anyone who will type in an e-mail address.

But not all FTP is anonymous. For example, after you get into a research project you may find it necessary to quickly move a file using FTP from your computer to your personal account on an Internet computer at a remote site, or to move a file with FTP between your personal account and someone else's account with another Internet Service Provider.

If you have an account (a log-in name and a secret password) on a service that also provides a remote FTP server, you'll probably eventually use FTP to transfer files into and out of your personal account space on that computer. But

Anonymous FTP cannot do that for you. Anonymous FTP is designed to access public areas and freely available files, not to access your personal account space and your private files.

So, in some cases, you'll log in, giving your account name and password, to use "nonanonymous" FTP to send or receive files. At other times you'll be anonymous and won't need a password. But not to worry, Anonymous FTP is used in all of the examples in this chapter, so you will not necessarily need to have a personal account on an FTP server to try out FTP.

Caution   *Anonymous FTP can be addictive! This tool is so powerful and easy to use that you may be tempted to fill up your hard drive with free materials that you won't actually need or use. Be discriminating. Be careful that you only bring home files you have room to store and use!*

Three Methods of FTP

In its simplest form, FTP is primitive and has almost no bells and whistles. But in its more recent Windows incarnation, FTP is one of the most flexible, powerful, and informative Internet research tools.

The Windows-based FTP program demonstrated in this chapter requires you to be running some form of WinSock "socket" to allow Windows 3.1 to use Internet standard TCP/IP, as we first mentioned in Chapter 1. We'll show you where and how to obtain the software to install a Windows Winsocket, and we'll do it using FTP to get the WinSock program from a remote computer. And because you may not yet have the Windows FTP software installed, we'll first demonstrate the old reliable command-line FTP method, just to be sure you can do FTP, even if you don't have Windows or a WinSock program running.

At the end of this chapter, we'll also briefly cover FTPMail, BITFTP, and TRICKLE services that are slower because they rely on e-mail (and often are processed on a lower-priority basis), but they can be just as capable as the "live-action" FTP that you'll want to use if you possibly can. If you only have e-mail access to the Internet, or if FTP access is much more costly for you than e-mail and you have lots of time for some e-mail back-and-forth with remote computers, FTPMail and BITFTP may be just the thing for you. And the TRICKLE service is a valuable way to keep up-to-date on the research software you're using.

FTP Passwords

Before we can begin the first demonstration of FTP, we need to discuss passwords. Remember, File Transfer Protocol makes it possible to transfer files from one computer (the FTP server or host) on the Internet to another server or to your personal computer. To use an FTP program, you'll actually log into two hosts in order to transfer a file from one to (or through) the other. But you'll only need one personal password account—the one with your own ISP—to take advantage of the vast storehouse of information available from archive sites. To obtain access to those sites, you use a "general purpose" password on any of the thousands of computers that allow Anonymous FTP. Logging in through Anonymous FTP usually involves one of the following three scenarios:

Anonymous FTP Log-in Identities and Passwords

Your Anonymous FTP password is technically one of the following three possibilities:

Standard Method

```
Log-in:    anonymous
Password:  yourname@e-mail.address
```

Method One

```
Log-in:    anonymous
Password:  guest
```

Method Two

```
Log-in:    ftp
Password:  yourname@_____
```

Years ago, the Standard Method (and sometimes Method One) prevailed on almost all FTP sites worldwide. But recently, Method Two has swept around the Net, and today Method Two is acceptable on almost all sites. If an FTP site rebuffs an approach using Method Two, try using the Standard Method, and then try Method One. If all three methods are rejected, something else is wrong.

FTP Sites That Fail

Commonly an FTP site will reject log-ins when it is too busy to handle more traffic. Many site administrators set a maximum number of anonymous users that will be allowed at any one time, and/or a maximum number of nonlocal users. You've just come along at a time when too many people are already visiting, or during the site's local working hours. Sometimes a site will also be unavailable for more technical reasons, such as a network link that is out of service, routine scheduled maintenance, or reorganization due to new management, and so on.

Or, occasionally an FTP site is withdrawn from the Internet, and only allows local access. Often this is due to lack of funding for maintenance of the resource. Likewise, old FTP servers sometimes reach the end of their useful life, and are taken out of service.

If the site you are trying to reach is not responding after repeated attempts over a period of several days, it is time to find an alternate site that has the same resource material. To find alternate FTP sites, use Archie (Chapter 4) or check the FTP sites and mirror sites listed later in this chapter.

Another way to deal with a persistent failure to connect to an FTP site is to switch to a different means of connection. Gopher clients can usually make an FTP transfer, and Chapter 12 shows you how to use a Gopher server to dynamically visit many of the most popular FTP sites and obtain the research files you need. FTP site administrators often favor Gopher visitors, because they only use a host channel momentarily, rather than the usual FTP user, who personally holds the channel continuously from log-in to "bye." Recently more World Wide Web sites have also added FTP capability, and a Web browser such as Netscape can retrieve the files (but more about that later).

Caution

Most FTP archive servers have other jobs to do as well. Please respect the needs of the host site's primary users and restrict your FTP access whenever possible to evening hours (generally between 7:00 PM and 6:00 AM) at the host's time zone.

It is especially important to respect this caution for FTP servers on another continent because these Internet links can be somewhat slow and/or may be near capacity at all times of the day.

Tip

Evening, go East—Waking, go West

North American FTP users can extend their reach late in the afternoon by using European FTP sites where it is already evening. And in the morning North American FTP users can get a jump on the day by using FTP sites in Asia, Australia, and New Zealand where it is still night.

Note

Microsoft Windows 95 has TCP/IP capability built-in, so there's no need to have a WinSock program running in order to use the Windows WS_FTP program.

There is also another version of WS_FTP designed to work with Windows in 32-bit mode. Your copy of Windows 3.1 is probably still running in the original, regular 16-bit mode. But if you have already installed the free Microsoft "beta-test" upgrade to 32-bit processing, you should use the 32-bit version of WS_FTP. The FTP addresses for where to obtain these programs are given below. And, because you already know from Chapter 4 that Archie can be used to search over 1,000 of the major FTP sites in the world, you can find these valuable FTP programs at other sites, too. WS_FTP32 was actually developed on a Windows 95 system. You have to use the MS TCP/IP. (You can't use a 16-bit network stack on a 32-bit operating system for a 32-bit application.)

Is That File Binary or ASCII?

As noted above, ASCII text files can be read by anyone, and they will transfer correctly over almost any part of the Internet. But anything fancier or more complex than ASCII may run into trouble. And, nowadays, most files available by FTP are fancier than ASCII.

In nontechnical terms, ASCII uses only the regular letters you can see on your keyboard, and does not use the programming codes necessary to run a computer program file (such as a file that ends with .com or .exe). ASCII also does not include and cannot handle the codes used by PKZip and other compression programs, nor the codes needed to transfer a graphic or sound file from a remote FTP server to your computer.

ASCII Text	Binary Files
readme.txt	graphics
00index.txt	sounds
filename.txt	pkziped.zip
uuencode.uu	gnuziped.gz
README	WordPerfect
Index	PostScript
	AmiPro
	winword.doc
	WordStar
	program.exe
	program.com
	library.dll

If you are transferring anything more complex than pure ASCII text, you'll need to use a more powerful mode of FTP transport. You'll need to change modes to "binary," so that the strange codes programmers use (such as "§©ª") can be transmitted along with the regular keyboard codes. Binary file transfers won't damage an ASCII file, but an ASCII file transfer will destroy a binary file.

To switch modes using the command-line method of FTP, you type the name of the mode you want at the ftp prompt. For example, to switch from ASCII to binary, you would type:

```
ftp binary
```

Or, to switch to ASCII from binary, you would type:

```
ftp ascii
```

In the event you don't know what mode is now on, you can type:

```
ftp stat
```

This will get you a detailed description of the status of your FTP connection with the remote server.

Some FTP servers automatically start your session in binary mode as soon as you log in. But others assume you will want ASCII, so you can't be too careful. Because the "status" command gives a verbose answer, you may want to just send the "binary" command instead, and be done with it. Again, binary file transfers won't damage an ASCII file, but an ASCII file transfer will destroy a binary file every time.

Tip

Here are two abbreviations for the FTP mode commands that work on most systems. Before relying on these abbreviations, however, be sure to check if they work on the systems you use by testing them using the status command just mentioned.

Shortest	Abbreviated	Full
i	bin	type binary
a	asc	type ascii (works on only a few systems)

There are also transfer modes more complex than binary, such as TENEX. If you try the ASCII and binary methods shown here without success, ask your local computer gurus if you should be using TENEX mode instead. This topic is also covered in greater depth in the FTP FAQ and the FTP RFC (#1635), which are also discussed in the next section.

Compression and Decoding Software

FTP accounts for a large proportion of the Internet's traffic, and is one of the core tools in the TCP/IP suite. Because of FTP's central position, many complex techniques have developed to take advantage of FTP services in the most efficient way.

Files available for FTP are stored on or near the FTP host server. At larger FTP sites the number of bytes of stored files easily reaches into many gigabytes. These huge repositories often store their files in compressed form, in order to hold even more files available for FTP. For you to use these files after you retrieve them by FTP, you must uncompress them using exactly the right program and procedure.

PKZip and the Compression FAQ

The simplest and most common compression software used in DOS/Windows environments is PKZip. Shortly, we will show you where to get a copy of this shareware program using FTP, and demonstrate how to use it.

Unfortunately, PKZip is not the only compression currently in use on the Internet. Far from it. There are around three dozen compression methods in use, and they can be combined in many more ways. This topic deserves and requires its own FAQ, and the Compression FAQ is on our FTP shopping list. It is pretty technical stuff, but sometimes you'll have to use it, because a file you must have is compressed in some new unfamiliar way.

The first indicator that a file is compressed is the extension at the end of the filename. Many compression methods are confined to one or two operating systems or platforms, but some of them work across platforms and operating systems with ease. The Compression FAQ maintained by David Lemson at the University of Illinois (e-mail at lemson@uiuc.edv) is the best technical instruction manual and covers all of the compression programs and where to obtain each of them by FTP.

"How to Use Anonymous FTP"—RFC #1635

This official Internet RFC (Request for Comments) #1635 is titled "How to Use Anonymous FTP." The FTP RFC also has a filename of *rfc1635.txt* and is available in several RFC repositories. A list of FTP repositories of RFCs is given later in this chapter.

RFC #1635 discusses the most common compression methods, helps the reader with several FTP examples, discusses FTP netiquette, and explains the use of UUENCODE to allow binary files to be transferred over ASCII connections. The FTP RFC #1635 is less comprehensive than the FTP FAQ, but it is also less technical and much easier to read than the FTP FAQ.

This document is sometimes packaged with a huge list of FTP sites in a file that has grown enormous. In early 1995, even when PKZiped, it was around a third of a megabyte (333,334 bytes), and well over a megabyte when PKUnziped. So, because the site listing is so large, if your drive space is limited, you may want to find a copy of the FAQ without the site listing. The FAQ itself is around 25 pages, and when compressed with PKZip it is only around 25,000 bytes.

Tip

Several alternate FTP sites contain most or all of the Usenet FAQs at Massachusetts Institute of Technology's RTFM (Read the "Fine" Manual) site. If you want to retrieve a FAQ from the Usenet .answers archives, you might also like to try the mirror FTP archive sites shown in the section on mirror FTP sites later in this chapter.

UUENCODE and WINcode

As mentioned earlier, some older network equipment and software is unable to handle binary files without translating them to ASCII text. One program you can use to translate files is a Windows program called WINcode. WINcode is freeware, and is on our FTP shopping list.

Tip

Keeping up with the Newest Software

To keep research software up-to-date, keep a small file on your hard disk called versions.txt. This file can contain the names, version numbers, and DOS file dates for your most critical research software. When you see a copy of a software program on a remote FTP site, check your versions list to see if it might be a newer rendition than the one you currently have. This simple list can also help prevent you from bringing home files that you already have!

For another way to keep up-to-date on your software, please see the section on the TRICKLE software update service at the end of this chapter.

FTP Command Line Examples

We're about to embark on our first FTP shopping spree. To properly prepare for our session we need our shopping list. The following is the "shopping list" from the beginning of this chapter, shown in a slightly more elaborate form that is more conducive to command-line FTP.

Beginner's FTP List		
Host FTP Server	Subdirectory	Exact Filename
ftp.cc.utexas.edu	/microlib/dos/archivers	pkz204g.exe
oak.oakland.edu	/pub3/simtel-win3/winsock	ws_ftp.zip
oak.oakland.edu	/pub3/simtel-win3/winsock	twsk20b.zip
oak.oakland.edu	/pub3/simtel-win3/encode	wncod261.zip
oak.oakland.edu	/SimTel/msdos/info	ftp-list.zip

Beginner's FTP List		
Host FTP Server	Subdirectory	Exact Filename
`ds.internic.net`	`/rfc`	`rfc1635.txt`
`ftp.cso.uiuc.edu`	`/doc/pcnet`	`compression`

To get these seven files you will need around one and a half megabytes (1,500,000 bytes) of available storage space. Whether you are FTP-ing the files to your personal account space on an Internet Service Provider's computer or onto your own hard drive, be sure you have room for these arriving files! Once you have the files, remember that they are in compressed form. They will take up much more space when you uncompress them.

If your storage space is very limited, you might want to postpone FTP-ing the file, wncode261.zip. Also, rather than getting ftp-list.zip, which is also quite large, you may want to instead get the much smaller file FAQ from the directory/pub/usenet-by-group/news.answers/ftp-list on the FTP server rtfm.mit.edu. Another way to get this document is by FTPMail. An FTPMail script to get this document is provided later in this chapter.

BTW (by the way), the server rtfm.mit.edu is named after another common Internet abbreviation, usually directed toward "newbies" who ask unnecessary questions that are already covered in the most introductory written material—which everyone is expected to read before asking questions.

Tip

Once you've got the files on your hard disk, it's a good idea to make back up copies of the compressed files on a floppy disk, before you uncompress and read or install them.

Command-line FTP requires that you have access to a computer that is connected to the Internet. Most often this will be on a Local Area Network, on a terminal connected to a network server, or it will be a service available from your Internet Service Provider as part of an Internet account.

Note

If you are a Macintosh user, you'll want to use Fetch to follow along with the examples, and you can skip getting the files pkz204g.exe, ws_ftp.zip, twsk20b.zip, and wncod261.zip because they are Windows programs and won't do you much good unless you intend to use them on a PowerMac in the "simulated" Windows environment! Fetch is available from Dartmouth College. Ask a friend to FTP a copy Fetch_2.1.2.sit.hqx for you from ftp.dartmouth.edu in the directory /pub/mac.

Getting that First File with Command-Line FTP

Once you have a UNIX command prompt before you (in this example the prompt is world%, for World Software Tool and Die), to start an FTP session you type *ftp* and press Enter, as shown. Your local FTP client program will be called into action, and quickly respond with a new ftp prompt to signify that you are now using the FTP protocol on your local FTP client. You have not yet connected to a remote site, but you are prepared to because you have invoked the FTP protocol.

```
world% ftp
ftp
```

Now, to connect to a remote FTP server, give the instruction *open* followed by the FTP address of the remote server you want to visit. The remote server will reply, asking you what account you wish to use for this FTP session. If you had an account on the remote machine, you could log in and give your password as usual. But this example is to show you how to use the general purpose "anonymous" FTP account.

The FTP server at the address ftp.cc.utexas.edu has a copy of the first file on our shopping list, so we'll go there first. When asked for my name, notice (below) that one of your authors entered *anonymous*. The remote FTP host then asked me for a password, and I entered my e-mail address as my password. When I typed my password, none of the characters were visible on the screen, as a security precaution.

```
ftp open ftp.cc.utexas.edu
Connected to sheba.cc.utexas.edu.
220 sheba.cc.utexas.edu FTP server ready.
(Version 6.20 Fri Apr 9 23:43:10 CDT 1993)
Name (ftp.cc.utexas.edu:kinnaman): anonymous
331 Guest login ok, send e-mail address as password.
Password:
```

Caution   *Be aware. Most code lists in this chapter are truncated. They will most likely look slightly different when you use FTP.*

Note   *Don't be distracted by the numbers at the beginning of most lines that the remote FTP server sends back. They are meaningful, but the wording and exact meaning varies from site to site. It's more important now to read the words and ignore the numbers!*

After I type my e-mail address and press return, the remote FTP server sends me a welcome message followed at the end by an ftp prompt.

```
230-Welcome to
230-The University of Texas at Austin
230-Computation Center archive
230-Access is allowed all day, but preferably outside the
   hours of
230-6am-6pm Central time. Local time is Sun Mar 19 21:05:05
   1995.
230-All transfers are logged with your hostname and email
   address.
230-If you don't like this policy, disconnect now!
230-This is an experimental FTP server. If your FTP client
   crashes or
230-hangs shortly after login, please try using a dash (-)
   as the first
230-character of your password—this will turn off the
   informational
230-messages that may be confusing your ftp client.
230-***** NOTICE *****
230-Due to security problems, as of 3/8/95, we will no
   longer allow the
230-uploading of files via anonymous access. We regret any
   inconvenience
230-this may cause to *legitimate* users.
230-E-mail comments or questions to
   "remark@ftp.cc.utexas.edu."
230-Please read the file README
230-it was last modified on Thu May 19 15:41:06 1994—304
   days ago
230-Guest login ok, access restrictions apply.
Remote system type is UNIX.
Using binary mode to transfer files.
ftp
```

The shopping list tells us that the file we want is in the directory microlib/dos/archivers, so we must change directories using the command *cd*. After changing directories, I checked to be sure I was actually in the directory I thought by using the command *pwd* for print working directory.

```
ftp cd microlib/dos/archivers
250 CWD command successful.
ftp pwd
257 "/microlib/dos/archivers" is current directory.
ftp
```

And since the file we want is binary, we'll set the transfer mode to binary, as shown next.

```
ftp type binary
200 Type set to I.
ftp
```

I'm in the right directory, and in the right mode. So now I can use the Get command to FTP the file from the remote server to my local hard drive or into my space at an Internet Service Provider.

```
ftp get pkz204g.exe
local: pkz204g.exe remote: pkz204g.exe
200 PORT command successful.
150 Opening BINARY mode data connection for pkz204g.exe
    (202574 bytes).
226 Transfer complete.
202574 bytes received in 2.44 seconds (80.96 Kbytes/s)
ftp
```

Notice that this FTP server reports on the local and remote filenames involved in the transfer. That reminds me that if the UNIX filename on the FTP server was not a legal DOS filename, I could rename the file with the FTP *get* command so that when it arrives at my location it has an acceptable name. To rename a file with the FTP *get* command, you type something like this:

```
ftp get ReallyLong.UNIX.filename newname.dos
```

Tip

If you forget to rename the file, you can still use UNIX to rename it once it's on your home directory on your service provider. The UNIX syntax is mv, which is the same as move. So on your service provider you could type at the $ or % prompt:

```
$mv ReallyLong.UNIX.filename newname.dos
```

The mv command actually moves the file to a new location and deletes the old file, so it is also used to move files around a UNIX directory system as well.

Caution

Windows 95 supports long filenames. Windows 95 also has a system of mapping longer names with corresponding older style 8.3 names (that's the old eight-character dot three-character system) so the names will be compatible with older Windows 3.x and DOS software. But disk and file management utilities written for those older DOS and Windows 3.x applications cannot support long filenames until updated versions are released. Use caution if you are just getting used to Windows 95, and, for the time being, until software catches up, it may be a good idea to maintain a system of the old 8.3 filenames.

I've retrieved my first FTP file and I'm ready to disconnect, so I type *bye*. FTP has no provision for you to politely say thank you; just say *bye*.

```
ftp bye
221 Goodbye.
```

One item on the shopping list is now on my hard drive.

Beginner's FTP list		
Host FTP Server	**Subdirectory**	**Exact Filename**
✔ftp.cc.utexas.edu	/microlib/dos/archivers	pkz204g.exe
oak.oakland.edu	/pub3/simtel-win3/winsock	ws_ftp.zip
oak.oakland.edu	/pub3/simtel-win3/winsock	twsk20b.zip
oak.oakland.edu	/pub3/simtel-win3/encode	wncod261.zip
oak.oakland.edu	/SimTel/msdos/info	ftp-list.zip
ds.internic.net	/rfc	rfc1635.txt
ftp.cso.uiuc.edu	/doc/pcnet	compression

Download the file to your hard drive from your home directory, if it's not already on your hard drive. If not, create a subdirectory, move pkz204g.exe into that directory and type the name—it's a self-extracting file and its components will appear in the directory (usually) as separate filenames.

Note

You create a new directory on your hard drive called c:\pkzip204 by exiting to DOS, typing cd [Enter] and md \pkzip204 [Enter]. Then, change directories to the new directory by typing cd \pkzip204 [Enter]. Copy the file pkz204g.exe into the new directory. Then, while \pkzip204 is the active directory, type the name of the file pkz204g.exe [Enter] to have it self-extract.

Read and study the PKZip instruction files that you just extracted before you go any further, because it is fundamental to FTP success that you can use PKZip, or more immediately, that you can use PKUnzip. Four of the remaining six files on the shopping list are PKZipped, so you will need to be able to uncompress them.

Getting More Files with Command-Line FTP

The next example is slightly more complex, because we must find files in three different places in the oak.oakland.edu FTP server. Notice the subdirectory names shown on the shopping list for the Oakland University site (which is actually in Michigan, by the way). Two files come from the directory/pub3/simtel-win3/winsock, but the other two files are each in different places. This example, then, shows you how to move around an FTP site from directory to directory, moving up and down the directories and subdirectories at will. Because you won't always have a shopping list to guide you, this example will also show you how to find out which files are in each of the directories you visit along the way.

Here is what it looks like when you FTP to the Oakland site and change directories to the /pub3/simtel-win3/winsock directory. Note that the UNIX prompt on my local server is matrix:/usr/home/kinnaman for this example because I used a different account.

```
matrix:/usr/home/kinnamanftp
ftp open oak.oakland.edu
Connected to oak.oakland.edu.
220-oak.oakland.edu FTP server (Version wu-2.4(8) Wed Jan
    18 20:05:05 EST 1995) ready.
Name (oak.oakland.edu:kinnaman): ftp
331-Guest login ok, send your complete e-mail address as
    password.
Password:
230-Welcome to
230-THE OAK SOFTWARE REPOSITORY
230-A service of Oakland University, Rochester Michigan
230-If you have trouble using OAK with your ftp client,
    please try using
230-a dash (-) as the first character of your password—this
    will turn
230-off the continuation messages that may be confusing
    your ftp client.
230-OAK is a UNIX machine, and filenames are case sensitive.
230-Access is allowed at any time. If you have any unusual
    problems,
```

```
230-please report them via electronic mail to
    archives@Oakland.Edu
230-You are user #353 out of 400 maximum users on Tue Mar
    21 13:04:31 1995.
230-Oak is also on the World Wide Web, URL:
    http://www.acs.oakland.edu/oak.html
230-File searching is now available! Example command: site
    exec index 4dos
230-Please read the file README
230-it was last modified on Wed Nov 9 16:32:22 1994 - 132
    days ago
230-Guest login ok, access restrictions apply.
Remote system type is UNIX.
Using binary mode to transfer files.
ftp
```

The shopping list calls for us to now change directories to pub3/simtel-win3/winsock, and then we'll have a look at what is in that directory by typing the *dir* command. The FTP protocol allows this DOS-like command (dir) to be used on UNIX hosts.

```
ftp cd pub3/simtel-win3/winsock
250 CWD command successful.
ftp pwd
257 "/pub3/simtel-win3/winsock" is current directory.
ftp dir
200 PORT command successful.
150 Opening ASCII mode data connection for /bin/ls.
total 10847
rw-r—r—  1 w8sdz  OAK    3453 Mar 13 02:15 00_index.txt
rw-r—r—  1 w8sdz  OAK    1516803 Mar 1 20:01 atisml02.zip
rw-r—r—  1 w8sdz  OAK    287073 Mar 17 1994 cello101.zip
226 Transfer complete.
ftp
```

The extreme right side of the preceding directory listing shows the filenames available. Notice they all end with .zip in this directory, except the very first one, which is an ASCII text file giving you the contents of the directory.

Usually, you would first get the README and 00INDEX files in a new directory that you had not visited before. But this time you have a shopping list all prepared, and don't actually need to see the README and INDEX files in each directory. Also note that the size of each file in bytes is shown, between the date and the word "OAK" in this listing.

The shopping list says we want two files that are in this directory, ws_ftp.zip and twsk20b.zip. Here is how to get them:

```
ftp type binary
200 Type set to I.
ftp get ws_ftp.zip
200 PORT command successful.
150 Opening BINARY mode data connection for ws_ftp.zip
    (116700 bytes).
226 Transfer complete.
116700 bytes received in 23 seconds (5 Kbytes/s)
ftp get twsk20b.zip
200 PORT command successful.
150 Opening BINARY mode data connection for twsk20b.zip
    (179015 bytes).
226 Transfer complete.
179015 bytes received in 44 seconds (3.9 Kbytes/s)
ftp
```

Now we're finished in the first directory at this site. We need to switch to the second directory. Here's how the *cd ..*, *pwd*, and *dir* commands can be used to move up one directory and see what's available there. The command *cd ..* means move up one directory. Please note: There is one space between the *cd* and the two periods.

```
ftp cd ..
250-This MS-Windows collection is a mirror of SimTel, the
    Coast to Coast
250-Software Repository . Questions about or comments on
    this
250-collection should be sent to lrobbins@SimTel.Coast.NET.
250-Please read the file README.COPYRIGHT
250-it was last modified on Sat Feb 18 00:19:30 1995 - 31
    days ago
250-Please read the file README.MIRRORING
250-it was last modified on Sat Jan 28 14:50:23 1995 - 52
    days ago
250-Please read the file README.descriptions
```

```
250-it was last modified on Wed Mar 15 01:24:26 1995 - 6
    days ago
250-Please read the file README.dir-list
250-it was last modified on Sun Feb 12 18:12:42 1995 - 37
    days ago
250-Please read the file README.file-formats
250-it was last modified on Fri Dec 23 19:29:27 1994 - 88
    days ago
250-Please read the file README.how-to-upload
250-it was last modified on Sat Feb 18 11:51:12 1995 - 31
    days ago
250-Please read the file README.simtel-cdrom
250-it was last modified on Sat Feb 4 11:07:38 1995 - 45
    days ago
250 CWD command successful.
```

The next directory we need to look in is /pub3/simtel-win3/encode, so now we'll change directories and ask for a directory listing.

```
ftp cd encode
250 CWD command successful.
ftp pwd
257 "/pub/simtel-win3/encode" is current directory.
ftp dir
200 PORT command successful.
150 Opening ASCII mode data connection for /bin/ls.
total 805
rw-r—r—  1 w8sdz   OAK      830 Mar  4 10:31 00_index.txt
rw-r—r—  1 w8sdz   OAK      19465 Feb 12 12:12 aaauue.zip
rw-r—r—  1 w8sdz   OAK      96426 Sep  3 1992 extrct34.zip
rw-r—r—  1 w8sdz   OAK      177030 Sep 21 1994 uucod314.zip
rw-r—r—  1 w8sdz   OAK      110945 Feb 26 14:19 uudvw04a.zip
rw-r—r—  1 w8sdz   OAK      266083 Nov  9 02:21 wncod261.zip
rw-r—r—  1 w8sdz   OAK      133836 Sep 20 1994 xferp100.zip
226 Transfer complete.
ftp
```

Next we want to get the file wncod261.zip, so here is what the process looks like:

```
ftp get wncod261.zip
200 PORT command successful.
150 Opening BINARY mode data connection for wncod261.zip
    (266083 bytes).
226 Transfer complete.
266083 bytes received in 66 seconds (3.9 Kbytes/s)
ftp
```

The next directory on the shopping list is on a whole different branch of the directory tree, so we'll change directories all the way back up to the top FTP directory and then go down that branch. Here is a special *cd* command to jump all the way to the top directory. Please note there is a space between the *cd* and the forward slash (or virgule).

```
ftp cd /
250 CWD command successful.
ftp pwd
257 "/" is current directory.
ftp dir
200 PORT command successful.
150 Opening ASCII mode data connection for /bin/ls.
total 1122
rw-r-r—    1 w8sdz    OAK          0 Nov 13 14:41 .notar
drwxr-x--  2 root     operator  8192 Dec 31 16:44 .quotas
drwx——  2 root     system    8192 Dec 30 19:16 .tags
226 Transfer complete.
ftp
```

Deleted from the preceding directory listing, there is a subdirectory called SimTel, which is what we are looking for.

```
ftp cd SimTel
250-The files in this directory tree are a mirror of
    SimTel, the Coast to
250-Coast Software Repository . Please read
    README.COPYRIGHT for
250-information on distribution rights.
250-Please read the file README.COPYRIGHT
```

```
250-it was last modified on Sat Feb 18 00:19:30 1995 - 31
    days ago
250-Please read the file README.MIRRORING
250-it was last modified on Sat Jan 28 14:50:23 1995 - 52
    days ago
250 CWD command successful.
ftp dir
200 PORT command successful.
150 Opening ASCII mode data connection for /bin/ls.
total 24
rw-r-r-  1 w8sdz  OAK          172 Jan 28 15:05 .message
rw-r-r-  1 w8sdz  OAK            0 Jan 28 15:05 .notar
rw-r-r-  3 w8sdz  OAK         4596 Feb 18 00:19
README.COPYRIGHT
rw-r-r-  3 w8sdz  OAK         1573 Jan 28 14:50
README.MIRRORING
drwxr-xr-x 220 w8sdz  OAK      8192 Mar 20 22:34 msdos
drwxr-xr-x 81 w8sdz   OAK      8192 Mar 19 22:03 win3
226 Transfer complete.
ftp
```

This listing says there is a subdirectory (remember that the "d" in the leftmost column means it's a directory) called msdos, which is one step closer to our final destination at this FTP site.

```
ftp cd msdos
250-This MS-DOS collection is a mirror of SimTel, the Coast
    to Coast
250-Software Repository . Questions about or comments on
    this
250-collection should be sent to w8sdz@SimTel.Coast.NET.
250-Please read the file README.COPYRIGHT
250 CWD command successful.
ftp pwd
257 "/SimTel/msdos" is current directory.
ftp
```

To change to one more directory down the branch, we now type *cd info*:

```
ftp cd info
250 CWD command successful.
```

```
ftp pwd
257 "/SimTel/msdos/info" is current directory.
ftp
```

What's SimTel?

SimTel was originally a huge collection of MS-DOS software stored on a computer at the U.S. Army's White Sands Missile Range. The collection was closed in 1993 and the prime site is now the one at Oakland University at Rochester, Michigan. The Oakland collection and its mirror sites around the world are updated regularly as new software is added.

Now that we are in the directory we want (/SimTel/msdos/info), let's look for the file we're after (ftp-list.zip) by asking for a directory listing. Note that the directory listing is so long that it quickly scrolls past, and nobody but Superman can read that fast.

To stop the scrolling there are several tricks. The most effective scroll commands are pressing both the [Ctrl] and [Pause] keys at the same time. If that doesn't work, try the old-fashioned DOS command of pressing the [Ctrl] and [s] keys to stop the scrolling, and [Ctrl] and [q] to resume scrolling.In this case another option is to retrieve the first file 00_index.txt and read it, because the index file contains the directory information we need.

```
ftp dir
200 PORT command successful.
150 Opening ASCII mode data connection for /bin/ls.
total 29146
rw-r-r-  1 w8sdz  OAK      15574 Mar 3 01:14 00_index.txt
rw-r-r-  1 w8sdz  OAK       3620 Jun 8 1991 401bugs.zip
rw-r-r-  1 w8sdz  OAK       2566 Jul 18 1987 640xtmod.zip
rw-r-r-  1 w8sdz  OAK       9460 Dec 12 1988 896k-mem.txt
rw-r-r-  1 w8sdz  OAK       9149 Aug 19 1991 addhelp.zip
226 Transfer complete.
ftp
```

To retrieve the directory listing in the form of the file 00_index.txt, displaying only one page or screen at a time, here is another special UNIX-like FTP command. Note that there is a space before the |*more* at the end of the command. And only the first few lines of the file are shown below.

```
ftp get 00_index.txt |more
```

```
200 PORT command successful.
150 Opening BINARY mode data connection for 00_index.txt
(15574 bytes).
NOTE: This list was created on Fri Mar 3 01:14:14 EST 1995
Some files may have been added or deleted since that date.
See file SimTel/msdos/filedocs/aareadme.txt for additional
information.
NOTE: Type B is Binary; Type A is ASCII
Directory SimTel/msdos/info/
Filename      Type Length Date    Description
================================================
401bugs.zip  B    3620    910608 2 bugs found in MSDOS 4.01,
with test programs
640xtmod.zip B    2566    870718 Put 640K on an IBM 256K
motherboard
896k-mem.txt A    9460    881212 Expand IBM PC-XT motherboard
memory to 896K
addhelp.zip  B    9149    910819 Change or add to the DOS
5.0 help file
```

The shopping list says we need only one file in the SimTel/msdos/info directory—ftp-list.zip, so let's get it. Then, once we've closed the FTP session with Oakland University with the word *bye*, let's ask UNIX if the files we just got with FTP are actually now in our home or personal directory at our Internet Service Provider's computer. The UNIX equivalent of the *dir* command is *ls*, for list.

```
ftp get ftp-list.zip
200 PORT command successful.
150 Opening BINARY mode data connection for ftp-list.zip
(332144 bytes).
226 Transfer complete.
332144 bytes received in 1.2e+02 seconds (2.7 Kbytes/s)
ftp bye
221 Goodbye.
matrix:/usr/home/kinnaman1s
ftp-list.zip  mail twsk20b.zip   wncod261.zip  ws_ftp.zip
matrix:/usr/home/kinnaman
```

So the transfer worked, and the files are now in our local space.

Beginner's FTP list		
Host FTP Server	**Subdirectory**	**Exact Filename**
✔ftp.cc.utexas.edu	/microlib/dos/archivers	pkz204g.exe
✔oak.oakland.edu	/pub3/simtel-win3/winsock	ws_ftp.zip
✔oak.oakland.edu	/pub3/simtel-win3/winsock	twsk20b.zip
✔oak.oakland.edu	/pub3/simtel-win3/encode	wncod261.zip
✔oak.oakland.edu	/SimTel/msdos/info	ftp-list.zip
ds.internic.net	/rfc	rfc1635.txt
ftp.cso.uiuc.edu	/doc/pcnet	compression

Lots of help is available, too. While you are at an ftp prompt, you can type *help*, or, before or after an FTP session, you can type *man ftp* at the UNIX prompt. Both of these methods will get you more detail than most people ever need about FTP! One thing not covered here is the *mget* command that allows you to retrieve many files at once if they begin with the same letters. Check it out.

Summary of Basic FTP Commands Used in Examples

This table is a brief review of a few FTP commands.

Command	Results
ascii	Prepares to transfer simple text files with ASCII characters only
binary	Prepares to transfer more complex files,, such as programs or compressed file
status	Displays whether the next transfer will be in ASCII or binary mode
cd director	Changes the working directory on the remote FTP server to the named directory
cd ..	Changes the working directory up one level
cd /	Changes the working directory to the top-level FTP directory
pwd	Displays the name of the remote FTP host's present working director
get filename	Copies the filename from the remote computer to your hard drive or your account at an Internet Service Provider
mget filename	Copies a group of files beginning with the same word-root.

Command	Results
by	Closes the connection to the remote FTP server and ends your FTP client program session on your local computer

To retrieve the remaining two files on our list we'll use WS_FTP. So, now you should store backup copies and unzip the files twsk20b.zip and ws_ftp.zip in their own new DOS directories, and carefully follow the instructions to install each of them in turn. That way we can use the modern new convenience of a Windows-based FTP client: WS_FTP.

Credit Where Credit Is Due

The WS_FTP program is freeware for noncommercial users, but being free doesn't make it less valuable. It was written by U.S. Army Master Sergeant John A. Junod, who lives in Martinez, Georgia. An expert programmer in several languages, Junod creates easy-to-use free software, and gives it to anyone who wants it.

Sergeant Junod expects to continue his U.S. Army career until at least 1998 (he began service in 1978). He helped set up the first army.mil Internet name server and has been involved in the Internet and TCP/IP since 1986 when he began helping to develop the large cross-platform campus TCP/IP network at the U.S. Military Academy at West Point (ftp.usma.edu).

Although Sergeant Junod is now stationed at Fort Gordon, Georgia, many of his fine programs are still in use at West Point, and his free software programs are available for FTP at West Point's FTP site.Sergeant Junod's programs at ftp.usma.edu include WS_Ping, WS_FTP, WS_FTP32 and WS_Watch.

He upgrades the FTP programs (and all the others) regularly on his own time, keeping them at the cutting edge. By giving away his many expert programs, Sergeant Junod has made, and continues to make, major contributions "giving back to the Net."

To personally thank Sergeant Junod, or to recommend a new feature to any of his programs, contact him at:

John A. Junod

267 Hillwood Street

Martinez, GA 30907

USA

E-mail: `junodj@css583.gordon.army.mil`

FTP Examples with WS_FTP

The remaining FTP shopping examples assume you have TCP/IP (such as Trumpet WinSock or other WinSock from a commercial suite) now running in Windows 3.1, or you have Windows 95 with built-in TCP/IP on your computer. We'll also assume you've got a direct connection to the Internet through your school or workplace, or at least a SLIP/PPP account logged in, and the WS_FTP client software running, by meticulously, sequentially following all the instructions for both Trumpet and the WS_FTP program. Except the very first time, when you open the WS_FTP program by double-clicking on the icon, it opens and looks a little like Figure 5-1.

You can either connect with the last site from your previous session, or you can click on the profile selection drop-down menu to choose from a list of all the sites you've visited and saved before. To visit a new site, open the Connect box by clicking on the Connect button in the lower left corner, and fill in the FTP address you want to visit. You also must give a log-in and password that you want used, or the remote site will refuse your FTP visit with little explanation.

When you click on OK, WS_FTP will try to connect to the remote FTP server. After you are logged on to an FTP server, the address of that server appears in the bar at the top of the WS_FTP window, as shown in Figure 5-2. The FTP site's available directories are shown in the upper right quadrant, and the files in the current directory are shown in the lower right quadrant.

Figure 5-1.
WS_FTP opens ready for action—with the last site you visited preloaded! All you need to do it click on "Connect."

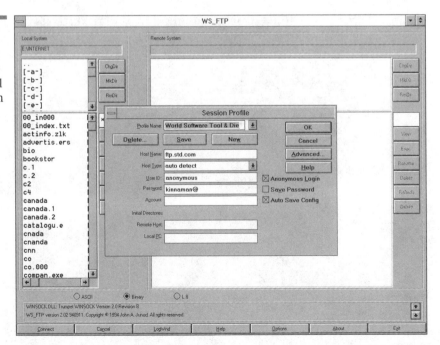

Figure 5-2.
This is the top-level directory at InterNic. The site's FTP address shows on the bar at the top of the window.

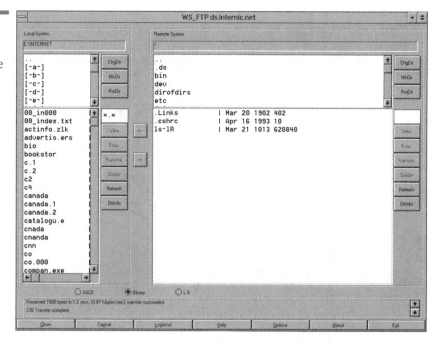

You can now change directories by using the ChgDir button. Just type in the name of the directory you want, and click on OK. An example of changing directories is shown next. Although you can also double-click on a highlighted directory in order to switch to that directory, sometimes, on some computers, this shortcut may cause Windows to freeze up.

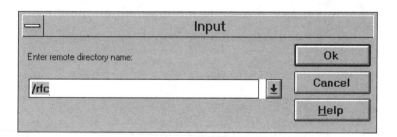

Before you retrieve any files, let's set one safety precaution. Open the Options dialog box by clicking on the Options button. Here is what you should see:

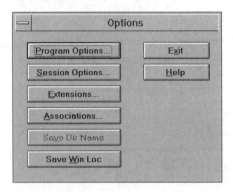

Now click on the Session Options button and click on the boxes for Send Unique and for Receive Unique. Close the dialog box by clicking on Save, and close the Options box by clicking on Exit. This precaution prevents the UNIX disaster of copying a file with the same name onto a directory that already has a file with that name, thereby writing over the previous file with the new file of the same name, with absolutely no warning. UNIX just assumes you meant to write over the old file (didn't you?), unless you check these boxes! These options will cause a slight change in the filename to be made, before it lands on your hard drive, if an overwrite is about to occur—thereby saving both files.

One of the best visual features of this program is that while you are retrieving a file with WS_FTP you are able to watch the progress of the transfer on a graphic "thermometer" in the file transfer box, as shown in Figures 5-3 and 5-4.

As you can see, Figures 5-3 and 5-4 represent the last two file transfers on the shopping list, and complete the examples showing you how to FTP. Now, that wasn't so bad, was it?

The current version of WS_FTP is available at the FTP address ftp.usma.edu in the directory /pub/.

✔Beginner's FTP list		
Host FTP Server	**Subdirectory**	**Exact Filename**
✔ftp.cc.utexas.edu	/microlib/dos/archivers	pkz204g.exe
✔oak.oakland.edu	/pub3/simtel-win3/winsock	ws_ftp.zip
✔oak.oakland.edu	/pub3/simtel-win3/winsock	twsk20b.zip
✔oak.oakland.edu	/pub3/simtel-win3/encode	wncod261.zip
✔oak.oakland.edu	/SimTel/msdos/info	ftp-list.zip
✔ds.internic.net	/rfc	rfc1635.txt
✔ftp.cso.uiuc.edu	/doc/pcnet	compression

Figure 5-3.
The thermometer says we have transferred 31 percent of the file rfc1635.txt from ds.internic.net.

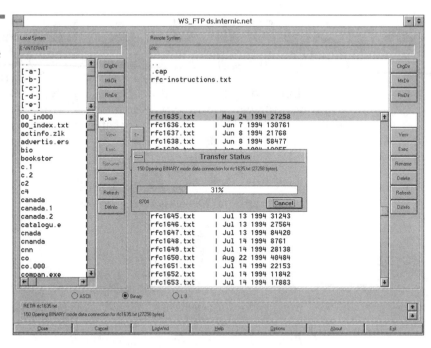

Figure 5-4.
39 percent of the file named "compression" has been transferred from ftp.cso.uiuc.edu.

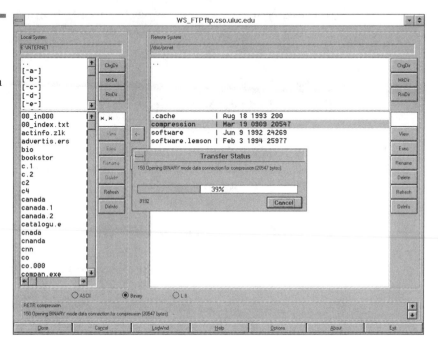

Key FTP Sites for the Changing Internet

The Internet is a high-speed moving target. It never holds still. By the time this book is printed and in your hands, significant new resources will be available that don't exist as we're writing. Because of the vastness of the Internet's FTP archives, and because they are ever changing, we will give you only a few samples of what is available in five arbitrary categories:

» English Literature

» Health Care Issues

» International Business

» Internet Information Tools

» Windows and Macintosh Software Repositories

Note

Two very popular sites that are found by Archie are not on the FTP site lists found throughout the remainder of this chapter. After weeks of unsuccessful attempts to visit them, these few sites were abandoned on the basis of frustration. We want you to be successful when you FTP, not frustrated.

At the time of this writing the sites listed below contained items that well fit the category shown. But, as has been said, the Internet is ever-changing, and you may find larger or smaller collections when you visit. As they say on the Net, your mileage may vary!

Tip

Finding Other FTP Sites with Archie

Because these are only intended to be samples, and not comprehensive listings, you probably will not find your chosen research topic included. To find FTP sites for any other topic, turn back to Chapter 4 and do an Archie search using the appropriate keywords.

FTP Sites for English Literature

The number and quality of English-language electronic texts available on the Internet is increasing rapidly. Each of these sites has full-text digital documents available for researchers to obtain using FTP.

FTP Addresses	Directories
North America	
`epas.utoronto.ca`	`/pub/cch/english/shakespeare`
`etext.lib.virginia.edu`	`/pub/britpo`
`freebsd.cdrom.com`	`/.15/obi/.5/gutenberg`
`ftp.etext.org`	`/pub`
`ftp.std.com`	`/obi`
`ftp.uu.net/obi`	`/doc/literary`
`wiretap.spies.com`	`/Library/Classic`
Europe	
`ftp.demon.com.uk`	`/pub/etexts`
`ftp.funet.fi`	`/pub/doc/literary/etext/Poe`
`ftp.sunet.se`	`/pub/etext/ota/pub/etext/wiretap-classic-library`
`ftp.uni-trier.de`	`/pub/buecher/obi`
`locust.cic.net`	`/pub/Fiction/Shakespeare`
`ota.ox.ac.uk`	`/pub/ota/public/english`
`src.doc.ic.ac.uk`	`/Project-Gutenberg`
`ugle.unit.no`	`/pub/misc/shakespeare`
`unix.hensa.ac.uk`	`/pub/uunet/doc/literary/obi`
Australia	
`goanna.cs.rmit.oz.au`	`/pub/etext/Classics/Shakespeare`

FTP Sites for Health Care Information

Health care reform in the United States remains unresolved. Canadians, while acknowledging that their medical system has faults, are much more satisfied with the medical care they receive and the price they pay for it than practically any other developed country. Here are some sites with useful information about the debate in the U.S., and about many other health care resources. The fine collection at the University of Trier in Germany is oriented toward the everyday health care consumer, and covers a wide range of health care topics.

FTP Addresses	Directories
North America	
`ftp.uci.edi`	`/med-ed`
`lhc.nlm.nih.gov`	`/big/collection`
`nigel.msen.com`	`/pub/vendor/a-albionic/gopher/health`

```
rtfm.mit.edu            /pub/usenet-by-hierarchy/alt/support
                        /pub/usenet-by-hierarchy/sci/med
sunsite.unc.edu         /pub/academic/political-
                        science/whitehouse-healthcare.archive
                        /pub/academic/political-science
                        /whitehouse-papers
                        /pub/academic/political-science/Health-
                        Security-Act/pub/academic/sci.econ.re-
                        search/Health
```

Europe
```
ftp.demon.co.uk         /pub/diabetes
ftp.uni-trier.de        /pub/buecher/obi/customers/nonprofits
                        /empowerment-ctr/pub/buecher/obi/USG
                        /Health.Care.Security.Plan
```

FTP Sites for International Business

Here are some FTP sites for research in international trade. Topics covered extensively by these sites include NAFTA, GATT, and trade with the newly emerging Eastern European countries.

FTP Addresses	Directories
`igc.org`	`/pub/TRADE`
`oak.oakland.edu`	`/SimTel/msdos/info/online.zip`
`nigel.msen.com`	`/pub/vendor/a-albionic/gopher` `/conspiracy/NWO`
`cs.dal.ca`	`/comp.archives/ca.politics`

`kekule.osc.edu`	`/pub/central_eastern_europe/russian`
	`/relcom/news/pub/central_eastern_europe`
	`/ukrainian/relcom/news`

`freebsd.cdrom.com`	`/.10/japanese/monash/.15/obi/Patents` `/Documents`
`ftp.spies.com`	`/Gov/NAFTA`
`ftp.mty.itesm.mx`	`/pub/mexico/faqs`

`coombs.anu.edu.au`	`/coombspapers/coombsarchives`
	`/economics-rspacs/coombspapers`
	`/coombsarchives/international-relations`

`unix.hensa.ac.uk`	`/pub/uunet/doc/papers/coombspapers`
	`/coombsarchives/economics-rspacs/pub`
	`/uunet/doc/papers/coombspapers`
	`/coombsarchives/international-relations`

```
ftp.uu.net                /doc/papers/coombspapers/coombsarchives
                          /international-relations
ftp.iij.ad.jp             /pub/academic/economics/.old-nafta
                          /NAFTA-by-section/pub/academic
                          /economics/sci.econ.research/Q-and-A
                          /pub/academic/political-science
                          /whitehouse-papers/1993
bluehouse.go.kr           /whitehouse/political-science/nafta
                          /whitehouse/political-science
                          /whitehouse-papers/1993
uceng.us.edu              /pub/wuarchive/doc/coombspapers
                          /coombsarchives/international-relations
```

FTP Sites for Internet Information and Tools

Here are locations where you can FTP documents and software tools needed for your research on the Internet. The Internet Hunt archives contain the research methods and results for the monthly Internet Hunt contest. The winning contestants share their advanced research skills with you, for free.Official Internet documents (RFCs, FYIs, STDs, and so on) and Usenet FAQs are available at several sites listed later in this chapter in the section on mirror repositories.

FTP Addresses	Directories
North America	
`access.usask.ca`	`/pub/hytelnet`
`boombox.micro.umn.edu`	`/pub/gopher`
`ftp.cic.net`	`/pub/hunt/about/`
`ftp.cni.org`	`/pub/net-guides/i-hunt`
`ftp.cs.dal.ca`	`/htmlasst`
`ftp.csd.uwm.edu`	`/pub/inet.services.txt`
`ftp.ncsa.uiuc.edu`	`/mac/mosaic/pc/telnet`
`ftp.rpi.edu`	`/pub/communications`
`ftp.sura.net`	`/pub/nic`
`ftp.qualcomm.com`	`/mac/eudora`
`watsun.cc.columbia.edu`	`/kermit`
Europe	
`ftp.nic.surfnet.nl`	`/mirror-archive/resources/internet-hunt/about/`
`info.cern.ch`	`/pub/www`
`lister.cc.ic.ac.uk`	`/pub/wingopher`

```
micro.hensa.ac.uk          /kermit
```

Australia/Asia
```
baudin.cc.utas.edu.au      /pc/trumpet
ftp.latrobe.edu.au         /pub/network/gopher
```

FTP Sites for Windows/DOS and Macintosh Software

Here are some places where you can use FTP to retrieve Macintosh software, followed by places to retrieve software for the Windows and DOS platforms.

Macintosh Software FTP Sites

These worldwide locations have good collections of Macintosh software.

FTP Addresses   **Directories**

North America
```
ftp.apple.com              /dts
ftp.cs.dal.ca              /mac
ftp.dartmouth.edu          /pub/mac
ftp.ncsa.uiuc.edu          /mac/telnet
ra.nrl.navy.mil            /MacSciTech
romulus.ucs.uoknor.edu     /mirrors/mac
sumex-aim.stanford.edu     /pub/info-mac
```

Europe
```
ftp.funet.fi               /pub/mac
ftp.luth.se                /pub/mac
ftp.pasteur.fr             /pub/Mac
ftp.uni-kl.de              /pub0/mac
garbo.uwasa.fi             /mac
nic.funet.fi               /mac
power.ci.uv.es             /pub/mac
src.doc.ic.ac.uk            /mac-sumex/mac-umich
```

Australia/Asia
```
ftp.comp.vuw.ac.nz         /mac
ftp.hk.super.net           /mac
ftp.ocs.mq.edu.au          /Mac
```

```
plaza.aarnet.edu.au      /micros/mac
```

Windows/DOS software FTP sites

These worldwide locations have good collections of DOS/Windows software.

FTP Addresses   **Directories**

North America

```
ftp.cica.indiana.edu     /pub/pc/win3
merit.edu                /pub/ppp
sunsite.unc.edu           /pub/micro/pc-stuff/ms-windows
oak.oakland.edu          /SimTel/msdos
wuarchive.wustl.edu      /pub/MSDOS_UPLOADS
```

Europe

```
garbo.uwasa.fi           /pc/windows
micros.hensa.ac.uk        /mirrors/cica/win3/winsock
nic.funet.fi              /msdos/winnt/msdos/windows/winsock
src.doc.ic.ac.uk          /windows3/dos/mirror/simtel-win3
```

Australia/Asia

```
baudin.cc.utas.edu.au    /pc/win3
brother.cc.monash.edu.au  /pub/win3
csuvax1.murdoch.edu.au    /pub/pc/windows
ftp.cc.monash.edu.au     /pub/win3
ftp.hk.super.net          /pub/dos/pub/windows
```

Tip

Remember to set your file type to binary when you are downloading executable, compressed, or word-processor formatted files. At the ftp prompt, type:

```
ftp binary
```

Mirror FTP Sites

This section gives you mirror FTP addresses for seven major collections:

» Center for Innovative Computer Applications, Indiana University, Bloomington, Indiana

» Garbo Software Archives, University of Vaasa, Finland

» Internet Information and Standards—RFCs, FYIs, STDs, and more

» Massachusetts Institute of Technology's Usenet FAQ repository

» SimTel Coast to Coast Software Repository

» Stanford University's Info-Mac Macintosh Software Collection

» The University of Michigan's Macintosh software repository

These FTP sites are so popular and valuable that they are imitated in whole or in part by several other sites around the world. One prime collection is mirrored or shadowed, which means that the identical files are maintained at multiple sites. This is in keeping with the successful decentralized nature of the Internet, and makes the whole Net more efficient, useful, valuable, and convenient.

Most mirror arrangements also include regular updates to distribute additions and new versions of the documents and software in the collection, as well as to refresh the existing files from the original files. Generally, as a matter of netiquette, you should first access the mirror-family FTP sites on your own geographical continent, rather than sites overseas. This conserves the Internet's precious intercontinental network resources and often will increase the likelihood you'll be allowed access to a busy FTP site. That's why these mirror sites are sorted by continent.

Caution

Although these FTP addresses and directory names have been verified as correct at the time of this writing, unfortunately, things may change. Remember, the Net changes daily.

CICA Indiana University

The Center for Innovative Computer Applications at Indiana University in Bloomington, Indiana, has a famous collection of great software. Here are the worldwide mirrors of that collection:

FTP Addresses	Directories
North America	
`archive.orst.edu`	`/pub/mirrors/ftp.cica.indiana.edu/win3`
`ftp.cdrom.com`	`/pub/cica`
`ftp.marcam.com`	`/win3`
`gatekeeper.dec.com`	`/pub/micro/msdos/win3`
`mirrors.aol.com`	`/pub/cica/pc/win3`
`mrcnext.cso.uiuc.edu`	`/pub/win3`
`wuarchive.wustl.edu`	`/systems/ibmpc/win3`

Australia/Asia

`ftp.cau.ac.kr`	`/pub/win3`
`ftp.hk.super.net`	`/mirror/cica`
`ftp.iij.ad.jp`	`/pub/win3`
`ftp.monash.edu.au`	`/pub/win3`
`ftp.nectec.or.th`	`/pub/mirrors/win3`
`nctuccca.edu.tw`	`/PC/windows/cica`

Europe

`ftp.cyf-kr.edu.pl`	`/pub/mirror/win3`
`ftp.uni-paderborn.de`	`/Cica`
`ftp.uni-stuttgart.de`	`/pub/systems/pc/win3-cica`
`ftp.unipd.it`	`/mirror/win3`
`info.nic.surfnet.nl`	`/mirror-archive/software/cica-win3`
`nic.switch.ch`	`/mirror/win3`
`src.doc.ic.ac.uk`	`/packages/ibmpc/windows3`

Middle East

`ftp.technion.ac.il`	`/pub/unsupported/mswin/cica`

Garbo Software Mirrors

Following are worldwide mirrors of the excellent Garbo software collection maintained at the University of Vaasa in Finland:

FTP Addresses	**Directories**
North America	
`wuarchive.wustl.edu`	`/mirrors/garbo.uwasa.fi`
	`/systems/msdos/garbo.uwasa.fi`
`ftp.cdrom.com`	`/pub/garbo/macpub/garbo/pc/pub/garbo`
	`/windows`
Europe	
`cnuce_arch.cnr.it`	`/pub/msdos/garbo.uwasa.fi`
`ftp.germany.eu.net`	`/pub/comp/msdos/mirror.garbo`
`garbo.uwasa.fi`	`/pub/pub/mac/pub/pc/pub/windows`
`pascal.ibp.fr`	`/pub8/pc/garbo`
`ftp.ibp.fr`	`/pub/pc/garbo`

Africa

`owl.und.ac.za`	`/mirrors/garbo/pc`

Australia/Asia

`archie.au`	`/micros/pc/garbo/pc/micros/pc/garbo/windows`
`ftp.bhp.com.au`	`/pc/garbo/pc/pc/garbo/windows`
`ftp.sogang.ac.kr`	`/msdos_garbo`
`nctuccca.edu.tw`	`/PC-MSDOS/Garbo-pc`
`nctuccca.edu.tw`	`/PC/garbo`
`plaza.aarnet.edu.au`	`/micros/pc/garbo`

Internet Information and Standards—RFCs, FYIs, STDs, and More

These sites hold the Internet's documents about the Internet itself. These are wonderful places for learning about the Internet, and they contain information for all users, from beginning to advanced. The acronyms for these document collections may be understood as follows:

Acronym	Meaning
fyi	for your information
rfc	request for comments
std	standards

FTP Addresses	Directories
`ds.internic.net`	`/fyi/internet-drafts/rfc/std`
`nic.ddn.mil`	`/fyi/internet-drafts/rfc/std`
`nic.merit.edu`	`/documents/fyi/documents/internet-drafts/documents/rfc/documents/std`
`nic.switch.ch`	`/docs/faq/fyi/docs/rfc`
`ftp.uu.net`	`/inet/internet-drafts/rfc`

Massachusetts Institute of Technology—Usenet FAQs

Here are several alternate FTP sites that contain most or all of the Usenet FAQs at Massachusetts Institute of Technology's RTFM (Read the "Fine" Manual) site. If you want to retrieve a FAQ from the Usenet .answers archives, you might like to try the following FTP archive sites, especially if they are closer than Massachusetts.

FTP Addresses	Directories
North America	
`ftp.uu.net`	`/usenet/news.answers`
`rtfm.mit.edu`	`/pub/usenet-by-group/news.answers`
Europe	
`ftp.germany.eu.net`	`/pub/newsarchive/news.answers`
`ftp.sunet.se`	`/pub/usenet`
`ftp.uni-paderborn.de`	`/pub/FAQ`
`nic.switchch`	`/docs/faq/faqs`
`grasp1.univ-lyon1.fr`	`/pub/faq`
Asia	
`ftp.hk.super.net`	`/mirror/faqs`
`hwarang.postech.ac.kr`	`/pub/usenet/news.answers`
`nctuccca.edu.tw`	`/Usenet/FAQ`

SimTel Software Mirrors

This is a large collection of software on almost any subject maintained by the SimTel Coast to Coast Software Repository . Some sites do not have the same directory structure as the primary SimTel site at Oakland University in Rochester, Michigan.

FTP Addresses	Directories
North America	
`oak.oakland.edu`	`/Simtel`
`ftp.uoknor.edu`	`/mirrors/SimTel/msdos/mirrors/SimTel/win3`
`ftp.uu.net`	`/msdos/simtel`
`wuarchive.wustl.edu`	`/systems/ibmpc/simtel/msdos/systems/ibmpc/simtel/win3`
Europe	
`micros.hensa.ac.uk`	`/mirrors/simtel/msdos/mirrors/simtel/win3`
`src.doc.ic.ac.uk`	`/pub/packages/simtel/pub/packages/simtel-win3`

`ftp.funet.fi`	`/pub/mirrors/oak.oakland.edu/Simtel` `/msdos/pub/mirrors/oak.oakland.edu` `/Simtel/win3`
`ftp.ibp.fr`	`/pub/pc/SimTel/msdos/pub/pc/SimTel` `/win3`
`ftp.uni-paderborn.de`	`/SimTel/msdos/SimTel/win3`
`ftp.nic.surfnet.nl`	`/mirror-archive/software/simtel-msdos` `/mirror-archive/software/simtel-win3`
`ftp.cyf-kr.edu.pl`	`/pub/mirror/simtel/msdos/pub/mirror` `/simtel/win3`
`ftp.sunet.se`	`/pub/pc/mirror/SimTel/msdos/pub/pc` `/mirror/SimTel/win3`
`ftp.switch.ch`	`/mirror/simtel/msdos/mirror/simtel` `/win3`

Middle East/Africa

`ftp.technion.ac.il`	`/pub/unsupported/simtel/msdos/pub` `/unsupported/simtel/win3`
`ftp.sun.ac.za`	`/pub/simtel/msdos/pub/simtel/win3`

Australia/Asia

`archie.au`	`/micros/pc/SimTel/msdos/micros/pc` `/SimTel/win3`
`ftp.cs.cuhk.hk`	`/pub/simtel/msdos　/pub/simtel/win3`
`ftp.nectec.or.th`	`/pub/mirrors/SimTel/msdos/pub` `/mirrors/SimTel/win3`
`nctuccca.edu.tw`	`/PC/simtel`

Stanford University's Info-Mac Macintosh Software Archive

It's likely that you will not be able to connect to this very busy site at Stanford University. So, it's fortunate that many mirror sites are available.

FTP Addresses	Directories
North America	
`ftp.amug.org`	`/pub/info-mac`
`ftp.hawaii.edu`	`/mirrors/info-mac`
`ftp.ucs.ubc.ca`	`/pub/mac/info-mac`
`ftp.uu.net`	`/systems/mac/info-mac`
`grind.isca.uiowa.edu`	`/mac/infomac`

```
wuarchive.wustl.edu        /systems/mac/info-mac
```

Europe
```
ftp.cs.tu-berlin.de        /pub/mac/info-mac
ftp.fenk.wau.nl            /pub/mac/info-mac
ftp.francenet.fr            /pub/miroirs/info-mac
ftp.funet.fi               /pub/mac/info-mac
ftp.ibp.fr                 /pub/mac/info-mac
ftp.jyu.fi                 /info-mac
ftp.lth.se                 /mac/info-mac
ftp.rrzn.uni-hannover.de   /pub/info-mac
ftp.sunet.se               /pub/mac/info-mac
ftp.switch.ch              /mirror/info-mac
ftp.uni-stuttgart.de        /pub/systems/mac/info-mac
ftp.univie.ac.at           /mac/info-mac
info.nic.surfnet.nl         /mirror-archive/software/info-mac
src.doc.ic.ac.uk           /packages/info-mac
```

Middle East
```
ftp.technion.ac.il         /pub/unsupported/mac/info-mac
```

Australia/Asia
```
archie.au                  /micros/mac/info-mac
ftp.center.osaka-u.ac.jp   /info-mac
ftp.edu.tw                 /Macintosh/info-mac
ftp.iij.ad.jp              /pub/info-mac
ftp.nus.sg                 /pub/mac
ftp.pcvan.or.jp            /pub/info-mac
ftp.riken.go.jp            /pub/info-mac
hwarang.postech.ac.kr       /pub/mac/info-mac
king.ncb.gov.sg            /info-mac
```

University of Michigan Macintosh Software Archive

These sites are mirrors of the Macintosh software repository at the University of Michigan. The home site "carpediem" in Michigan is almost impossible to connect with, so you really shouldn't bother trying unless you are on campus at Michigan!

FTP Addresses	Directories
North America	
`carpediem.cc.itd.umich.edu`	`/pub/mac`
`ftp.pht.com`	`/pub/mac/umich`
`mirror.archive.umich.edu`	`/mirrors/umich`
`mirrors.aol.com`	`/pub/mac`
`wuarchive.wustl.edu`	`/systems/mac/umich.edu`
Europe	
`ftp.sunet.se`	`/pub/mac/umich`
`src.doc.ic.ac.uk`	`/computing/systems/mac`
Australia/Asia	
`archie.au`	`/micros/mac/umich`

Using FTP Without Direct Internet Access

Next we'll show you three ways you can use FTP to get your research done, even if you only have an e-mail account. If you cannot access the Internet directly to use FTP, you can still get the job done, but it will take a bit more effort and time.

FTP by FTPMail

FTPMail is a great service for people without direct access to Internet FTP. It takes longer, and is more resource-intensive than either plain or anonymous FTP, so don't use FTPMail unless you need it.

To find out more about FTPMail, send e-mail to *ftpmail* at whatever address that is closest to you, with the word *help* as the body of the message. Also, if you intend to use the service much, consider sending the help message to the address below in Germany, and to the two USA sites because the help messages were written or modified by different people, and each one explains some things better than the others. Each help file also contains sample scripts for your study, to learn to write your own FTPMail requests. The Australian site also offers Archie services by e-mail, so their help message is expanded to include the Archie commands.

FTP by E-mail Sites	Country
North America	
`ftpmail@sunsite.unc.edu`	USA
`ftpmail@ftp.uu.net`	USA

Australia

`ftpmail@cs.uow.edu.au`   Australia

Europe

`ftpmail@src.doc.ic.ac.uk`   England
`ftpmail@grasp.insa-lyon.fr`   France
`ftpmail@ftp.uni-stuttgart.de`   Germany
`ftpmail@ieunet.ie`   Ireland

Once you have read a couple of the help files, you should be ready to try out this service. Here is the general form of an FTPMail script:

```
open <site> <username> <password>
cd <directory>
dir              # To obtain a directory listing
get <file>          # To retrieve a file
quit
```

For an example test script, try replacing the words *yourname@email.address.net* with your actual e-mail address below:

```
open rtfm.mit.edu anonymous yourname@email.address.net
cd /pub/usenet/news.answers/ftp-list
get faq
quit
```

Then send the script to the FTPMail server shown above that is geographically closest to you. What you'll get back is the latest version of the Anonymous FTP Frequently Asked Questions (FAQ) List.

As you can see, an FTPMail script is very similar to the actual sequence of commands you would type if you were using the "live-action" command-line FTP method. Many of the regular FTP commands are available to FTPMail users. The help messages mentioned above are designed to be all the training you need to use FTPMail, so that's where you should start.

Caution   *Please read and abide by the guidelines that each FTPMail server has placed in its help files. Most FTPMail servers want you to use their own copies of files, so please try retrieving files from the site itself first. In general, most of the files you need are* *already available at the first FTPMail site, so it's a waste of resources to ask the FTPMail server to connect to a regular FTP server, especially if it's just retrieving a file it already has!*

Bitnet's BITFTP Service

The former TRICKLE server in Germany has been converted to a Bitnet FTP server, and because it is intended to service only the Bitnet community, it has many special options and features that make no sense for the regular Internet user. If you are on Bitnet, get the instructions on how to use this special service by sending the message *help* to BITFTP@BITFTP.BITNET.

Bitnet's TRICKLE Software Service

TRICKLE's main purpose is to provide a service similar to FTPMail throughout Europe (and to the remainder of the international Bitnet community). But North Americans can use one of the minor TRICKLE commands to keep current on new versions of software.

Europe

Austria	`TRICKLE@AEARN`
Netherlands	`TRICKLE@HEARN`
Poland	`TRICKLE@PLEARN`

Middle East

Israel	`TRICKLE@TAUNIVM`

Caution

Be particularly careful to use all CAPITAL letters when dealing with TRICKLE servers. Maybe it's because they are part of Bitnet, but they have an unnerving habit of not responding at all if you make the slightest typing error. If you don't get a response within a couple hours, send your message again, very carefully!

All TRICKLE (also called RED) servers contain large amounts of very popular software. The software is frequently refreshed with new copies from the original source.

Although it is somewhat counter-intuitive, do not use an Internet-style address to address mail to these Bitnet servers, even if you know how to translate the Bitnet alias into an Internet address. They either don't respond at all, or they respond much slower if you do not use their Bitnet address.

TRICKLE has two main commands, /PDDIR and /PDGET, and many minor commands. If you send the command /PDDIR it will cause a TRICKLE server to send back a directory or subdirectory listing, and /PDGET is used to have files sent to you by e-mail.

Note

Unless you are a Bitnet user, you should probably instead use FTPMail, which is covered in the previous section, rather than the TRICKLE /PDGET command to have software delivered to you. The /PDGET part of TRICKLE is primarily for Bitnet users and for Europeans who for some reason have no ready access to FTP services.

But the rest of us can use the software update service TRICKLE offers, by ordering a free "subscription" to any new versions of our favorite software, without overly burdening the TRICKLE servers.

Finding Directories and Software

Before you can subscribe to a TRICKLE software file (or a directory of software) and just sit back and wait for a new version to come out and be delivered, you first must find out which TRICKLE server contains the files you want, and then you must find the exact directory name and the filename as it is used on that TRICKLE server.

To find out which server contains software you would be interested in, you send the following message to each of the four servers listed above:

`/PDDIR`

The four servers will send back the names of all the directories (or folders) in their current software collections. Of course, if you find the same directory listed on two servers, use the TRICKLE server closest to you

Once you have identified a server and directory of interest, ask for a listing of the files in the directory. The next example shows you the response received from the Austrian TRICKLE server when it received the message"/PDDIR."

```
From TRICKLE@AEARN.BITNET Sat Mar 11 23:29:10 1995
Date:   12 Mar 1995 06:18:55
From:   "RED File Server Version 3.01"
 @AEARN.BITNET
To:  kinnaman@world.std.com
Subject:   Re: Your command file "KINNAMAN MAIL" of 03/12/95
           06:18:54
/PDDIR
Greetings from TRICKLE@AEARN.
```

```
The names of the available directories are: MISC MSDOS SIGM
PC-BLUE CPM
ARCHIVES UNIX-C MACINTOS OS2 AMIGA WINDOWS
Try: /PDDIR   of the above names
Completed in 1 seconds.
```

One of the directories on the server is WINDOWS, and to find out what is in the WINDOWS directory, you should send the following command:

```
/PDDIR
```

Here is the response the TRICKLE server sent back.

```
From:   TRICKLE@AEARN.BITNET Sun Mar 5 11:50:10 1995
Date:   5 Mar 1995 18:44:49
From:   "RED File Server Version 3.01"
 @AEARN.BITNET
To:   kinnaman@world.std.com
Subject:   Re: Your command file "KINNAMAN MAIL" of 03/05/95
            18:44:49
/PDDIR
List of subdirectories for:
ACCESS      DEMO       DESKTOP     DRIVERS     EXCEL
            FONTS      GAMES       ICONS       MISC
PAGEMKR     PATCHES    PDOXWIN     PENDING_UPLOADS PIM
PROGRAMR    SDL        SOUNDS      TOOLBOOK    UTIL
WINMAG      WINSOCK    WINWORD     WPWIN       WRK
Use "/PDDIR .subdir" to search a specific directory.
Completed in 0 seconds.
```

So, now we know the WINDOWS directory has a subdirectory called WINSOCK. To find out what files are in the WINSOCK subdirectory, just send this message:

```
PDDIR.WINSOCK
```

To save space, only a small portion of the files listed in the WINDOWS.WINSOCK subdirectory are shown. Please notice that several files used in examples earlier in this chapter are on the Austrian TRICKLE server, for example, WINSOCK.ZIP, WS_FTP.ZIP, and WSFTP32.ZIP.

```
From TRICKLE@AEARN.BITNET Sun Mar 5 12:04:35 1995
Date:   5 Mar 1995 18:52:20
From:   "RED File Server Version 3.01"
@AEARN.BITNET
```

```
To:  KINNAMAN@WORLD.STD.COM
Subject:  Re:/PDDIR.WINSOCK
.WINSOCKINDEX              6922 27-02-95
.WINSOCKATISML01.ZIP       1236373 13-02-95
.WINSOCKBSDCHAT.ZIP        23435 27-07-94
.WINSOCKCELLO.ZIP          328429 11-07-94
.WINSOCKCFING10.ZIP        121924 24-01-95
```

This edited list shows only a small portion of the available software in the Austrian TRICKLE server's WINDOWS.WINSOCK directory. The right-hand columns show the size and archive date for each file.

Once you've discovered software files that you want to stay current on, and you know which subdirectory they reside in, you can "subscribe" to them, and for one year you will automatically receive all newer versions soon after they reach the European Bitnet portion of the Internet.

You can subscribe to any single file on the server, and whenever a new file of that name arrives, a /PDGET command will be automatically entered for you, and you will quickly receive that new file. Here is the general form of the message to use.

SUBDIRFILENAME.ZIP
/SUB <DIRECTORY.SUBDIR>FILENAME.ZIP

Or you can turn off your previous subscription using a very similar command:

SUBDIRFILENAME.ZIP
/UNSUB <DIRECTORY.SUBDIR>FILENAME.ZIP

You can also subscribe to an entire subdirectory, so that you get free copies of all new or changed software files coming into that subdirectory.

SUBDIR
/SUB <DIRECTORY.SUBDIR>*

The unsubscribe command for entire subdirectories is:

SUBDIR
/UNSUB <DIRECTORY.SUBDIR>*

Review all of your subscriptions at any one TRICKLE server by sending this command to the server:

/SUB QUERY

Tip

Remember, this service is designed especially for Bitnet users and Europeans who cannot use regular Internet FTP services. If you use this service from the Internet side, rather than on Bitnet, a few of the options and commands in the FAQ and in the return mail from the servers just don't work. The commands demonstrated here do work, as of this writing. It's a great service, but don't expect it to do everything!

Note

To get detailed instructions on all the TRICKLE commands, or to learn how to contribute software to TRICKLE, send an e-mail message help to TRICKLE@HEARN.BITNET, or any of the other servers listed above.

TRICKLE also has a dedicated mailing list for discussion of the software TRICKLE collects and distributes. To subscribe, send an e-mail message to listserv@nic.surfnet.nl and in the body of the message say:

```
subscribe red-ug Your Name
```

To unsubscribe, send e-mail to the same administrative address, but in the body say:

```
signoff red-ug
```

FTP—Pandora's Box

It's possible you may find that FTP is too powerful. Your hard drive and your disk space at your Internet Service Provider may fill up "overnight" with materials you thought were absolutely necessary for your research project. To help you deal with this possible glut of new information, we next provide you with some ideas for handling material once you bring it home. Without some way of dealing with the millions of files of available information, Internet FTP could be your Pandora's Box—opening all the world to you, and overwhelming you, too.

MIT Treasure House

The RTFM archive at the Massachusetts Institute of Technology doesn't just hold technical information for people who use the Internet. It's a treasure house of FAQs and other files related to many of the thousands of Usenet News Groups. It's also a good place—perhaps—to get the latest information on that group's subject. The volunteers or staffers who write the FAQs update them frequently.

The RTFM archive is one good place to start if you're embarking on a research project and you're looking for an appropriate Usenet newsgroup to monitor. There are two ways to get the FAQs at MIT, if you're starting from the top. One is to search the subdirectories by name. The second is by hierarchy or group.

Figure 5-5.
Using Free Agent to search for a cancer Usenet group.

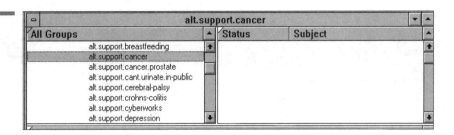

Let's take a group we've already discussed, *comp.answers*. We could find many FAQs in a subdirectory called comp.answers in the name directories. If we tried the group system, instead, we would first look under the *comp* subdirectory and then find the *answers* subdirectory. Stored there are many computer FAQs—the index file by itself is 100K. Now let's try another subject, cancer, as a real life example, and see what MIT has to offer.

You have a couple of alternatives in searching for information about cancer. The most obvious are the sci. or sci.med hierarchy or the alt. hierarchy. If you have a newsreader such as Free Agent that lets you search through all 11,000 or so Usenet groups, you can search for the keyword "*cancer*" and find there's one, "alt.cancer" as shown in Figure 5-5.

If you're using News Xpress, you can use a word processor to search the on-disk .newsrc file for the word *cancer*. You also may have to scroll through the subdirectories at the site, like a good old fashioned fishing expedition, depending, of course, on your subject.

In this case, we'll use Chameleon's FTP utility, because it has one advantage for large scale searches, a filter that cuts down the search time. The Chameleon filter only searches by the first letters in a text string. So I tried sci. and sci.med and found no references to cancer in the RTFM FTP files. So next I tried "*alt*" in the RTFM hierarchy directories. Using the letter "C," I found no hits for "cancer." The next try, using "*supp*" to get to the "support" subdirectory I did get a hit as shown in Figure 5-6. I clicked on support and then again tried the letter "C" in the filter box, as shown in Figure 5-7. The result was a successful hit "cancer," indicating there was a group called alt.support.cancer.

Finally you click the *cancer* subdirectory to find what files are available and find one, as shown in Figure 5-8, a list of psychology support groups, which includes not only cancer, but almost every other support newsgroup on the Net. A good place to start.

A search for another subject might yield more, or it might yield nothing. Again, we make the point that Internet FTP and the MIT Treasure House are just two tools among many. You should not neglect using Archie to try to find files with the name *cancer* elsewhere on the Net or a Web search engine or Veronica to locate the material you need.

Figure 5-6.
Searching the alt level in RTFM using Chameleon's FTP utility

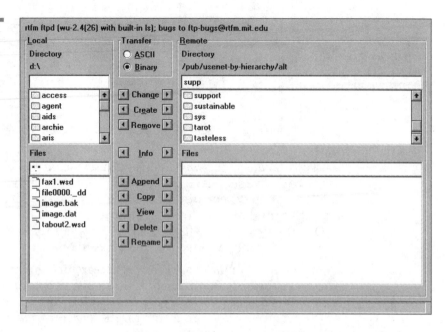

Figure 5-7.
Using the Chameleon filter to locate the cancer subdirectory

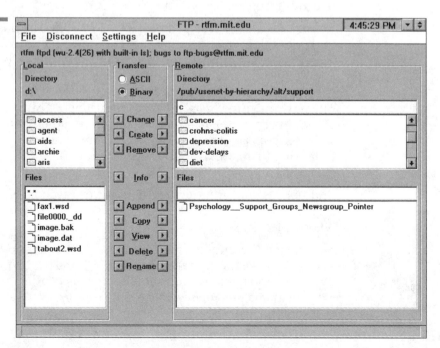

Figure 5-8.
The support file in the
alt.support.cancer
subdirectory

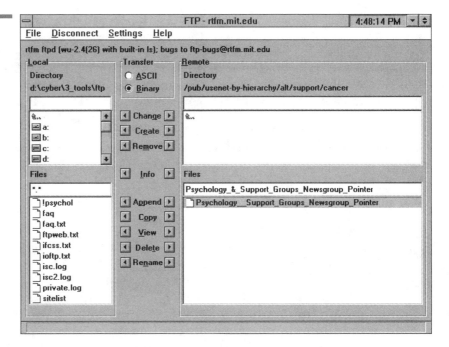

Filenames Can Be Misleading

When you're doing any kind of research, the obvious answer isn't always the correct one.

Here's an example. Last fall, one of the authors was looking for a new Canadian government briefing paper on privacy on the "information highway" at the Canadian Department of Industry's "debra" FTP site, using an old fashioned UNIX search.

I first searched in the subdirectory debra.dgbt.doc.ca/pub/isc—which is what the notice posted on a couple of mailing lists recommended. The *dir* command brought this result:

```
dir
total 6046
rw-r-r- 1 222    222    980 Oct 5 18:00 .Links
rw-r-r- 1 222    222    185 Feb 2 1994 .message
rw-r-r- 1 222    222    322 Jan 6 1994 .sig
rw-rw-r-1 222    222    18552 May 4 1994 00documents.style.guide
rw-r-r- 1 222    222    3053 May 12 12:00 00lisez
```

The search found three files relating to privacy and I quickly used the *"get"* command to retrieve them to my home directory on my service provider. Because, I was doing a manual UNIX search, I had to change the names to DOS 8.3 style before downloading them to my PC. I then opened the files and found they were the wrong ones—they were political statements on privacy from the previous Conservative government that was wiped out in the 1993 Canadian federal election. A footnote for my research, perhaps, but not what I was looking for. So I went back and took another look and tried the Canadian.Information.Highway subdirectory. I went up the subdirectory and again tried the directory command. This was the result:

```
dir
total 1111
rw-r-r—   1 222    222      168 Jul 20 11:32.name
rw-rwxr—  2 222    222    34126 Apr 20 1994
Advisory.Council.Membership.txt
rw-rwxr—  2 222    222   107128 Apr 20 1994
Advisory.Council.Membership.wp
rw-rwxr—  1 222    222    95048 Apr 8 1994
Building.Canada's.Info.Infrastructure.April94.txt
rw-rwxr—  1 222    222   120353 Apr 8 1994
Building.Canada's.Info.Infrastructure.April94.wp51
rw-rwxr—  1 222    222    31782 Mar 23 1994
CANARIE.executive.summary
Competition.Act.and.Info.Highway.eng-francais.txt
rw-rw-r—  2 222    222    81012 May 5 1994
Competition.Act.and.Info.Highway.eng-francais.wp
rw-r-r—   1 222    222    11984 Oct 26 13:42
Education.Opportunities.on.Infohighway.txt
lrwxrwxrwx 1 222   222       25 Jul 20 11:27
Info.Highway.Advisory.Council
```

You'll notice that the bolded entry *lrwxrwxrwx* is one we haven't seen before in this book. It's not a directory nor a file, but a pointer, advising you to manually switch to yet another subdirectory Info.Highway.Advisory.Council -/dbd/ftp/pub/info-highway

I switched to that subdirectory and found the file I needed:

```
total 189
rw-r-r— 1 204   1      154 Oct 18 1994 README
rw-r-r— 1 204   1    52741 Oct 18 1994 priv_e.asc
```

```
rw-r-r- 1 204    1         61738 Oct 18 1994 priv_e.rtf
rw-r-r- 1 204    1         76626 Oct 18 1994 priv_f.rtf
```

The name was already in DOS 8.3 format, so I downloaded it.

John Iliff and His Window on the Internet FTP File

One of the files you should retrieve—especially if you're new to the Internet—is a handy Windows help file that offers a simple guide to the Internet called "Window to the Internet." (see Figure 5-9). It was created by John Iliff, at the Pinellas Park Public Library in Florida.

Iliff is also a co-moderator for the PUBLIB and PUBLIB-NET mailing lists. He developed the help file to give people "a quick read on the Internet." It's available from *snoopy.tblc.lib.fl.us* in the pub directory. The filename is *nethlp.zip*.

Iliff says he created the help file "using Word 6 and the Windows help Compiler HC31. The creative process was simple—I just put information in that people were *constantly* asking me at my reference desk."

Figure 5-9.
The window to the Internet help file

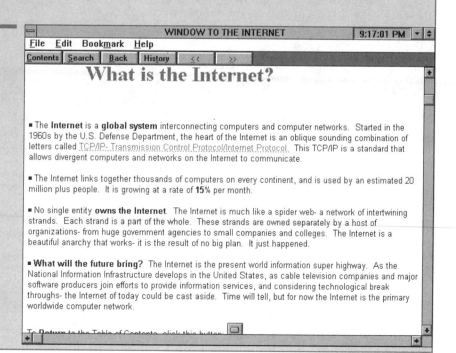

Iliff has a 486 with a 14.4 modem. "I have a PPP connection, and use the Chameleon suite of Net software," he says, "but I also use TIA and Trumpet at times as well for a SLIP connection (to save money). In the four years I've used the Internet I've always done some form of dial-up. I think I was among the very first of the end user types—those not affiliated with a major research institution or Defense Department entity—who found ways to surf the Net.

"It can be an all consuming endeavor. I can mark my life, in many respects, as pre-Net and post-Net. I work at a reference desk in a public library where we get, literally, thousands of questions every month," Iliff says. "I find the Internet useful in helping to answer many of those questions. "

Iliff says recent changes have made searching the Internet easier. "First Gopher and early Web line browsers provided a more uniform approach to info on the Net (as opposed to Telneting to an individual site). I think it is getting more complex, though, in that there is such an explosion of information. Three years ago sites were added to the tune of one a day, or even per week. Now dozens and dozens of useful sites are added per day. It is extremely difficult to keep up with.

"I could give you one for virtually every day I work. Today I used the Net, for example, to help a high school student do a paper on Tunisia. I printed out a copy of a report on Tunisia from the CIA World Factbook, for example. I also helped a person interested in starting a small business by giving publications from the U. S. Small Business Administration. The Net, for us, is a revolution in the information we can provide. "

Tips for Researchers

Iliff has a number of tips for researchers. "I think the best advice I can give," he says, "is to spend a considerable amount of time exploring the resources, to take notes, to set bookmarks, and to remember that this is a constantly changing research tool. If you *ever think you've arrived, then you are doomed—this is technology that requires always knowing there is much, much more to learn.*

"I think the worst instance was when a fellow insisted everything ever published was now available full text through the Library of Congress. When it was explained this was clearly not the case the fellow dismissed us as uninformed.

"I think the worst that folks can do with research on the Internet is expect it to do what it can't (at least at present). There are some incredible misconceptions about the technology out there.

"Most of the information I get for people has to be on paper or saved to disk," he adds. *"It's got to be walk and wear. Thus, it's shoot it off the Net and into my library user's hand."*

Iliff believes that Net researchers should be versatile. "I can't think of anything other than learning to be comfortable with a variety of Net software [programs]," he advises. *"For example, if my PPP account is down, [it's good] to be comfortable to dial-in to a UNIX site and use Lynx seamlessly and quickly. Flexibility is my biggest trick."*

Iliff has one warning about the future. "I think the Net will get only more and more overwhelming—there is getting to be so much information," he says. *"I think it all comes down to having an understanding of how information is organized. Librarians have been organizing information since ancient times—look at Alexandria. My advice to anyone who wants to understand the Net, and to be able to use the Net, would be to look at how librarians search for and organize information. Use those techniques and the seeming morass of the Net will seem manageable."*

6

What Is the Internet?

Now that you have some basic information about the Internet, and you've gone online and explored, it's time to take a little time out, go back, and take a look at the Internet itself.

Every Internet book tells a little history of the Net. We've left it to this chapter because we knew you wanted to get the feel of the Net and would have skipped over the history stuff anyway. But this chapter doesn't have the "usual" history stuff.

So let's define what we mean by the Internet and what the readers of this book—researchers—need to know about the Net. The Internet is computers. The Internet is packet switching networks and service providers, but it's mainly *people*—the people who dreamed up and then designed the networks, the people who wrote the software, and the people who use the Net. So when this chapter asks "What is the Internet?" we mean the people.

Now you're going to meet some of them, Net creators and Net users. Not your usual "history."

Present at Creation: Len Kleinrock, UCLA

The story is well known; the Internet began as ARPANET. In 1969, the United States Department of Defense's Advanced Research Projects Agency decided to set up a decentralized computer network that could, in theory, survive a nuclear war. The network was designed to reroute messages if any one link went down. Thus emergency communications could be maintained by routing the message around the problem computer. The first Net connections linked four universities: the University of California at Los Angeles, UC Santa Barbara, Stanford University, and the University of Utah. Leonard Kleinrock was at UCLA.

Today, Kleinrock is chairman of the Computer Science Department at UCLA. In 1988, Kleinrock chaired a committee that wrote a key report to push the National Research and Education Network, NREN. And in 1994, he was responsible for another report to look at the National Information Infrastructure (NII) in the United States.

"I was asking the question, basically, what should be NSF's [National Science Foundation] role, what should be the architecture of an NII, what should the government do, and how do we concern ourselves about the research, education, and library communities," Kleinrock recalls.

"I created the major report that came out in May [1994], called Realizing the Information Future: The Internet and Beyond, and that basically took Washington by storm. I spent the whole summer with one of the other authors, briefing everybody and his brother up to the presidential science adviser, the head of congressional subcommittees, etc., promoting an architecture and other things."

Kleinrock was educated at the City College of New York and the Massachusetts Institute of Technology. He joined the faculty at UCLA in 1963. His research interests focus on the evaluation and design of many kinds of computer and electronic networks. Since 1969, he has been a UCLA principal investigator for the Defense Advanced Research Projects Agency. He led the group at UCLA when it became the first node on the ARPANET in 1969 and headed the effort at UCLA when it served as the ARPANET Measurement Center as well.

"My Ph.D. dissertation at MIT in December '62 was on laying the foundations for packet-switch networks. Analysis, design, protocols, etc.," Kleinrock says. "I then came here to UCLA. No one in the early '60s was interested in data networks, but in the mid to late '60s, the Advanced Research Projects Agency (ARPA) got interested because they wanted to connect their machines together to do resource sharing.

"I was on the early team in 1967 to specify what the packet-network would be. We created the specs, sent it out for questions and proposal. In January '69, Bolt, Beranek, and Newman won the contract to build the network based on these specs. They were supposed to select a minicomputer and lease the lines, and write the code. And they did that.

"What was it like in those early days? Wonderful. In the very early days, nobody wanted to connect to a network. A typical principal investigator was asked to join the network because ARPA wanted to share his computing machines with all the other researchers . . . and the typical response by a PI (principle investigator) was 'I don't want to join! Why? Because I don't want other people to use my machine!'

"I said, 'well wait a minute, you're going to be able to use other people's machines.' He said, 'Oh, no, no. I'm not interested.'

"So I extracted from each of them some idea as to how they would use the network if they were connected. I asked how many teletypes' worth would you allow into your time-shared system, and they said 'I have no idea.'

"I said, 'how about two or three?' and they said, 'Yeah, two or three.' I said, 'How much would you use these various sites,' and I extracted numbers from them."

Kleinrock then published the results of his survey in a paper and then went to work convincing people they should do it.

"Pretty soon, they loved it," Kleinrock says, and what was to become the Internet was born.

"When the first message was passed between our host computer and the first node in the network," he reports, "we had a variety of people here at UCLA." It was the Tuesday after Labor Day, September 2, 1969.

"It was a monumental day," Kleinrock says. "We had in our laboratory here, of course, the computer science guys, we had the engineering people, we had the UCLA administration. It was a big event, you know; we had Bolt Berinek Newman, we had ARPA, we had ATT long lines (because we couldn't connect their lines), we had GTE, the local telephone company, we had Honeywell who built and supplied the mini computers that BBN modified, we had the Scientific Data Systems, who were builders of our host machine Sigma 7, we had everyone and their brother, and they were all ready to point the finger at the other guy if it didn't work, and the fact is, it worked.

"That first day we were moving bits back and forth; next day we were moving messages back and forth, so it was a big success. They rolled out one node per month til December, so we had four nodes. We were also selected to be the ARPANET network measurement center, so we began running tests and right to '75 the network grew."

"What was the vision at that point, you might ask? What did we think we were creating? And the answer is," Kleinrock says, "we were solving a very important engineering problem that would connect computers together; so we would have data computer-to-computer communication."

"We had no idea we would have 30 million users at this point. Nobody at the time anticipated that. Nobody anticipated e-mail at that point; it came a few years later.

"So [it was] an important engineering event, but it was not recognized as a mammoth moment, the way the man on the moon was. It happened in '69 also, as did Charles Manson, as did Woodstock. Those four happened. Let's look at the man on the moon, which had all the attention. It cost $25 billion and eight years of effort. Ours was a few million dollars' effort and eight months of effort, and the effect I think of one versus the other is not even comparable. But we had no idea that this was happening. The first message had no interesting information in it, it didn't say 'Watson, come here, I want you,' or 'What has God wrought?' or anything else. '

"Since then, I've been with the network all the time. In those early days," Kleinrock says, "the network was very hard to use because there was no common protocol on order to use a remote machine, you had to know the command language, the operating system, you had to understand the guts of that system from your location. So there was relatively little traffic until a host-to-host protocol was created, and that took two more years—in October of '71 it first was fully specified.

"Most of the traffic was caused either by measurement traffic that I and my facility were generating, or by people who migrated from one of those sites to another site and wanted to use this original machine because they understood the remote machine.

"We were basically the ones whose job it was to break the network, and it was easily done," Kleinrock chuckled. "So BBN was not very thrilled with us, because we kept showing them the mistakes they made . . . We found all kinds of deadlocks and crashes in the network for a variety of reasons, be they hardware or software failures . . . all sorts of things that you wouldn't anticipate, things that were pieces of software that had faults in them that people couldn't anticipate ahead of time, but once they occurred, we could easily fix them. And that's true in today's systems as well, when networks crash and you get brownout, ATT systems crash. It's because there's some weird condition there that has never been exposed before . . . ."

October of 1972 was a major date in the development of the Internet. An international conference on computer communications, ICC '72, was held in Washington D.C. At the conference Kleinrock and his colleagues held the first public demonstration of the ARPANET. Until then, it had been a private network involving ARPANET contractors, researchers, and some U. S. government officials. The entire network community of people created demonstrations to run at that conference.

"That was a landmark event because it demonstrated to the public how easy it was to use the network," Kleinrock says. "There were some really jazzy demonstrations [such a] distributed processing. We had all kinds of remote file transfer; you could log on from Washington to the UCLA machine to pull up a file out of Boston, compile it at UCLA, and send the printed results back to Washington. In those days, that was really exciting. And all kinds of artificial intelligence projects and games and simulations were demonstrated. As a result, the public became aware of this network and many more people joined the network shortly thereafter.

"Things pretty much stayed that way until the mid '70's," when we had more than one kind of network that wanted to participate in this," Kleinrock says. "We had the ARPANET; also, at UCLA, we were spearheading an effort in satellite backup switching, which was funded by ARPA, which had a very different protocol from ARPANET, and we also had another effort in ground radio packet switching, which is the other, third, network. So, there's a need for these three networks to talk to each other, and that's what gave rise to the need to develop TCP/IP."

That's when Robert Kahn and Vinton G. Cerf joined the project and both worked on the development of the protocol. Cerf had been a programmer working on Kleinrock's project at UCLA. The Internet began to develop in the late '70s with TCP/IP.

The Net was growing, CSNET, a network linking some computer science departments, joined in 1980. ARPANET had split off MILNET, for U. S. military communications, in 1983.

Then, in the mid 1980s, the United States National Science Foundation established its super computer centers around the country, and they started to connect them. That led to the creation of NSFnet in 1987, which became the backbone network of the Internet.

ARPANET began to back out and the NSF took over in the United States. "Instead of running a pilot program," Kleinrock says, "NSF decided to run a full-participation program across all sciences. And so the entire science community then began to play networking games, and that persisted until the commercial sector said, 'wait a minute, all these scientists are using networking on a network subsidized by the U. S. government, but there's a business here, we should be able to sell this service at ATT and the other long lines companies."

In 1991, the commercial groups started their own network, called CIX, or the Commercial Internet Exchange, and Kleinrock was called on once more to look at the future of the Internet.

"My committee came on to do the second report, *Realizing the Information Future*," Kleinrock says. "NSF was busy backing out, they were wondering whether their plans for backing out made sense, and what the future of their participation should be. Meanwhile, the commercial world was recognizing that there's a huge business opportunity here, and the entertainment world suddenly jumped on the bandwagon. In addition, in '93, the Clinton administration moved in talking about the NII. The Internet was exploding because of the commercial people moving in. And our report suddenly found itself at center stage—that's why it was such an important report, trying to resolve some of these issues—and as you see now, [the Internet] is going highly commercial.

When the World Wide Web suddenly happened, that was a big surprise to everybody two years ago. [It] has taken off; it's going to dominate network traffic very soon. So, end of story."

Tips for Researchers

"Most of these really really hot applications on the network were never anticipated," Kleinrock says, "E-mail was an ad-hoc add-on. The World Wide Web was something for physicists and it took over . . . it's a phenomenon.

"The latest thing that I'm working on—that I believe will be a major shift in the way that people do computing and will affect the Internet as well—is the notion of nomadic computing, where I can take my laptop anywhere, plug in anywhere and do computing while I'm moving, either connected or not. When I arrive someplace else, I'll be able to have my files automatically synchronized, I'll be able to find out what my local environment looks like, and my local environment will recognize what I look like.

"The notion of nomadic computing, I think, is a major change in the way people are going to do computing, and you know, the PDA's [Personal Digital Assistants] and the pagers and the cellular telephones and the notebook computers—you take all that on the road with you. You feel like a warrior going to battle.

"All those are going to be integrated and part of a system that understands that the basic paradigm is people on the move, changing locations. When I move from my desk to my conference table, and I take my laptop from one place to another, I've made a nomadic move, and the system has to be able to follow me and recognize I've got less time activity and different needs as I move around."

Putting on the Net: Michael Hart, Project Gutenberg

For more than twenty years, Michael Hart has had a dream, to see most of the world's great literature online and accessible to millions of people around the world. He's a professor of Electronic Text at Illinois Benedictine College in Lisle, Illinois, and executive director of Project Gutenberg.

Illinois Benedictine pays Hart a thousand dollars a month. Other money comes from donations and computer support comes from the University of Illinois at Champaign-Urbana.

Project Gutenberg is one of the best-known—and most massive—efforts on the Internet. Hart's sig file notes that he was User #100 on the Net. Asked how he knows, Hart says, "Oh, as a guess, but it's probably a pretty accurate one."

Hart's inspiration is Johann Gutenberg, the German printer who created modern movable type in Mainz, Germany, in 1440. Gutenberg's invention spread almost as fast as the Internet has and created the first information explosion. More books appeared in the following decades than had in the previous two millennia. Prices plunged, books that were once the preserve of the clergy and the nobility, were cheap enough for thousands.

Now Hart wants to use the computer to get at least ten thousand books in digital form by the year 2001. He hopes to reach one billion readers.

In a Christmas 1994 message to the Internet, Hart wrote: "This is about my 24th Christmas since getting on the Internet, and that was just about 24 years ago when I was 24 years old in 1971. Since then, the '70s, the '80s, and now half of the '90s have passed, things changed for the Internet, and never more than this year, which marked the 25th year of the Internet.

"For the first time, we have the capability for everyone on a universal scale, literally, to have information, education, and literacy at their fingertips, should they choose to be informed, educated, or literate.

"There are approximately 365 million computers today, and if just one of them were used each day to produce an etext we could all share, then we would all be members of a sort of a book of the day group.

"1995 is the 100th Anniversary of the Carnegie Public Library System and we would love to celebrate that anniversary by starting Electronic Public Libraries in the same mold.

"As the U.S. Adult Literacy Report stated, we were in a virtual epidemic of illiteracy these past few decades, with adult literacy falling to the appalling level of about 50 percent.

"Perhaps the best possible use of the Internet is to fight this epidemic and to make the cures for illiteracy and ignorance available so cheaply that there can never again be any excuse for ignorance and illiteracy—forever."

So how did that 24-year-old student become involved in such a huge, lifelong project?

"I first got on it pretty much by luck," Hart explains. "My brother's best friend and my best friend were mainframe operators at the materials research lab at the University of Illinois. I hung out there to do my homework, hiding in the air-conditioning when it was hot . . . [It was 1971] they gave me a free account, put a hundred million dollars worth of play money in it, and said, 'Do something.'

"I was not a programmer of any sort. I had read the FORTRAN manual and had nightmares of FORTRAN all night, and decided I wasn't going to be a programmer. I also didn't think that any program that was being written in 1971 would be in use ten years later, so I tried to think of something that was more permanent.

"It happened to be around the bicentennial of the [American] Revolution and I had a copy of the Declaration of Independence, one of those little parchments they were handing out back then, so I typed that in."

Hart and his friends sent out a note to general.com, one the first newsgroups and said: "Here's the instructions for getting the Declaration of Independence if you want it." The following year they added the U. S. Bill of Rights and the Constitution.

"They wouldn't let us do anything very big," Hart says, "because the computer only had two drives and they were only five megabytes a piece."

"I said we would eventually have the Bible and Shakespeare up there and they looked at me like I was nuts. I said, 'No, you wait, you wait, the disks will get bigger.'

"They said, They're not on our disks, you're not going to," Hart says, laughing at the memory. "You know, these [disks] were the huge things that looked like cake carriers—and had five megs. But they gave me enough space to play around with, and I guess, weaseling accounts here and there."

During this time, Hart received his degree in man-to-machine interfaces, at the University of Illinois's department of individual plans of study. "I studied a lot of math, psychology, sociology, music, biology, and a bunch of languages," Hart says. "I wanted to put a library on the Internet."

"Until 1988, nobody really paid any attention to what we were doing. The Internet was pretty small. The Usenet groups and chat groups were very ingrained. You only talked to the people you knew there, and unless you knew somebody who was interested in what you did, it was pretty boring. A lot of the early stuff was just, you know—my mainframe is crashing in this particular manner, who knows how to help?

"Around '83, Usenet got going, but most of the Usenet groups were very specific SIGs [special interest groups], and they weren't anything I was interested in.

"Somewhere around '87 or '88, there was a huge jump from approximately 35,000 to a quarter of a million users, and it kind of jumped from conversations about really specific esoteric stuff to conversations about everything. All of a sudden you could talk about anything. I got the first note from somebody that said anything other than: 'You want to put Shakespeare on a computer? You must be crazy.'

"That was all the responses I'd gotten for seventeen years, and then I got what I wanted—'Hey, electronic books, neat idea, let's do some.' It pretty much picked up. We decided to do mostly history of democracy stuff—Gettysburg Address, inaugural addresses, Magna Cartas—plus Shakespeare and the Bible."

Hart doesn't know who sent him the King James Version of the Bible. "He never sent me his name. He just sent me the disks. I just had to assume it was somebody who wanted the Bible out there for everybody. He did a good job too. We've only found a couple of errors in it. My guess is that since it was so good, a whole group of people worked on it and proofread it with each other.

"The real breakthrough for us came when we did *Alice's Adventures in Wonderland.* We did that in '88 and did *Peter Pan* in '88, and those things appealed to every age, rich or poor . . . and all of a sudden we started getting huge amounts of feedback. From there, we went on to do a fairly decent children's collection, including *Anne of Green Gables.*"

Project Gutenberg then expanded into what Hart calls "heavy literature," more Shakespeare, Milton reference materials, Roget's thesaurus, Webster's dictionary, the Encyclopedia Britannica. They also added computer material such as *Zen and the Art of the Internet* and the *Hacker's Jargon Dictionary.*

Other books included Moby Dick, The Scarlet Letter, The CIA World Fact Book, The Call of the Wild, The Man from Snowy River, The Turn of the Screw, Heart of Darkness, Caesar's Commentaries in Latin, Sons and Lovers, and the I Ching.

"I think it was in 1989," Hart recalls, "when the executive director of Common Knowledge (a lobby group that wanted the holdings of the Library of Congress available on CD-ROM) was on the phone with me, and I heard a crash that literally sounded like a tree fell through the roof of her house."

"She ran off, and . . . she came back laughing. Her son had found *Alice's Adventures in Wonderland* on her computer . . . and had been coming home from school, reading it after school every day." Every day more kids followed him home from school to read this thing on her computer. They had finally got so many of them piled up on the chair in front of the computer that the chair had just burst into fifty pieces.

"The kids had just gone everywhere. And she told me this whole story, and, all of a sudden, the light went on over my head that Gutenberg was not going to be what I thought it was going to be . . . It was going to be what other people turned it into being. It just never occurred to me that a dozen kids of junior high school age would follow somebody home to read a book on-screen. I just all of a sudden realized . . . Eric, was his name . . . and for Eric, *Alice's Adventures in Wonderland* for his whole life was going to be in his head on a computer screen and not on paper."

Project Gutenberg also has the original illustrations from *Alice* available as .GIF files (see Figure 6-1). "You can either get just a text file, or you can take the text file and put all the GIFs with it," Hart says. "There are forty-two illustrations [in *Alice*] and there are fifty for Through the Looking Glass." The GIFs take up seven times as much space as the book.

Figure 6-1.
John Tenniel's original Mad Hatter's Tea Party illustration from the Project Gutenberg *Alice's Adventures in Wonderland* file.

Illustrations have added to appeal to Project Gutenberg's audience. "We got a lot more space, a lot more bandwidth—and a lot more feedback," Hart says. "There are definitely people out there that like the pictures."

Project Gutenberg recently got permission to use the recently discovered, 2,000-year-old cave paintings in France, although, so far, feedback has been slow. "I thought that we would get a lot of feedback from that too," he says. "But the illustrations either aren't ringing people's bells, or they're ringing people's that are of the MTV generation, and they just don't talk back. It's hard to say."

Project Gutenberg's home base is computers at the University of Illinois at Champaign-Urbana. "We run off a NeXT machine that has seven hard drives on it, each one of about a gigabyte," Hart says. "We send out maybe 60 or 70 gigabytes from there every month. And there are mirror sites that just automatically pick up all our stuff as we post them all over the world."

The material on Project Gutenberg is mostly keyed in by more than 450 volunteers, although some more modern folks are using scanners. "We're pretty hands-off bosses," Hart says, "If they want to type it in on an Atari 400, that's fine with me, as long it comes out so that everybody can read it on the screen."

Project Gutenberg is, of course, a research gold mine, although according to Hart, few people print out the material. It usually remains on the screen and disk.

"A lot of people use them [the books] as reference works, but a lot of people do read 'em end to end, even people who are older than I am," he says. "There's no real way of telling. If you've got a screen that you're happy with and there's no bother with that—and they're getting more and more variations on screens, so probably it'll happen better and better. But not too many people print them out."

Researchers use Project Gutenberg for comparing books and doing language searches, or just use the dictionary and the thesaurus.

The growth of technology and computers means a bright future for Project Gutenberg, Hart says, "If a trend from our five megabyte drive twenty years ago, to five gigabyte drive today for the same amount of money, if that continues, [we'll have a] five terabyte drive for fifteen hundred bucks, twenty years from now, which will hold pretty much everything out of the Library of Congress."

Hart's plan to put the world's great literature onto disk is controversial, in a digital era when many writers are afraid of losing rights and income. He opposes proposals from Senator Orrin G. Hatch to reform U. S. copyright law that would extend some copyright from seventy-five years, as it now is, to ninety.

U.S. copyright law changed in 1978. Before then a work could be copyrighted for 28 years and then renewed for 28 years. It was then that the United States joined the rest of the world by making copyright in a work last for the life of the author plus fifty years after death. In works created as "work for hire" or by corporations, copyright lasts for 75 years.

The difference in American law with the rest of the world often lead to works being in the public domain in the United States but not in other nations. (We'll discuss the implications of international copyright law for online researchers in a later chapter.)

The American law has a provision that called for works created before January 1, 1978, but not yet published that would remain in copyright until December 31, 2002. For U.S. works published before January 1, 1978, U. S. statutory copyright was extended for 47 years, making the total duration of copyright 75 years.

"The problem is that 99 percent of all the information in the country is copyrighted," Hart says. "They say information is doubling every fifteen years, or something like that?

"So half of our information is under fifteen years old, three-quarters of it's under thirty years old, seven-eighths of it's under 45 years old, fifteen-sixteenths of it's under sixty years old, and thirty-one thirty-seconds of it is under seventy-five years old. I may have invented the term, 'holding the Library of Congress in the palm of your hand,' when I predicted these five-terabyte drives, but I always said as a footnote, I have some belief that they won't let you put the Library of Congress in the palm of your hand when you can.

"[U. S. Vice President Al] Gore says he's worried about the information rich versus the information poor. I say, well, it's already got 98.23 percent of all the stuff that's in physics is under copyright, and if they push this one farther, they're just going to move it up to 99.18, or whatever it is. The thing is, they're only going to add one percent to their own profits, but they're going to take away half of everything that's in the public domain.

"When *Winnie the Pooh* was copyrighted in 1926, the [U.S.] law was that you wait until 1982 and then *Winnie the Pooh* gets out of jail and can go anywhere," Hart says. "In 1982, they had revoked that law in '75 and put another nineteen years on it to make it go to 2001. Now they're trying to revoke that one again, because 2001 is coming along, and make it be 2021."

(The author *of Winnie the Pooh*, A. A. Milne, died in 1956. In most of the world, *Winnie* falls into public domain in 2006.)

"I personally [think] they're not playing fair. I do not advocate stealing people's books and putting them on the Net, you know—even if they're things like *Neuromancer*, which kind of encouraged it. I would prefer to have it be half and half.

"I think that big, you know—it would be okay to have half the information be under copyright and half of it be in the public domain. But if the way you're talking about it their fear of getting ripped off makes them rip you off first. This is kind of like the first-strike versus Russia—business. If they're saying, 'Well, we're afraid they're going to steal our stuff, so we're going to rip it all off and make it all copyrighted now—[that] adds an *ex post facto* law. That's kind of creepy to think that 99 percent of all the information is basically already under copyright.

"We have had a history of limited distribution, where basically the only thing that was unlimited was air. This whole philosophy that any one person can type in *Alice's Adventures in Wonderland* in a couple of days and that everybody for the rest of history could have one, that is not being adopted by our colleges, or anything else.

"It's changed from technology to politics. All my life I've been trying to find ways of getting more stuff into the box. Now all of a sudden those people, with the advent of publicity on the Internet, have said, 'We don't want everybody to have all that information.'

"[There's a] 53 percent adult literacy rate in the United States. That means already that half of all the written books in the country can't be read [online] by anybody. Right? So, they're trying to make it worse. They're trying to copyright it even further, and I just look at that as they want a monopoly on information, or something.

"Now, tell me what's going to end the world if everybody gets *Winnie the Pooh* and Hemingway?

Finding Project Gutenberg

The easiest way to locate Project Gutenberg's files is through the project's World Wide Web site at http://jg.cso.uiuc.edu/PG/welcome.html, shown in Figure 6.2.

The Web page has easy-to-read pointers to Project Gutenberg's main FTP site and two mirror sites. As shown by the icons in Figure 6-3, the user gets a choice of retrieving either the plain text or a zipped version of the file.

If you want to use FTP directly, check the Project Gutenberg Mirror Sites list first to see if there is a Gutenberg mirror site locally.

If not try:

```
ftp mrcnext.cso.uiuc.edu
login:anonymous
password: yourname@your.machine
cd pub
cd etext
cd etext95 [or 94, 93, 92, 91 or 90. 70s and 80s are in
          /etext90]
get filename [(be sure to set bin, if you get the .zip
          files])
```

Figure 6-2.
The Project Gutenberg
Home Page

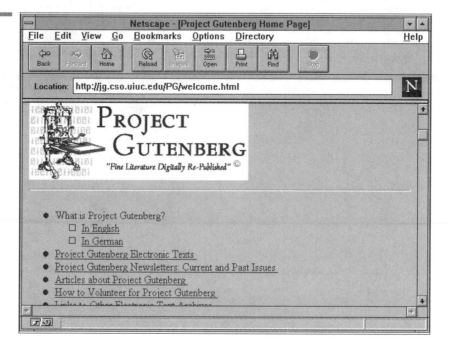

Figure 6-3.
The Project Gutenberg
Web pointer page

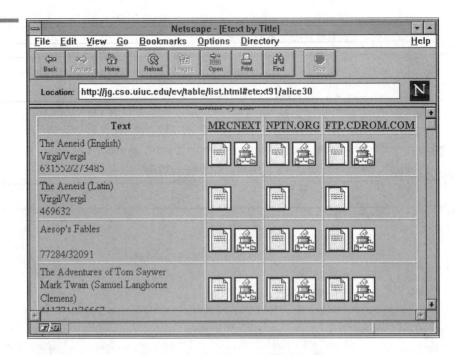

Figure 6-4.
Alice and the Cheshire
Cat, from the Project
Gutenberg file

```
get more files
quit
```

To subscribe to the Project Gutenberg newsletter, send the following a message to:

```
listserv@vmd.cso.uiuc.edu or listserv@uiucvmd.bitnet:
sub gutnberg your name
```

Leave the subject line blank.

Project Gutenberg Mirror Sites

In the United States:

```
etext.archive.umich.edu = 192.131.22.7
ftp.etext.org   (192.131.228)
    cd /pub/Gutenberg
ftp.cdrom.com = 192.153.46.2
freebsd.cdrom.com   (192.216.222.5)
    cd /.5 and /.6 and /.3
ftp.wustl.edu = wuarchive.wustl.edu = 128.252.135.4
nptn.org = 192.55.234.52,
oak.oakland.edu = 141.210.10.117
ftp.uu.net   (192.48.96.9)
    /doc/literary/gutenberg/etext93
ftp sunsite.unc.edu
    cd /pub/docs/books
inforM.umd.edu
calypso-2.oit.unc.edu (198.86.40.81)
    cd /pub/docs/books
ftp.scri.fsu.edu (144.174.128.34)
    cd /pub/dduke
mailer.cc.fsu.edu (128.186.6.103)
    cd /pub/dduke
halcyon.com (198.137.231.1)
    /dec/.0/data
```

Canada:

Many Project Gutenberg mirror site—but far from all—are available at:

`mindlink.bc.ca`

Log in as a guest.

France:

`ftp.cnam.fr = 163.173.128.6`

Germany:

`alice.fmi.uni-passau.de  (132.231.1.180)`
`    cd /pub`

United Kingdom:

`unix.hensa.ac.uk:/pub/uunet/doc/literary/gutenberg/etext94`
`src.doc.ic.ac.uk:/media/literary/collections/`
`                project_gutenberg`

Japan:

`ftp news3.yasuda-u.jp.ac`
`    cd users/pub/gutenberg/etext91, 92, 93, 94`

Singapore:

There's also a World Wide Web site in Singapore (much of it is in Chinese).

`http://www.technet.sg/singapore-server.html`
`http://www.np.ac.sg:9080`

Remembering the Holocaust: William Connelly, U.S.

Bill Connelly is a librarian at the United States Holocaust Research Institute Library and Museum in Washington, D.C., and one of the many librarians who help the growing number of online researchers. The museum's home page is shown in figure 6-5.

"I'm hardly what you could call an Internet guru," Connelly says. "I just send lots of e-mail in response to questions posted on a couple of lists I subscribe to. If I sometimes tack on the odd bibliography generated from our library's catalog, well . . . I mean, it's not like I've retrieved it from a server hidden in an asteroid belt.

Figure 6-5.
The U.S. Holocaust
Memorial Museum
home page

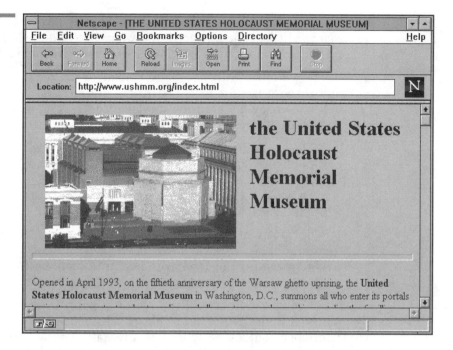

"Having an Internet address means more work for librarians, Connelly says. "Nowadays, anyone in the world who can lay their hands on a PC rigged with a modem can lob a request for information into my inbox in less time than it takes for me to get a cup of coffee. Generally, this is a grand thing, unless the java's been on the burner all night again, of course.

"E-mail's a fine thing too. Researchers can network and correspond at a hitherto unheard of pace, and the quality of research can benefit thereby. But there is also a vexing 'down side' to all this sudden immediacy of access. Many times it's clear from requests I receive that the sender hasn't bothered to pay a visit to one of their local library.

"The fact that about 80 to 90 percent of such 'lay-z-boy' messages I get are received from university addresses, those with *.edu* at the tail, is appalling when one considers the real dynamics at work here and the possible consequences. Don't learn to find an answer yourself, just sit back and let someone else tell you what's what and where it's at.

"The Holocaust Memorial, is a monument warning what can happen when enough people shrug off the task of sorting out the truth on their own, and become willing to eat up whatever's put on the table in front of them.

"Will the Internet, which rewards the slap-dash and lazy with an info glut that might fool the unwary into feeling they'd done a thorough research of a matter, result in a rapid atrophying of people's bibliographic research muscles?

"Is Veronica truly the handmaiden of the devil, luring the slothful and unwary with her siren-song of instant gratification? It all brings to mind that well-known saying about eternal vigilance . . . (Don't e-mail me for the full quote, go to your library. They miss you.)

"Eternal vigilance was also a recurring theme during last year's [1994] Computers in Libraries Conference, held here in Washington. There it was termed 'judging the quality' of material available on the Net. That's the thing about a book in a library: You look at it, and immediately you've got some idea where it came from, who put it together, how old it is, and so on.

"So much of what's available via the Net is of unknown provenance, spurious quality, or debatable reliability. Ask around. Do you know anyone on the Internet who'd like to have a liver transplant based on a surgical technique that's been floating around from file to file and server to server on the Net?

"I could (and have) filled hard disks with textual (and other) information retrieved from the Net, and I have since made much of it available to visiting researchers, but always with a plainly stated caveat, labeled on the cover, that the materials are *Internet Downloads*, followed by a verbal advisory that as such they should be viewed with an especially critical gaze, as damned near *apocryphal* items.

"Such is the present state of things on the Net: it's easy to get tangled in the dross out there. But I believe that the future will see more and more *reliable* servers asserting their *trustworthiness*, and that citing materials retrieved from these sites will gain a measure of research respectability, as these arrive replete with sources and a general air of vettedness necessary for reliable research.

"To match this vettedness visually, improving graphical interfaces will allow for an appearance of bookish reliability." For example, Connelly says, "in the not-so-distant future, it will be possible for someone accessing our specialized online catalog here at the museum to use it to access files containing digitally scanned images of the actual pages of an book or document indicated in a search of the catalog.

"The system will offer the user with the right equipment a display of an actual image of the work itself, coffee stains, dog-ears, penciled marginal scribbles, and all.

"So what do I mean by 'not-too-distant future?' All I'll say is that in the next couple of months, I will be receiving a software update for our online catalog that allows for such visual image tagging. Now if I only had a mega-gajillion gigabytes to store 50,000 volumes on.

"I was a dedicatd Net-lurker for a few months, but I don't have as much time to do it now," Connelly says. "I'm more interested nowadays in getting our own stuff on out.

"I haven't had a chance to play with Mosaic too much yet. I can see that it's rather different than the text-based system I was used to with Delphi. I like Gopher, but that's just what I'm used to. As a librarian, I appreciate Hytelnet, the collected online library catalogs utility available via some gophers. Veronica's swell too, but I only tend to use it when searching for programs. The fact is, most of my online searching is done through fee-based or subscription services I have access to through the library such as OCLC or by using our large collection of reference CDs, such as Encyclopedia of Associations, Books-In-Print, [or the] Social Sciences Citation Index. These services are not generally available on the Net, not for free anyhow.

"Apart from the Library of Congress's Marvel service, I seldom use the Net for hard reference, which is to say, research in response to specific queries. When I am on the Net it's more of a foraging exercise, rather like bird watching."

Tips for Researchers

Connelly has a number of tips for researchers, both offline and online. "Be wary of what you find," he says, "and buy a large bag of salted sunflower seeds. They help pass the time."

An Elementary or High School Student

"We have a special department at the Holocaust Memorial Museum which supplies all manner of information and organizes programs for students and their teachers—the Educational Resources Department. In addition, any researcher, regardless of age, is welcome to visit the library.

"As far as Internet services via e-mail are concerned, unless a researcher mentions his or her age, I don't feel compelled to ask. That's one desirable aspect of the Internet culture: the ether is the great leveler.

"I have had conversations with the many correspondents whose tender ages were volunteered from the outset—that leads me to guess that one might have an easier time explaining the process of unzipping a compressed file to the average seventh grader than with most tenured professors."

A Scholar

Connelly says help for scholars by Internet (e-mail) usually means he sends a reply with an attached DOS-file bibliography containing the results of a search of the Holocaust Research Institute's library's online catalog on the subject they are researching. He also sometimes sends an advisory that some other useful or requested material is being sent by snail mail.

As well, Connelly and some of his colleagues at the museum frequently post responses to requests for information posted on H-NET's "Holocaust List" (an Internet mailing list devoted to holocaust issues and research).

"Since I work in a library, my own responses tend to be simple suggestions for possible bibliographic sources for information or verbatim excerpts from such materials, which I then cite," Connelly says. "(Although) I just about smothered some professor at Amherst with Internet stuff on and about Ernst Zundel, the Holocaust Denier, which is a subject he was researching. The prof couldn't believe the stuff he was getting. Unfortunately, it was all too easy since the Holocaust Denial groups are very very active on the Net. It just goes to show that what I said above about eternal vigilance is true."

A Journalist

"Journalists receive the same services as any other scholars," Connelly says. "When they are researching the Museum itself, they are referred to the Museum's Public Affairs Department. My personal experience indicates that journalists largely seem to prefer the telephone. This also holds true for a related occupational group; fact checkers calling from publishing houses and magazines. They usually want quick answers to complex questions, and generally are disappointed by offers of bibliographies."

Tracking Alzheimer's on the Internet: Dr. J. Edward Jackson, UCSD

J. Edward Jackson, M.D. is an Associate Professor of Medicine, an Associate Clinical Professor of Pharmacology, and the director of the Seniors' Only Care Clinic, at the UCSD Alzheimer's Disease Research Center at the University of California, San Diego.

Dr. Jackson has been doing online research in his field for the past two or three years. He mostly uses the U. S. National Academy of Medicine's Medline service, and says his online research time has increased as more sources become available.

His main advice for those doing online research on the Internet and elsewhere: "Know what you're looking for," Dr. Jackson says. "If [you're] using a commercial service, know the rates—one can get stung very badly using, for example, databases on CompuServe that have additional charges."

Jackson uses specific mailing lists that serve what he calls "a quasi-research function of keeping one abreast of what others think are significant issues and how problems are being approached—ranging from very theoretical to quite concrete." He is a member of ADCnet (which is a list restricted to only Alzheimer's Disease Research Centers and the NIA Dementias in Aging staff).

"Another major component of my Internet activity is on the providing end—responding to questions posed on the lists that I monitor," states Jackson. "The role of the Internet for communication, especially. across time zones, is astounding. This is particularly helpful for those of us on the West Coast who are confronted by things being closed or at lunch when we start making calls to the East.

"The Internet forms an increasingly key communications role for a number of multicenter programs, such as California's state Alzheimer's program," Jackson adds. "The Net allows messages to be left for response at the convenience of both parties, which is particularly helpful if one is in [a] clinic or lab or library when the message arrives.

"Increased international access will see increased use in coordinating international research," Dr. Jackson predicts. "We do not yet have Net connections for the folks we work with in China, but these are in the cards at some point this decade."

Tips for Researchers

"The ability of networked communications to generate enormous amounts of mail electronically or on paper cannot be underestimated," Dr. Jackson says. "Thus, as you know, the Net can be an incredible time sink. This makes filters on messages particularly important.

"If I had an Internet mail handler as nice as Orest Skypunch's program for CompuServe Recon, I'd be thrilled." (Internet mail filters are discussed the Chapter 8, "Focusing Your Aims.")

Network Cyberspace: George Lewis, NBC News

George Lewis is a veteran, Los Angeles-based, correspondent for NBC News who covers the Internet and cyberspace for the network.

"We've done stories where we've used Internet e-mail to make initial contact with our sources when we couldn't get through by telephone," Lewis reports in a December 1994 e-mail interview. "It has also been a big source of research information on stories involving information technology. An upcoming story is on advocacy groups using the Internet and [we did] a previous story on advertisers using the Internet that showed off World Wide Web pages. So the Net has been a source of visuals for us.

"I've been on the net for about a year," Lewis explains. "I subscribe to several mailing lists, read several newsgroups, and routinely browse WWW pages. I'm on the lookout for new applications of information technology that might be of interest to our viewers."

One of the greatest problems on the Internet, Lewis says, is finding ways to verify the information that comes in via the Internet. "Tell your readers to take some of it with a grain of salt," Lewis advises.

The NBC correspondent predicts more changes ahead for the Internet. "I see intelligent agents helping us widdle down the glut of information that will be appearing on the Internet. I see people charging for some information that is now free."

Tips for Researchers

Lewis advises Net researchers, "to be patient and to be prepared for the many quirks of the Net. It isn't as easy as logging into Nexis/Lexis, but it's a helluva lot cheaper!"

His favorite site is the University of Colorado's Harvest Broker, which has thousands of Web pages and a "nifty search tool for locating information by keywords." It can be found at:

`http://harvest.cs.colorado.edu/brokers/www-home-page`

He also suggests: "Do your net surfing at 3:00 a.m. when the highway isn't too crowded."

The Evolving Internet: Dan Tinker, University of Toronto

Dan Tinker is one of the many scientists around the world who are part of the project to map the human genome—all the genes in the human body.

"The Internet," Tinker says, "is becoming the only source of large quantities of data. With the growth of the genome project biologists now really need access to the kind of mega-databases that particle physicists used to need, and there's only one way to get it, and that's the Internet."

The Net is also a good source for specialized software for biological and other forms of research. "I do a lot of development, not only in my research," Tinker says, "but to allow other people to have access to things to use it for teaching purposes, so I need access to the public software."

"Enormous amounts of software for every purpose under the sun are available," Tinker says, "hundreds and hundreds of gigabytes of public-domain software: graphics processors, plotter graphs, fitting equations, statistical packages, databases—any scientific function that you can imagine is supported by enormous repositories. You couldn't administer your system without those and without accessing that software.

"A third advantage to the Internet," Tinker says, "is that it allows scientists to follow the ends of what's hot in the various research fields. At one time the only way to [keep up] was to read the journals religiously, which I still do [with] some of them. With some [other] journals, I read many less journals that I used to, because many of them are out of date, many of them are years old . . . and as far as my primary source now of keeping up with what's going on in the fields of biochemistry that I'm interested in, the Internet is it."

Tinker's main sources of information are the Bionet newsgroups. "That was started off, really, by people with a lot of vision, and now you couldn't get along without it. The thing that's been most amazing to me is that when I first became aware that Usenet news existed and the Internet existed—it wasn't even called the Internet—I went over to the computer center and asked for help to set it up and they said, 'Well, you have to get an account on the mainframe' . . . and the only way to access that account was to dial in through a modem . . . and when I did that, I found out that there was only one newsgroup that was devoted to biomedical research, and it was called sci.med.

"There were about maybe ten or twelve messages a week on it. This was in 1985. And I found that I could read all the newsgroups in one day. All the news posted in one day, you could read it in 1985, in every session. And that was astounding.

"I then became dissatisfied with the costs and the effect that when I logged on to their mainframe, if I didn't log on every day, they wiped out yesterday's news. They weren't keeping it long enough, so I thought, 'Well, I'll get my own system.' So I had my own system at home, the UNIX system.

"I got all the biological newsgroups, and it was just on a PC. Now, I couldn't, you know, I'd have to buy a gigabyte disk just to keep up with the volumes of messages in biology, in bio.sci, in the whole of biology. And so you get things like evolution, ecology, and taxonomy. It's just amazing, and that's my awareness service, what's going on in the fields that I'm interested in, [the Internet] that's much more up to date, much more popular, much easier to track than the journals.

"I would predict that in five to ten years that most of the journals will be online," Tinker says. "There'll be simply no need for them [on paper]."

Tinker is a beta-tester for a University of Toronto project that hopes to provide article-level access to the literature on the Net.

"The idea being that you will put your profile of interests in the computer," he explains. "Then every day when you log on, you will get a list of what's available by titles that match your interest profile. If you want to look at that, you can, you'll be able to click on it and get an abstract, and say, I think I need this article, click on it and it arrives—royalties are automatically paid for. So whether its your department or you personally are paying for it, I mean it's not that it's free, but it's freedom . . . we'll be able to get this stuff . . . by disk or by fax."

Sunrise on the Internet: William Graves, UNC

One of the most popular destinations on the Internet is the Sunsite at the University of North Carolina at Chapel Hill. UNC Chapel Hill is also the home of William Graves, the University's Associate Provost for Information Technology.

"That means I'm the chief information officer for the network and academic computing, student LANs, classroom technology and interactive video," Graves says. "I'm also head of what we call the Institute for Academic Technology, which has IBM funding its university operation."

It's a U. S. national center for computer research. The center has about five thousand educators visiting every year for tours and to take courses. Like Tinker, Graves believes the Internet is changing scholarly publishing. He points to physicists who now publish pre-prints of academic papers on the Internet.

"It changes the nature of scholarly publications, or at least the way it allows people to have access to what used to be very limited, pre-print distribution [snail mail] list," Graves says. "If you weren't on that person's list, you wouldn't see that person's papers. It was a limited list. But everyone insisted you see it, so it went on the Internet.

"We spend a lot of time at the university trying to build an information policy. Who's going to connect whom, and who's going to put what resources on there . . . and who has access to them. Those are things that aren't very well understood. The Internet is becoming more and more viable as a place for getting information, the kind you get in the library, but it's certainly not there yet. It's getting better and better, but the what's there is still a pretty serious question. When you find something there, how do you know it's authentic? If you're looking at a copy of something, how do you [know if] it's the same as the original? All those kinds of questions are unclear."

To Graves, one thing is becoming clear, the Net is increasing collaboration among researchers. "One of the main values for a student—in fact for all of us—is to realize that this is a way (in the student case) to be in contact with other students about the work you're doing. This whole thing's a collaboration. You understand that amongst scholars, and we should understand that amongst students—the old model with teaching has every student on his own. It's competitive model instead of a collaborative model, and I think that can change so that more and more students are helping together with the learning—and they don't just send social notes but send notes to each other about what they're supposed to be doing, what they're learning, what their questions are.

"We do offer courses for students that . . . show them how all the tools that you know about by now work. In fact, we have students now teaching student lab [classes] to teach each other. So it's pretty popular here.

"We have a maritime library here at the University of North Carolina—must be one of the top ten or twenty in terms of oldest, and that sort of thing. It includes a very rare book collection. It includes the Southern historical collection and the Southern folklore collection. It's pretty unique stuff, and we were in this wonderful building one night and a group of university visitors, including alumni, were there and had a wonderful dinner. It was a fine old mahogany-paneled room with these rare old books, and it was just wonderful. And the very next day I was able to show these folks some of the same things they'd seen, but in the digital form on the Internet. It opened their eyes, because it says, 'okay,' this place is a place you no longer have to come to. It's wonderful to come here, but not everyone can do that."

Tips for Researchers

Graves says he evaluates the material he finds on the Internet, a little differently from the way he evaluates any other material.

"I just couldn't live without e-mail . . . and some lists, although I'm not an over-subscriber, I think you have to use it wisely," Graves says. "If I'm looking for something and I find it, I'll take a glance at it. If it looks interesting, I'll read it a little further or look at it a little further. And if I decide it interests me, then I might actually try and find out who did it. Then you'll need to communicate with that person or ask around to other people—is this reliable or not? And that's unlike what you do with other materials, except that you have some assurance—something's published in book or in a journal with some form of peer review. That seems to me to be the main difference."

More Tips for Researchers

*Keep trying

*Moderate your expectations

*Use the right tools for the work to be done

*Have fun . . . give room for serendipity

—George H. Brett II, Director
  Center for Networked Information Discovery & Retrieval Information
  Technologies
  Research Triangle Park
  North Carolina

The Internet is so vast that it is possible to lose yourself and lots of time wandering aimlessly about. Students should have a focus and purpose and learn the search tools to be successful with Internet research. We need to remember that the Internet does not replace the traditional sources of information, but it does add tremendously to our information resources, including access to mentors at universities and corporations.

—Barbara Fife
  Ed Tech Resource Teacher
  Northville Public Schools
  Northville, Michigan

Be patient. It takes time to learn where to look. If you expect immediate, short-term turnaround on a research expedition, you better already know where things are. Generally, the best way to figure that out in a hurry is to ask someone with an interest in the field, or someone who's already done what you're trying to do.

—Heather Newman,
  Tucson, Arizona citizen

Despite the hype, the Internet doesn't have everything. Generally, there will be a lot out there you didn't expect to see, but a lot of what you thought would be there doesn't exist.

The information you can contribute to the Net is just as important to others as the information you get is important to you. With all the hype about the commercialization of the Net, the amount of scientific and professional information is still growing rapidly. The best way to ensure the growth of the amount of information on the Net is to contribute good, solid information (i.e. research results).

—Brandon Plewe
  State University of New York at Buffalo
  Creator of the Virtual Tourist Web site

The Internet Is Only a Tool

From its beginnings with one node in a crowded room at UCLA in the fall of 1969, to today's millions of users, the Internet has been a tool, and just one of the many resources available to researchers. As the people we have met in this chapter have said, when you venture onto the information super hype-way, keep your eyes open and wary of what you find, for there will be some treasures and some fool's gold, just like in the rest of the world.

7
Netiquette

This chapter describes Internet culture and what is called "netiquette." Netiquette is the Internet's set of rules and practices of courtesy and etiquette. Too many new Internet researchers violate the Internet's netiquette by asking simple questions that could easily be answered by reading a FAQ (Frequently Asked Questions) file. Some new researchers make other blunders that distract others and waste their time. This chapter can help you avoid these errors, and can help smooth out your research process and make it more productive.

Many rules fill this chapter, and some statements may seem overly restrictive or limiting, but please be advised—these rules are *not* comprehensive. Nor are they universal. Each "neighborhood" of the Internet community has its own rules and expectations. Just as you would not go to an Italian restaurant expecting to remove your shoes, sit on cushions on the floor, eat sushi, and drink heated *sake* wine, you should not expect the rules for one part of the Internet to apply equally to all other parts.

So, knowing the rules and practices in this chapter, or the standards of behavior for any one Internet locale, will not suffice for the whole Internet. If you know and practice the recommendations in this chapter, however, you are much more likely to discover the prevailing rules in a new part of the Net *before* you get into trouble.

Be Nice to Other People

When you enter the "foreign" environment of the Internet to do research, you will inevitably encounter bewildering and confusing situations and events. It can be like suddenly landing in a foreign country for which there's no travel guide to inform you of local customs. This will sometimes cause strong emotions. Combine these emotions with the fact that some people "take it out on the machine" when a human-machine interaction does not provide immediate satisfaction, and you have a formula for disaster. Because Internet work is often done alone, and because we often don't recognize our own "operator errors," it is easy to become upset and frustrated, which somehow allows us to over-respond to the (next) situation. But, don't take it out on the *people!*

For example, experts and clueless newbies can often be found together in the same areas of the Internet, so it is usually not safe to assume you are addressing either one or the other when you write e-mail to a newsgroup or mailing list. Some groups are famous for their helpfulness and tolerance, and others are known for their severity. So, how are you to know which is which?

The simplest answer is that you must always "lurk before you leap." On the Internet, lurking means to hang around, *reading* the messages but *not writing* any messages until you get the feel of the place. Lurking also includes other human-computer activities that are invisible to the people in the group—such as retrieving a newsgroup's FAQ from the RTFM FAQ repository at the Massachusetts Institute of Technology, or asking the LISTSERV robot if any files or archives are associated with a certain mailing list. We explained how to retrieve FAQs in Chapter 5 and how to search LISTSERV archives in Chapter 4.

Some people can lurk for a few days or a week and get right into synchronization with a newsgroup or mailing list. Others are more comfortable waiting months and months before they make their first contribution. You should wait at least as long as it takes you to read a few days of contributions. And, as we'll discuss later in this chapter, you should also expect and be prepared to make a positive contribution, not merely absorb the good information available in a new neighborhood.

Note   *If a group's activity level is high, you may be able to get the feel of the group faster, because you have a larger sample of behavior to model your own actions upon. If a group has 50 or more new messages a day, after only two or three days of reading all of them you should have a pretty good idea of how that group operates! But, to be sure, you should still read the FAQ if there is one. And, for Internet mailing lists, you should carefully read the material you were sent when you first subscribed. Those initial messages often contain references and instructions for proper acclimatization.*

Although it may seem trite, another way to be nice to other people on the Internet is to say "please" and "thank you." Some people neglect this polite practice in their everyday worlds, but on the Internet, remember, people cannot see your gestures or your eyes, so they cannot tell that you sincerely appreciate their help and their attention. A few words of kindness often go a long way toward making the Net a better place for all concerned.

Personal E-Mail Is Between Two People

It is *not* permissible to forward, bounce, or otherwise share private e-mail that was originally directed to you without the writer's knowledge and agreement. Most people recognize the right of privacy in a personal postal mail message. You wouldn't read someone else's postal letter mail, even if it was legal to do so. The same rule applies to e-mail, even though the law in this area is not yet clear.

If you intend to publish, copy, distribute, or quote material from an e-mail message, a newsgroup, or a mailing list, completely aside from legal considerations in Chapter 10, at minimum you must ask the original writer and the mailing list moderator (or owner) for permission. This is a simple courtesy to the original writer, as well as a legal obligation.

Caution

One of the worst pitfalls is a case when one is tempted to share an item with a friend or research colleague without the permission or knowledge of the original writer. And, unless that friend or colleague is also known to the original writer, there may be a small danger that such an indiscretion will be discovered. But this sort of discourtesy is not an acceptable practice in polite society. If one cannot openly admit one did such a thing, perhaps one should not do it.

If you happen to discover a method to snoop in other people's e-mail, don't do it—it's private, personal mail. It's like finding a lost letter that is already stamped and addressed. No matter how much curiosity, you have you shouldn't open it and read it. While it's true that e-mail is not secure unless it is encrypted, nobody wants to worry about people reading e-mail on the sly. It's personal, private and it's not yours, so just keep out!

Don't Send Uninvited E-Mail

Electronic mail is very private and personal for many people. Like postal "junk mail," unsolicited e-mail is distasteful to many Net citizens. Because the Net allows you to completely mold your own personal information environment, selecting and subscribing to things specifically, idiosyncratically of interest to you, it is jarring and sometimes quite unpleasant to receive unsolicited e-mail.

Unbidden e-mail is even more disturbing if it does not have a distinct personal nature, but is instead commercial or impersonally demanding.

Students occasionally make the mistake of assuming newsgroups and Internet mailing lists are automatically available for their school-related research. While some mailing lists are, in fact, designed just for students, most are not. Before a grade school, high school, or college student uses a mailing list for any "homework-related" purposes, they should obtain permission from the mailing list's moderator or owner, and also obtain advance approval from their teacher, instructor, or professor.

Another of the many manifestations of uninvited e-mail is the disreputable practice of "subscribing" others to a mailing list without their knowledge or consent. This usually can be done only by a mailing list owner, electronic mail node postmaster, or someone with similar authority and security access to a mailing list. Because of their positions, these people should know better than to allow unsolicited e-mail to proliferate.

But sometimes it seems compellingly logical that *everyone* interested in X^1 and subscribed to the X^1 group would also be enthralled with and want to immediately subscribe to the X^2 group, and normal privacy and netiquette safeguards are overridden. In these cases, only a negative option is left to the persons who were thus imposed upon with unsolicited e-mail; to maintain control of their own e-mail inbox they are required to perform an unsubscribe operation *without having ever subscribed* in the first place.

But proper netiquette requires that people be given positive options, so that they are completely in control, in advance, of all incoming mail. One of the strongest reasons why this "positive option" ethic is part of the Internet derives from the costs associated with incoming mail. In some parts of the world, and with some Internet service providers, people must pay for their e-mail based on the number of incoming messages, or by the size of incoming messages in bytes, or both. Sending unsolicited e-mail to these people can force them to spend money on something they are uninterested in, and did not choose of their own accord. Even if they are generally interested in the topic, they should still be allowed to control their own costs by positively choosing the mail they will receive. So, it ends up being an invasion of privacy unless you let others completely control their own e-mail.

Be a Good Neighbor

Each Net community includes distinct neighborhoods. Although these neighborhoods vary in their style and demeanor, they often share common traits:

» Respect for each other's time and privacy

» Tolerance for many personal opinions

» Tolerance for personal growth and exploration

» Willingness to freely share information

These qualities are put into action daily throughout the Net. To avoid wasting the time of your neighbors, you should thoroughly prepare each e-mail message. Your e-mail contributions to mailing lists and newsgroups and your e-mail requests for information should be well written. Carefully crafted e-mail is quicker and easier to read, understand, and to respond to. These advantages save time, and make the Net work more efficiently for everybody.

Well written e-mail is not just spell-checked and grammatically correct, it is also concise, short, and to the point, usually not more than two screens of information (*one* is preferred). This helps readers who process hundreds of messages each day to take the time to read your whole message. If you send long rambling messages they will most likely not be read—they will be deleted immediately.

Some Net communities allow large e-mail messages to be posted, with the provision that they are identified as *(long)* on the Subject line or on the first line of the message body. While this convention is within the netiquette of some Net communities, it does little to improve the likelihood that your message will be read—it merely reduces the chance that you will be flamed for posting over-long e-mail messages.

So, if you have a lengthy outgoing message in mind, try to cut it into several smaller messages. If a world-renowned expert responds to your message, you won't want them to address only one tiny aspect of a multipart message. This frustrating end can be escaped by simply avoiding compound queries in the first place. For clear communication on the Net, it's best to ask one single question at a time, and to indicate, if appropriate, that there may be follow-ups.

The same principle applies to answering questions in newsgroups and mailing lists. Simple, direct answers to simple queries are easiest for readers to follow. If necessary, a larger posting can be responded to in a series of increments. A brief quote of the question or previous message is given (don't forget to be clear about the original writer's intent and identity), followed by your response and another brief quote from the original writer's previous message with your response, and so on.

But reading long messages on a computer screen can be quite tedious, and you should expect a *much* smaller audience if you use this method. Many people just delete messages longer than two or three screens, often because the combination of display software and hardware they use may make the message difficult to see and read. Also, the "brief quote-response, brief quote-response" style is much used in rivalry inspired "is too!/is not!" debates that eventually are read only by the debaters themselves.

Out of courtesy and respect for the Net community and your neighbors, most debates that degenerate to the "is so!, is not!" stage should move out of the newsgroup or mailing list where they started and be carried on in private e-mail. When a debate approaches this level, courteous neighbors pleasantly and conscientiously suggest that the contentious discussion should be continued off-list, and anyone wishing to follow the debate is welcome to request to be included in the off-list repartee.

Good neighbors go out of their way to make it clear that they have good intentions toward each other, even in their everyday activities. Because the normal visual and aural cues are missing from the *textual* world of the Internet, you must find ways to be especially clear about your intent. Without the opportunity for your reader to see your face and gestures, and to hear your voice inflections, you must supply textual clues about what you really mean. At least two variations of new textual devices are developing on the Net.

Emoticons, such as :-) and 8+(give textual clues about the writer's intent. (If these marks don't make any sense to you, turn your head sideways to the left and look at them again.) They seem a little colloquial, but they can be useful because they help your reader know what you mean. They can protect the meaning of your words, and help convey your message, especially when you are using humor or irony. Humor and irony are particularly dangerous on the Internet, because you lose the ability to use voice, gesture, timing, and other nonverbal cues to reinforce your true meaning, and your readers do not read at the same time, place, or pace that you write.

Note   *In some parts of the Net, emoticons are regarded with disdain. Just to keep life interesting, people who use, or overuse, them are sometimes flamed.*

Another textual device on the Internet seems to be coming from the worlds of IRC and MUSEs (Internet Relay Chat and MultiUser Simulated Environments), and from CompuServe. Its simplicity is disarming. After a statement, you place the word that describes the visual "gesture" you would make if you were having a face-to-face conversation. The descriptive word or words are often enclosed in carets or parentheses: grin <frown>, smile <pout>, giggle. Some of these significations are becoming popular enough that their *abbreviations* are developing meaning, so that a <g> is already widely understood as a grin!

Keep Your Neighborhood Tidy and Clear

All e-mail messages can be made more attractive and more readable by use of visual tools such as indentation, separator lines, bulleted lists, and white space.

When you draft your e-mail messages, appearance and clarity are paramount, especially if you want people to actually read them.

Every single public e-mail message that you send should be up to your professional, businesslike standard. Sometimes it is tempting to not bother with spell checking, or with correcting typos prior to sending a message. Sometimes these extra steps seem unimportant because Net citizens are so forgiving and tolerant of minor textual peccadilloes. But the success of your research will likely rest on the credibility you establish, and 100 percent of your credibility is based on the appearance, clarity of construction, and thoughtfulness of your e-mail.

Ask yourself, is it clear who said what to whom? Is my intention stated clearly? Does my *Subject:* line allow disinterested readers to eliminate this message, thus saving them time? Have I set the stage, laid the groundwork, and placed my message in context, so that my readers will understand what I mean to say and why I am saying it? Have I made clear to the reader exactly what I want them to do?

Caution

A common mistake in newsgroups and especially in mailing lists is to assume readers will understand arcane references, acronyms, and abbreviations. This probably happens because of the erroneous assumption that anyone subscribing to the same newsgroups must have the same common experiences and background. But nothing could be further from the truth, and in fact this faulty assumption dramatically reduces the audience for a posting, because people may not understand the meaning of a message without knowing the special abbreviations and acronyms used. It can also insult and waste the time of all the people who do not happen to know or recall the special abbreviations or references.

Remember that foreign and interdisciplinary colleagues, students, and interested lay persons and professional experts from other fields often subscribe to newsgroups and mailing lists. People subscribe to particular groups for many different reasons. Many of them will be alienated by posts stuffed with obscure acronyms or abbreviations and excess jargon, and their time will be wasted. The abbreviations, jargon, or acronyms that you do use should be commonly understood.

Be Flexible and Forgiving

One of the most important principles of research netiquette is to be flexible and forgiving. E-mail, by its spontaneous nature, contains spelling and grammar errors that the writer missed. It does nobody any good to fuss and flame after the fact about these minor errors. If you can understand the message, go on as if it was spelled and punctuated correctly, and had perfect grammar. And just try to catch all the boo-boos in your own next message before sending it! Proofreading e-mail on a computer screen is difficult, so Net citizens have developed a tolerant attitude.

Another remarkable part of the netiquette principle of flexibility is the practice of offering quick gratuitous apologies. If a communication problem has arisen, by definition it required two or more parties to be involved. All parties had a part in the origin of the problem, and there is no sense in fighting over whose fault it is. So, when this happens on the Net, *any* party, ideally, quickly apologizes for not communicating clearly and makes another more deliberate attempt to clarify the misunderstanding. This method is amazing in its simplicity and effectiveness. The good will that such flexibility and tolerance generates keeps many interest groups running smoothly and comfortably year after year.

One last comment on flexibility: there are Internet groups that you will not understand. They may not understand you, either. Nobody is eclectic enough to be part of all these thousands of communities and neighborhoods. Whether it's alt.sex.hampsters.duct-tape or alt.business.multilevel, there simply will be groups that are beyond your grasp or that may even be repugnant to you.

How should you deal with these variant groups? That's simple: just ignore them. Don't visit that neighborhood of the Net. Simply don't get in their faces, and they won't bother you. It wastes everyone's time to argue against the premise of a group you don't believe in or understand. You and they are not required to agree on anything, except that you may disagree—and you should stay away.

Stay Calm in a Flame War

When someone posts an inflammatory statement, there usually is no need to post a response at all, just delete it and move on. Be warned: it may be flame-bait, intended precisely to provoke you to respond. If you must respond, why not respond privately, one-to-one? A private response prevents the provocateur from stirring up the group, and saves bandwidth.

If a flame war erupts, stay calm. Try to minimize emotional responses. Let your temper, outrage, or pain subside before you draft your response (if you must respond), and then wait a few hours before rereading and actually sending the message. The Net, like our human real-life communities, is home to many kinds of people. Do your best to tolerate individual differences in expression and demeanor, and don't join flame wars. If you must write something, try to be a calming, steadying influence, and try to work off-list to soothe nerves and find commonalities on both sides of the debate.

A flame war in progress can seem apocalyptic. After a few days, however, it often carries much less significance. Have the sense and dignity to remain calm and moderate any responses.

Be a Lifelong Learner

The first thing to do when visiting a new part of the Net is get your bearings. Carefully read and save all the messages sent when you first subscribe to a new mailing list. And when you start a subscription to a Usenet newsgroup, be sure you always read the FAQ *before* posting a question.

An attitude of lifelong learning is maturing on the Net, and you should try to embrace it. To acclimate to a new area of the Net, you'll need to learn new customs and new ways of seeing and doing things. Here are some ways you can get in tune with this new learning attitude.

Seek Out and Respect Local Rules

When you enter a new part of the Net, watch for differences that you have not seen before in other parts of the Net. Some mailing lists, for instance, pride themselves on having lots of personal messages between two members of the group posted to the whole group as a form of sharing. This is anathema to most groups because it seems to lower the signal to noise ratio. But in the groups where it is welcomed it is part of the ethos and purpose of the group, and it is reassuring and gives these groups a singular flair.

Read and carefully re-read the FAQ and any other charter documents. Take them seriously. They are the collected wisdom of many people, and will give you a better understanding of how the group operates and what behavior is expected.

If you've checked with the RTFM (see above) FAQ repository (noted in Chapter 5) and been unable to find a FAQ for the group or topic, send a personal note to two or three of the people who frequently post messages in that area, asking them for direction and advice. Ask them who are the group's leaders, and if there is someone who is "in charge" or providing other services to the group as a whole.

Some high-volume mailing lists have *Subject:* codes that are used to help readers know more about the content of the message. A code given on the subject line may mean a specific subtopic is addressed in the message.

Or the subject line code could also indicate where in the group's process this message fits in. For instance, on the mailing list for reference librarians, Stumpers, *Subject:* lines have taken on a special significance. The list deals with dozens of questions each week, and they have decided to help themselves keep track of the questions and answers by using the question's subject as the subject line for answers. Any subject line that begins with the percent character (%) signifies to the readers that that piece of e-mail is a *partial* answer to the previous question with the same subject line. If a subject line begins with an exclamation point (!), it means that that message contains a complete, final or definitive answer to the question. This can prevent someone from bothering to work on researching a question, if it has already been answered.

This sort of custom in mailing lists can also develop without documentation, so you cannot always rely on a FAQ or charter document to find *all* the rules. This is another reason to read and lurk for a while before you begin to post messages.

Sources of More Netiquette Rules

Here are some references for further study of Internet netiquette:

Arlene Rinaldi's Personal Home Page

`rinaldi@acc.fau.edu`

`http://www.fau.edu/rinaldi/netiquette.html`

The Net User Guidelines And Netiquette

`gopher://zeus.esusda.gov:70/00/internet/docs-gen/rinaldi-netiquette.txt`

***Netiquette*, by Virginia Shea (Albion Books)**

`http://www.netsurf.com/nsm/v01/01/albion/albion.html`

`http://dab.psi.net/ChapterOne/computers/browse/netiquette.html`

Patrick Douglas Crispin

`pcrispe1@ua1vm.ua.edu`

Patrick Douglas Crispin's Roadmap Workshop #07—Netiquette

`http://bcn.boulder.co.us/help/Roadmap/msg10.html`

Internet Etiquette by Stan Horwitz

`stan@vm.temple.edu`
`ftp://ftp.temple.edu/pub/info/help-net/netiquette.infohn`

Various Guides to Usenet Netiquette

`http://www.uchicago.edu/a.docs/TechSupport/usenet-etiquette.html`

`http://www.uchicago.edu/a.resource-guide/ChapThingsNetiquette.html`

`http://scwww.ucs.indiana.edu/FAQ/USAGN/`

`http://www.hut.fi/~jkorpela/Welcome/appiv.htm`

http://www.eff.org:80/ftp/Net_info/Introductory/netiquette.faq

CU-SeeMe Etiquette

`http://btree.lerc.nasa.gov/NASA_TV/netiquette.html`

And let's end this netiquette reference section with two versions of a favorite of mine:

Brad Templeton

`brad@alto.clari.net`

Dear Emily Postnews by Brad Templeton

`http://www.clari.net/brad/emily.html`

`http://www.cis.ohio-state.edu/hypertext/faq/usenet/usenet/emily-post`
`    news/part1/faq.html`

Internet businessperson, creative artist, and author Brad Templeton wrote this back in the late 1987 or 1988 as a satire of some "silly" Net practices of the day. You'll notice that the preface note on the second version of the document is *not* given on the first version at ClariNet, where Brad works. This and similar notes have been added to several versions of the document over the years *by persons other than the author,* to warn the occasional "incredibly thick" reader that this satirical advice is *all wrong!*

About *Dear Emily Postnews,* Brad says "I wrote it as a satire, not for the new user section of the Net, but just for the sake of writing a satire." Friends liked the piece so much that they convinced Brad to post it to the Usenet newsgroup rec.humor.funny (which Brad moderates), and the rest is history, so to speak.

Although it was written purely as a satire, Brad admits that this bit of humor also performed a useful educational function, "It actually had a strong effect. By showing certain activities as *silly* rather than wrong, it discouraged them a fair deal. Double signatures for example, are very rare now, as are some other things satirized, but they were very common back then. There is no form of education about what's silly that is better than satire." Brad also has weighed in on copyright issues on the Net; if you're interested check out this URL:

```
http://www.clari.net/brad/copymyths.html
```

Give Back to the Net

Find a way that you can contribute to the Net community. You have special knowledge, or skills, that are needed on the Net. It's part of your role to find these personal characteristics and bring them to the Net as a contribution to the community at large. Everyone is expected to creatively participate in ways that fulfill their own needs while they also help others.

Net Citizenship Requires Participation

Just as political citizenship requires participation in decisions through voting, jury membership, and similar civic activities, so also Net citizenship requires participation.

Lurking, the practice of becoming familiar with the intellectual terrain before striking out on your own, *is* the right way to become acculturated to new Net neighborhoods. But eventually, you'll want to engage someone or some topic, and do something other than watch.

One of the biggest advantages of participation is that when you ask for help your name will be recognized. There is nothing more rude than popping into a discussion asking for help, and including a statement that you are not a member of the discussion, so any answers should be sent to your personal e-mail address. And nothing is deleted more quickly than these rude upstart demands.

Note

One group that breaks this "pop-in rule" quite often is journalists. They're looking for story material in a hurry, especially if they're on deadline. And as we say elsewhere in this book, dropping in on a newsgroup or mailing list is often a good way of finding sources.

When Jerry Garcia, the founder and leader of the Grateful Dead died suddenly on August 9, 1995, the Internet responded quickly—and that became part of the story. Reporters for wire services, newspapers and television networks reported what the Dead Heads on the Net were saying about the loss of one of America's best known rock musicians.

If reporters or researchers identify themselves, it's not really much different than making a phone call. Some people will ignore you, others will volunteer valuable information. And reporters should always return to the site, thank the people for the information and let them know where they can read or see the resulting story.

How you participate is up to you, and how the community responds is also largely up to you and your reputation among the group. If you have been a participating member, through thick and thin, you will certainly get a better response than some flash-in-the-pan "no account" that has never visited or contributed before.

Help the Newbies

Everything you can do to help prepare and train the newbies in your neighborhood will pay off, too. Send them personal mail, encouraging them to keep on learning, and suggesting they read one of the many beginning books about the Internet. Some helpful "basic training" documents are even available at no cost on the Internet, for example:

» Zen and the Art of the Internet

» Big Dummy's Guide to the Internet

» SURAnet's Resource Guide

» Internet RFCs and FYIs

By gently directing clueless newbies to these resources and to your favorite books about the Internet, you help the entire Net community to educate its young, as it were. An African proverb says that it takes a whole village to raise a child. It's also true that each of us on the Internet has a responsibility to help newbies grow to become the best Net citizens they can be. Even Net gurus had to start somewhere, and were once newbies themselves, as we all were.

Share Information with People

The Internet comprises immense stores of information, but it is inhabited by people. Vast amounts of information are everywhere. Bewildering arrays of complexly related and unrelated information of every kind abound. And there is more of it than any human mind can encompass in a hundred years.

Specific addresses and "how to" instructions are given throughout this book for many valuable tools that can help you make sense of this glut of information. But the nature of the Internet is that more information will be added continually. So the real treasure maps of the Internet are knowledgeable and sharing human beings.

The greatest power of the Internet is people helping people. At first, if you're a newbie, you can usually only help other newbies, except in a narrowly defined or non-Internet related area. Later, with skills learned from this book and experience, you will be in a position to pass on know-how and tricks that others will need. It's part of the Internet ethic and netiquette to help others navigate the Net and tame the maze, at least occasionally.

You need not spend all day every day helping others, unless you work on one of the many online help desks that are springing up. But you'll find it helps us all if you can regularly provide instructions, crib sheets, shortcuts, and outright helpful advice to others with lesser (or alternative) skills. This helpful atmosphere will also help you, the next time you venture into an unknown part of the Net!

Summarize for Your Supper

Another part of the Net ethic is to provide an information service to your community, as a recompense for their help to you. When you ask a topical question of a newsgroup or mailing list, it is customary to summarize the responses received both privately and on the newsgroup or mailing list. You begin the process by asking your question, and you end the process by providing a brief, edited summary of the important results and meaning of the summary for group members.

Sometimes the summary will be only a couple of factual sentences, but other times your report will call for writing a detailed summary, carefully attributing short quotes to their authors, and providing the context to show the overall flow and meaning of the quotes in answer to the question you asked.

This practice of summarizing back to the group strengthens the group by offering education to its members, and by assuring them that their contributions are valuable and useful to the community at large. Even if you do not promise to summarize in your request, you should do it as a matter of netiquette.

Communicate Clearly

Spelling and grammar are not enough. Your communication skills are all you have to sustain your Net research, so every way that you can improve your communication is worth the effort. Take the time, when drafting an e-mail message, to think over what you really mean. Make sure you express yourself as concisely and precisely as possible. Precision is especially important when dealing with the complexities of Net software and hardware, because so many things can go awry. With only the information that "the software won't work," people are likely to assume operator error. But with the precise information that "When I intend to send a message and press control and x together, nothing happens, but it used to tell me the message was being sent and a copy was being put in my sent-mail folder," a prospective helper has much better information to work with.

In writing e-mail messages, establish an historical and motivational context, and clearly tell the reader of your e-mail what the overall meaning or single purpose of your message is. Shore up that point with particulars and details, but stick to that one issue and don't throw in tangential matters unless they help to better explain your goal.

Every Message Carries Your Name

Don't let the fact that you are alone, typing on a computer behind a locked door, make you feel invulnerable to the consequences of any naughtiness you get into over the telephone line with your computer. Every message carries your name, or enough technical information to find your name, and records are kept that will usually allow the origin of your message to be found out.

Flippant, off-the-cuff remarks can be damaging both on and off the Net. On the Net, your words can be broadcast to hundreds and thousands of people in seconds, and they are likely to be recorded for some period, for review by further thousands. Remember this audience when you write e-mail messages to newsgroups and mailing lists, so you can avoid being recorded in Net history as a clueless dork, or whatever similar appellation becomes popular in the next century.

Spelling and Grammar

Although we stressed earlier that one must not fuss over spelling and grammar errors in ordinary e-mail, it is also incumbent on every e-mail user to write messages as clearly as possible. While minor errors are not to be considered earth-shaking, the value of comprehensibility and clarity can't be over-stressed.

Messages that are easy to read and easy to understand are more likely to be read and understood. More people will respond. If you want responses, spell check your messages! Re-read them for grammar. Give specific examples. Remove redundant and unnecessary words and phrases. Explain all acronyms and special terms. Leave nothing to doubt.

The spontaneity of e-mail is not ruined by complete sentences and good English! Spontaneity is *improved* by clarity and comprehension!

One Topic Per Message

Including more than one topic in an e-mail message has two serious disadvantages:

1. You increase the chances that people will just delete your message without reading it because it is longer.

2. You increase the chances that your readers will be confused and reply to only part of your message.

Either way, you lose. By ignoring this dictum (one topic per message), you can waste the time of your readers, and reduce the value of any responses you do receive. It may seem inefficient to ask only one question at a time, but it is not. It forces you to carefully analyze your questions, to prioritize them, and to divide them into their component parts.

Restricting yourself to only one topic per message may reveal parts of the question to which you already have answers. By reminding you to parse your questions into smaller and smaller pieces, it helps you notice any assumptions you've made, reminds you to state the givens of the problem and the context and intent of your question.

Test Your Message Before Broadcast

The principle here is to limit the damage you cause while you are learning how to send messages. Limit the damage by experimenting on a very small and controlled scale before escalating to full broadcast mode.

Note   *If you don't yet know the details of your e-mail program, this advice may also apply to your learning the basics of e-mail logistics (discussed in Chapter 4).*

First and most simple, send *yourself* your first draft. E-mail the message to your own e-mail address. See what it looks like. Read it with fresh eyes, as if it was coming from a stranger—would the intent and meaning of the message be clear? Are there unfortunate line breaks or other cosmetic features that obscure the meaning?

Next, send the test message to a friend or a few colleagues, with a cc: copy to yourself. Ask them for feedback and advice. This will give you more time and feedback to refine your posting so it accomplishes exactly what you want it to. By testing your message, you will be sure that simple errors have been avoided.

When you actually do post your first message on a newsgroup or mailing list, wait at least 18 hours before you post it to a second group, if you are posting to more than one group. This will allow you to correct any simple misconceptions that crop up from the first posting, before you compound the difficulty by adding hundreds or thousands of additional readers.

Also, be sure to save a copy of your final outgoing message, so that you can refer to it while you interpret the responses you receive.

Conserve Network Resources

The health and vitality of the whole Internet is your responsibility. You should always think about how to best accomplish your Net tasks, and learn to simplify the task and conserve resources whenever possible. If everyone started wasting bandwidth by sending and getting unnecessary messages and files, the Net we depend on could slow down or stop altogether. Parts of the Net reach overload traffic levels every day, and engineers are always working around the clock somewhere to clear out backlogged queues and keep the Net running.

Every time you retrieve across the Atlantic Ocean from Europe to North America a file that you easily could have retrieved directly from North America, you're stretching the Net's capacity. Ask yourself if it is really necessary. The Internet's intercontinental connections are a precious resource which we all must conserve.

If possible, use local Internet sites, or at least sites in your own state, province, or region. Each time you use the Internet, ask yourself if there are geographically closer sites that could serve the same purpose. For instance, many Gopher and World Wide Web clients want to connect to a set home page when they are first turned on or opened. If possible, configure yours to initially connect to a *local* site that is in your own city or state. This will perhaps be less exciting, but it serves three excellent purposes:

1. Your client program will probably open and connect a little faster with a geographically closer home page.

2. It demonstrates the performance of your local portion of the Net, and can quickly let you know if important local links are out of service.

3. You will have conserved network resources by only using a *local* connection to do the mundane, everyday task of opening the program.

Carefully Check the *To:* Line of Each Outgoing Message

Learn to use your e-mail software to mail to only those e-mail addresses that are appropriate. Some e-mail programs reply to everyone imaginable when you press the *Reply* button, requiring you to then edit out any inappropriate addresses. People in the early stages of learning their e-mail program are commonly embarrassed by sending personal mail to entire groups, rather than to an individual colleague. Sometimes the excitement of finding an old friend's e-mail address just overwhelms them, and they forget to carefully inspect the outgoing mail addresses that they are sending the message to.

Most routine clerical functions can be performed privately and automatically on the Net. But one of the most annoying newbie errors is to send e-mail "subscribe" and "unsubscribe" requests to the *people* on a mailing list instead of the clerical robot that handles routine subscription matters for that mailing list. As you might imagine, this same error happens when newbies want a copy of the group's FAQ or charter. The clerical robot always has a different address than the people on the mailing list.

Note   *How does one address the robot? Here's a clue! A mailing list's automated clerical robot's address usually starts with one of these four naming conventions:*

```
listserv@
listproc@
majordomo@
listname-request@
```

If you don't use an address like one of these above, you may be mailing to the people on a mailing list, rather than the clerical robot for the list.

Sending unnecessary, irrelevant administrative e-mail to hundreds of people on the mailing list who can do nothing about your request is not considered within the netiquette of most lists. Send your request to the automated robot, and if the robot gives you trouble, send a help request to *one* person, not the whole list!

Likewise, don't send test messages, "me too" messages, or messages to be "sure" you're still subscribed to a mailing list to the entire list. If you must send a message to the "people address," please have the courtesy to have something to say.

There is no point in wasting the whole group's time merely because you have a doubt about your single subscription. Instead, send a message to the mailing list robot or one individual. Or, on Usenet, send your test message to the alt.test or misc.test newsgroup. Messages that are not within the charter of a mailing list or newsgroup have no business being posted, especially for nonsubstantive "me too" drivel. The rule is that each and every message should contribute to the group's purpose, or be posted elsewhere.

Send Personal E-Mail Rather Than Posting to the Entire Group

It can be embarrassing to mistakenly send a personal message to a group of hundreds. It also can be unpleasant to ask the wrong question in a group that you are not yet familiar with. Why not just send a personal message to a single person?

Sometimes the newness of having a large group of people who are actually interested in the same topic hypnotizes us, and we waste the time of the whole group instead of carefully crafting our questions for maximum usefulness. If you are new or unsure, try out your question on one individual (a frequent poster, for instance), and see if they agree that you should ask the question of the whole group. Carefully directing your message to an individual or two can often accomplish the same good, and does not waste the time of the whole group.

Send to the Correct Group Rather Than Several

When you address an e-mail message, you have control over where it is sent. It is better to send your message to one group that is directly involved and interested in the topic of the message than to send it to 10 groups that *might* be interested. You'll waste the time of fewer people, and you'll be more likely to get valuable responses. Choose your target group(s) carefully, and you'll use less bandwidth to accomplish your purpose with less wasted time and effort for everyone.

If you doubt the appropriateness of posting to a *seemingly related* mailing list or newsgroup, send a personal message instead, exploring the purpose and appropriateness of your research question with only one or two people, such as the group's moderator, mailing list "owner," frequent posters, or thoughtful individuals who have made contributions that you respect. This method requires time to study the group's charter, and time to read current or archived messages, but it is not nearly so time consuming as postal correspondence. Student research on the Net should *always* follow this rule, if Usenet newsgroups or mailing lists are involved. If you send a question that somehow becomes labeled as a "spam," the likelihood of your receiving useful replies plunges dramatically.

Note

The pejorative term "spam" means an e-mail message sent to unrelated mailing lists or newsgroups (usually several or many groups) that is not within the charter purpose of those groups. It's junk mail, sent in a scattershot way, hoping to get a lucky response. But because it is so disrespectful of the purpose of the group(s) offended, it almost always backfires.

Many people just return spam immediately to its sender, thereby demonstrating their rejection of the off-topic message. Because this can cause service interruptions for other, innocent parties (due to extreme e-mail congestion), it is not considered good netiquette. Hurting innocent parties is not the intent of rejecting the spam by returning it, but it can easily happen.

Behave Lawfully and Humanely

Moving, storing, processing, or otherwise being involved with threatening, harassing, seditious, treasonous, and other material that is dangerous to national security can get you in trouble on or off the Internet. One programmer, for instance, is now facing serious U.S. national security charges because his encryption program was released onto the Net, allowing international access to a program the American government would have preferred to keep under wraps. There is no question that the program was internationally dispersed by FTP, but the programmer merely placed his product on the Internet in an FTP-accessible space, and did not actively distribute it.

Research in these and similar areas is always tricky, and doing it on the Internet will increase the difficulty, and the need for caution. Chapter 10 discusses many of the legal issues you should be aware of on the Internet, but for now remember that even though you may feel a little like you're riding the frontier in the wild west (because you are, in a way), even so, the rule of law and the Golden Rule are still in effect.

Likewise, the rules of good behavior you learned at your mother's knee still apply. Strong language is seldom appropriate. On the Internet you seldom get to see, hear, or touch your correspondent, but the rules of polite behavior still matter. Presumption, insensitivity, and rudeness in all of its forms are still inappropriate, and will likely cause trouble for you sooner or later.

It is often tempting to test out a new persona, or to try a new way of carrying yourself in the fresh, seemingly isolated environment of the Net. Such experiments are fine, but they are never a license to be hurtful, crude, or rude. Personal, verbal behavior on the Net is usually recorded for at least a few days, if not months or in perpetuity, and can therefore seldom be effectively denied.

So, the standard has developed that you should not say or do anything on the Internet that you would not be comfortable with seeing or hearing on the evening news tonight. Even though you can't see the person you're addressing, always act as if you are in the same room, face to face.

Help Newbies Find Their Way

Recently, millions of people have entered the Net community, each one for the first time. While some have had good preparation and training for Net citizenship, many have not. As each additional Internet service provider opens its Net gateway, it unleashes new hordes of *clueless newbies* on the Net community.

An example of this is the way that, in the early 1990s, America Online (AOL) grew to be one of the largest North American dial-up service providers by offering an easy to use Graphical User Interface (GUI) for internal messages, live chat, and information databases. AOL cultivated in their users an attitude that information should be easy to use and that "everything" was available within the insulated, protected world of AOL.

When AOL opened a gateway allowing these unprepared users to join Internet newsgroups and mailing lists, the AOL users often made fools of themselves. They often did not distinguish between services that AOL provided and controlled and resources on the Internet itself. They insisted that they were *paying for* the service they received from an Internet mailing list, for instance, and expected service to be delivered promptly! They sent messages to entire groups of people that should have been addressed carefully to one or two people. They expected and demanded *help* with ordinary clerical and personal tasks that everyone else had always done for themselves.

Because a wave of mass arrogance, ignorance and misbehavior seemed to begin all at once when AOL loosed its customers on the Net, *clueless AOL newbies* began to be harshly criticized and shunned. Since this unfortunate event, AOL has worked to better prepare its customers for Net citizenship, but the taint of an *@aol.com* address still haunts some less tolerant Net neighborhoods. And AOL has not yet found a way to force all of its customers to learn about the Net before trying their shenanigans.

In fact, no Net provider has yet instituted a Infobahn driver's license, so to speak, but many providers and services have learned from AOL's experience and are continuously improving their efforts to educate and train their customers about Net customs, Net skills, and netiquette.

The Infobahn Litter Crew expects further waves of clueless newbies to wash into the Internet in future months, as CompuServe, Delphi, and other service providers allow their users to enter the Internet proper. The Litter Crew collects methods and techniques to help newbies learn the ways of the Net. If you discover or develop a new way to help newbies learn about the Internet, the Infobahn Litter Crew wants to hear from you! Write to them at ILC@dotorg.org or P.O. Box 524, Austin, Texas USA 78767-0524.

Remember That the Internet Is International

Many researchers have become used to working and communicating within their own cloistered academic and research circles, and some do not naturally think of broader audiences and new ways to communicate. This probably explains many embarrassing moments on the Internet when wrong assumptions lead to unsuccessful communication.

Idiom, jargon, acronyms, and abbreviation are not as useful on the Internet, because they unnecessarily alienate large parts of your audience. Remember that jokes often don't translate well, and many members of the Internet community are not native English speakers.

Your readers may be world-renowned experts who just do not speak English well, much less know about the latest fad, media event, or catch phrase in your region. Use care to make your message clear to all kinds of other people, because the Internet is a community that welcomes everyone, internationally.

Because we live on a spinning, globe, it may be sunrise for me and evening for my correspondent simultaneously. Keep these time differences in mind and allow considerable leeway for local holidays in other parts of the world. E-mail is very fast, but it also has brief and not-so-brief delays. And people don't always read their e-mail as often as you might expect or desire.

Don't Deceive or Mislead Others

Remember, the Net is a decentralized and eclectic place. There are many kinds of software and hardware using the TCP/IP protocol on the Net. And, well, some software is easier to cheat with than other software, and some software is actually easy to use to fool people about who sent a particular message. Why is this a problem? Because it is unethical, in some cases it is illegal, and in almost all cases e-mail forgery is discovered and some folks, particularly security officials and authorities, do not take it kindly.

If you begin a personal or research relationship over the Net, it is not acceptable to embellish or exaggerate your qualities and accomplishments simply because you are on another continent or in a different region. People are now physically traveling around the world to meet their Net buddies and colleagues, and deceptions of any kind are not a good basis upon which to build a working relationship. Just because you can begin a ruse knowing your reader cannot "possibly" see you does not mean you can ultimately carry it off.

Please note, this netiquette rule applies to all identity deception but does *not* apply to anonymous remailing. Anonymous remailing is an accepted part of several large regions of the Internet, and is not prohibited or even discouraged in most of the remainder of the Net. Some private matters are more easily handled anonymously, and good netiquette accepts this principle. Anonymous e-mail is not deceptive by its nature—rather, it is private by its nature. If the average person receives anonymous postal mail they are immediately curious, and naturally want to be careful of the veracity and sincerity of the sender. Anonymous e-mail is no different.

By heeding the warnings given in this chapter, your research should be more productive and lead to fewer dead ends on the information superhighway. If you wish to study netiquette in even more detail, please see the section "Be a Lifelong Learner" above for several additional sources of Netiquette information.

8

Focusing Your Aims

The Net is seductive, hypnotic. There is so much out there, tempting you to visit all the kingdoms of the Net in a moment of time by clicking the mouse.

You're a researcher, you have a job to do, and despite all the distractions on the Net, you have to finish that job. So you have to focus your aims. This chapter will help you do that. With more than 13,000 Usenet groups already in existence, with thousands of Web home pages and Gopher sites, not to mention gigabytes of e-mail, there is a lot to sift through to find the gems of information for your research project.

In Chapter 3, "Getting Ready for Research" we heard advice from Barbara Tuchman to "divide and distill." So, how do you do that?

One of the best ways is to use an outliner, not just to outline, but to focus your aims, as a thought processor and an organizer. Any outlining software will help you do that. From an outline you can organize your hard drive, either on your PC or the home directory of your Internet account. You can also use the same organizing scheme in your paper files (and there will be lots of paper—believe it!) and in the categories in a free-form text retrieval database (which we highly recommend if you're going to be doing research on the Net.)

Outline Before You Start

A research project, as we have said, is like a journey, a trek, a quest. The ancient heroes usually knew what the goal of the quest was—the Holy Grail, marriage to the princess, or finding a long-lost father. An outline, for any project, gives you that goal to shoot for, and thus helps organize your thoughts.

Teachers of dramatic writing often advise young playwrights or novelists to "know your ending." Usually that ending changes as the project progresses, but that initial ending provides the goal that lets you take the first step toward the completion of your project.

If you're writing an academic paper or an essay, you're doing the same thing—with one key exception. Your ending is up front in the abstract of your thesis.

In a story, you're taking the reader on a step by step journey to the dramatic ending, whether that story is nonfiction or fiction. In a paper, you're often proving a case, taking the reader step by step through the evidence that supports your thesis and, if you're honest, the evidence that's against the thesis as well. In either case, it's a good idea to start with an outline.

Remember the outline from high school? We all do and we all hated it. Jon Franklin has a whole chapter on outlines in his well-crafted book *Writing for Story* (New American Library, 1986). He calls that high school outline, complete with Roman numerals, the "English Teacher's Revenge." (Franklin's book is one of the best around for those who want to know how to research, organize and write nonfiction.)

Outlining software is the best answer to Franklin's English Teacher's Revenge. You don't have to write Roman Numerals on a piece of foolscap. If outlining on paper is a barrier to your thoughts, using the proper software can enhance your creative thoughts.

An outline is really a first rough draft. How often have you had a great idea, written a few pages and then run out of steam? Or had a great idea for a new development in your field and rushed to the word processor and then found the idea went nowhere? If you go to the outliner first (and almost every word processor comes with some sort of outliner) and write using the outliner, you quickly find out where the holes are in your story, research project, or thesis. You quickly find that spot where you would stop writing, because your ideas seem to dry up.

Just let your thoughts flow. Create a few first level categories to rough out your project. Find where your ending is or what thesis you're trying to prove. Then fill in the blanks, using as many levels as you need (and your software permits).

If one category doesn't come immediately, leave it blank and go on to the next, with just the number created by the outlining software. If something doesn't work, stop (you haven't invested too much effort yet, after all) and analyze why it doesn't work. Now is the time to decide whether to go on with the project, to figure exactly what is wrong and what is right and work to solve those problems. If it's just one of those bright ideas that go nowhere, put the idea aside and go on to something that will work.

Let's get back to the Internet for a moment. Once you have the outline, then you can go to those Internet tools and decide which ones you're going to use on your project. Each one of the steps in the outline is a step you're going to fill in with your research on the Internet, in the library, and in person.

Remember how easy it is to be overwhelmed on the Net by all those megabytes of information from around the globe. An outline will let you have some idea of the categories you're interested in. Then you can ignore (to the best of your ability) all those Usenet headers and Web pointers that have nothing to do with your project. In the end, as material builds up on your hard drive or home directory, you'll find that you will *have* to focus, and ignore everything that doesn't match what you want.

One of this book's authors uses an old DOS shareware product, PCOutline, by Brown Bag software. (It came bundled with WordStar products during the 1980s and is still available from some shareware suppliers and on CompuServe.) With a few keyboard commands, and no mouse to click, PCOutline lets your fingers fly over the keyboard. The important keys in PCOutline are [Ctrl], [Enter], and the arrow keys that let you create a new entry and then decide its level in the outline. With those key commands you can outline as fast as your thoughts go.

With PCOutline, you can move categories up and down as you please, by marking a line with [Ctrl]+[M]. You can move whole parts of an outline to a new area.

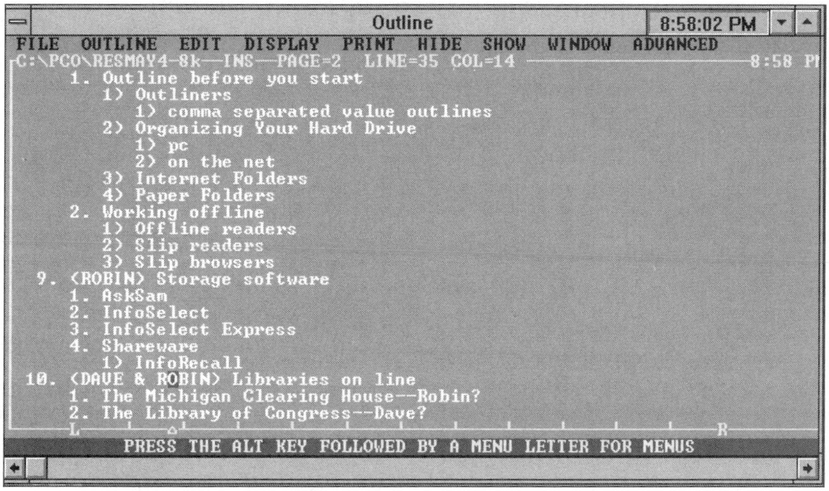

Figure 8-1.

An outline for this chapter in PCOutline

Other outliners are similar. Learn the outliner that comes with your word processor (WordPerfect, for example, has a powerful one). If it has keyboard commands, learn them, so that as your thoughts occur, you can write them down.

Once you've learned the outliner, get to work on your research project. If it's a story-based project, whether it's fiction or nonfiction, you have a germ of an idea: a situation, a character, a beginning. Open your outliner and enter those ideas. Now you have to know where you're going. So figure out that ending. The hero triumphs (or is defeated). The nonfiction character is born, has a career, gets married, and eventually dies. Now you have a beginning and an end. Fill in the middle.

If it's an academic research project, or anything else where you have to prove a case or a thesis, begin with that. A defense lawyer wants to prove that his client is not guilty, so that lawyer would then outline each of the steps in proving that case. A doctor wants to prove to colleagues that a new treatment is safe and effective. So the doctor outlines the proof, step by step, using the clinical cases that prove it. If you're a reporter and you're doing a story, you may have your lead and now you're going on the Net to get details. The outline gives you the blanks that you, as a reporter, have to fill in to get the story.

Don't be afraid to change the outline. As you do your research, new ideas will come to you. Add the new information to your outline. It's not cast in stone. If something doesn't work, drop it. If an idea works better somewhere else in the outline, move it to where it does work. In this way, the outline works for those people who like to outline before they write and those people who think and build as they write. Adding material to the outline lets you see your project in a nutshell.

When all the research is done, or if you've reached your cutoff point or date, the project is half written already. It's a dynamic, living thing, and will change again before it's complete. An outline will keep you on the right road, or it might, as with road maps, help you find a more scenic route that still reaches your destination, but in a more colorful way.

Finally, that outline is a selling tool, whether it's a book or a research (and grant) proposal. With a good outline, your project is there, in miniature. You can hand it to your agent, your publisher, your professor, your boss and get the go-ahead.

Outlines and Comma-Separated Values

Outlining software gives you another advantage. You can transfer your outline to all kinds of other software and use it to organize your material. For example, you could transfer the outline to software that lets you print labels for use on file folders in a filing cabinet, ready to receive printouts and notes that fit that part of your outline.If you are familiar with databases, or mailing lists, you will have heard that one of the common ways for exchanging data between databases is with files using *comma separated values (CSV)*, also known as *comma delimited values (CDV)*. A CSV file for an address database often looks like this:

```
John Smith,123 Washington Blvd.,Hometown,CA,99999,USA
Mary Jones,456 Macdonald St.,Smalltown,ON,L1A B9C,Canada
```

The computer and database software read the information between the commas and put it into a database field. Then the computer and software look for the next comma and put the next item into the next field in the database.

At the end of each line is the *carriage return* (ASCII 13) that tells the computer and software that that's the end of the current data set and it should begin a new entry with the data on the next line. Using the carriage return as the final delimiter, it's easy to turn your outline into a small database, then import it into other software that will enhance your research.

So, using your outliner (depending on the software), export your outline to ASCII or use the "Save As" function and save the outline as plain ASCII text.

Let's take the example of an early outline for this book:

```
Chapter 8. Focusing Your Aims
1. Outline before you start
        1) Outliners
            1) Comma separated value outlines
        2) Organizing Your Hard Drive
            1) PC
            2) On the Net
            3) Internet Folders
            4) Paper Folders
2. Working offline
        1) Offline readers
        2) SLIP readers
        3) SLIP browsers

Chapter 9. Libraries Online
1. The Michigan Clearing House
2. The Library of Congress
3. Telneting to Libraries
```

Once you save your outline to ASCII, a carriage return will end each line—just the delimiter that a database program needs. So now you use your word processor (in its ASCII mode of course), and you can flatten the outline like this:

```
Chapter 8. Focusing Your Aims
Chapter 9. Libraries Online
```

and create a category for each chapter, or you can use your judgment and create the kinds of sub-categories you think would work. For example:

```
8., Focusing Your Aims
8.1.1, Focusing Your Aims, Outliners
8.1.2,Focusing Your Aims, Organizing Your Hard Drive
8.2.,Focusing Your Aims, Working offline
9., Libraries Online
9.1, Libraries Online, The Michigan Clearing House
9.2, Libraries Online, The Library of Congress
9.3, Libraries Online, Telneting to Libraries
```

You can make it as complex—or as simple—as you need.

Caution
Remember the old adage—Keep It Simple, Stupid (KISS). Even if you are expanding your original outline as you research and write, use only the simplest categories to organize your paper folders, Internet folders, and hard drive. Simplicity will help you find things faster and as more information comes in, the organization will not overwhelm you.

Let's take a simple example. You've organized your outline, and now you're going to organize your paper file folders in the same way. If you have a labeling program, such as Avery's LabelPro or LabelPro for Windows, it's easy, because LabelPro is made to import CSV files.

In LabelPro for Windows, for example, you would use the *Merge* function on the menu bar and click on the *Link to List* function (see Figure 8-2) to display the Link to List dialog box (shown in Figure 8-3).

Figure 8-2.
Linking menu options in
Avery's LabelPro

Figure 8-3.
The Link to List dialog box

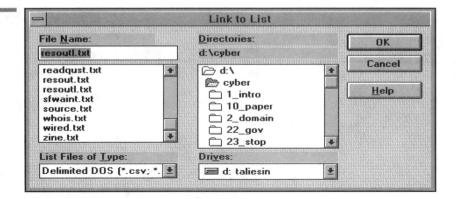

In the Link to List dialog box, choose *Delimited DOS (*.csv)* as file type and then link LabelPro to the ASCII version of your outline.

Once you've linked LabelPro for Windows to the ASCII outline, click on the label on the screen and then, on the menu bar, click on *Merge* again and choose *Merge Fields*. The Merge Fields dialog box is shown in Figure 8-4. If you have one line in your outline, it's simple; there is one line in the merge fields dialog box. If you have categories separated by commas, then you can have multiline labels, and it appears on the print preview function of LabelPro, as shown in Figure 8-5.

Now you have labels for file folders that match your outline. The same procedure works for note taking or organizing the material you take in from the Net, whether it's e-mail, Usenet information, or from the World Wide Web. If the project is small, then InfoSelect, a software program, is probably your best bet. If you have a large, ongoing project, then a powerful free-form text retrieval database such as AskSam for Windows is a good idea. Both programs will import

Figure 8-4.
The Merge Fields dialog box

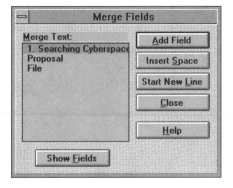

Figure 8-5.

The Print Preview Box showing a final label

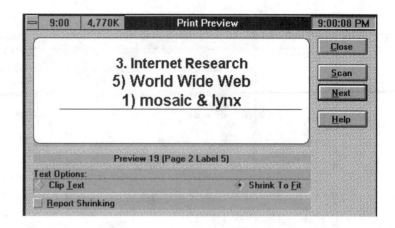

comma-separated value files in a way that creates ready-made note pages. In InfoSelect for Windows, for example, you can import your CSV version of the outline by choosing *Import* and *Database* from the *File* menu (see Figure 8-6).

Once you've imported the CSV file, each category in your outline becomes a new InfoSelect window page for your notes, as shown in Figure 8-7.

Figure 8-6.

Choosing Import and Database in InfoSelect

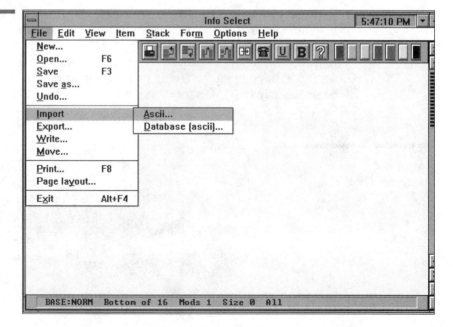

Figure 8-7.
Note Windows created by importing a CSV file into InfoSelect

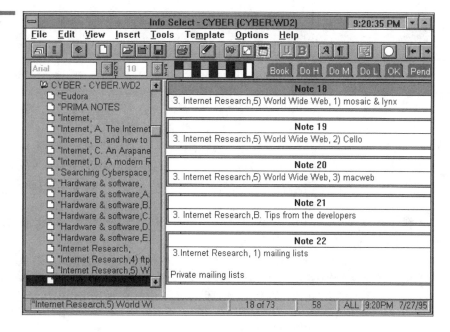

Folders

The Internet has traditionally organized material into "folders." Many e-mail programs allow you to create folders to sort material, an essential feature if you're dealing with a lot of information. Pine, Eudora, Delrina's Internet Messenger Yarn, and Netmanage's Chameleon are just a few programs that create folders to hold e-mail.

Tip

In the language of the Net, a folder usually retains the letter or Usenet format. That lets you reply to and forward messages just as if they were in your inbox. If you save the messages as ASCII text, then to reply to the message you have to do it manually by typing the address yourself and importing or retyping the original message.

Pine is a UNIX, mainframe-based e-mail and news reading program. It organizes its folders in your Pine directory on the mainframe's hard disk. Programs such as Yarn, Eudora, and Chameleon organize the folders on the hard drive of your PC. Internet Messenger gives you the best of both worlds if you're dialing into a compatible UNIX system; it permits you to mirror your folders on your PC at home and on the UNIX host at your office or service provider—an ideal solution if you do a lot of work at both locations.

Use your outline as a *guide* to creating folders. Too few and you will be unable to find the material you want in a hurry. Too many and, as information grows, you may not remember where everything is.

You should also create special folders for personal mail to keep it separate from your research project, for any hobby or other information not related to your immediate project, and to store such important messages as instructions for listservs, mailing lists, and FAQs you frequently consult.

Filters

Once you've organized your folders, see if your mail program allows you to filter the messages. It's a lot easier if the software presorts your mail for you. That way you can choose which material to read first and which to put aside to another day if you're busy.

On some UNIX systems, using Pine, the system must have another piece of software to do the filtering (also called delivery filtering on some UNIX systems). Check with your system operator if programs such as Procmail, Deliver or Filter are available. Then you set up the folders, using the Setup/Config command of Pine and closing "enable-incoming-folders." Then use the Add command to create the folders in Pine.

Filtering is similar and simpler in Netmanage's Chameleon. In the mail function, you choose *Services* from the menu bar and then click on *Rules*, which brings up the dialog box shown in Figure 8-8.

You then fill in the dialog box to fit the filter and folder you want. If it's a "Subject," that's an easy choice, but note that message headers can change over time, so you may have to have several rules all pointing to one folder.

If you're filtering all the mail from one mailing list to a single folder, it's usually best to use the "From" address, because all the messages usually come through one address. Similarly, if you want all the mail from one colleague sent to one filter, then use the "From" function.

Tip

If your software does not save the outbox after messages are dispatched, create a "sent" folder for those messages so you have a record. Send a Blind Carbon Copy (Bcc) to yourself and then use the "To" filter to send the message in to a "Sent" folder.

It helps to have those messages on hand, especially if one bounces because of a mistyped Internet address. Then all you have to do is forward the sent message, retyping the address correctly.

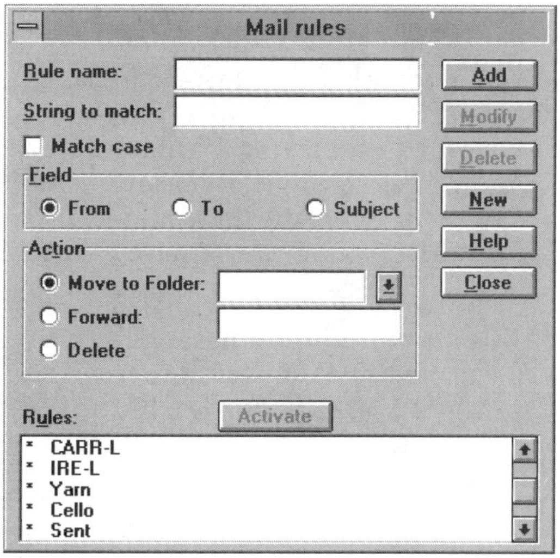

Figure 8-8.
The Chameleon Mail
Rules dialog box

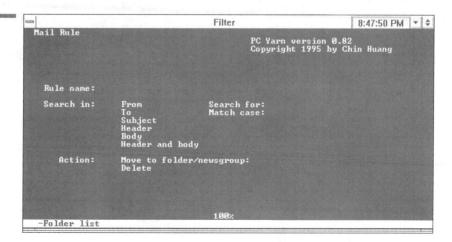

Yarn, the DOS offline news reader, also permits you to filter incoming messages and to search the entire body of messages for keywords, as shown in Figure 8-9.

There's one last function to filters that is a big help. The "delete" option, which operates as a kill file and allows you to prescreen messages you wouldn't want to read anyway and that only clutter up your folders.

Figure 8-9.
The filter function in
Yarn

Organizing Your Hard Drive

You're going to have a lot of material on your hard drive as your Internet research progresses. That means that you should organize the subdirectories on your hard drive (or if you are using Windows 95, the Win95 folders) to match your outline. Again, keep it simple, be flexible, and find out what works for you. If you are consistent in organizing your e-mail folders, your paper file folders, and your hard drive, then you will have taken a major step toward maintaining control of your material. A sample hard drive organization appears in Figure 8-10.

One of the problems with DOS is that it sorts by the first character, so that, if you are using numbers, the numbers will sort by 1, 10, 11, 12, 2, 20, 21, and so on—not exactly how we learned to count in school. Alphabetical order, of course, presents no such problem.

You should plan on using special subdirectories for letters, as opposed to research, and other special features such as a contacts database, picture files, and so on. One of the advantages of using the computer is speed, and the better organized you are on your hard drive, the more you can take advantage of that speed.

Working Offline

We briefly discussed working offline in Chapter 1, and now's the time to take a closer look at the subject.

Figure 8-10.
Organizing the hard drive for this book

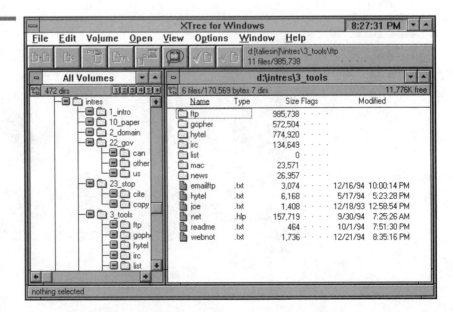

Working offline has recently become easier. In the early days of the Net, researchers were tied to their UNIX home directories and worked out their own ways of organizing material.

With all the powerful new software available for the PC, it's smart, in most cases, to get the material off the Net and onto your own system, where it's at your fingertips and where you can organize it the way you want. So your aim should be to find the research material on the Net, evaluate it, download the most crucial information in a readable format such as ASCII, and then store it as plain text or in some form of database.

For years people have been using various word processor formats to store their files. That means a lot of material is stored using a lot of different formats, and you'll need to use the *find* or *index* function of the word processor to retrieve specific information.

As we mentioned before, a popular alternative is the free-form text retrieval database, which allows large amounts of material to be stored in one file. Information is easily retrieved using keyword or Boolean searches. The aim of this chapter is to help you get that material off the Net in a way that you can store it and find it again, no matter what storage strategy you use.

It's also a good idea to subdivide the material, whether in word processing or text database format, in different subdirectories as we discussed above.

One of the most frustrating problems for newcomers to the Net is dealing with the quirky and obscure commands on the UNIX mail and newsreaders used on some systems. Offline readers, QWK SOUP for those with UNIX shell accounts, and a variety of SLIP and PPP readers for those with TCP/IP connections make life a lot easier.

The programs we'll discuss are liked by some people and disliked by others—they have both good features and poorly designed features. The advantage of working on the Net is that the programs are either free or have free versions and you can experiment to find which system works best for you.

QWK SOUP Offline Readers

As we mentioned in the first chapter, QWK SOUP, organizes your e-mail and newsgroups into packets and zips them into one file. You can then download the packet using your communications. SOUP stands for "Simple Offline Usenet Packet."

This section discusses one QWK SOUP DOS offline news and mail reader called Yarn (MacSOUP is the equivalent for the Macintosh).

If you are limited by your service provider to a UNIX shell account, or if you are dealing with a large volume of messages and articles and don't want to waste storage space on Windows-compatible files, then QWK SOUP is a good system to work with. You might prefer to work with Windows and SLIP/PPP; we'll discuss that next.

Yarn

The most popular QWK SOUP-style offline reader for DOS is Yarn, created as freeware by Chin Huang. Yarn is a suite of programs for the PC that allow you to efficiently handle a large volume of news and mail offline. This section will highlight those features of Yarn and related programs that are advantageous to researchers. Complete documentation comes with each program.

Two other freeware products enhance Yarn, Yes, created by Per Goetterup, and WinYarn, created by Stanley Wong. If you are going to send or receive files using MIME (Multipurpose Internet Mail Extension), you will also need a fourth program called Metamail.

Yarn requires PKZIP to uncompress and compress the news and mail packets, plus an available DOS editor. The default is the MS DOS Edit program, but for more efficient word processing, consider a shareware mini word processor such as VDE.

The fact that these four products (and some others) work together is not unusual on the Net. Often programs are enhanced by people in different parts of the world who come together electronically to produce a new product.

If you think about it, if you look at a piece of commercial software, there are all those .exe and .com files that make up the megabytes of those programs, so using a commercial program is not much different from loading those four programs. The first thing you have to do before you download Yarn and its supporting software is to find out if your service provider supports the QWK SOUP format.

If your service provider does support QWK SOUP, you will find that once you go online using your communications program, such as Wincomm or Crosstalk, that your service provider will have a script, batch file, or program provided that will take your mail and newsgroups, compress them using a PKZIP-compatible UNIX program, and then download them to your hard drive (with the help, of course, of your communications program). A second script would watch for zipped replies uploaded by your communications program, unzip them, and then post the e-mail and newsgroup articles.

Yarn is designed as a multiuser program so that a number of people using the same PC can each have their own mail and news subdirectories. That means you will need at least two first-level subdirectories to run Yarn.

You first set up the Yarn directory (usually C:\Yarn) by running the install program. In this case, with Version .083, Yarn comes with English and French documentation (it is created in Canada), so to start the English version of the install program you type *English c:\yarn*.

The next step is to set up your user or home directory. If you are a single user, you can choose your name or *home* or *Internet*. If you have multiple users on a home PC, the directories should have the names of the users (John, Joan, Joe, and so on). Create the subdirectory using the DOS *MD* command or your file manager. Then run the Yarn program *Adduser* and fill in the name of the home directory, your name and user ID, the name of your service provider, and your edit program (*Edit* or *VDE*). Finally, you have to fill in the name of the reply packet. That's the PKZIPped packet that contains the news and mail you want to post on the Net. The name you need will come from your service provider and will interact with the unpacking script or program after it's uploaded to your service provider. Then you add the information to your autoexec.bat file:

```
Set Yarn=C:\Yarn Set Home=C:\Internet Set TZ=EST5EDT
```

The last entry sets the time zone in the difference from Greenwich Mean Time. For Eastern Time it is, as shown, Greenwich plus five hours. For Pacific, it would be Greenwich plus eight hours.

Yarn has a large custom configuration file that lets you choose colors and other features. It's stored in the \home\yarn subdirectory so each user can configure the system to his or her own needs. Much of the configuration file is created when you run the AddUser program. But Yarn is so feature-rich that some parts of the configuration file are worth taking a look at.

```
# The save to file command writes this line at the start of
  each saved message.
# The default is to write no line at the beginning of the
  message.
save-mail-header = Message %a of %C:
```

This part of the Yarn configuration file is one of the more important features of Yarn for a researcher, especially if you are importing ASCII text into a free-form database of some kind.

This allows you to put a delimiter between the stories if you save them in a file for importing into the database. The import feature of the text database program then automatically uses the delimiter to separate information into different pages.

An industry-standard delimiter for most text retrieval systems is the tilde ~ (ASCII 126), so that if you want a tilde between files as you store (and append) the files you would add the tilde to the configuration file as follows:

```
save-mail-header = ~Message %a of %C:
```

With this command, Yarn will create the delimiter and a number. For example, a message from the mailbox would be created like this:

```
~Message 22 of INBOX:
```

Caution

In this case there is a conflict between two industry standards. The tilde (~) is a common delimiter used by text databases. The tilde is often also an element in many World Wide Web addresses. Worse, sometimes there are as many as twenty or thirty tildes in some too-fancy signature files. This means using the tilde as delimiter could create scores of blank pages in a text retrieval database. With Yarn, however, you can use any character you want as a delimiter and then change the delimiter in the options file of most text retrieval software.

Note

There is now yet another use for the tilde (~). Windows 95 uses it when it shortens long file names to the traditional DOS 8.3 file names.

This is what Microsoft Tech Support advises:

The infamous ~.

The tilde will always be used for the 7th character in a short filename that is generated from a long filename. This is hard-coded into the Fat file system driver of Windows 95 and Windows NT (both use the exact same code to generate short filenames). The basic algorithm for creating a short filename is pretty much as follows:

1. *Remove any unacceptable DOS characters*
2. *Remove any spaces*
3. *Truncate at 6 characters*
4. *Add the ~ and the sequence number of the file*
5. *Use the first 3 characters after the last period to form the extension*

The Windows 95 Resource kit should go into more detail, plus examples.

To add MIME support to Yarn, you add the Metamail program to the Yarn subdirectory (or make sure it's in your path) and then add the following lines to the configuration file:

```
decode-mime=metamail %
```

Once you've configured Yarn to your satisfaction, you can run the Filter program to set up filters for your mail (as discussed above) to send it to easy-to-handle folders.

Once you're ready to go online, you use your communications program to connect. You then have to set up your user profile so it will work with the script or program that creates the SOUP packets. This means that you have to manually subscribe to the newsgroups you want, using the standard UNIX newsreader program on your service provider. That newsreader program creates a *.newsrc* file, which the SOUP script will read so it will know which newsgroups to download.

You have two ways to create .newsrc files. You can either do it manually with the UNIX word-processing program such as Joe or VI, or by using the standard UNIX newsreading program provided by your service provider. For the best advice, check with the system operator or the help person in charge of SOUP for your system.

If, for example, you use the standard UNIX TRN (threaded newsreader) program and you want to subscribe to the newsgroup that discusses offline readers, *alt.usenet.offline-reader*, you would use the following script:

```
$trn
```

No unread news in subscribed newsgroups. To subscribe to a newnewsgroup use the g<newsgroup command.

```
********End of newsgroups—what next? [qnp]
```

Next, you type in the name of the newsgroup:

```
********End of newsgroups-whatnext?[qnp] alt.usenet.offline-reader
```

The system will reply:

```
Newsgroup alt.usenet.offline-reader is currently
    unsubscribed to—subscribe [y/n] y
```

You'll get another prompt:

```
********* 451 unread articles in alt.usenet.offline-reader—read
    now [+ynq]
```

Because you're going to download those articles using Yarn you can type *n* for no. But if there are too many articles, you can type a *c*, which tells the .newsrc file that you've read all the articles. That means the next time you go online there will be a smaller number of articles (unless it's a very high-volume newsgroup).

After you've chosen n or c you once again get the following prompt (or something similar, since this prompt is system-specific):

`********End of newsgroups—what next? [qnp]—`

Here you can either hit q to quit TRN or g to subscribe to other newsgroups and then quit when you're finished.

Tip

If you're away for more than a few days, on vacation or away on business, and want to catch up on all your newsgroups when you return, go back online and use the c command (in TRN) to mark all those files as read to save downloading and reading time.

Once you've created the .newsrc file, on some systems you have to create a second file for Yarn to read, called *.newspack*. Create it with your UNIX word processor so that it contains a list (spelling and case count!) of your newsgroups. The SOUP generator reads the .newspack file to see which newsgroups to download, goes to the .newsrc file to make sure you've subscribed to the groups and then zips your mail and newsgroups into a packet and downloads them to your hard drive.

Once you've got the packet on your hard drive, you run Yarn's Import program, which unzips the packet, reads the names of the newsgroups, and places them into Yarn. You then get a menu like the one shown in Figure 8-11. You highlight and press *Enter* for the newsgroup you want or *I* for the mail inbox.

Once you're in Yarn, you can choose articles to read from the menu. Yarn has many sophisticated key commands, based on the traditional Internet TRN and tin newsreaders. They take a little learning and practice, but once you've mastered them, you can quickly scan your newsgroups and read and save the information you want, discarding the rest.

Caution

Yarn commands, at both the article selection and reading level, like the original UNIX commands are case sensitive, which means that it matters if you capitalize any letters.

Yarn saves material in two formats: *folders* and *files*. You can move an e-mail message or Usenet article to a specific folder by using o (lower case) from the article or message level. Folders are active; that means you can create a reply or forward a message directly from the folder. To save to a text file, you use the s

Figure 8-11.
The Yarn menu page

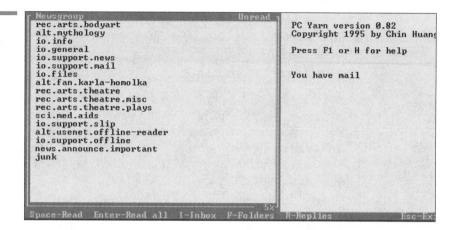

```
Newsgroup                               Unread
rec.arts.bodyart                              PC Yarn version 0.82
alt.mythology                                 Copyright 1995 by Chin Huan
io.info
io.general                                    Press F1 or H for help
io.support.news
io.support.mail
io.files                                      You have mail
alt.fan.karla-homolka
rec.arts.theatre
rec.arts.theatre.misc
rec.arts.theatre.plays
sci.med.aids
io.support.slip
alt.usenet.offline-reader
io.support.offline
news.announce.important
junk
                                    5%
Space-Read  Enter-Read all  I-Inbox  F-Folders  R-Replies        Esc-Ex
```

command, where you will be prompted for a filename. Yarn automatically adds the delimiter we discussed earlier, so once you've finished saving the material you need, you can either import it into a text database or read the files with your word processor.

To answer a message, you press *R* (uppercase) to reply quoting the original article or *r* (lowercase) to reply starting with a clean slate. Yarn then opens the word processing program you've chosen and you can then type the message. To post a mail message you press *M* (uppercase), or, to post an article, press *a* (lowercase), and again Yarn activates the word processing program. To forward a message you press *m* (lowercase) from the mail menu or *F* (uppercase, for quoting) or *f* (lowercase, for no quotes) from a Usenet article.

Once you've finished and you exit from Yarn, the program automatically zips all your replies and new messages or articles into a packet ready for uploading.

Although Yarn has many powerful features, it does have one significant limitation. There are, at this writing, no print commands. To print a message or article you have to use the save (*s*) command and, when you get the file prompt, type in the DOS *prn* command to send the material your printer.

Despite a high learning curve (which was common on the Internet for years in any case), Yarn has thousands of users around the world. For once you've learned it, it simplifies the handling of information—and that's a key advantage for researchers.

Yes

Yes is an editor shell for Yarn created by Per Goetterup. It adds a couple of interesting features to Yarn, including multiple signature files. That's helpful if you want to have a serious signature file for your professional mailing lists and newsgroups and a more flamboyant one for hobby or other personal-interest groups. It also lets you add a custom quote, if you wish, to the bottom of the signature file.

Yes also includes a utility called *Ypost* that you'll need if you want to add attached files to the messages you're sending out.

Yes comes with its own install program, which sets up the program, modifies the Yarn configuration file to work with Yes, and sets up Yes's configuration file. You then create your various signature files, all with a *.sig* suffix, and then create a pointer file called *assign.yes* that should contain the names of your newsgroup and its matching signature file. Goetterup has also added a utility called *Yfolder* that allows users to change the order of messages or articles in a Yarn folder.

WinYarn

WinYarn is a Windows front-end for Yarn that puts the common Yarn commands in an easy-to-use Windows format. You install the main files in a \Winyarn subdirectory. WinYarn is written in Visual Basic so it requires *.vbx files and VBRUN300.DLL in the \Windows\System directory.

You then run the program makeini.exe from the Program Manager. That brings up the Windows Notepad program that lets you fill in the blanks of the .INI file with values such as the name and location of the Yarn program and where you download the packets and store the reply packets for uploading. It also lets you decide whether to use WinYarn and Yarn in a window or at full screen. The winyarn.ini file is stored in your Yarn subdirectory when you save with the Notepad. The WinYarn buttons then allow you to perform most of Yarn's functions using Windows buttons, as shown in Figure 8-12.

Figure 8-12.
The WinYarn file folder page

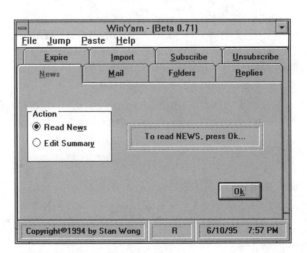

To retrieve by FTP Yarn, Yes, and WinYarn, try the Simtel site at oak.oakland.edu in /pub/msdos/offline or its mirror sites. Yes can also be found in the author's home site at:

```
ftp://login.dknet.dk/pub/pg/yesxxx.zip
```

And WinYarn can be found at:

```
ftp.cica.indiana.edu:/pub/pc/win3/uploads/winyrnxx.zipftp.g
    ate.net:/pub/users/myob/winyrnxx.zip
```

Newsgroup:

```
alt.usenet.off-line.reader
```

Also try comp.os.msdos.mail at:

```
newsnews.software.readerscomp.mail.uucp,comp.mail.misccomp.
    os.msdos.appscomp.os.ms-windows.apps.comm
```

Mailing list:

Send a subscription message to:

```
listproc@lists.colorado.edu
subscribe yarn-list firstname lastname
```

FAQ:

The Offline FAQ is found in RTFM.mit.edu in subdirectory alt.usenet.offline-reader, which also contains "Yet another Offline FAQ." It is also regularly posted on:

```
alt.usenet.offline-reader and other groups
```

Metamail:

```
ftp://thumper.bellcore.com/pub/nsb/mmxxdos.zip
```

For Mac Users:

```
ftp://ftp.gte.com/pub/MacSoup
```

Look in the comp.sys.mac.comm FAQ for more information.

SLIP/PPP Mail and News Readers

The accelerating growth of the Internet has, as we said before, brought an explosion in the use of Windows software that uses the TCP/IP protocols to connect to a service provider using SLIP or PPP.

This means you have a choice among Windows mail and news readers. There are Commercial systems such as Chameleon and Internet In A Box, freeware mail readers such as Eudora (which also has a more powerful commercial version), and newsreaders such as Free Agent (free beta versions with a commercial version in the works), News Xpress (freeware) and Trumpet Newsreader (shareware).

So what's the best mail and newsreader for research? The choice is yours. This section, however, concentrates on the latest addition to Net software, Free Agent, because it is created so the user has the choice of working both online and offline.

Again, working offline gives you time—time to think about what you want to download and read, and time to carefully consider those replies you are typing (as we discussed in Chapter 7).

In offline mode, Free Agent permits you to download a list of headers in all your newsgroups, pick only those headers for articles you want to read, and ignore the rest. It's a great time-saver and, if you are focused on your project, a good tool.

Free Agent also has a powerful keyword searching function, which saves even more time and energy. If you are wondering if there are newsgroups on a certain subject, for example, Free Agent will let you quickly search the names of the thousands of newsgroups in seconds to see if anything comes up. Once you have the name of the appropriate newsgroup, Free Agent then permits you to go online and grab fifty sample headers to see if the subject you are researching is a regular topic on that newsgroup. Other software gives you the choice of either manually searching online or, like Yarn, grabbing the text of all the available articles, downloading them, and then searching through them all when you open the newsreader.

Free Agent is still being developed at this writing. The current beta is .55, but there is active discussion on its strengths and weaknesses on alt.usenet.offline-reader and the developer, Forté, welcomes input from its Net users.

As shown in Figure 8-13, Free Agent's main screen allows you to see the newsgroups, the headers, and the messages in three different windows. This organization makes it easier for the researcher to scroll through the information and find if there is anything worth reading and saving. By hitting Z, in the active window, Free Agent expands that window to full size.

Figure 8-13.
Free Agent

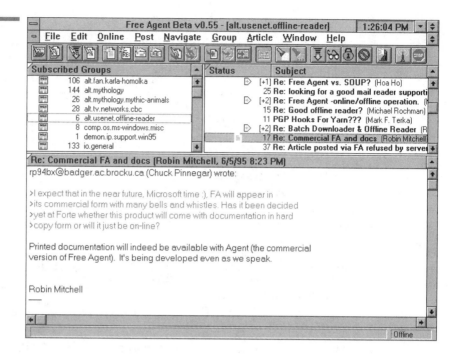

To configure Free Agent for offline operation, you go to the File menu and click on Preferences. When the file folder screen appears, click on Offline Operation and your choices are presented as shown in Figure 8-14.

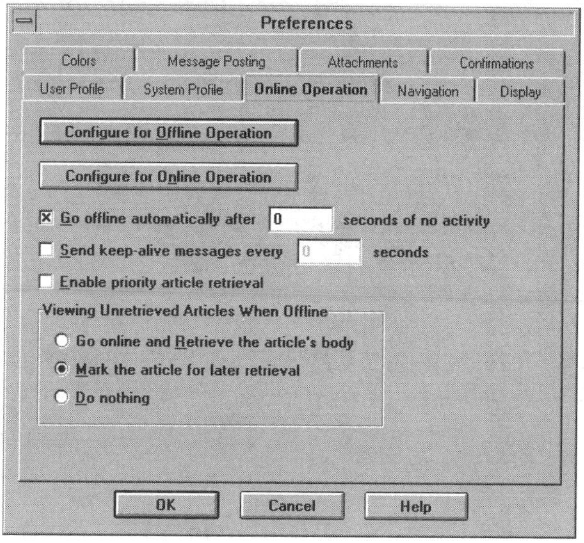

Figure 8-14.
Configuring Free Agent for offline operation

Once you've downloaded the articles you want, you can save them to a file. Unfortunately, at this writing, none of the SLIP/PPP readers give you the option of inserting a delimiter between appended files.

And as for mail, Eudora is currently the most popular freeware online/offline mail reader. It allows you to go online, pick up your mail (if you have a live connection to the Net, it picks up your mail as it comes in), and store it in folders for later reading. Eudora is built around the Net tradition of folders; if you're using Eudora it's a good idea to organize your mail into folders using the outline you've already created. (See how that one step helps you organize everything else?) The freeware version of Eudora has limited text-storagecapability. Unlike other readers, the freeware version of Eudora doesn't allow you to append one message to another. They all have to be stored in separate text files. Often those text files appear unformatted and have to be reformatted by your word processor.

Netmanage's Chameleon (the commercial version) has a powerful mail reader that lets you organize your information into folders or create large text files by using the "append" command. You can use these files later in a text retrieval database or word-processor.

Forté says it will soon release Agent, a commercial version of Free Agent, which will have mail handling features similar to its free beta newsreader. When choosing a mail reader, make sure that it has MIME support so you can attach large binary files to your mail. That way you can compress word processing, graphic, or other files using a program such as PKZIP and then send them easily to their intended destination. You should also check with the intended recipient before sending the files, to make sure that person can handle attached files—otherwise they will find their mailbox jammed with what appears to be gibberish.

It's also good netiquette to never send an attached file to a mailing list. Not everyone wants those files and many recipients won't have the software to handle them anyway.

Free Agent: `ftp.forteinc.com/pub/agent/agentxxx.zip`

Web: `http://www.forteinc.com/forte`

E-mail: `agent-info@forteinc.com.`

News Xpress: `ftp.hk.super.net`

Eudora: `ftp.qualcomm.com/guest/eudora/windows/xxx`

Working Offline with Web Browsers

We've discussed the World Wide Web and Web browsers such as Mosaic, Cello, and Netscape earlier. When you find a gem of information on the Web, how do you work with it?

With all the pretty graphics available on the Web, it's still text that most researchers need, and at this point in Web browser development little attention has been paid to the need for researchers and other Web users to store the text on their hard drives.

If you simply save the Web page you've found as an HTML file, you will find it filled with pointers and commands that clutter up the text. Fortunately, there are solutions.

Netscape 1.x

Although Netscape is, at present, the most powerful Web browser available, its current text-saving utility is poor. To get plain text information from Netscape, you have to mail the material to yourself. Unfortunately, as shown in Figure 8-15, Netscape adds the caret for quoting material to the text. So once it's in your mailbox, you have to use your word processor to remove the carets to use the plain text.

Cello

The current version of Netscape limits mail files to 30K, so if you run into a bigger text file on the World Wide Web, you will have to save it as an HTML file and use a program called HTML Converter to strip all the pointers.

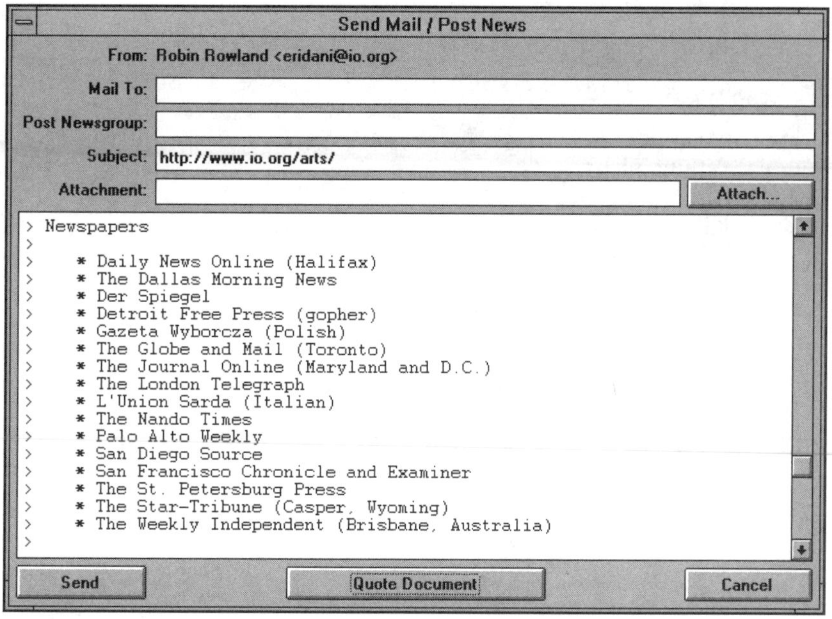

Figure 8-15.
Mailing plain text to yourself in Netscape

```
Send Mail / Post News
From: Robin Rowland <eridani@io.org>
Mail To:
Post Newsgroup:
Subject: http://www.io.org/arts/
Attachment:                                                    Attach...

> Newspapers
>
>      * Daily News Online (Halifax)
>      * The Dallas Morning News
>      * Der Spiegel
>      * Detroit Free Press (gopher)
>      * Gazeta Wyborcza (Polish)
>      * The Globe and Mail (Toronto)
>      * The Journal Online (Maryland and D.C.)
>      * The London Telegraph
>      * L'Union Sarda (Italian)
>      * The Nando Times
>      * Palo Alto Weekly
>      * San Diego Source
>      * San Francisco Chronicle and Examiner
>      * The St. Petersburg Press
>      * The Star-Tribune (Casper, Wyoming)
>      * The Weekly Independent (Brisbane, Australia)
>

   Send              Quote Document              Cancel
```

Cello, one of the original Net browsers, has one advantage, probably because it was developed at Cornell University and the developers recognized the need for researchers to save information as plain text—and that's just what it can do.

First you have to use Cello's *Configure* option to *Choose Your Own Editor*. The default is the Windows Notepad, but with its 32K limit, Notepad is often too small to handle large files. Many Cello users recommend a freeware editor for Windows called Programmer's File Editor to capture Web text and store it as ASCII files, as shown in Figure 8-16.

Using the Edit option on the menu bar, you choose Save as Plain text from the options that come up. Once you have the text in the editor, it's easy to save it to the proper subdirectory and then read it.

The new version of Cello (2.0), which should be available in late 1995, should have the same feature and should be able to match most of Netscape's more powerful features.

HTMLcon

HTMLcon is a DOS HTML conversion utility that strips commands from HTML files and saves them as plain ASCII text. If you create a standard Windows .pif file for HTMLcon, you can store it in the same Windows group as your Web browser, and simply input the name of the file you saved and the name of the text file you want, as shown in Figure 8-17.

Figure 8-16.
Using Programmer's File Editor to capture plain text from the World Wide Web

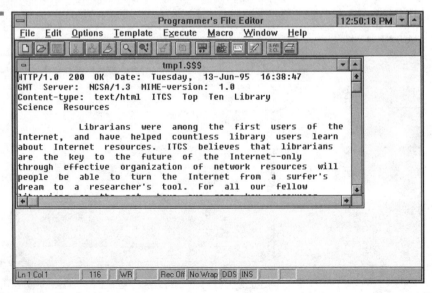

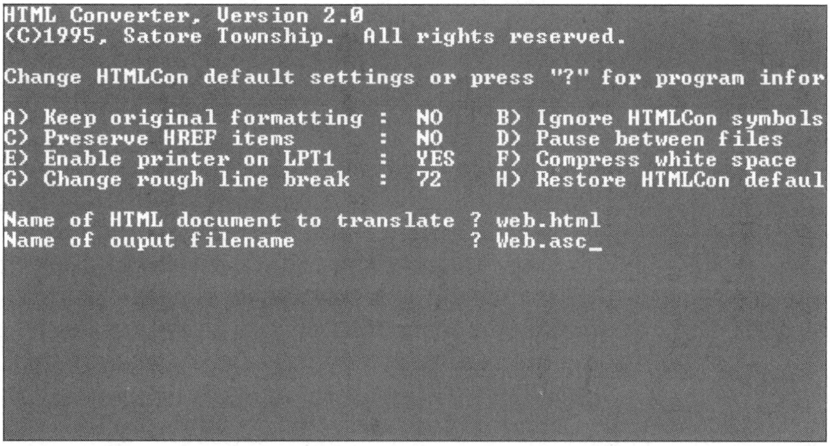

Figure 8-17.
Converting HTML files
with HTMLcon

```
HTML Converter, Version 2.0
(C)1995, Satore Township.  All rights reserved.

Change HTMLCon default settings or press "?" for program infor

A) Keep original formatting :  NO    B) Ignore HTMLCon symbols
C) Preserve HREF items       :  NO    D) Pause between files
E) Enable printer on LPT1    :  YES   F) Compress white space
G) Change rough line break   :  72    H) Restore HTMLCon defaul

Name of HTML document to translate ? web.html
Name of ouput filename             ? Web.asc_
```

Programmer's File Editor:

E-mail:
A.Phillips@lancaster.ac.uk

FTP:
micros.hensa.ac.uk

systemwsmr-simtel20.army.mil

ftp.cica.indiana.edu

HTMLcon:
ftp.crl.com/ftp/users/ro/mikell/ftp

WWW:
http://www.crl.com/~mikekell

Online Temptation: Don't Be an Information Pack Rat

If you've set up your software and subdirectories so you can work offline, there's one last problem you have to be aware of. Information overload is not only a problem on the Net, it's a problem off the Net as well. You'll want to save many of those e-mail messages, Usenet articles, and Web pages as your research progresses. But soon you'll find that you've accumulated so much you don't know how to deal with it.

Don't be an Internet information pack rat. Here are a few hints that will help keep your Internet life uncluttered:

» If the information can be left online on a Web page or Gopher site, and you don't need to store it on your hard drive, leave it on the Net. Bookmark the page with your Web browser or Gopher client and go back to it when you need it.

» Take care in deciding what you save off the Net. As you get busier, you'll find you have less and less time to handle all the e-mail and Usenet articles. So decide at the outset: is this information *essential* to your project? Then you can save it. Is it something you *need*? Then you should probably save it. Is it something that would be *nice to have*? You probably don't need it, so think hard before you save it. Is it information you *might just need someday*? You'll probably never use it and it will only clutter up your files. Be ruthless in purging material from your mailbox and newsgroups. Otherwise, you'll spend too much time reading and storing information you'll never use.

» Even if you have been ruthless in evaluating and choosing what information you will store on your computer, you're going to be tempted to print it out, and you'll find yourself overwhelmed with paper. Paper is still easier to read than a computer screen. Again, be ruthless in deciding what you're going to print, and print only the material that is absolutely essential to your work. Then file it right away in the file system you've created with your outliner. That way you'll find it quickly. Don't let it pile up beside your printer.

One last word. These hints are just guidelines, part of the research road map. You'll make your life easier if you recreate them in a way to suit your work style. Researchers have had paper piled on their desks for centuries. Now they have floppy disks piled on their desks as well. That's never going to change. In the late 20th century, the amount of information is growing exponentially and that means you're going to have be careful that your research road doesn't lead you to the wrong side of town. You don't want to be stuck in an information swamp.

9

Libraries on the Internet

Librarians were among the first people to recognize the importance of the Net. In the old ARPANET days, there were only a few librarians and researchers on the Net. Then, as library catalogs moved from three-by-five cards to computers in the 1980s, government and university libraries created the first Net connections. Then, and to a large extent still today, the Internet was a line into the library catalog. Users usually had to telnet in and use their PC as a dumb terminal, using the commands created for whatever cataloging software that library had.

In the past few years, there have been efforts to create Gopher and the World Wide Web links to libraries both large and small. Gopher links are quite common and some of these are still primitive. It's possible that eventually the creation of enhanced Web browsing software that can talk with library catalogs and their software around the world will make accessing libraries as easy as connecting to the rest of the Web.

The technical term for electronic library catalog access is OPAC, which means Online Public Access Catalogs. You'll probably be most interested in your local public or university library. These usually will have both Internet and local dial-up access. Many Freenets have connections with local public and university libraries.

More and more libraries are also offering *public access terminals*, often with full or limited Internet access. It's probably worth a phone call and then a personal visit to the library you want to use for your research. In most public libraries and some universities libraries with public access terminals, you can walk in, sign up for a time, usually in 15 minute blocks, and then do the work you want. For others you need a library card and perhaps a password. Universities have different access rules for students, visiting scholars, alumni, and the public, so it's a good idea to find out what the policies are—and, in some cases, whether or not they're within your budget. To find out more, call or visit.

If you wish, you can get lists of library catalogs before you embark on an online search. Art St. George of the University of New Mexico and Don Larson of the University of Maryland have created a large list, with almost 9,000 entries of Internet and dial-up libraries, Campus Wide Information Systems and bulletin board systems. It can be retrieved from FTP to ariel.unm.edu. Change to the library directory and retrieve the file Internet.library. There is also a large list of libraries around the world with the online access by FTP from ftp.utdallas.edu in the /pub/staff/billy subdirectory. The file is called libguide. Additional Gopher and Web links for library and library catalog access are at the end of this chapter, in the "Online Net Access to Library Catalogs" section.

With over 9,000 online libraries (and that number is growing), we can't look at them all. So what we will do is take an in-depth look at one of the more dynamic library programs at the University of Michigan. Then we'll look at some national libraries, the Library of Congress, the British Library, the National Library of Canada, and the National Library of Australia. Finally, we'll give you some examples using Telnet, Gopher, and the World Wide Web to find material in library catalogs, and then leads to other library resources on the Net.

The University of Michigan

The University of Michigan School of Information and Library Studies is one of the most active and innovative on the Internet. Best known is Michigan's Clearinghouse for Subject-Oriented Internet Resource Guides. It's jointly sponsored by the university and Argus Associates of Ann Arbor. It has hundreds of topics with, according to the university, a "special emphasis on guides that provide evaluative information." The Clearinghouse can be reached through the World Wide Web, Gopher, and FTP.

Another is GoMLink, "an electronic library of thousands of Internet resources arranged much like a public library" that specializes in information about the state of Michigan, including government information services and library catalogs.

Other projects include one where most-used journals may now be printed directly from an electronic catalog called MIRLYN; Internet access to Dissertations Abstracts International, developing an Electronic Reference Shelf;

Figure 9-1.
The University of
Michigan Clearinghouse

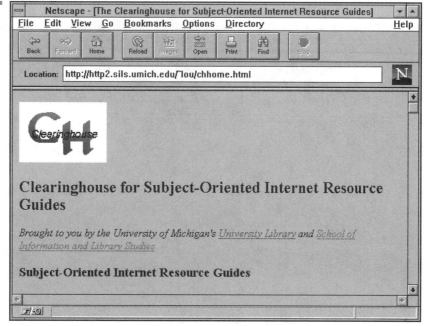

and the Humanities Text Initiative that creates and maintains an online text system called Social Science Data System, described as "a menu-driven means of extracting data from social science data sets via the World Wide Web."

The University of Michigan can be reached on the World Wide Web at http://http2.sils.umich.edu, by Gopher at gopher.lib.umich.edu and by FTP at una.hh.lilb.umich.edu. Figure 9-1 shows you the home page of the Clearinghouse's Web site.

The University of Michigan also offers the *Internet Resource Directory*, a bibliography of Internet resources in education, created by Judi Harris. It's a collaborative effort of the University of Michigan with teachers taking telecomputing at the University of Nebraska.

It can be found at gopher://una.hh.lib.umich.edu in directory inetdirsstacks or via FTP at una.hh.lib.umich.edu, in the directory inetdirsstacks and files education:harris1, education:harris2, education:harris3, and education:harris4.

The Michigan Clearinghouse

The Michigan Clearinghouse for Subject-Oriented Internet Resource Guides grew out of Lou Rosenfeld's class on the Internet at the School of Information and Library Studies. The subjects covered by the Michigan Clearinghouse can be found at the Clearinghouse for Subject-Oriented Internet Resource Guides: HTML Versions. This site is brought to you by the University of Michigan's University Library and School of Information and Library Studies.

The following are HTML versions of some of the guides already in the Clearinghouse, as well as many others. But first, here is a partial list of the Clearinghouse's categories which place Internet resources by subject.

» Adult/Distance Education

» Africa

» Biotechnology

» Cancer

» Cyberpreneurship

» Demography and Population Studies

» Employment Opportunities & Job Resources

» International Affairs

» Journalism

» Medical Resources

» Social Sciences

» U.S. Federal Government

» Women's Legal and Public Policy Issues

If you have questions and/or comments about the subject listing, they are welcomed by Louis Rosenfeld at i-guides@umich.edu. Rosenfeld is a doctoral student and an instructor at the School of Information and Library Studies at the University of Michigan.

"I've been involved with the Net for about four years," Rosenfeld says. "I have that library perspective of understanding information, what's quality information, how do we design information so that people want to use it."

Rosenfeld began working for the university library as a Masters student a little after Gopher had just started to take off. "We were really hoping to work on building a subject-oriented Gopher," Rosenfeld says. "A lot of Gophers were just a list of things in a kind of incoherent organization." Rosenfeld decided to build a subject tree, an approach quite common in the computer world.

"We wanted to figure out ways to create that subject content," Rosenfeld says. He recruited students from the school for an independent study group and helped them identify areas of interest, from philosophy to German history.

"They went out and identified and described and evaluated the resources on the Internet in those areas," Rosenfeld says. "They created guides, or plain text documents that you could actually access. . . . We probably did some pioneering work in that area, not only identifying what was out there, but creating an information package that was more useable than say just a list of groups that had some thing to do with subject texts.

"There already were guides available . . . but what a lot of those did was just present a list of resources in a very haphazard fashion . . . here's all the user groups, here's all the FTP sites. . . . We felt that users were probably more interested in what the information was as opposed to the tool that delivered it. So, we were to identify organizational schemes for the information packages or guides. For example, if it was history it might be a chronological organization, if it was in computer science maybe there were organizational schemes used by that discipline already that we could utilize.

"A lot of the previous work in this area was just identifying what was there, and not trying to assess the value or the quality. In the early days, when there wasn't very much on the Net, that was fine. . . . Today, as time has moved on and as more information is available and more people are producing stuff, you need to do two things: you need to identify not only what's there, but assess it and evaluate it, the quality.

"You have to look at a listserv not only to look at it and tell people how to get to it, but to describe what kinds of discussion goes on there: [is it so] sophomoric or scholarly or high volume that you wouldn't want to bother subscribing? So we work in that area."

Rosenfeld says the task now is to focus in on a narrower domain. "One of the first batches these people did was one on philosophy. You could never really do a comprehensive guide to philosophy today, because there's just so much more information now. So I encourage them to not cast their nets so wide. I encourage getting in more depth in narrower areas."

When Rosenfeld returned to the faculty to take his Ph.D., he co-taught a course called "Internet Resource Discovery and Organization." Working in pairs, his students created about a dozen guides. "We found that they were working, on average, 20 hours a week apiece, and they were working in pairs, so this is quite addictive. One of the reasons it was successful was that, unlike the kind of work that many students might do in any kind of class, this work was more real for them because their work was made available to broad communities of users by the Internet. So, not only were our students producing a product, they were producing a product that was going to be used by many thousands of people, and it had the students' names on it.

"A little over a year ago, I decided it would make sense to pull together other guides that people had done that were subject-oriented, such as 'Electric Mystics' and 'Not Just Cows.'"

Adding other guides allowed students to look at them as examples. "The students now had even greater motivation to really produce quality and work hard because their guides were being used by other people on the Internet. And what I created was what I eventually called the Clearinghouse For Subject-Oriented Internet Resource Guide. If I did it again today, I would have picked a much shorter, better name. (I couldn't really think of anything [else] that late at night.)

"I pulled together probably 15 of these guides initially in August of 1993, and at the end of August, I got the monthly stats for our Gopher and noticed that 7,000 uses of those guides had been logged."

There had been no announcement, people just found it by themselves. "Just navigating and Net surfing and stumbling through serendipity," Rosenfeld says. "I decided to pursue that and make the Clearinghouse a real thing, and try to make it comprehensive . . . to try to include all the guides I could possibly find that were subject-oriented."

Rosenfeld continued his policy of creating narrow, focused, high-quality guides. "People would come to me at that time and say 'This is a good idea. Why don't you keep all the how-to guides on hand as well,' and I would say 'Well, that's another clearinghouse for someone else to do,' because the more you take on, the less quality it will be."

When Rosenfeld was interviewed in December, 1994, the Clearinghouse had 115,000 uses per month.

"There's a demand for what I call value-added repackaging of information on the Net," Rosenfeld says. It had, at that time, 150 guides, of which 25 were created by his students; the others came from other sources. "The fact that you put it together and standardize its presentation, and you make it available through major tools and you publicize it, makes it a very valuable resource," Rosenfeld says. "The sum is greater than the parts."

How do Rosenfeld and his students evaluate material on the Internet?

"It depends primarily on the audience," Rosenfeld says." We have our students find an audience, specific people who know the subject area, the type of people who use this information, and they have a sense of what they want and what constitutes quality."

These experts help the students do that kind of work when they create their guides. "What is quality, what are you looking to evaluate?" he says. "You want to evaluate things like currency: is the information up to date, is it kept updated? You want to evaluate information on authority: where does the information come from, is it an institution or an individual or entity or company or whatever that you trust? Is it the *National Enquirer* or *The New York Times*? So, authority is another big issue. What kind of audience are you dealing with? Are they scholars, are they practitioners, what kind of connectivity do they have?

"Right now, the class I'm doing now . . . we're having them do both HTML versions of their guides and in ASCII because you've got to think of your audience. State-of-the-art is HTML, it's cool and people really love it and it's fun, but I made them do ASCII versions because there's still a majority of people that are going to be accessing it through the VT-100 environment. So they can get just plain text versions.

"When you get into this issue of how do you do ASCII as opposed to HTML for the Web, you get into a lot of design issues. I changed the name of the course the second time around, what I'm just finishing teaching, to 'Internet Resource, Discovery, Organization, and Design'."

"You have to teach the class about design, because how you design these packages of information is very important.

"Those are issues you'd have to take into account when you're creating these guides. So that's actually another issue of how you evaluate information: on its design. Is it useable? For mailing lists and Usenet groups, we also add in things like the level of discussion, the nature of the people who seem to be participating, and the volume. That's really very important to people.

"We also evaluate on the presence or lack of *meta information*, that's information about the information, not the resource," Rosenfeld says. "You know that authority is important, you know that audience is important, you know that currency, all these things [are important], but you don't know what they are in a specific information resource unless there's meta information provided. In other words, something has to tell you who the authority is, who created the information. Something has to tell you how often it's updated. Something has to give you a little history. So that's meta information.

"The things I'm telling you are what librarians are known to be good at and what we learn in our professional training. This is the sort of thing that librarians have done institutionally for years. So that's the ways we look at evaluation.

"Then basically, [what you have to do] is solve the problem of design, where you've got markers and the GIFs and somebody wants to actually download something, and cite it."

The Internet is a lot different from three-by-five-card library catalogs.

Other subject-oriented sources:

`gopher://info.anu.edu.au`

The Electronic Library Internet Resources by subject

`gopher://watserv2.uwaterloo.ca`

Electronic Resources Around the World

University of Waterloo's Library Finding Information Area

Resources by Discipline.

National Libraries

The best places to start library research on the Internet are the great national libraries. They're often at the forefront of innovation on the connections between the Internet and libraries, and they often have connections to other libraries around the world.

U.S. Library of Congress

The United States Library of Congress is rapidly expanding the online services available on the Internet by adding World Wide Web services to the LC Marvel Gopher services that have been available for years. At this writing the Library of Congress Web site already has several special collections, links to exhibitions and events, and their topical digital library collections, a what's new review, and a review of the Library's services and publications.

The menu for Library of Congress services includes the U.S. Copyright Office, the National Library Service for the Blind and Physically Handicapped, Newspapers and Current Periodicals, the American Folklife Center, Library of Congress Publications, Cataloging Distribution Service (CDS) 1995 Sales Catalog, Library of Congress Publications from LC Marvel, Conferences and Seminars Sponsored by the Library of Congress, a Seminar on Cataloging Digital Documents, and Network Advisory Committee Network Planning Papers, and links to other United States federal and state government information (to be discussed again in Chapter 14). Figure 9-2 shows the Library of Congress WWW home page.

The LC Marvel Gopher contains links to information about the Library of Congress such as LC Marvel events, facilities, publications, and services; what's new on LC Marvel; research and reference resources, including public services; libraries and publishers technical services; copyright; Library of Congress employee information; U.S. Congress; broader government information; the Library of Congress LOCIS online system (the same system used by the U.S. Congress and their staff), the Library of Congress Anonymous FTP site, and the FEDLINK ALIX bulletin board system; a global electronic library (by subject); other Internet resources; and a way to search the LC Marvel Gopher menus. Figure 9-3 shows the top menu of the LC Marvel Gopher.

Figure 9-2.
The U.S. Library of Congress information is available on the World Wide Web

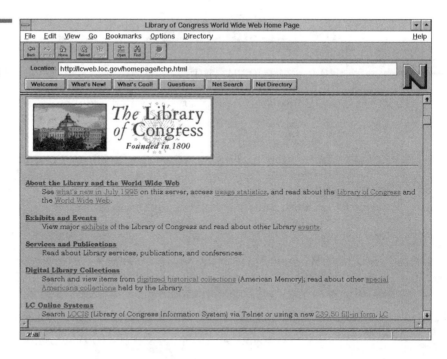

Figure 9-3.
The U.S. Library of Congress LC Marvel Gopher is linked to other information sources

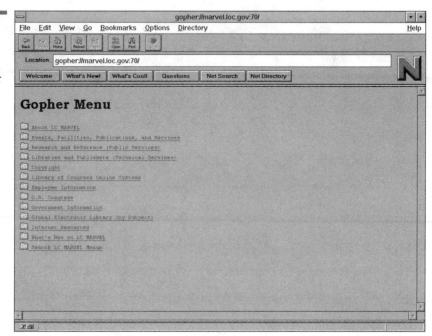

The National Library of Canada

Canada's National Library overlooks the Ottawa River just a couple of blocks from Parliament Hill. Electronically it can be found in English at http://www.nlc-bnc.ca/ehome.htm, although most of the library's services are available on its Gopher server: gopher://gopher.nlc-bnc.ca:70. Figure 9-4 shows the first page of the National Library of Canada's Web site.

The National Library's Web server has links to the NL Gopher, supplying information in English and French, about the National Library, Canadian libraries, and Canadian Internet resources. Canadian Information by Subject is a project under development that will provide subject access to Web sources of Canadian information. The Open Government Pilot, undertaken by Industry Canada, uses the Web to provide greater access to the Canadian government through information networks.

The library's Gopher server is a gateway to a large number of Canadian resources:

» Canadian library catalogues and Gopher servers

» Catalogues and Gopher servers, by geographic location

» Catalogues and Gopher servers, by type of library

» Ottawa/Hull libraries

» Federal library catalogues and Gopher servers

Figure 9-4.
The National Library of Canada Web home page.

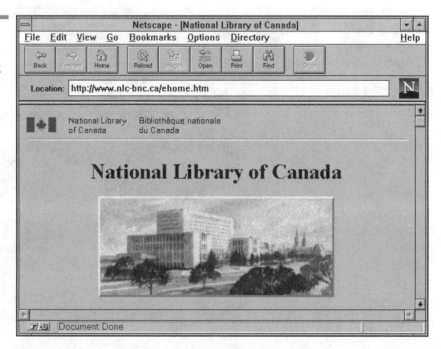

» Council of Federal Libraries

» List of Canadian Depository Libraries (via Statistics Canada)

» Directory of Canadian University Data Libraries and Archives

» Canadian resource sharing

» Canadian Library Association (via NCFreenet)

There is also a complete Gopher menu available in French with access to libraries across Canada. Figure 9-5 gives you a view of the library's Gopher menu.

Partial Gopher Menu

» Acadia University Library (catalogue)

» Brandon University Library (Manitoba)

» Concordia University Library (catalogue)

» Dalhousie University Library (Halifax)

» Electronic Library Network (ELN, British Columbia)

» Lakehead University Library (Thunder Bay, Ontario)

» Malaspina University-College Library (catalogue)

» Memorial University of Newfoundland Library (catalogue)

Figure 9-5.
The National Library of Canada Gopher links you to both information about libraries and to library catalogs.

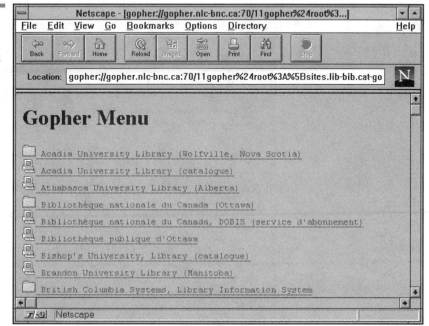

» National Library of Canada (Ottawa)

» Natural Resources Canada, Surveys, Mapping, and Remote Sensing Library

» Nova Scotia Provincial Library (catalogue)

» Ottawa Public Library

» Ryerson Polytechnic Institute Library Services (Toronto)

» Saskatoon Public Library (Saskatchewan)

» Technical University of Nova Scotia Library

» University College of Cape Breton Library (Nova Scotia)

» University of Saskatchewan Library

» York University Libraries (Toronto)

The British Library

The British Library is one of the world's oldest and best known national libraries. Although much of it is now in a modern building with ten million volumes in the London area known as St. Pancras, it was once part of the British Museum in Bloomsbury. Generations of scholars and researchers worked under the museum's great dome.

Figure 9-6.
The British Library Web page

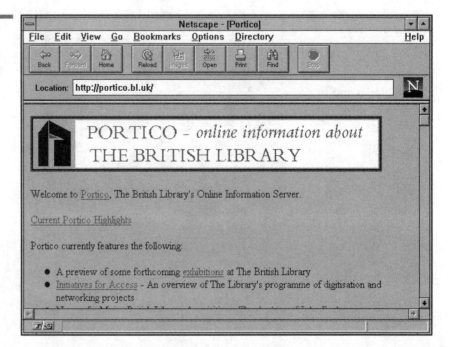

Now, like other national libraries, the British Library is working on getting wired. Its World Wide Web address is http://portico.bl.uk and its Gopher address is gopher://portico.bl.uk:70. Figure 9-6 shows the British Library's Web page.

Like many Internet computers, the British Library's computer has a special name—Portico, defined as "a row of columns supporting a roof around or at the entrance of a building."

The library says that since its Gopher service was launched on 27 July 1994 (notice how new everything is on the Internet?) over 370,000 transactions on the system have been logged and 120,000 text files retrieved by users. In the first week of the Portico WWW server (from 27 March 1995) there were some 20,000 hits. The library notes that it is still under construction and access to files is not yet complete.

The British Library Gopher uses text documents that gives access to directories of collections and other services. "They are dated at the end to show the currency of the information and provide contact points for further information."

The library's "Network OPAC" allows access to the major British Library catalogues, including the current science, music, and humanities files and the retrospective catalogue of holdings dating back to the beginning of printing. The library also recently added files on monographs bringing the total of computerized records to 6.5 million. The Network OPAC is now available over JANET, the U.K. Joint Academic Network. About 150 sites in Britain have access. It requires the installation of special client software. For information e-mail to jan.ashton@uk.bl.

Off the Net, the British Library is experimenting with electronic and multimedia storage of photographs and other documents. One project involves digitizing the original thousand-year-old manuscript of the Beowulf epic. Test images are available on the Internet and are available by anonymous FTP from the London server othello.bl.uk in the directory sys/pub/mss/beowulf and in Kentucky at beowulf.engl.uky.edu in the directory ftp/pub/beowulf.

The library is also scanning old newspapers onto optical disk as a replacement for microfilm, which will probably be a relief to the eyes of generations of researchers who have scanned miles of microfilm.

The British Library's Web server is also the gateway to other research resources in Britain, including Oxford's Bodleian Library. The gateway can be found at:

`http://portico.bl.uk/otherwww.html`

Internet Search Tools and General Guides to the World Wide Web

» The Virtual Tourist—WWW World Map

» WWW Servers in Europe—Country Maps

» Search the ALIWEB Database

» The Harvest Information Discovery and Access System

» Lycos: The Catalog of the Internet

» Yahoo: A Guide to WWW

» Bulletin Board for Libraries—BUBL

» NISS Information Gateway

» BARD—Bodleian Access to Remote Databases

» Global Network Navigator—GNN

» Exploring the Internet—University of York

—*From Portico:The British Library's Online Information Server*

The National Library of Australia

The National Library of Australia can be found at http://www.nla.gov.au. Australia's national library was also one of the pioneers in getting library resources on the Internet.

As shown in Figure 9-7, it has a well-developed World Wide Web server that not only has access to the National Library but to other Australian research sites around the world.

» Examples of Starting Points

Figure 9-7.
The National Library of Australia Web page

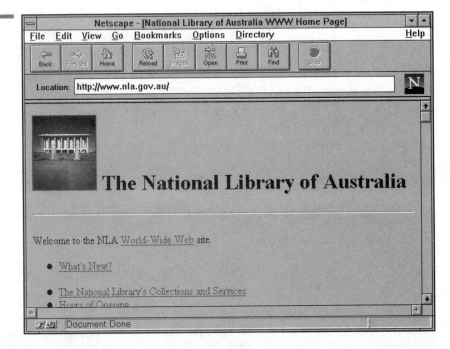

- » EINet galaxy
- » Entering the World Wide Web: A guide to Cyberspace
- » The Whole Internet Catalog (O'Reilly and Associates)
- » Internet Resources list (EIT)
- » Yanoff list (mirrored at Monash University, Melbourne, Australia)
- » Arrangements by Subject
- » WWW Virtual Library (by Subject) (CERN)
- » Clearinghouse for Subject-Oriented Internet Resource Guides (University of Michigan)
- » Web of Wonder
- » Joel's Hierarchical Subject Index
- » Interesting Sites
- » ITS top ten Internet sites
- » The Best of the Web (Buffalo)
- » Gopher Jewels
- » GNN Best of the Net

Online Net Access to Library Catalogs

Several efforts are going forward to provide library catalog access via the World Wide Web and Gopher Internet service protocols. This section details four collections of links to libraries all over the world. The next section provides a wide range of other library-related resources, including an example of how to find electronic mailing lists related to libraries (or anything or any other topic you might choose).

LIBCAT—Metronet

LIBCAT includes live hyperlinks to over a thousand libraries worldwide. LIBCAT has live Gopher and WWW links, and gives detailed access information about hundreds of public and special purpose libraries. It also includes the special collections at each library, so you can find resources that are available nowhere else. Figure 9-8 shows the LIBCAT home page.

LIBCAT also has special instructions for America Online (AOL) users so they can access LIBCAT through the AOL Gopher client. The URL for LIBCAT is:

`http://www.metronet.lib.mn.us:70/0h/vendor/maven/lc/lc1.html`

Figure 9-8.
LIBCAT at Metronet uses
a feline logo

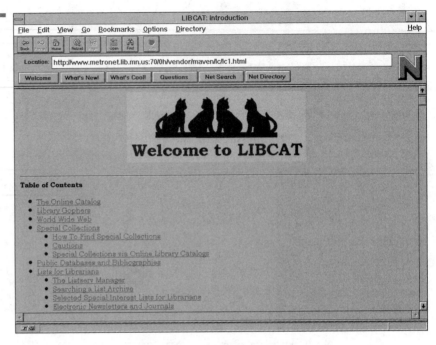

Library Catalogs with Web Interfaces

Another compilation of online library catalogs is at North Carolina State University, maintained by Eric Morgan. It includes a link to the unique database Morgan calls the *Alex Catalog of Electronic Texts on the Internet*, a database of about 1800 online books and other texts. Figure 9-9 shows the top of the *Library Catalogs with Web Interfaces* Web page. The URL for this site is:

```
http://www.lib.ncsu.edu/staff/morgan/alcuin/wwwed-catalogs.
     html
```

Library Information Servers via WWW—University of Washington

Thomas Dowling, tdowling@u.washington.edu, Networked Information Librarian at the University of Washington Libraries in Seattle, Washington, maintains a large list of hot links to Internet-accessible libraries and to information service companies on the Net. Figure 9-10 shows you the top of Thomas Dowling's *Library Information Servers* via WWW home page. The URL for Dowling's site is:

```
http://www.lib.washington.edu/~tdowling/libweb.html
```

Figure 9-9.

Eric Morgan's collection of library catalog hot links and electronic text site

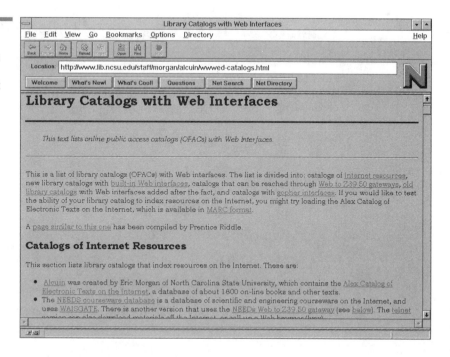

Figure 9-10.

Thomas Dowling has a large international set of Library Information Servers available via WWW

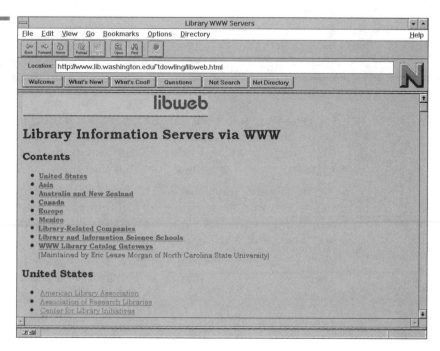

YaleInfo—Telnet College and University Library Access

YaleInfo, housed at Yale University, is a special Gopher allowing telnet access to hundreds of libraries throughout the electronic world. The top level menu allows you to choose from the following options:

» Africa

» Americas

» Asia and Pacific

» Europe and the Middle East

» Manuscript archives at Johns Hopkins University

» Instructions for how to use the various catalogs

» How to get a printed list of libraries

The listings under the Americas menu include seven locations:

» Brazil

» Canada

» Chile

» Mexico

» Puerto Rico

» United States

» Venezuela

When you select the Canada menu, you'll find over 60 direct telnet links to Canadian college and university libraries. Each link is accompanied by a text file that gives log-in and password information and any special instructions necessary, as well as contact information in case the system is not working.

The United States menu is further subdivided into menus for each of the states. For example, the states of California and Texas each have about 40 live telnet links to college and university libraries, and the states of Illinois, Michigan, and North Carolina each have about a dozen telnet links.

To access this Gopher, and make telnet connections to the many libraries available, point your Gopher or Web browser at the following URL:

```
gopher://libgopher.yale.edu:70/11/
```

For further information send e-mail to gophlib@libgopher.yale.edu. This resource is mirrored at the University of Texas at Dallas at this URL:

```
gopher://gopher.utdallas.edu:70/11/internet/Libraries
```

It is also mirrored with additional live links to active library bulletin board systems at the Swedish University Network Gopher:

```
gopher://gopher.sunet.se:70/11/Libraries/yaleinfo
```

An ASCII text version of this resource can also be retrieved by anonymous FTP from ftp://ftp.utdallas.edu:/pub/staff/billy/libguide/. Be sure to *check the date* to see if it is up-to-date enough for your research purposes.

Other Library Resources on the Internet

This section provides the Internet researcher with a variety of library resources. Library networks in Belgium and Britain; medical library and legal library hot link collections; the international ISSN serials network; literary, reference, and special collections hot links; as well as research library organizations are all available on the Internet.

Belnet—Belgian Academic Network

In 1994 a workgroup representing libraries and documentation centers in Belgium was set up to point to different library-related resources on the Internet. It includes links to information about library catalogues, information about Belgian library projects, library WWW and Gopher servers, library-related WWW experiments (including WWW gateways to library catalogues), standards for library and information systems, library organizations, library system suppliers, proceedings from library conferences, and a calendar of forthcoming events (congresses, courses, workshops). Figure 9-11 shows you the Belnet User Forum Workgroup on Libraries opening page. The URL for the Belnet User Forum Workgroup on Libraries is:

```
http://www.ua.ac.be/WGLIB/root.html
```

Figure 9-11.
Belnet's User Forum
Workgroup on Libraries
provides links about
library information
worldwide

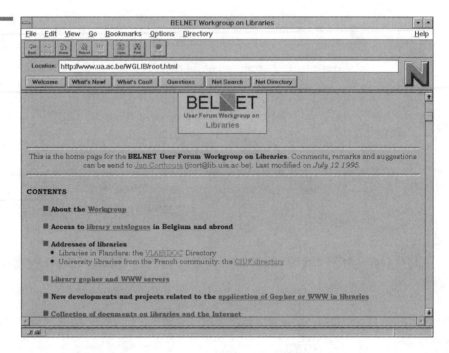

British Association for Information and Library Education and Research—Bailer

Bailer is an association of all teaching and research staff in the 17 information and library schools and departments in universities in the United Kingdom and the Republic of Ireland. Bailer maintains a Web page on the Internet at this URL:

```
http://epip.lut.ac.uk:80/bailer/
```

The Bailer Web page includes links to librarian affairs and resources throughout the United Kingdom and Ireland, and has links to schools of information and library science in the United States.

Project Bartleby: The Public Library of the Internet

Columbia University's Project Bartleby allows you to access hypertext books from the other side of the planet without leaving your desk. Here is the list of literary and other documents now available:

» Bartlett, John. 1901. *Familiar Quotations*, 9th ed.

» Chapman, George, trans. 1857. *The Odysseys of Homer.*

» Dickinson, Emily. 1896. Poems.

» Inaugural Addresses of the Presidents of the United States, 1989.

» Keats, John. 1884. Poetical Works.

» *Melville, Herman. 1853. Bartleby, the Scrivener. A Story of Wall-Street.*

» Shelley, Percy Bysshe. 1901. Complete Poetical Works.

» Strunk, William, Jr. 1918. *The Elements of Style.*

» Whitman, Walt. 1900. *Leaves of Grass.*

» Wilde, Oscar. 1881. Poems.

» Wordsworth, William. 1888. Complete Poetical Works.

Project Bartleby also includes a search engine to scan all of these books for words of your choice. This allows researchers to rapidly identify texts and page numbers that might be of interest. The URL for this project is:

`http://www.cc.columbia.edu/acis/bartleby/`

Electronic Information Service—University of North Carolina

The Reference Department of Davis Library at the University of North Carolina at Chapel Hill provides this Electronic Information Service. This service includes electronic journal and electronic text collections, Web pages of other libraries and library catalog access throughout the world, state and federal document collections, as well as unique databases only available at the University of North Carolina. To access this resource, point your Web browser to:

`http://sunsite.unc.edu/reference/`

InfoSurf Library Gopher—University of California, Santa Barbara

This Gopher includes links to reference materials, special collections, electronic journals, library tutorials (how to use the catalog, and so on), and over 70 links to other library Gophers. It also includes Telnet access to the LC Marvel Gopher at the U.S. Library of Congress, the Los Angeles Public Library, and the YaleInfo collection of Telnet library resources mentioned previously.

Law Library Catalogs—Rutgers University

Rutgers University School of Law at Newark maintains a set of hyperlinks to other law libraries and government resources on the Internet. The URL for this legal resource is:

`http://www.rutgers.edu/lawschool.html`

U.S. National Library of Medicine

The U.S. National Library of Medicine maintains a hypertext multimedia Web presence at this URL:

`http://www.nlm.nih.gov/`

It includes a listing of what is new on the service, hours of operation of the regular facilities, maps and instructions on finding and using services, conference announcements, telephone and e-mail contact lists, and several links to other medical reference sources. Figure 9-12 shows the opening page for the U.S. National Library of Medicine.

Figure 9-12.
The National Library of Medicine links you to their own and other Internet resources

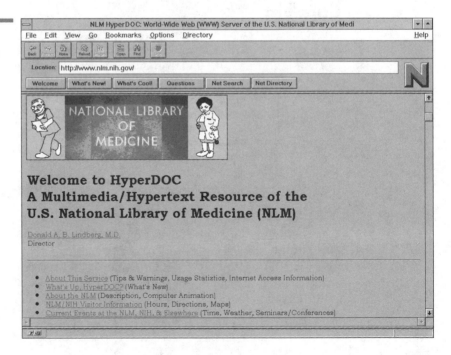

The U.S. National Library of Medicine also makes available a recent report on the preparation of health science librarians at this URL:

`http://www.nlm.nih.gov/ep.dir/rfa_libr_training.dir/title.html`

Research Library Organizations

There are also two large organizations that serve research libraries available on the Net. They are the Association of Research Libraries (ARL), and Research Libraries Group, Inc. (RLG). Each has a Web presence.

Association Of Research Libraries—ARL

ARL identifies and influences forces affecting the future of research libraries in the process of scholarly communication. ARL is comprised of libraries that serve major North American research institutions. ARL maintains a Gopher at this URL:

`gopher://arl.cni.org:70/11/arl`

Research Libraries Group, Inc.—RLG

The Research Libraries Group, Inc. (RLG) is a not-for-profit membership corporation of universities, archives, historical societies, museums, and other institutions. RLG is devoted to improving access to information that supports research and learning. RLG was founded in 1974 by Harvard, Yale, and Columbia universities and The New York Public Library.

As of 1995, RLG is an international alliance of more than 140 members providing sophisticated technical resources worldwide. RLG's *Eureka* search system and RLG's *Ariel* document delivery service over the Internet are two of these advanced services to watch in the future. The URL for the RLG home page is:

`http://www-rlg.stanford.edu/welcome.html`

Library Mailing Lists

Hundreds of library-related mailing lists populate the Internet. Reference librarians work together to solve their toughest assignments on the list Stumpers-L, government document librarians communicate on GOVDOC-L, librarians in New York communicate on NYSLAA-L, and southeast Asian librarians use SEALIB-S. To get a large list of Internet mailing lists (around 200) about libraries and librarianship, send an e-mail message to the LISTSERV server at Nodak, LISTSERV@vm1.nodak.edu, with the following message:

```
list global /librar
```

The list you'll get back gives the name and address of almost all library-related LISTSERV lists. Of course, if you're looking for LISTSERV lists on any other topic, all you do is substitute the other topic for the *librar* in this search.

Most of these mailing lists maintain archives that can be searched for research that has already been done on any topic you choose. For example, the reference librarian's Stumpers-L Archive, at Concordia University in Illinois, is available by Gopher at this URL:

```
gopher://gopher.cuis.edu:70/11gopher_root2%3A%5Bstumpers-1%5D
```

The Gopher at Concordia University also contains the instructions for subscribing to Stumpers-L.

10

Stop Signs on the Infobahn

In late 1994, an ad for a nanny appeared on many of the Internet's job-hunting newsgroups. A family in Northern Ireland with five children wanted a nanny who would "be prepared to take on their ways, watch them, read to them, teach them, learn from them, hug them, tickle them, play with them, control them, serve them and especially love them. . . ." The ad had a condition of employment: "Females only please, no junkies! Nationality or standard English doesn't matter."

This ad, with its "females only" qualification, appeared across North America and, thus, violated sex discrimination laws in many states and provinces. The Northern Ireland Equal Opportunities Office Commission says the ad also is illegal there.

The Internet is international. Information crosses national boundaries in the flick of an eye. The law is far behind, treading its measured pace as it has for centuries. Cases grind their slow way through the courts while information flies around the world at the speed of light.

Researchers working on the Internet must be aware of the law. If they are working internationally, or if they post something that could appear in another country, researchers should at least be aware of the differences in law between their own country and other nations.

This chapter uses a broad definition of the term "research," and it assumes that the information included in your research will eventually either be published in hardcopy or posted on the Net. The problems of research and publication faced by investigative reporters are—when it comes to the Internet—similar to those faced by academic and other researchers. Thus, we are taking a traditional approach, one used in journalism and law schools. We'll look at the significant cases involving the law and the Internet and use those cases to illustrate how the Net is facing new legal challenges. Since there are, as yet, no definitive rulings from courts, case law is the only guide available for researchers and writers.

Crimes are being committed on the Internet. Or are they crimes? Promoting hatred is a crime in many countries. In the United States, where the First Amendment to the Constitution protects almost all forms of free speech, promoting hatred is not a crime (acting on hatred, of course, is a crime in any jurisdiction).

What should rule the Internet? Net culture or Common Law? If law, whose law? Can the Internet be policed? What happens when the outside world collides with the Internet? When that collision occurs—and it has—existing law is being used, however awkwardly, to decide questions of copyright, libel, and censorship. Those laws will continue to be used until the politicians, lawyers, and judges catch up. Something similar happened many years ago, when the automobile first appeared on the streets. In the case of a fatal accident in those days, police in many jurisdictions automatically charged the driver with manslaughter. That was before vehicular homicide, criminal negligence, dangerous driving, or drunk driving laws appeared on the books.

Caution

This chapter reports on the legal questions facing Internet researchers. It does not contain specific legal advice, especially because the Internet crosses state, provincial, and national boundaries.

If needed, you should obtain legal advice only from a lawyer licensed to practice in your jurisdiction. You should seek a lawyer who is both competent in the specialized area you are concerned with and who has some knowledge of the Internet and computers. That lawyer should be able to protect your rights and explain your responsibilities.

A researcher working on the Internet—especially a researcher publishing on the Net itself or in traditional media such as journals, books, newspapers, or television—should be aware of the following areas of law:

» Copyright

» Patent law

» Trade secrets

» Defamation (libel and slander)

» Misrepresentation (sometimes called "identity hacking" on the Internet)

» Censorship (obscenity and court-imposed publication bans)

Cyberlaw

In 1995, only a handful of lawyers in each Western country practice what has been called "cyberlaw." Some of those lawyers are already debating who can use the term "cyberlaw."

Anita Brenner, a lawyer practicing in Pasadena, California, reported in her newsletter, "Cyberlaw IX: The Howling," that there already was a Cyberlaw listserv run by Professor Trotter Hardy of the Marshall-Wythe School of Law, College of William and Mary. Brenner reports that Cyberlaw "ran afoul" of an online educational service with the already trademarked names Cyberlaw and Cyberlex, run by Jonathan Rosener. The listserv has been changed to Cyberia-l.

The Internet began in the United States, and it's likely that the future legal shape of the Net will be decided in the United States. "By far the majority of traffic is generated and circulated in the United States, so current practice is often shaped by U.S. policies and law," says Arnold-Moore, of the University of Melbourne Law School in his World Wide Web site called "The Legal Pitfalls in Cyberspace." Nevertheless, some of the most important cases, at least in the areas of libel and censorship, have taken place outside the United States. Net-watching lawyers in both the United States and in other countries know of those cases, even if their more paper-bound colleagues do not.

In the United States, at least one case of alleged libel has taken place on the Internet. This case, involving a Washington-based journalist, Brock Meeks, and Suarez Corporation, was settled before going to trial. The first case of libel on the Internet to be heard by a court took place in Western Australia in 1994. It involved two anthropologists named David Rindos and Gilbert Hardwick. A third case, still pending, will take place in Great Britain. There are other cases, not on the Internet itself, that could determine how libel is defined in the online world. Two key cases are in the United States: *Cubby versus CompuServe* and a case pending against Prodigy.

Copyright has always been a vexing question online. Software piracy is the best known, but researchers face more troubling questions. Often material is taken from one source, repeated on the Net, and then reposted. A common, although illegal, practice is to grab material from a wire service or newspaper database and repost it, without permission, on a mailing list or newsgroup. The information usually crosses international boundaries. Material posted by an American can appear in France or Japan. What happens to copyright law then? What happens when something originating in the United States is downloaded, copied, and printed in France? Or vice versa?

Pressure to censor the Internet has begun to build. There's a battle brewing in the United States over the censorship of the Internet. In June 1995, the United States Senate passed Senator James Exon's "Decency in Communications Act," which aims at controlling sexually explicit communications over the Internet, commercial online services and bulletin boards. The Senate passed the bill after explicit material was downloaded and shown on the Senate floor. The bill holds responsible those who originate such messages.

This bill, however, may run into opposition from the House of Representatives since House Speaker Newt Gingrich says it is probably unconstitutional, stating it's "clearly a violation of free speech and it's a violation of the right of adults to communicate with each other."

At the same time Senator Exon was introducing his bill in the United States, a Canadian criminal court imposed a publication ban on the details of a controversial murder case involving two suspects named Paul Bernardo and Karla Homolka. The ban proved almost impossible to enforce on the Internet (and hard to enforce as well on commercial services like Genie). The failure of the ban (at least as far as the Internet is concerned) in the Homolka/Bernardo case shows how hard it is to censor the net.

Whose law applies?

The cautious answer from lawyers in the United States, Canada, and Australia is, *it depends*. Whether it's a criminal matter, a case of copyright infringement, or libel a local court will have to decide whether it has jurisdiction in the case. Important to the plaintiff in a civil case is whether the defendant has assets in that country to make it worthwhile to sue.

If the politicians do not intervene and create written laws, the question will probably be decided case by case. The Internet is, at present, most popular in countries whose legal traditions are based on English Common Law: the United States, Canada, the United Kingdom, and Australia. Common Law is based on the collected wisdom of judges, and the idea of precedent. Newer decisions are most often based on earlier cases, hence the importance of decisions by a country's Supreme Court. So, in theory, and allowing for local statute law, the libel case in Australia could act as a guide for a judge in the United States or

Canada. It should be noted that the word *guide* is important. Computer law is so new that no online case in any country has yet reached a court that can give a decision binding on other judges.

The growing popularity of the Internet makes the international situation even more complicated when you add European countries (plus the state of Louisiana and the province of Quebec) that have a different legal tradition known as Civil Law, based on the Napoleonic Code. The situation is further complicated with the emerging electronic giants in Asia: Japan, Taiwan, Singapore, and the People's Republic of China. The law in Asian countries is based largely on their own cultural and legal traditions together with some of the laws imposed by European colonial powers. (In the winter of 1995, the United States imposed trade sanctions on the People's Republic of China in response to China's widespread and profitable pirating industry that copies movies, compact discs, and computer software worth millions of dollars.)

So what does a researcher have to know? This chapter outlines the basic law a researcher should understand. But advice can be summed up as common sense. Don't take and copy any significant amount of material that has been created by someone else. If you're going to use material from the Internet as part of something you are publishing, get permission first. Don't defame another person; don't get carried away in a nasty flame war. Otherwise you might find yourself in court, either in your home town, or somewhere far away.

The Long Arm of the Law

Laws existed before the Internet, before the world of computers, but is now colliding with computers and the Internet myth—the ethic that "anything goes" on the electronic frontier. So even the most innocent posting may now result in the "long arm of the law" reaching into that basement with a lot more than a slap on the wrist. For years, the Internet was largely a private preserve for university and industry researchers, students, hackers, power users, and other Net nerds. They created their own anarchistic Net culture.

There's only one problem. A lot of new folks have just cruised into this electronic town, and they've brought along a sheriff and deputies and judges to tame the frontier.

"What I find is a feeling that [the people on the Internet] are pioneers, and therefore they are doing something that is great for the world," says Robert Wilkes, a Toronto-based lawyer who specializes in computer law. "And because they are doing something that is great, they should be allowed to do whatever they please. That is not necessarily so. What you're finding is a problem of respecting the laws that exist. . . . You buy a computer and you sit in your basement and you have access to the world. Because you're in your home and you're working on your computer, you think there are no laws. It's your own place . . . people do not understand that they fit within the laws that are out there. Freedom of speech is not an unlimited right; it never has been. It's very strong in the United States and it's very strong in Canada. But," Wilkes adds, "that brings us to libel and slander. You're not allowed to say anything you want. Just because you're in your basement and there's no one around, you're not allowed to broadcast to everyone in the world misinformation about other people."

Ignoring the law because one is online is what Wilkes calls "the concept of willful blindness," whether it's copying something illegally or participating in a flame war. "You just decide that you're not going to look, [but that stance] in our law does not get you out of responsibility."

Dan Burk, a law professor at George Mason University in Arlington, Virginia, has a similar view on Net culture and the law. "Right now there's an enormous amount of copyright violation going on on the Internet, frequently very innocent," Burk says. "The Internet grew up as a scientific tool. Scientists tend to exchange data very freely; it's part of the scientific norms or culture. They don't tend to stop and think about copyright or other sorts of problems. This culture says 'here's a great news article' and they just send it out. The [U.S.] Copyright Act provides statutory damages for each act of infringement. You send a *New York Times* article to 100,000 people on the Internet—the *Times* is not going to appreciate that. They don't have to prove actual damage. All they have to do is show you've infringed, and they can get a statutory amount and you could be liable for hundreds of thousands or millions of dollars under those provisions. So people have to be aware."

Copyright

Copyright laws exist, in most cases, to protect the people who have created something, whether it is a poem, a book like this one, a movie, or a piece of software. The need for copyright grew out of the Gutenberg revolution. Printing allowed the reproduction of books. The people who created books—and whose income depended on those books—needed protection to make sure that someone else would not print their book and make off with the profits.

Today the "right to copy" has been translated into the legalese of the United States Copyright Act to say:

Copyright protection subsists . . . in original works of authorship fixed in any tangible medium of expression, now known or later developed, from which they can be perceived, reproduced, or otherwise communicated, either directly or with the aid of a machine or device.

In a simpler definition in the Canadian Copyright Act, copyright is determined to be:

the sole right to produce or reproduce the work or any substantial part thereof in any material form whatever, to perform . . . the work or any substantial part thereof in public or if the work is unpublished the work or any substantial part thereof. . . .

Two international treaties, known as the Berne Convention and the Universal Copyright Convention, govern much worldwide copyright law. More than one hundred countries, including the United States and Canada, have signed these treaties. They give U.S. authors protection in the United States, and some protection in other countries. This is known to lawyers as "national treatment," meaning that the rights of a foreign author in the United States are the same as those granted to a U.S. citizen and vice versa.

Copyright laws, and laws governing patents (protecting inventors) and trade secrets (protecting something being developed by an individual, institution, or company), cover what is known as *intellectual property*. Normally, the author of a work has copyright. If there are two or more authors (as in the case of this book), then the authors have "joint ownership" under copyright law. If a person creating a work is an employee, then usually the company that employs that person is the "author" for purposes of copyright. The employee, under U.S. law, is doing what is called "work for hire."

In most countries, an author's copyright exists from the moment of the creation of the work. The United States only recognized that right in the 1970s, with the passage of a new Copyright Act. The U.S. Copyright Act now states that "unpublished works are eligible for protection without regard to the nationality or domicile of the author." If, however, you wish to register your copyright once a work is published, U.S. law says, "works that are published in the United States are subject to mandatory deposit in the Library of Congress." To register a copyright, it is mandatory to deposit a publication with the Library of Congress; but you still have copyright protection for works even if you don't register your copyright. In Canada, on the other hand, there is no requirement for a copyright holder to register a work, although the Canadian Copyright Office does provide a registration service.

So what does this mean in the electronic world of the Internet? Robert Wilkes says, "It's not . . . that we don't have the laws, it's a matter of enforcing them and having people respect them. Copyright violations exist on the Internet and other online services because it's so easy to access the services and just too easy to copy something. "There's also the attitude that there is no law that applies. What we need," he emphasizes, "is an attitude shift, which comes from education . . . the public needs a way of knowing what they are allowed to do and not allowed to do. System operators and people who post material on the Internet must also find a way to make it easy for people to comply with copyright law.

Most of the civil violations of copyright law, which are resolved by lawsuits, come from software piracy although in at least one case copyright violation arose from the posting of excerpts from recorded music on CompuServe. Criminal violations, which result in police raids and criminal charges, have come from pirating software. Most researchers will not be involved in either situation.

Screen Display versus Hard Copy

Both U.S. and Canadian copyright laws are designed to protect things that exist in material form, Brian Macleod Rogers (a Toronto-based lawyer) says. The first question a lawyer asks is whether merely displaying material form on a screen is sufficient to meet traditional copyright criterion.

"What's meant by material form? There's no question that when you make a copy of something, when you turn on the LaserJet and produce something hard, that you're copying. A strong argument could be made that you're copying if you download it. . . . Certainly taking a file and putting it somewhere on your system puts it in a material form. But just putting it up on the screen, when you're searching for the data you want, is a different matter," Rogers says. "I don't think under the present law that it would be covered."

Michael Jacobs, a San Francisco lawyer specializing in intellectual property issues in the computer world, agrees. He compares reading something on a computer screen to browsing in a bookstore. A person can go into a book store and browse, without intending to pay for the magazine or book unless there's something that person considers worth buying.

In most cases, at this point, this legal dilemma shouldn't affect a researcher. Downloading or printing for your own use is covered by the fair use provisions of copyright law. The problem arises when material is systematically distributed in whatever form, to others.

The first step, explains Jacobs, is to determine why something was put on the Internet in the first place. Commercial databases such as Dialog or Lexis/Nexis post material with the consent of the copyright owner. Not only that, they can charge you whenever you access the service and pay the producer a royalty fee. "If a company allows downloading, it is implied that there is permission to transmit and make at least a second copy," Jacobs says. "The people who generally place material on the Internet are making it available to the public. Government and other information is often provided for free. The best way to protect yourself is to not make the information available on the Internet."

Often material that is posted on the Internet allows copying for personal use but requires permission for commercial reproduction. A problem arises once a researcher either redistributes the material to colleagues or completes the research and publishes the material.

Copyright law allows researchers a great deal of latitude, but researchers should also be aware that, if they use material from international sources, the laws may also have significant differences.

Fair Use—Fair Dealing

In the United States copyright rules allow someone to collect material for research or to quote short passages. This is known as *fair use*; in Canada it's known as *fair dealing*. Michael Jacobs says researchers have the fair-use right to copy limited material off the Net, without infringing on copyright law. On fair use, Section 107 of the U.S. Copyright Act allows copying "for purposes such as criticism, comment, news reporting, teaching (including multiple copies for classroom use), scholarship or research." Section 27 of the Canadian Copyright Act allows "any fair dealing for purposes of private study, research, criticism, review or newspaper summary."

The difference between the two acts is small, but significant. Canadian law does not consider a teacher using multiple copies in a classroom to be fair dealing. That could mean that if a teacher in either country retrieves material from a U.S. Gopher site, it can be copied and distributed to a class. If it comes from a Canadian gopher site, the teacher may need permission, unless, as is common on some Internet sites, a notice allows reproduction for non-commercial use. Fair use is a common defense to action for copyright infringement. If a user successfully proves something is covered by fair use or fair dealing, then there is no legal obligation to get permission or to pay royalties.

"The United States and other countries have similar provisions on fair use," Dan Burk says. "In the U.S., the four factors for fair use are:

1. How much of the work was taken? Did you take some excerpts from the article or did you republish the whole thing? There's a traditional example used by most experts. It's acceptable under fair use to reprint a few lines from a book, but reproducing a few lines from a short work, such as a poem or a song, requires permission from the copyright owner.

2. What kind of a work is it? Is it something that was intended to be freely shared like a piece of shareware, or is it something written by the *New York Times* or by someone as part of their livelihood?

3. The next thing the courts are going to look for—the biggest thing they're going to look at—is what does it do to the market for this

item? If you have taken a piece of software, and have spread it around the network to a thousand people, a thousand people are not going to go out and buy that product. That's a biggie, that question of the market.

4. If people want to quote something, they should not take the whole thing. They need to think about who they're sending it to, how big a group they're sending it to. It may be enough to say there's a really great article in the *New York Times* today; why not look it up?

But what is fair use in the case of an online service or bulletin board? So far no cases before the courts have tackled that issue.

Sharing Reference Material

It's common for researchers to share material among members of a research team. So what happens if someone downloads a document from an Internet site and then redistributes it among colleagues?

"There may be a point at which someone is in breach of copyright," Brian Macleod Rogers says. "It's not clear at the point of a researcher sharing material with other members of the research team. If they download something into their hard drive and communicate to others within an office or within the company or outside and they get caught in the copying and redistribution. . . ."

It appears that the number of copies and how the material is used may be relevant. In a recent U.S. case, *American Geophysical Union vs. Texaco*, Texaco was accused of violating copyright laws when its company researchers and librarians photocopied complete articles from scientific or technical journals. Texaco distributed the journals to its research employees, and let them make copies and keep them in their files.

The American Geophysical Union and 82 other publishers of scientific journals sued Texaco. The publishers were members of Copyright Clearance Center, Inc., an agency that collected fees for photocopying. The Copyright Clearance Center administers the fee-for-usage process in the United States. Texaco had not obtained a license from the clearance center but claimed in its defense that its copying was fair use.

The lawyers picked a test subject at random to represent all the photocopying done by Texaco employees, and a lower court found that the wholesale copying of articles for commercial research purposes did violate U.S. fair use law, because Texaco could easily have obtained permission from the journals themselves or through the Copyright Clearance Center.

The case was appealed to the U.S. Court of Appeals, Second Circuit, in Manhattan. Chief Judge Jon O. Newman upheld the lower court, ruling that creating the copies was not fair use "because the dominant purpose of the use is 'archival'—to assemble a set of papers for future reference, thereby serving the same purpose for which additional subscriptions are nominally sold, or for which photocopying licenses may be obtained."

What then of the Internet, where electronic journals are appearing and where copying is so much easier? Both Michael Jacobs and Heather Rafter, another San Francisco lawyer who watches computers and the law, say the Texaco case, which is expected to go to the United States Supreme Court, will eventually have a bearing on copying material from the Internet, especially if the material is distributed from hard drive to hard drive or accessible to many people on a Local Area Network. Rafter recommends getting permission from the copyright holder before any distribution.

Already some organizations are already charging—or metering out—for Internet services and some service providers charge by the byte for incoming and outgoing data. Michael Jacobs says there may eventually be some form of metering of the physical transfer of information on the Internet. "But," he warns, "there are serious pricing issues." Most information on the Internet is now free, and he wonders if people will pay when there are available alternatives such as public libraries or book stores.

Reproduction and Quoting

The best advice is to get permission before quoting a substantial amount of any material, whether it's from a book or from the Internet, and whether you're going to use it on the Internet itself or quote it in a newspaper, magazine article, or book.

"There is the general defense to copyright infringement," Brian Macleod Rogers says. "Is there substantial taking of a work? If you really taking a few paragraphs out of a much longer work, then it doesn't amount to a substantial amount if it's a lengthy work. Obviously, if it's a two-stanza poem, that would be different. On the Internet we have all those traditional copyright rules applied to a different setting. The real question for copyright issues is that it's really difficult for people to keep track of illegal infringement of copyright on the Internet. When you take something from a [commercial] database, obviously that's traceable and for some databases you have to pay. But once you've got [data], where you send it to on the Internet is anybody's guess. It's like a groundhog, only when its head pops above the ground, does anyone know. Meanwhile, there are a thousand tunnels of communication where there may have been some infringement."

The most common violation of copyright on the Internet is what is called "leakage" of newspaper or wire service articles, pulled from an online service and then reposted. In late 1994, at least one individual apologized in a widely posted message for reposting Associated Press dispatches. More and more wire service, television, and newspaper stories are appearing online. The official position of the Associated Press (AP) is that all the material is copyrighted.

When it comes to postings from individuals, it's considered good netiquette to request permission to repost an e-mail letter or Usenet article. It's very tempting simply to hit the "forward" button and send a notice to a destination where it wasn't originally intended to go. At the very least, it's polite to carbon copy the repost to the original sender to let that person know where it went. "It's a general principal that should apply anyway, to protect yourself," Roger says. "It's not required for private study or research, but when you publish it's obviously recommended and it is the traditional ethic for anybody in the academic world. You have footnotes coming out your ear." (Although in academic tradition, footnotes are mandatory, in some forms of popular writing footnotes are considered a barrier to communication. It's the researcher/writer's call.)

Citing Online References

The academic community has not yet come to an agreement on a style for citing references found online on the Internet. However, one suggested style is beginning to emerge:

```
Author, Date, Title, Periodical (if any), Available:
(Path)
```

For example:

Arnold-Moore, Tim, 1994, Legal Pitfalls in Cyberspace: Defamation on Computer Networks [Online] Available: World Wide Web http//144.110.144.11/law/defame.html

For more information see *Electronic Style: A Guide to Citing Electronic Information* by Xia Li and Nancy Crane, published in 1995 by Meckler.

Plagiarism

The worst form of copyright violation is, of course, plagiarism, the deliberate theft of someone else's work and passing it off as one's own. Something new has begun since the introduction of the personal computer, often called "cut and paste plagiarism." It's probably already occurred on the Internet, because it is so easy to cut and paste using any kind of word processor; it's also easy to be tempted to plagiarize. Often that plagiarism is deliberate, carried out for whatever reason—laziness, stupidity, lack of time—a deliberate theft. Some people, however, are warning that there is a danger of inadvertent plagiarism when fingers slip and material is inserted into a word processing file and its origin lost. The best advice again is to be careful. If you cut and paste material, make sure there is some note of its original source. If you are using a Microsoft Windows application, drag and drop from the original window to a destination window, rather than using a blind Clipboard. Again, if there is a substantial amount of material, get permission from the original author.

Moral Rights

Another aspect of copyright that Net researchers must be aware of is *moral rights*—the right of a creator to protect the integrity of a work. For a nation that prides itself on freedom of expression and its First Amendment, moral rights are strangely weakest in the United States. At present, the United States considers "economic rights" to be more important than "moral rights" as far as authors and other creators are concerned.

"The United States has joined the Berne Convention, so technically we give moral rights, but we really don't," says Dan Burk. "We've done piecemeal things that recognize certain aspects of moral rights. But the rights you would think of as moral rights, such as integrity or attribution, don't really exist as such in the United States. With some exceptions for visual artists, those kind of rights are very thin in the United States."

Moral rights came to the public attention in the United States in the fight over the colorization of old movies—directors wanted to preserve the look of the old black-and-white movies. The owners of the rights to movies wanted to use computers to add color to the old black-and-white frames—and in most cases, the owners won. The controversy resulted in the Visual Artists Rights Act of 1990 that gives American visual artists limited moral rights to their work. Some Americans have also argued that distortion of their work can be redressed by defamation law. They argue that substantial distortion or destruction of a work can damage an artist's reputation.

Moral rights go beyond the prevention of copying. The laws that exist in most countries outside the United States guarantee certain rights to a creator. European countries following the Civil Law tradition define the protection of moral rights as a basic human right. A work is an extension of the creator's personality, thus Civil Law considers a distortion of a created work to be an attack on the creator. Canada, a Common Law country, has a strong moral rights clause in its Copyright Act, and the courts have upheld the moral rights of artists in battles with big corporations that have bought and then attempted to modify their work. There are three components to moral rights:

» **Right of Paternity.** The right of paternity is the right of the creator of a work to claim authorship, to remain anonymous, or to use a pseudonym or pen name.

» **Right of Integrity.** This is the right of the creator to prevent the modification, mutilation, or destruction of a work.

» **Right of Association.** This is the right of the creator to prevent the use of a work if it is associated with a product, service, cause, or institution. This is similar to the right granted to television and sports personalities to protect their name from being used as product endorsements without permission.

"Again, researchers have to be aware. You may be able to put things on the Net in the U.S. and it would be perfectly legal, but it could contravene Canadian or European moral rights laws," says Virginia law professor Dan Burk.

"You have to look at a practical situation," Robert Wilkes says. "If you're creating software that was designed to be used in a functional way on an accounting system, your moral rights are not going to be strong. [The program] was meant to be modified, it was meant to be passed on. If, on the other hand, you are creating some form of artistic work that just happens to be transmitted through a computer, then you may get a very strong moral right." The United States has what is known as "first sale doctrine" that, with some exceptions, allows someone who has bought a copyrighted work to dispose of it any way he or she sees fit. The two exceptions to this rule are, interestingly enough, computer programs and recordings, both of which can be digitally copied.

So where do researchers or other people using the Net have to be aware of moral rights? The most frequently cited example is the use of computer-generated art that can be easily modified using either a paint or morphing program. If someone takes another artist's work off an Internet FTP site in Canada, Europe, or any country that protects its citizen's moral rights, and then modifies the file, technically that is a violation of moral rights. Similarly, if someone takes a copyright text file, and uses a substantial portion, that is a violation of copyright. If someone distorts or mutilates that file in some way, that would be a violation of moral rights. So again, the lawyers caution, forget Net practice and don't take, use, or distort any files that don't belong to you.

Neighboring Rights

Neighboring rights are a subset of moral rights, protected by the international treaty known as the Rome Convention. Copyright has traditionally protected the author of a work. Neighboring rights are rights granted to those who use a literary property to create a work, usually a performance of some kind. In Europe, neighboring rights are usually granted to performers and producers of sound recordings, performers of audiovisual works, and to broadcasters such as television stations.

In the United States, the rights of performers and producers of sound recordings are already protected under copyright law. Neither the United States nor Canada are signatories to the Rome Convention although Canada recently announced plans to introduce neighboring rights legislation.

Where do neighboring rights apply on the Internet? The lawyers and experts say neighboring rights are an area to watch as the Net offers multimedia and as World Wide Web pages offer music or film clips. Under neighboring rights, the person designing the Web page would have to clear the rights to the music through the composer, and the sound itself through the producer and the performer. Someone who picks up a WAV or other sound file on an FTP site, or a film clip, and intends to reuse it (other than using it privately) should be aware that all the rights should be cleared before any reuse.

Patent Law

People on the Internet who are doing research that could result in a patent have to be especially careful says Dan Burk, "especially if they work for an academic institution, or they have some sort of data that could lead to a patentable invention. Any publication of that data in most of the world, prior to filing a patent application, will negate your ability to get a patent. If you put out enough information that someone could understand the invention and use it before you filed a patent application, almost everywhere in the world that means it's been thrown into the public domain and you can no longer get a patent. In the United States, you have a one-year grace period after you have published it. But again, researchers tend to freely share data. They don't stop to think that by sharing this with my friends on the network, I now have prevented myself from getting a patent in most of Europe, Australia, or Japan. And I've started the clock ticking in the United States." Others are more cautious. Posting on a newsgroup *may* be the equivalent of publishing in print, but, as with other Internet issues, there is, as yet, no case law to guide judges and lawyers.

Burk says he was talking to a friend at a major research institution and mentioned the problems with sharing patentable information on the Net. Burk said his friend replied, "I never thought of that. Our researchers are online all the time sharing stuff. We've probably thrown all kinds of inventions out in the public domain."

Trade Secrets

For researchers working for a corporation, protecting trade secrets is as important as protecting patent rights. Again the lawyers warn that researchers should be careful about what they say on the Internet. "A trade secret is only secret as long as it remains secret," Burk says. "Secret doesn't mean you have to keep it absolutely unknown to the rest of the world. If you have a confidentiality agreement with another person, you can disclose that to them and they are responsible to maintain your secret, to keep it confidential. If you make things available on the network," Burk says, "you're not going to have a confidentiality agreement with five thousand people who read this listserv. You can very easily lose some valuable trade secret rights that your university, your institution, or your corporation might want to try and maintain."

People have to think very carefully about misrouted e-mail messages. It's very easy to send something to the wrong address and it could go to your competitor. It has happened with faxes, and then they know your secret. Researchers have to think seriously about using some form of encryption if they think they have something that the institution wants to guard."

Wilkes agrees. "If I had a trade secret and I told it to you, there may be a way we can prepare because we can get a confidentiality agreement, but once it's on the Internet it's gone. How do you minimize the impact of what's happening? That's extremely difficult. If it's put on one of the newsgroups, it's gone you can't get it back."

Defamation

A flame war erupts when two or more people on the Internet or any online system get into a serious argument. The people involved are not face to face, so fists, or worse, cannot fly. But the arguments can become heated, the insults personal.

Flame wars are part of Internet culture. They can go on forever, and are often boring for almost everyone except the people involved. Until recently, many of the flame wars or other rash statements people made on the Internet have been accepted as part of life on the Net.

Now flame wars, or other rash statements, are bringing libel suits to the poster involved for "digital defamation." Again, there are international complications. Flame wars, like real wars, can cross national boundaries. That raises the question of whose law applies. The United States, with its First Amendment tradition, has relatively loose libel laws. Canada, Britain, and Australia have stricter libel laws. European countries, with their Civil Law tradition, also have strict libel laws. Once again we ask, whose law applies?

First, what is a simple definition of libel? It's a statement (most often a false statement) that damages someone's reputation in the eyes of a community. Most people on the Internet have seen statements in flame wars that could fit that definition. It's worth repeating what Robert Wilkes said earlier in this chapter: "You're not allowed to say anything you want, just because you're in your basement and there's no one around. You're not allowed to broadcast to everyone in the world misinformation about other people."

So where does a researcher come in to all this? The greatest danger, apart from libeling someone in a flame war, is in a researcher repeating a libelous statement that one finds online and then either passing it on by reposting it or by repeating the libel by publishing it. The courts in the United States, in Canada, Australia, and Britain have all held that knowingly republishing a libelous statement makes the person doing that republishing (or reposting) as guilty of libel as the first person.

"With regard to libel right now," Burk says, "you have to be very careful about what you're going to put out there on the Net. You may find yourself being sued in any of the 50 states, territories, or possibly anywhere in the world. For an individual researcher, being sued in another nation may not be that big a deal. If a U.S. researcher is being sued in Australia, you can say no big deal. Unless, somehow, your institution is involved. And the institution may very well have assets there."

Journalists are trained with a knowledge of their country's libel laws both in college and on the job. Media corporations have procedures for "lawyering" a story before it is published or broadcast. Most individuals on the Internet, however, know very little about libel law and do not have a lawyer checking their e-mail messages before they are sent out to the world. So be careful out there.

Internet Cases

There have been at least three cases of libel on the Internet, one in Australia, another in the United States, and a third in Great Britain.

Rindos vs. Hardwick

In March 1994, an anthropologist named David Rindos was denied tenure at an Australian university, and consequently there was a debate on the issue in the Usenet group sci.anthropology. Another anthropologist, Gilbert Hardwick, joined the discussion and made allegations of misconduct against Rindos who then sued Hardwick for libel.

Hardwick did not defend the suit, claiming he had no resources. A default judgment was entered, resulting in the Supreme Court of Western Australia awarding Rindos $40,000 (Australian). In awarding the damages for pain and suffering, the judge found that posting the message on the Net increased potential readership and noted that the message could remain on a system for weeks, could be printed out and further distributed, all compounding the libel.

Suarez Corporation Industries vs. Meeks

In this case, Brock Meeks, a journalist living in Fredicksburg, Virginia, and working in Washington, published an Internet news service called CyberWire Dispatch. Meeks received a solicitation on the Net for something called the Electronic Postal Service. After inquiring about EPS, Meeks received a mailing from a Canton, Ohio, mail-order business named Suarez Corporation Industries. Meeks then wrote an investigative piece about Suarez Corporation Industries for CyberWire Dispatch. Suarez saw the article on the Internet and sued for libel. Meeks denied he did anything wrong. Eventually, the case was settled. Meeks paid the plaintiff's $64 filing fee, admitted no liability and did not issue an apology, retraction or correction.

Although the Meeks case did not go to trial, his attorneys, Baker and Hostetler, made some interesting arguments in court documents filed in August, 1994. The United States Supreme Court has ruled that vitriolic speech is protected under the First Amendment. In *Milkovich vs. Lorain Journal* (1990), the court ruled, (and in earlier cases as well) that "loose, figurative or hyperbolic language," "imaginative expression" and "subjective assertions" were protected.

That doesn't mean, however, that the U.S. Supreme Court has given the green light for flame wars. In the same case, the Court held that the First Amendment doesn't create a wholesale exemption from "anything" that may be "labeled opinion."

Meeks' attorneys argued that by posting information on the Internet, Benjamin Suarez became a "public figure" and thus was subject to a higher standard of libel than an ordinary U.S. citizen.

Godfrey vs. Hallam-Baker

Laurence Godfrey is a Canadian physicist who worked at a nuclear research establishment in Hamburg. At the same research unit was another physicist named Philip Hallam-Baker. Godfrey left Hamburg and moved to London after his employer refused to move him and his Filipino wife to safe accommodations after threats from local racist groups. Hallam-Baker also moved, to Geneva to work at CERN, the Swiss research center (which also founded the World Wide Web).

In a writ, issued in London, Godfrey said Hallam-Baker posted seven "very defamatory" statements on the Internet, between April 19 and July 1, 1993. His lawyer, David Price, told the newspaper *The Mail on Sunday* that he was considering adding Internet service providers to the suit.

If a single viewer in Great Britain saw the defamatory messages, experts say, then he may have a case. Unlike the United States, English law has no requirement to prove malice. In addition, recent British cases seem to have narrowed the idea of "innocent dissemination," which could cover system operators and service providers.

Other Online Cases

Other cases warn you to be careful what you say online. Those cases will have a bearing on what happens on the Internet. The Rodney King beating case was not libel, but it's worth remembering that the e-mail messages that the officers sent from their cruisers were evidence in the criminal cases and civil lawsuits. One read: "Oops, I haven't beaten anyone so bad in a long time." Experts were able to undelete Oliver North's e-mail from the White House system during the Iran-Contra investigation. In *Hagler vs. Proctor & Gamble* a Texas jury awarded $15 million to a Proctor & Gamble employee who sued for defamatory statements posted on the company's internal bulletin board system. The case is now under appeal.

Cubby vs. CompuServe

In 1991, Cubby, Inc. sued CompuServe in the southern district of New York for alleged defamatory statements carried in an online publication called "Rumorville, U.S.A." Rumorville was created by Don Fitzpatrick Associates, a San Francisco-based television personnel head hunter. It appeared on the CompuServe Journalism Forum, run by Jim Cameron and Cameron Communications Inc., which had signed a contract with CompuServe to manage the Journalism Forum.

In this case the New York court found that CompuServe was not liable. CompuServe defended itself by saying it was a common carrier, like the telephone company, and that it had no knowledge and could not have knowledge of everything that went on. The court agreed, noting:

> *CompuServe has no more editorial control over such a publication than does a public library, book store, or newsstand and it would be no more feasible for CompuServe to examine every publication it carries for potentially defamatory statements than it would do for any other distributor.*

Stratton Oakmont vs. Prodigy

A key case of online libel in the United States could be *Stratton Oakmont vs. Prodigy*, which is now before the courts in Long Island, New York. A Long Island investment firm, Stratton Oakmont, and its president, Donald Porush, are suing Prodigy and a former employee, David Lusby, for $100 million, for libel and negligence. The company also seeks $100 million in punitive damages.

According to Stratton's complaint, three statements, posted under Lusby's ID, appeared on Prodigy's MoneyTalk forum in October 1994. These statements claimed that public stock offerings by Stratton Oakmont on behalf of a company named Solomon-Page were "fraud" and "criminal." Lusby had left Prodigy about a year before the statement and says his Prodigy account was kept active and was used to post offensive messages.

In May 1995, in a summary judgment, now under appeal, Justice Stuart L. Ain ruled that Prodigy was a publisher for purposes of the case and that the board leader or sysop, Charles Epstein, was Prodigy's agent. In his ruling, Justice Ain found two key differences between Prodigy and CompuServe. First, he wrote, "Prodigy holds itself out to the public and its members as controlling its computer bulletin boards." Second, "Prodigy implemented this control through its automatic screening program and Guidelines which board leaders are required to enforce."

There is a key difference between the Prodigy and CompuServe cases. Prodigy does attempt to monitor the messages on its system (something that is probably impossible on the Internet). "We have a machine that scans for unacceptable words," Carol Wallace, a Prodigy spokesperson, told the *New York Times*. Prodigy has always seen itself as a "family" bulletin board and says it has taken steps to remove "offensive language" from postings. In an affidavit filed in the case, however, Prodigy's lawyer, William Schneck, said "Prodigy does not 'edit' the messages or review their contents before they appear on the bulletin board. Prodigy has also said online that it is not liable for statements unless posted by an authorized spokesperson. However, some have questioned Prodigy's statement. The Anti-Defamation League (ADL) sued Prodigy in 1991 for alleged anti-Semitic remarks posted on the system. The case was settled and the ADL issued a statement that said Prodigy "amplified its guidelines" to exclude "expressions of bigotry, racism, and hatred."

Justice Ain also wrote that Prodigy made a conscious decision in the free market to use control to attract a family audience and added that other computer networks that did not make such a decision may be less liable (unless, of course, the Communications Decency Act changes the rules, at least in the United States).

There's another question, possibly harking back to the judge's decision in the Australian *Rindos* case. How many people saw the offensive posting? News reports have said that the statements remained on Prodigy for two weeks before they were removed.

Company Control and Disclaimers

Another problem facing researchers who work online, especially those employed by a company or institution, is that an organization is responsible for what goes out under the organization's Internet domain address. Some companies, such as Eastman Kodak, already restrict employees from posting notices on discussion groups where the Kodak address might be considered an endorsement by the company.

Law professor Dan Burk says that the standard disclaimer seen on many institutional or corporate Internet messages may not stand up in court. "They're not that persuasive," Burk says. "You may put a disclaimer on a message and the courts will take that into account as one factor. If the circumstances are such that you really were speaking for your corporation or someone could believe you were speaking for your corporation or were speaking for your institution or university or whatever, that would be taken into account. The fact that you have this boilerplate disclaimer that you put on every message you put out—the courts could say that's not going to be determinative." This perspective could have a chilling effect on the lively free speech on the Internet, because many people use company gateways to get onto the Net.

Forum Shopping

Lawyers warn that the international aspects of the Internet could result in what is called "forum shopping"—looking for a court and country where the plaintiff could get a favorable verdict and a high monetary award. In some ways this is an expansion of the idea of a change of venue in a criminal case. There a lawyer looks for a jurisdiction where a jury may be less biased. In forum shopping, a lawyer looks for the jurisdiction most favorable to the client. Let's take the example of libel. It's hard for a libel plaintiff to win a judgment in the United States. They must prove the libel was damaging and inaccurate, and in the case of a public figure, published with "malice." In Canada and other British Commonwealth countries, defendants must prove truth, fair comment, and publication in the public interest to defend themselves against libel. It would probably be hard to prove that a flame war on the Internet is publication in the public interest.

In Civil Law countries, the libel laws are even tougher, covering any attack on the honor or reputation or anything that causes the humiliation of a person or corporation. Negligent publication of false information is libel in Civil Law countries. Truth, which can be a defense in Common Law countries, can be libelous in Civil Law countries if the libelous truth was published with deliberate intent to injure the plaintiff. Another defense against libel is "privilege," that it is a fair and accurate account of a proceeding of a public body—such as a city council, state or provincial legislature, Congress or Parliament.

There was one well-known case of forum shopping in the 1980s. The Prime Minister of the Bahamas, Sir Lynden Pindling, sued NBC News for reports that alleged Pindling had connections with drug dealers. Pindling first sued in the Bahamian courts, but NBC refused to appear. Pindling wanted to avoid the U.S. courts so he then filed a $4 million libel suit in Canada, naming NBC and 17 Canadian cable companies that carried NBC's signal. In opening arguments, the lawyers for NBC tried to have the suit dismissed, claiming Pindling wasn't libeled in Canada, since the broadcast originated in the U.S. The judge, however, permitted the case to proceed and was settled in 1989 without going to trial.

So what court could hear an Internet libel case? "The court is likely to hear the case if the libel is published or likely to have been heard by somebody in that jurisdiction," Burk says, pointing to both the Godfrey case in Britain and the Brock Meeks case in the United States. " While Meeks wrote his CyberWire Dispatch from his home in Fredericksburg, Virginia, Suarez was based in Ohio and filed its suit there—and that's where it was seen on the Internet by Suarez. "In the opinion of most attorneys and scholars, Ohio probably could have asserted jurisdiction because again the rule is: where the libel is published, that's where the tort is thought to have occurred and presumably someone is thought to have read that message."

"The thing about U.S. courts is that they would then ask, is it too inconvenient or unfair to travel all the way to Ohio or find someone in Ohio to defend him. That fairness factor will be the other factor that they will look at. Once you get a judgment in another country, the question is obviously enforcing it," Burk says. "If there are assets available in that country, the person who gets the judgment may go after those assets. If there is nothing there to go after, or not enough, then they might come to the United States to get a U.S. court to try and enforce the judgment. And the U.S. courts are likely to enforce the judgment unless it's in violation of U.S. policy."

On the other hand, Canadian media lawyer Brian Rogers says, "The libel laws for plaintiffs in Canada are the most attractive in the world, even more attractive in some ways than the U.K., although U.K. damage awards have been better. We could expect that kind of forum shopping in the future."

Identity Hacking

Identity hacking is a nagging problem on the Internet, one of which researchers should be wary. Identity hacking occurs when someone finds a way to misrepresent their identity on the Internet, by hacking a false name and Internet address or adding a false name to a message posted through an anonymous server; therefore, always check the identity of a poster.

The best known recent case of identity hacking was a fake Associated Press dispatch that purported to report that Microsoft was taking over the Roman Catholic Church. The phony dispatch noted: "Microsoft Corp. and the Vatican announced that the Redmond software giant will acquire the Roman Catholic Church in exchange for an unspecified number of shares of Microsoft common stock. . . . Through the Microsoft Network, the company's new online service," the fake dispatch reported, "we will make the sacraments available online for the first time." It also noted, "The deal grants Microsoft exclusive electronic rights to the Bible and the Vatican's prized art collection, which includes works by such masters as Michelangelo and da Vinci."

Although many people on the Internet saw the joke and chuckled, others were offended and called both Microsoft and the Associated Press. Microsoft quickly issued a statement saying, "The story has no truth and was not generated by the company. . . . The company is not aware how the electronic message originated but maintains strict policies internally concerning the proper use of electronic communications." With the publication of the denial, the story died, but it is now part of Net legend.

Another case of identity hacking has a warning of "look before you leap" for unwary researchers who have only a little Internet knowledge. In late November, 1994, the provincial government of Ontario went online and the news media presented the provincial Premier Bob Rae, sending a message on the Internet. On December 3, a message appeared on the newsgroup ont.general, purporting to come from Rae. It was typed so that it appeared to come from the premier's Net address Premier@govonca.gov.on.ca and contained offensive and obscene statements. A closer look showed that the message was actually routed through an anonymous server in Cupertino, California, and had a disclaimer that read "This message is NOT from the person listed in the from line. It is from an automated software remailing service. . . ."

The message, ignored by most Net-knowledgeable people, was jumped on by opposition politicians in the Legislature when someone faxed a copy of the message to the opposition Conservative party. Sources in the Conservative party say the faxed message did not contain the disclaimer.

Mike Harris, the party leader, with his eye on an upcoming election, released the incomplete message in the legislature. Harris rose to claim, "It's a security problem, it's a serious problem." The Canadian Press news agency reported that Harris claimed that "computer experts" had told him the sender had special access to the premier's computers or had somehow appropriated the premier's address—all, apparently, without seeing the original message.

This story is simply a warning to all Net researchers to check and double-check the information you find on the Internet. There was, for example, a short lived "Fakemail" site in the United States that allowed a user to send mail from "anyone." The most popular address was elvis@graceland.

Censoring the Internet

Can the Internet be censored? The technical answer is likely no. Any system built to withstand a nuclear attack, and one that is growing so quickly, is hard to control—and therefore hard to censor. Politicians and police look at the Internet and see pornography and pedophilia and want it controlled. A couple from California was recently convicted for violating Tennessee's pornography law, because people in that state were able to dial into their California BBS and download explicit files. That raises the question of the U.S. Bible Belt trying to force its standards on the rest of the United States—and perhaps the world.

The most practical test of censoring the Net has occurred between the United States and Canada, in the sensational Paul Bernardo-Karla Homolka murder case. Bernardo was charged with the murder of two Ontario teenagers, Kristen French, who was killed in 1992, and Leslie Mahaffy, whose dismembered body was found in a lake in 1991. Bernardo was also charged with a series of rapes in the Toronto suburb of Scarborough in the equally sensational "Scarborough rapist" case.

Bernardo's estranged wife, Karla Homolka, was later charged with manslaughter in the case, and appeared in court in St. Catharines, Ontario in July of 1993. At that time, the trial judge, Francis Kovacs, imposed a sweeping ban on publication of evidence at the trial, in order to protect Bernardo's right to a fair trial. Canada has always differed from the United States on the issue of fair trial versus free press. Until recently, Canadian courts have always sided on the side of a fair trial. Publication bans are routine at bail hearings and preliminary hearings although the information from those hearings can be published at the end of the trial.

Justice Kovacs ruled that the press couldn't report any of the evidence heard in the courtroom. It could report the verdict and sentence, but not the plea. American reporters from Buffalo, also covering the trial, were barred from the court room.

The defense, which usually asks for publication bans, did not want a ban. The prosecuting Crown attorney did. Lawyers representing the media were there to challenge the ban, and it was after their arguments that Kovacs issued his ruling. The *Toronto Sun*, the *Toronto Star*, and the Thomson Newspaper chain, owner of the *Globe and Mail*, have all appealed Kovacs' ruling, together with the Canadian Broadcasting Corporation. The case is now headed for the Supreme Court of Canada. Public interest in the case was high, the press coverage both sensational and detailed. Despite charges of censorship, there has been blanket reporting in Canada on the Bernardo-Homolka case, hundreds of newspaper articles, many television reports, and magazine articles. A satirical magazine called *Frank* regularly published details of the case. The only thing the mainstream media has not published or broadcast is material covered by Kovacs' publication ban.

A few weeks after the publication ban began, a new newsgroup appeared on the Internet, alt.fan.karla-homolka, founded, as a joke, by a university student in Kitchener, Ontario, and quickly became the prime source for banned information.

A FAQ file containing supposed details of the murders, the trials, related cases, hearsay, the latest rumors, and anything relevant gained a wide audience on the Internet in Canada. Alt.fan.karla-homolka and many American publications reported what they said was the plea, but technically there is no way of checking the accuracy of the reports because the plea was sealed by the court. Then, on Tuesday, November 23, 1993, the *Washington Post* published its own story on the crime and the ban, and increased American interest in the case and a new audience came on board alt.fan.karla-homolka. It is suspected that the *Post* and later other U.S. media outlets, including the TV tabloid show, "A Current Affair," got leads on the case from alt.fan.karla-homolka.

With the *Washington Post* article as a catapult, a debate on censorship raged across the Net, from the alt.fan.karla-homolka newsgroup itself, and as far away as the tattooing and piercing newsgroup rec.arts.bodyart, to the Legal and Journalism forums on CompuServe, and the Science Fiction Round Tables on GEnie. Canadians who were unable to buy hard copies of the *Post* downloaded it from the *Post's* database on CompuServe. Justice Kovacs' decision also received wide circulation; it was posted on alt.fan.karla-homolka, on other Net newsgroups and on CompuServe.

Soon any article containing information about the case, banned or not, appeared on alt.fan.karla-homolka. It appears that if the people on the newsgroup were not going to obey a criminal court publication ban, they also had no qualms about wholesale violation of copyright laws.

There were major debates in the universities about whether to kill the karla-homolka newsgroup. Some did take it off their Internet system; others did not. One commercial service in Canada tried to remove any references to the case from all newsgroups, but as the debate spread it proved impossible to control. Students at universities that banned the newsgroup soon found ways to Telnet to sites that had the newsgroup. A number of offshore FTP sites came and went, containing the FAQ files, pirated newspaper articles, and GIF files of the accused. New newsgroups appeared as soon as old ones were banned in some locations.

Another Canadian student, using the pseudonym Abdul, set up a Karla Homolka mailing list (called Teale Tales, derived from one of Paul Bernardo's other names), using Texas-based io.com as an offshore gateway. Then came a short article in *Wired*, which also broke the ban, bringing more controversy in Canada. *Wired* immediately cried censorship, but in Canada no government agency banned *Wired*, although *Wired*, for its own reasons, likes to say so. In some areas, private sector distributors withdrew the magazine on advice of their lawyers. Most did not. Some had newsstands black out a couple of sentences that broke the ban. One ripped out the offending page.

There was also a debate on the merits of the ban itself, and whether Justice Kovacs should have issued the ban. Many American participants, standing by their tradition, said he shouldn't have, but then came another, even more sensational murder case in the summer of 1994. Former football star and actor O. J. Simpson was charged with the murders of his estranged wife, Nicole Brown, and waiter, Ron Goldman. Almost overnight, a number of O. J. Simpson newsgroups sprang up to discuss aspects of the case. Not a few people in debates on the Karla-Homolka group noted that the ban had prevented the media circus that surrounded the O. J. Simpson case. Nonethless, the existence of alt.fan.karla-homolka, the offshoot newsgroups, and the offshore FTP sites show just how hard it is to censor the Internet.

Figure 10-1.
Make way for the
Internet interstate!

—*The Globe and Mail, Toronto*

The Future of Law on the Internet

So what is going to happen in the future? Will the law keep up with the change on the world-wide Internet? Or will the Internet change the law? "The problem is understanding and relating to the laws we have in place and understanding where the differences are," Robert Wilkes says. "There may be areas that have to be improved, but not ignored. You can't ignore the old law. One thing about the Internet, with 20 million [users], it's not that important, not yet. What we're really worrying about is what we think the future is. The future may not be an Internet, but it will be something along those lines. A lot of people are going to be disappointed, because they're going to lose their Internet."

Governments are slowly, very slowly, trying to tackle the problem of law and the Internet, and as Wilkes predicted, they are tackling the economic issue of copyright first. The United States, Canadian and Australian governments have all issued reports on the future of copyright. The American report is known as the Lehman report, for its chief author, Bruce Lehman, assistant secretary of Commerce and Commissioner of Patents who was chair of the Working Group on Intellectual Property. It notes:

U.S. copyright industries are significant contributors to the United States' current trade accounts, reducing our balance of payments deficit by some $34 billion in 1990. Inadequacies in the present system of intellectual property protection for copyrights and neighboring or related rights and the consequent losses to these industries from piracy and from trade barriers arising from differences in forms of protection have been estimated to cause losses to these industries of $12 to 15 billion annually. Improved protection for copyrights and neighboring rights would contribute to reducing these losses and improving the balance of payments.

In other words, the United States believes that the anarchic nature of the Internet could cost some of its most powerful industries a lot of money—and that will motivate governments to act.

One question raised by the report is whether or not retrieving something on the Internet can be viewed as a violation of U.S. copyright law. The committee has recommended that the first sale doctrine not include "transmission," including transmission by the Internet. This means that while the first sale doctrine allows the owner of a book to dispose of it by, say, selling it to a used book store, the same right would not apply to something retrieved from the Internet. The Lehman report recommends extending software copyright law to data, including, some say, e-mail. Technically, that could require permission to read anything on the Net. Others say the fears are exaggerated. Part of the argument is that unless copyright holders are guaranteed some sort of protection, nothing significant will ever appear on the Internet.

Another controversial aspect of the report is a recommendation for removal of moral rights, a move that will certainly bring the United States into conflict with countries already concerned about U.S. domination of culture on this planet. The Lehman report continues:

Concerns have been raised over the extent and scope of moral rights in the world of digital communications. Some believe that the ability to modify and restructure existing works make moral rights more important than ever before. Others take the view that moral rights must be rethought in the digital world. We agree with this view. New thought must be given to the scope, extent, and waivability of moral rights in digitized information.

The Canadian report, "Study on New Media and Copyright," created by a consulting firm, calls for an expansion of copyright collectives and registries. It repeats the American concern about Net piracy, noting, "If Canadian creators see no value in the work they create, because their work is insufficiently protected (in terms of both their economic and moral rights), then there will be less incentive to create."

While the Lehman report takes a legalistic stance, perhaps reflecting the litigious nature of contemporary America, the Canadian report also calls for education of the user. The new media may, in fact, lead to totally new laws, as the information infrastructure (the favorite bureaucratic term), leads in unforeseen directions. It's clear the Net and the computer have already changed society in ways undreamed of just ten years ago. And as technology races ahead, politicians (and some judges) are plodding behind, most of them trying to create 1950s solutions for 21st century problems. Who knows what technology will bring in the next decade? Or what laws will be passed, and if those laws will work?

In the meantime, researchers on the Internet have to be aware that, for now, old laws still govern the new world of the Internet. Researchers should show respect for others by not stealing material, or reposting without permission, or by defaming someone in a flame war.

Finding It on the Internet

Material mentioned in this chapter can be found at various Internet sites, as explained here.

Copyright

The Lehman Report

"A Preliminary Draft of the Report of the Working Group on Intellectual Property Rights" (The "Lehman Report")

World Wide Web:
`http://iitf.doc.gov:70/1s/newitems`

The Copyright FAQ

FTP from rtfm.mit.edu in directory:

`/pub/usenet/news.answers/law/Copyright-FAQ`
`files part1 through part6`

Canadian Study on New Media and Copyright

FTP:
`debra.dgbt.doc.ca/pub/info-highway/copyright/`
`    nglfinal.dos`

(copy is in ASCII)

Gopher:
`debra.dgbt.doc.ca port`
`70/Industry Canada Documents`

World Wide Web:
`http:/debra.dgbt.doc.ca:80/info-highway/copyright`

Libel

Arnold-Moore, Tim, "Legal Pitfalls in Cyberspace: Defamation on Computer Networks"

World Wide Web:
`http://144.110.144.11/law/defame.html`

Banned Information

Banned Newsgroups FAQ

Posted approximately once a month to alt.censorship, alt.comp.acad-freedom.talk, alt.internet.services, news.misc, alt.answers, and news.answers.

FTP:
`rtfm.mit.edu`
`    /pub/usenet/news.answers/usenet/banned-groups-faq`

Supreme Court of Canada Decision

Dagenais versus CBC ("The Boys of St. Vincent" case)

FTP:
`io.com/pub/usr/abdul/scc-ban.txt`

General Legal Addresses

Anita Susan Brenner Home Pages

World Wide Web:
`http://www.cyberspace.org/u/brenner/www/homepage.html` and
`http://avalon.caltech.edu/`

U.S. Code

The U.S. Code (including the Code's Table of Popular Names)is available at:

World Wide Web:
`http://www.pls.com:8001/his/usc.html`

Indiana Law School

The Indiana University School of Law-Bloomington WWW server is a good starting point for law and legal issues.

World Wide Web:
`http://www.law.indiana.edu`

Legal Resource Locater

World Wide Web:
`http://www.dorsai.org/p-law/`

The International Centre for Criminal Law Reform and Criminal Justice Policy

"A Guide to Internet Resources in Criminal Law and Criminal Justice"

Gopher:
`view.ubc.ca`

World Wide Web:
`http://view.ubc.ca`

The Emory Law School

Emory Legal Information Technology Environment (ELITE) Project

World Wide Web:
`http://www.law.emory.edu/`

The Virtual Law Library Reference Desk

Washburn University's School of Law Library provides reference access to sources of legal information.

Telnet:
`law.wuacc.edu`

`login = reflaw`

World Wide Web:
`http://law.wuacc.edu/washlaw/reflaw/reflaw.html`

Westlaw Directory

A directory of lawyers and law firms in the United States

Gopher:
`wld.westlaw.com`
(select West's Legal Directory)

Privacy Rights Clearing House

World Wide Web:
`http://www.manymedia.com/prc/`

Gopher:
`gopher.acusd.edu`

FTP:
`ftp.acusd.edu`

Telnet:
`teetot.acusd.edu (local c teetot, login: privacy)`

CRDP-LAW

University of Montreal's Legal Information Servers includes "Le Centre de Recherche en Droit Public" (CRDP) and the Faculty of Law of the University of Montreal.

World Wide Web:
`http://www.droit.umontreal.ca/`

`http://www.droit.umontreal.ca/english.html`

Gopher:
`gopher.droit.umontreal.ca/`

FTP:
`ftp.droit.umontreal.ca/pub`

Canadian Law and Society Association

Gopher:
`gopher.cc.umanitoba.ca:70/11/faculties/law/clsa%09%09+`

Electronic Frontier Foundation

Gopher:
`gopher.eff.org`

World Wide Web:
`http://www.eff.org`

FTP:
`ftp.eff.org`

Electronic Frontier Foundation (Canada)

Gopher:
`gopher ee.mcgill.ca`

11

The E-mail Interview

The interview is an important component of many kinds of research, whether it's done in person, by telephone, by letter and fax, or now by electronic mail. Even though the World Wide Web is hot, as Gopher was just a couple of years ago, it's e-mail that remains at the heart of the success of not only the Internet, but the entire online world. In the past couple of years, we've seen the rise of the e-mail interview as the latest and in some cases the most successful online research tool.

Reporters and other researchers are using online queries for everything from finding quick answers to puzzling last-minute questions, or locating new sources of information to news-making, groundbreaking journalism such as John Seabrook's *E-mail from Bill*, a profile of Microsoft's Bill Gates that appeared in the *New Yorker* in January of 1994.

In many ways, the e-mail interview is *not* new. Most of the advice that applies to a telephone or personal interview should also apply to an online interview. In addition, you should also observe all the rules of netiquette for the Internet or any other online service you are using.

Few experts foresaw the e-mail explosion. Just 15 years ago, when the first commercial online services were being planned, few mentioned e-mail. The engineers planning teletext and videotex were talking about hardware and the executives were talking about profits from advertising dollars. The information was to come from "on high," so to speak, and the public would passively accept it. The analogy, of course, was television, and it was the wrong analogy.

Even on the Internet, back in the days when it was ARPANET, when it was a research tool, it was first thought the Internet would be used for "official" government business, but scientists and researchers soon found other uses for the Net; E-mail blossomed, and Usenet was born.

There are a couple of great advantages to electronic mail: time and money. One technical term for e-mail is *asynchronous communications*. It means something that happens at different times. Thus if you are writing a message to someone at 9:31 p.m. in eastern North America, it's 6:31 p.m. on the west coast, and you might be able to phone someone in California. If the phone's busy, you're out of luck, at least for now. It's also 3:31 a.m. the next morning in Berlin. If you phoned, you'd probably drag someone out of bed. It's 12:31 p.m., just past noon, in Australia, and you'd probably be able to reach the person you want, if you wanted to pay for a long-distance call down under.

Asynchronous communication solves the time-zone problem. You can post your e-mail message when it's most convenient for you, and the person you sent it to will receive it when it's most convenient for him. Your answer (if there is one) will appear in your mailbox, at your convenience, when you log on. You're not playing expensive telephone tag either locally, nationally, or internationally.

In one way, what's happening is just a modern return to an old way of communicating—the letter. For centuries, the only method of long-distance communication was by letter. Ancient Mesopotamia used clay tablets encased in clay envelopes. The Greeks and Romans used both wax tablets and parchment. From the 16th to the 19th centuries, Europeans and North Americans were superb letter writers.

The next step in communication, the telegraph, added the speed of early electronics, and cost shortened the verbiage. Letters and telegrams fill historical archives, and scholars have written long and sometimes fascinating, sometimes boring, work on the collected letters and telegrams of many famous men and women.

How did interviews take place before the Internet? If a newspaper had no resident correspondent or stringer in a small town, or if a scholar had no means of communicating other than a letter or telegram, then that was used. In the late 19th century, at the height of newspaper competition, editors and reporters would sometimes do a remote interview by telegram. They'd telegraph a series of questions to a famous or newsworthy person in the hopes that she would answer (collect of course). Sometimes she would. Even today, enterprising journalists and scholars submit questions to possible subjects by letter. Letters may get by gatekeepers (executive assistants and secretaries) where a phone call would not.

The telephone ended all that. Once, long ago, when someone used a telephone, it was part of a news story. In the years just before and after World War I, newspapers would often report when a politician used "the long-distance telephone"—it meant something important was going to happen. If police used long distance that meant a major investigation. The phone was faster, more efficient and eventually less expensive than a telegraph. It became part of our daily lives.

Today, using the Internet for research is, in many ways, still news. That won't last long; there are too many people joining the Net, and journalists, writers, and researchers are still in the forefront of those joiners. A few years from now, some scholar will write a treatise on the *Collected E-mail of the President* and a tabloid will publish some star's naughty e-mail messages.

You can now buy books on how to do telephone interviews. Once, when there were few telephones, there were no rules. People learned as they went along. As with netiquette, rules are emerging for the e-mail interview. It's different from a telephone interview and different from a personal interview—but not that much. Combine netiquette, the experience of years of telephone and personal interviews and a little common sense, and you'll probably come out all right. So let's begin.

Lurk and Research

Before you even think of conducting an e-mail interview, you have to know what your story is. It may be a breaking story and you're a journalist, making a fast visit to a Usenet group or a mailing list to catch an idea of what the online world thinks. You may be a doctor polling colleagues about a mysterious case or a biographer looking for background on a certain person.

Rule Number One: Do your homework before you go online. Nothing destroys the credibility of a researcher more than making a glaring error online. Not only will it dry up most sources of information, you're likely to get flamed for your error.

Subscribe to an appropriate mailing list. Mailing lists (which usually have more specific targets than Usenet newsgroups) and moderated newsgroups are often more reliable than wide-open Usenet groups where the noise-to-signal ratio is high.

Lurking is crucial to contacting potential sources. It's more than netiquette. Lurking gives the researcher a sense of the total volume of messages on a mailing list or newsgroup. Personalities emerge quickly.

So, do basic research, both on and offline, before you ask a single question. Visit any appropriate Web or Gopher sites that might be appropriate for your project. Do the library research you'd be doing anyway, and do it as well in the newsgroups and mailing lists that you've chosen.

Research and lurking means you'll ask better and more focused questions once you decide to do an interview. Countless unprepared talk-show hosts have found that out over the years. A little pre-research is also a sign of respect for the person you're interviewing. If you ask appropriate questions, the subject will respect you—and then you can get to the heart of the interview faster. Research, especially library research, will give you names, dates, events, places, and data that can add credibility and substance to your interview.

Serendipity has always played a key role in research. You'll never know when a name you've come across in your library research for your current project—or even earlier ones—will show up one day in a message header.

You also have to remember that there's very little that's new in this world, especially in news. The story you're working on has probably been done many times before. It may have different people and a different angle but you can be sure there's background data out there somewhere, either on the Net, in the library, or in a commercial research database.

Whether you're working on a news story, an in-depth profile, or an academic research project, and you're preparing for any interview—online, by telephone, or in person—you should find as much material on your subject before you write a line of e-mail or pick up the telephone. A few hours of background research will give you a better sense of your subject. Checking more in-depth material, like magazines and academic journals, will give information that provides the human touch, the unexpected characteristic, hobby, or interest. That obscure paper written by some long-forgotten professor might provide a new insight into current research.

Caution   *Remember to be skeptical. Often in the hurry to meet deadlines, reporters will go to a hard copy or online morgue and repeat errors in previous stories. Time is a factor, of course, but you should always go back to original sources. Then you should ask your source if the information in your research is correct. Then, ideally, you should confirm with other sources what your interviewee told you!*

As we've said before, you also have to know when to cut off your research. There will come a point when you have the background you need, when you've lurked long enough, and you've got to go online and talk to potential sources. Know when to say when.

Approaching Sources Online

You should establish yourself in the mailing list by making contributions. Post messages answering questions where you can help. If you can intelligently add to the discussion, add your own comments to an ongoing discussion. You'll become part of the neighborhood, and your personality will come through to the often thousands of people who are reading the list or newsgroup. So now you're ready to go online and approach the sources you've picked out by lurking.

Asking a Mailing List or Newsgroup

If you've lurked for a few days or weeks, you should by now have a sense of the group of people you'll be working with. It may be a largely professional group, such as the journalists on CARR-L mailing list or the scientists on the Bionet Usenet groups. It may be a mixture of fans and scholars such as you find on the alt.mythology newsgroup. You should know by now what questions are welcome and what aren't.

Students, for example, will often get flamed if they post a question that is obviously a "help me with my homework because I haven't done it" type of question. On the other hand, if you've done your homework, a tightly focused question will often get the answer you want.

The Internet, especially e-mail, has been called "the gift economy" by some people. That comes from the custom among many aboriginal people who have an economy that works through the exchange of gifts and favors rather than money for goods and services. It's the same on the Net, you ask, receive an answer, and then either give back or give forward when you're able to help the person who helped you or others.

When you post a general question, you should:

» **Identify yourself:** you're a student, a staff reporter or producer, a freelance writer, a professor, a business person.

» **Be clear about the purpose of the question.** If it's for a newspaper, say so. If it's background information for a television broadcast, let the mailing list or news group know that. Whether you're an academic planning to use the material in a paper, or a business person doing research for a new product, or if it's just for personal interest, always identify the reason you are posting the question. The reason for your question will help determine the answer you receive. Some people are reluctant to speak to the news media, but would be more willing to give information to help a fellow scholar or a student. Others take the opposite view, they will talk to the media (because there's something in it for them), but won't take the time to help a student.

» **Keep the question or questions sharp and focused.** People don't have time to write an entire essay, but they can answer specific questions. As we said in the chapter on netiquette, keep the message short.

» **Always suggest that anyone responding should reply by private e-mail.** E-mail saves bandwidth on your mailing list or newsgroup and permits you to post follow-up questions to the individual who replied to you. That doesn't mean you shouldn't keep looking for answers in the original newsgroup or mailing list. Often people will simply hit the reply button and send the message to everyone. A lively discussion may result—one that might give you more information.

» **Always evaluate the information you receive in reply to a general posting.** Check it against answers from other people or against research from other sources.

» **The answers you get will depend on the people involved in the mailing list or newsgroup when you ask the question.** Be prepared for the possibility that no one in that specific group will be able or want to answer the question. You may also be flooded with replies for the first couple of days and then receive nothing for a while.

If you're pulling material off a discussion group on a topic of current interest, you should always e-mail the poster(s) and ask permission to quote. It's good netiquette, even though you could argue that thousands of people have already read the comment. It's polite and may lead to the person providing you with more information. If the person says "no," to your permission request, and you feel the comment is still worth using, consider whether it can be used anonymously. Try "one poster on the newsgroup, etc.," and you will find that the poster will usually say yes to that request.

» **Be prepared to be shot down in flames.** Sometimes your idea won't work, you've missed something, or your boss or adviser has come up with a damned silly idea and told you to do it anyway. The replies you get to a general posting will tell you whether what you're doing is worthwhile and you should keep working on it or if you've acquired enough ammunition to tell your boss or adviser, "This isn't working, let's drop it" or "this angle seems more promising."

Networking on the Net

The Net is one of the best—and easiest places—for researchers to network and track down potential sources. As we've said before, the Net is people, not hardware and software, and people are almost always ready to point you to a good source or the right mailing list or newsgroup. Here's how to "network" with people on the Net:

» Find the proper newsgroup or mailing list. You can do that by checking directories, lists of mailing lists, and keeping the file that lists all current newsgroups.

» Lurk for a while.

» Post a general question outlining your research and asking for contacts via e-mail. Contact potential sources you've already identified on the mailing list or newsgroup privately.

» If you're answering a similar query and recommending that the poster contact someone you know, c.c. a copy of the message to your contact or, if necessary, ask permission to pass on the name before answering the query.

» Sometimes (not always) your message will be passed on to other people on other groups and your network of sources will grow.

» Never "spam" your query by posting the same message to a large number of newsgroups and mailing lists. As we've mentioned before, Net culture frowns on spamming. If you've done your homework, checked the mailing list or newsgroup, and lurked until you have absorbed the local culture, then you will know how to focus your question to that group. Take the time to write individual queries. Create a "boilerplate" basic message outlining your project and save it as a file. Then, before you post, tailor that boilerplate message to that group.

One of the authors used the following boilerplate message for most initial queries:

I'm co-writing a book for Prima Publishing called "Researching on the Internet." I've co-written two previous investigative non-fiction books, "King of the Mob" and "Undercover." It's not going to be just another software manual. "Researching on the Internet" won't just tell how a researcher can find material on the Internet, it will describe how information gets on the Net. That way it will be easier for the researchers to evaluate the material once they find it. It will also be a "people" book with sidebars profiling researchers and sysops who work on the Net.

I'm hoping you can tell me more about yourself and more about the work you do on the Internet.

If you will agree to be one of my contacts. I'd like to interview you about your work first by e-mail with a follow up by telephone. I also have a basic set of 14 short questions that I'm asking everyone. I'd also appreciate any other contacts you may suggest.Thanks in advance.

Best wishes,

Robin Rowland

The text was altered whenever possible to make the message as personal as possible for a potential source. It describes the project, establishes a set of author's credentials and then goes out to describe what the author wants from the source.

» Save all potential contacts in an address book. Go back to sources who have helped you or whom you've helped in the past.

» The Net is also often a great place to avoid gatekeepers and PR people. One of the authors had tried several times, with conventional methods, to contact one source for an earlier story. During research for this book, the source's e-mail address popped up unexpectedly in a list provided by someone else. An interview was quickly arranged with a focused e-mail query. Don't assume busy or famous people won't answer your query—they just might.

» Direct contact doesn't always work. Some executives still have secretaries or assistants screen their e-mail. Other people will use a filter to prioritize their e-mail and your query may end up in a low-priority mail box.

» Some people will reply saying they're too busy. Some will reply, agreeing to the interview, and then never answer the follow-up questions. Others won't reply at all.

» Don't ignore old fashioned paper in searching for people. More directories these days are listing e-mail addresses along with street address and phone number. Put your e-mail address on your business cards so sources can contact you. If someone gives you a business card with an e-mail address on it, make sure that e-mail address goes into your address book.

» Check with associations and organizations, either by phone or e-mail, as part of your homework. More and more are going online and certainly some of their members will do e-mail interviews.

» When you're finishing up a conventional phone or personal interview *always* ask for an e-mail address. If the source isn't online, they sometimes will say they can be contacted through a spouse, parent, or child who does have an e-mail address.

Tip

Always end an e-mail (or other interview) by asking your source if they can suggest any other contacts. It usually leads to new sources of information. Some reporters with chutzpah also ask subjects for names of people who oppose their point of view, adversaries, and enemies.

Tailor your signature file to your project. Many reporters put their affiliation in their sig files, and that often leads to new sources of information coming out of the woodwork.

Whether you're talking in person or to voice mail, always leave your e-mail address when you call long-distance. It's cheaper and easier for someone to return your message by e-mail rather than calling long distance.

Finding Family, Finding Friends

The Internet is often used for personal research as well as reporting and academic research.

Meaghan Walker is a self-employed computer consultant and Net researcher who lives in Port Alberni, on Vancouver Island, British Columbia. For Walker, seven days of Net research accomplished what seven years of fighting government bureaucracy could not.

Walker describes herself as three-quarters Indian. When she was six months old, Walker was adopted by a non-native family. When Meaghan was 14, her parents told her that she was adopted and that they had just learned that her birth mother had died.

That began Walker's long fight through the British Columbia bureaucracy. She filed a Freedom of Information request, asked for her Social Services file and filed with the Adoption Reunion Registry. The result was almost no information, except the fact that her birth mother had committed suicide in 1975 at age 23.

So Walker turned to the Internet and posted a message on three local newsgroups. Seven days later, a woman in Victoria, the provincial capital, asked a question. "What color are your eyes?"

The question provided the link. Walker's family, members of the Cowichan band, have a genetic quirk—blue eyes. Walker has blue eyes; her 16-month-old son has blond hair and blue eyes.

The Net contact in Victoria had gone to school with Walker's birth mother in Duncan, British Columbia. It turned out that Walker's original family name was Williams. "Every single Williams family for the past two generations has had one child with blond hair and blue eyes," Walker says.

That contact led to Walker's, 24-year-old sister, Naomi, who lived just 45 minutes away. Naomi's son also has blond hair and blue eyes. Naomi introduced her long-lost sister to eight aunts and uncles and their maternal grandfather, Doug Williams.

A query on the Net also brought this story from a California librarian:

"I started wondering about an old love of mine, who, the last time I saw him, said he was heading for Brazil. This was maybe nine years ago (I thought I was really getting the kiss-off, I mean Brazil?) Because I'm a librarian, I know about things such as Current Contents, which indexes professional publications. I hooked up with a university that had CC available, searched on my old love's name and got seven papers that he had written or co-written on the cacao plant.

"CC only lists initials and last name, but because he is a plant pathologist and because I pretty much believed there was cacao in Brazil, I thought "this is him!" I then went onto MELVYL, the University of California online system catalog, to see if these publications were in any nearby university library. I had luck there, too. This was getting exciting! The hunt was on.

"I then left my computer and drove over to the campus to look at actual publications. His name was spelled out in print so now I knew I had the right person. The publication even gave an address for where the research was performed. I know I could have just written a letter at that point, but I wanted to see if maybe, just maybe, he had e-mail anywhere.

"I started searching lots of files in Brazil because I had the name of the agency for which the research was performed. Luckily, I know Spanish, which got me through lots of text in Portuguese. The closest I could get was to a University in Itabuna, Bahia, Brazil. Because the address I had was in Itabuna, I wrote to the Internet postmaster at the university and asked if the agency was university or government or private, and was it on the Internet. I got a very quick reply saying it was a government agency, not yet available electronically. So I ended up writing an old-fashioned letter and sent it off.

"Many months later, over Thanksgiving vacation, I had a call from the ex-love, telling me he got my letter. However, this was on an answering machine since I wasn't home, so I still haven't talked to him. But the actual search in finding him was relatively easy and all done electronically. What fun."

ProfNet

Another way of finding sources of interviews is through ProfNet, a cooperative of university public information officers. At present, ProfNet aims its services at working staff and freelance journalists, although they say " we are exploring ways to broaden our cooperative approach. For example, we are test-piloting a ProfNet-like service aimed at helping corporations find academic experts to assist in technology transfer. And we have taken early steps toward creating a global experts database on the World Wide Web—a resource we intend to make accessible to the entire international community."

"ProfNet" ("Professors Network") is a cooperative of public information officers (PIOs) linked on the Internet to provide journalists and authors convenient access to expert sources. It is coordinated by the State University of New York at Stony Brook's Office of University Affairs.

At ProfNet's core is an e-mail distribution list that enables our news staff to send journalists' queries simultaneously to public information officers throughout North America and overseas. PIOs respond directly to the inquirer by e-mail, fax, phone, or hard mail—whatever route you specify.

ProfNet is not a listserv or bulletin board system. It is a by-invitation-only mailing list. Your query is placed directly into the e-mail boxes of our members.

As of December, 1994, our membership included 1,500 PIOs employed by 800 institutions in 17 countries. For the most part, our members represent colleges, universities, and a wide range of government, corporate, and non-profit entities oriented to scholarship and research.

How to Make a Query

In submitting queries, please specify your news organization, the nature of your project, the nature of the expertise you seek, your time frame, and the manner in which you wish PIOs to respond. The more detailed your query—and the more lead time you give us—the more successful your search will be. There is no fee for conducting ProfNet searches, nor is there any limit to the number or frequency of your queries.

You may deliver queries to ProfNet as follows:

*By Internet: scitech@quadnet.vyne.com

*By phone: 516-941-3736 or 800-PROFNET

*By fax: 516-689-1425

*By phone: 800-PROF-NET (800-776-3638) or (516-632-6332)

"PIOs ONLINE"

The Stony Brook Guide to PIOs Online provides e-mail addresses and other contact information (phone, fax, and hard mail) for public information officers who had joined ProfNet. Any academic PIO with an e-mail address is eligible to be listed in future editions. Cost is $20 U.S.

Why Conduct an E-mail Interview?

The traditional interview is usually done in person or by telephone. The aim is to get information. If it's for print, a notebook or tape recorder is used, and the interviewer is asking questions that can be used as quotes or background in published copy, ranging from a short news item to a full-length book. The broadcast interview, on the other hand, has the aim of finding a short sound bite that will fit into an overall script. As the years have gone by, the sound bite has gotten shorter, shrinking from as much as a minute in the early 1960s to a usual maximum of 25 seconds today. Only in traditional documentaries are longer clips used. The broadcast interview, whether it's taped or live, has other considerations. Producers and researchers are always looking not only for the right person but trying to find out if that person is a "good talker," someone who is articulate in the television or radio studio.

So what are the circumstances when you should use an e-mail interview?

» To answer short puzzlers, those questions where reference material isn't easily available

» To track down new sources for your research

» If you make first contact by e-mail, you've already overcome the "cold call barrier" that even experienced researchers face. Once you've exchanged a couple of e-mail messages with your source, picking up the phone is easy.

» To "pre-interview" a source you will later telephone or meet in person

» If the interview is highly technical

» To follow-up and fact check an earlier e-mail message, telephone call, or personal interview

» If a reporter or researcher is established in a newsgroup or mailing list, it creates an ongoing relationship with sources and potential sources.

E-mail has added a new tool for the interviewer, one that can enhance the interviewing process and take the media or academic interview in new and unforeseen directions.

The E-mail Interview

Let's say you've established contact and now you're ready to ask the questions. Take a look for a moment at the usual interview. If you telephone a source, he or she is at the office, or at home. It can be quick, over in a minute. You ask the question you need an answer to, thank the source, and hang up. It can be as long as a half hour or an hour and delve into many areas of the source's life, the event you're reporting, or the issue you're covering. All the time the interviewer is listening to the sound of the source's voice; the way he or she uses words, the tone of voice, pauses. This information helps tell the researcher more about the subject, adding to what the source is saying. At the same time (and interviewers often forget this) the source is listening to what *you* are saying. If you're in too much of a hurry, or you sound bored, or if you have your own agenda, that all will come through on the telephone.

The in-person interview gives the interviewer (and in the case of television, the audience) an even greater picture of the interview subject or television guest. The interviewer watches the subject's eyes, the body language and gestures, all for clues of what the subject is really saying. Television can, of course, sometimes deceive the interviewer, and the viewer, especially if the subject is trained as an actor or is experienced with television. A good television interviewer, such as Ted Koppel of *Nightline*, or the late Barbara Frum of CBC's *The Journal*, usually draws out some measure of truth from the TV guest. You don't have any of these extra clues with the e-mail interview.

Cocooning

When a television crew shows up at someone's office or home, there's a reporter and camera person, perhaps a sound person, and sometimes a producer as well. There's all that equipment and it's the job of the reporter (or the producer if they're alone) to make the subject forget that there's the camera, the lights, the lavaliere mike on their shirt, and believe that there's just a one-on-one conversation between the interviewer and the interviewee. It's the job of the interviewer to make the subject relax and concentrate on the questions. It's called *cocooning*. When you conduct an e-mail interview, your subject is, most often, already in a cocoon.

We've discussed how someone reacts differently if he's in his basement or den, typing e-mail or Usenet articles alone, with no one to bother him. We know that human emotions seldom come across in cold electronic type. That's why emoticons, such as the smiley :-), were invented. We've also seen how people will often feel that if they're in the privacy of their own home, laws in the outside world may not apply to them.

So if your source agrees to answer a few questions by e-mail, he or she will often be answering those questions in his or her own cocoon. His fingers fly over the keyboard typing answers in a different way than if talking on the telephone or facing a microphone. Thus, if your aim is to go to the heart of your subject, you may find some interesting insights into an individual's character, life, and work from an e-mail interview—something you might not get in person.

Then again, you might not. A number of people who had worked with computers and the Net, the same people who send out scores of e-mail messages, were reluctant to do e-mail interviews for this book, and they were interviewed the old-fashioned way, by phone. Others were the opposite, they were too busy to come to the phone but supplied long e-mail messages. In most research, you're dealing with people. Everyone's different. Be prepared to adapt to make your subject comfortable.

The E-mail Pre-interview

One area where the e-mail interview is valuable is in what's called the "pre-interview." Pre-interview is a broadcasting term. A researcher, producer, or reporter is looking for a good on-air subject for an interview. The "pre-interview" is used to check the person out. Is the person a "good talker?" Does he or she know the subject at hand? If the source is a bureaucrat or company official, are they high enough in the hierarchy to answer the questions?

There are rules for the pre-interview, A key one is that the researcher tells the source that she or he is looking for information. There's usually no commitment to booking a guest on a show, so the interviewer can draw out information over the telephone. Print reporters will often do the same thing, asking a few questions before decided whether to go ahead or to give the source a polite "thank you" and hang up.

The e-mail pre-interview is a new and valuable tool for anyone conducting research. Here's how the pre-interview can help you:

» It helps establish whether the source knows the subject you're interested in.

» It helps you avoid costly duplication. Does the source have new insight or is the source just repeating what someone else has said better?

» It keeps down the cost of long-distance calls. If you get the preliminaries out of the way, then you and the subject know what you're going to talk about ahead of time. The farther away the subject, the more valuable this information.

» If you're traveling out of town, e-mail is a cost-effective way to set up appointments. The questions you ask online provide an opening focus for the interview. This is especially helpful if you have limited time with each subject in each city you're visiting.

» A good pre-interview eliminates "housekeeping" questions such as general biographical information. (Many people keep an ASCII copy of their resume on their hard drives. Ask for it. Also, asking basic questions by e-mail helps you prepare. It will give you ideas for questions you ask when you're phoning or meeting the subject. It may give you ideas where you can do more research on the subject before you conduct the in-person interview.

For broadcasters, the type on the computer monitor cannot tell you if the person you've contacted is a "good talker." Sometimes people who are eloquent speakers are finger-tied at the keyboard and sometimes people who type beautiful prose are lousy taped interviews. With e-mail as one more tool, however, you're further ahead—you at least have more background information and possibly new sources, even if the person you're talking to doesn't work out. How much work you do, of course, depends, on whether you're working two hours ahead of an interview on an afternoon news show or preparing a multi-episode documentary.

The Questions

What do you ask in the e-mail interview? The suggestions for good e-mail netiquette also apply to the e-mail interview. Keep everything as tightly focused as possible. Here are some e-mail interview suggestions:

» **Ask housekeeping and biographical questions first.** That not only gets them out of the way, it starts your subject typing and makes it easier for them to answer later questions.

» **Plan your questions carefully.** Remember the focus of your story or research project. Know *what* you want and *why* you want it.

» **Keep your questions simple—but open-ended.** A simple question doesn't intimidate the source. An open-ended question allows the source to think about the answer and could lead to an answer you, the questioner, did not think of. The source may give you an unexpected answer. Simple questions also often show that you don't know as much as you thought.

» **Ask just one question at a time.** It's not only easier for the source, it's easier for you to find that answer on disk when it comes time to include it in your report. *Ask questions*—don't make statements, answer your own question, or start a flame war.

» **Don't be afraid to ask difficult questions.** All the source can do is leave them blank. Most often, they will answer. At the same time, consider whether the most personal of questions are appropriate for online or better at an in-person interview.

» **Remember that you're a researcher, not a prosecutor.** Craft your questions carefully.

» **Personalize your questions**, even if you're using a basic boiler plate template. Use your research to find and ask that question that no one else has asked.

» **Ask for anecdotes.** It doesn't matter whether you're a journalist, student, or academic, anecdotes and stories illustrate your research. If you're an academic with a fear of "anecdotal evidence," do your research first and then find the anecdotes that illustrate and dramatize your data and your thesis.

» **Never underestimate your source.** She or he probably does know more than you do—at least in some fields.

The e-mail interview is seldom a complete substitute for an in-person or telephone contact. However, it's a way of smoothing the way and finding insights you might not otherwise find.

Note

Always make it clear in your initial contact that the questions the source is answering are for publication either in the media or in an academic paper where she will be quoted. With asynchronous communications there are many possibilities for misunderstanding. No one can ask online "can we go off the record here" as they might in a personal interview. It's also the interviewee's responsibility not to include confidential or off-the-record information in an e-mail interview without reaching an agreement first with the researcher.

The E-mail Questionnaire

Should you use a questionnaire for your e-mail interview?

You can, but you should be aware that there is a questionnaire netiquette emerging as more people come on the Net. Here are some thoughts to consider:

» **Don't create a spam questionnaire.** That's a random questionnaire you post on one or more newsgroups or mailing lists. It will offend most of the people in the group, few people will answer it, and as with similar mail-in or telephone polls the answers will be unreliable—only those people with an agenda will answer. If you feel you want to post it anyway, ask the list-owner, newsgroup moderator, or sysop for permission.

» **Find your sources first** and then focus your questionnaire to the subject of your project.

» **Ask permission to send the questionnaire** when you make your initial contact with the source.

Let's take another look at the initial query:

If you will agree to be one of my contacts, I'd like to interview you about your work first by e-mail with a follow-up by telephone. I also have a basic set of 14 short questions that I'm asking everyone.

Not everyone agreed to this, but enough people did. We had a brief look at the questionnaire used for this book when we were discussing how to handle the material in a text-retrieval database. Now here's the complete questionnaire.

Here are the questions I'm asking everyone I'm talking to. It helps give me a sense of the breadth of the Internet. Please feel free to answer as many, or as few, as you see fit.

Name

Company

E-Mail

Phone

Date

1. *What main hardware and software do you use to access the Internet?*

2. *What mail reader and news reader do you use?*

3. *Do you have a favorite search system, such as Gopher, Veronica, Mosaic, and so on?*

4a. *What kind of research do you do on the Internet?*

4b. *How long?*

4c. *How has research on the Net changed in recent years?*

5. *Please tell me an Internet research success story?*

6. *Do you have an Internet research horror story?*

7. *What advice would you give to other people using the Internet to do research?*

8. *Since this book is called "Researching on the Internet," are there any questions you don't know the answers to that you'd like me to answer?*

9. *What is the main thing you wish people had told you when you started doing research on the Net?*

10. *What's your favorite location for finding information on the Internet?*

11. *What's your best software or Net surfing trick?*

12. *How do you organize your material once it's off the Net?*

13. *Any other advice you would give to researchers working on the Net?*

14. *What do you see in the future for the Internet?*

The questionnaire evolved as the project went along and the original questionnaire grew from ten to 14 questions. Often specific questions were added, aimed at a specific interview subject. Fifteen questions are a lot; 20 questions are probably a maximum. Be prepared for the fact that many of your correspondents will not answer all the questions or will simply say "N/A" to some. Once you have a response to the questionnaire, then you can ask specific follow-up questions as you wish.

The Follow-up

Once you've completed the e-mail interview, you should do a follow-up in person or by telephone. First, many researchers are aware—and wary—of the problem of identity hacking or mistaken identity on the Net. So, whenever possible, you should confirm the identity of your e-mail source with a phone call.

A phone call, or a visit, will also give you the chance to get an all-important "feel" for the person that you need to judge both the e-mail and in-person answers. Just hearing the person's voice will change the way you view that person, adding another dimension to your research.

An in-person visit, of course, will give you the color that you won't ever be able to get by reading an e-mail message. You will be able to see if that e-mail message came from a glass and steel corporate office tower, a one-bedroom apartment home business or an ivy-covered stone quadrangle at a university.

There are times, of course, when you can't do that follow-up, such as when your subject is on another continent and you don't have the budget for an airline flight or long-distance call. You should learn to judge and evaluate the answers from an e-mail interview just as you learn to evaluate material on a Web site or in a paper file. That comes with experience.

The Net is a virtual neighborhood that gives you many more opportunities to do research. The Net levels the playing field. A reporter on a small town paper or a grad student at a small college has as much access to the Net as a reporter for the *Washington Post* or *The New York Times* or a senior professor at a major university. The Net is erasing the boundaries between people and nations. It's just as easy to send an e-mail message to another continent as it is to send one to someone five blocks away. It is generally a friendly and informed neighborhood and many times, you'll find that the people in your community will often (although not always) be willing to answer your questions.

E-mail Success Stories

"In 1992, I organized eight authors (plus myself) to write a paper that reviewed the state of a major research field in astronomy (determining distances to galaxies). Each author described a different technique. The eight sections were e-mailed/FTP-ed to me where I edited them into a draft version of the final paper. That draft was placed in a public FTP archive for the authors to retrieve. They then commented on all the sections, e-mailing their thoughts to me to be merged. The comments were distributed to all authors, a second draft was created, and the process was repeated one more time.

"The authors were from all over the U.S. and Canada. Traveling was unreasonable for the multiple drafts and regular mail was inconveniently slow. The Internet provided an excellent vehicle to make this large collaboration a possibility."
—*George Jacoby National Optical Astronomy Observatories*

"I've asked for (and gotten) lots of "real people" to comment on general subjects on the Net. On rec.arts.tv.soaps and alt.fan.oj-simpson, I found people to comment on America's fascination with O.J. On rec.arts.tv, I found folks addicted to televised trials. That sort of thing."
—*Heather Newman, Tucson (Arizona.) citizen*

"Recently, the University of Southern California sent me a printed list of all of their experts who are available to the media. I sent them e-mail congratulating them on publishing the Internet addresses of the people on the list. This resulted in an exchange of messages that led to us shooting a story on the new USC "cybrary," an Internet-equipped library."
—*George Lewis, NBC News*

The Delphi Study: Academic E-mail

Michael Barnes is a Ph.D. student in the Psychosocial Stress Research Program at Florida State University who is using the Internet and e-mail to complete a *Delphi study* for his dissertation. He explained it this way in an e-mail interview:

"My research will be with professionals who work with the families of children who have been physically traumatized and admitted into hospitals for critical medical care, so I am interested in lists that would include critical-care medical professionals, emergency room physicians/nurses, hospital social workers, and others.

"A Delphi study is a methodology in which experts on a certain subject are polled about the subject in the hope of developing some type of consensus about an aspect of that subject. It was developed by scientists at the Rand Corporation in the late 1950s and early 60s as a means of consensus building and [making] future predictions concerning bombing sites in the U.S., in the event of an attack on our country.

"Generally, the researcher develops a set of five or six general questions concerning the topic of interest and asks the experts to respond with as much detail as possible for each question.

"An example from my study will be that experts will be asked to identify various response patterns of families after the traumatic injury of the child. The experts will be asked not only to identify the patterns but to provide as much information as possible about each (such as perceived reasons for the reaction, factors associated with the development of the pattern, inhibitions of the pattern, and so on).

"Once each of the experts has responded, the researcher and associates analyze the information and create a second questionnaire that consists of specific statements that address all possible answers/factors for each question on the original questionnaire.

"Each statement will then have a scale beside it. Each expert will then vote whether they strongly agree [or] disagree that that specific factor is indeed an appropriate response for that answer. This is where we begin to identify a consensus between experts about the research topic. This list can be quite long and very time—consuming for experts to complete. Some Delphi studies will then send a third questionnaire to the experts with the results of the second questionnaire, giving the experts the opportunity to change their own opinion about each question. Most in recent years have not undertaken the third questionnaire because of the exhaustion factors discussed by experts.

"In recent years, this methodology has been utilized in the field of marriage and family therapy on several occasions because it allows the researchers to inductively identify factors that are difficult to operationalize for strictly quantitative research. The methodology is valuable for theory development in cases where the existing theory is weak or non-existent (which is the case in my area of study).

"I believe that the methodology is tailor–made for the Internet. The major problem will be the recruitment of subjects/experts via the Internet. It is for this reason that I am looking for various discussion groups, listservs, and so on that may include academics and practitioners who have access to the Net.

"The definition of expert is not specific and is the responsibility of the researcher to decide. Most others have included specific levels of training, experience, publications in a specific area, and presentations at professional meetings on a specific topic. I can't believe that I'll deviate from a somewhat standard criteria. The issue is gaining access to the individuals who have these specific experiences/credentials.

"There have been various studies concerning the phenomenon of electronic bulletin boards and how they influence communication and social interaction, but I've only been able to identify a few with limited value to my research. If we can pull this project off, we may be the ones who can set the standard for developing a research methodology for recruitment and data collection on the Internet."

12

Finding the Right Information with Gopher

Gopher is one of the most powerful research tools on the Internet. Gopher can search and retrieve any kind of file using menus or the search tools, Veronica and Jughead. And Gopher has FTP (File Transfer Protocol) and telnet functions built right in, so it can connect to and retrieve files from remote sites without you ever needing to know about FTP or telnet!

This chapter provides you with the Internet addresses of over a dozen mighty Gophers. But having a number of these starting points will soon be less important to you, because most of these starting points will fade in importance as you find menus in *Gopherspace* that meet your own particular needs, menus that have information on your own research topics. And any solitary Gopher address will also diminish in importance as you discover that most Gophers are connected to each other in one way or another!

Tip   **Ready for Gopher Addresses?**

If you are already familiar with Gopher and how to use it, you may want to turn immediately to the section in this chapter called "A Beginning Inventory of Gopher Bookmarks." There we share some of the best Gopher addresses for all kinds of research.

Because almost all the Gopher servers in the world are interconnected, they are collectively referred to as Gopherspace. This chapter shows you how to do research using the Veronica tool for searching *all* of Gopherspace at one time or using the Jughead tool to search *distinct parts of Gopherspace.*

Additionally, this chapter points you to several Gopher servers that in turn point to other Gopher servers based on the subject matter of the information you are researching. The importance of subject-oriented Gophers will become clear as we delve more deeply into using Gopher as a research tool.

And, finally, this chapter also includes a summary of the popular UNIX Gopher client commands that researchers should know and a list of over two dozen sites you can telnet to in order to use a remote Gopher client—in case you have no access to a Gopher client locally.

Gopher Basics

Gopher is one of the Internet's most powerful but under-recognized tools. Gopher is a menu-based software program that allows you to choose interesting topics from a series of menus. As you make choices along the way, you navigate closer to information on your research topic, and you bring home any information you want. Gopher also allows you to access many different types of Internet files and resources while simplifying your work by showing all these different kinds of files and resources in a single, uniform, straightforward menu.

Gopher menus are usually hierarchically structured, so that major topics at the top menu are subdivided into increasingly finer minor subject menus, with levels of menus branching from broad topics into more and more limited and specific subject areas. Every Gopher menu is made up of items (or, actually, *pointers to* items), and/or *pointers to* other menus.

So, Gopherspace is made up of menus that point to other menus. This may be confusing right now, but when you use Gopher the distinction between items and menus becomes easy. When there are no more options (menus), you have discovered an item! It's like a pot of gold at the end of the rainbow—your reward for researching with Gopher.

Because Gophers do all the work of finding the items and menus on each menu, *you* don't have to remember the rules for each resource (Telnet or FTP, for example) or where the items are actually stored. Instead, you just focus on your research topic and keep on pointing and clicking. Gopher remembers the stored menu addresses and the Telnet and FTP rules for you, and all you need to do is point the Gopher to menu items you want to explore further, recording your progress with *bookmarks* along the way.

Tip

Regardless of which software Gopher client you use, there are several tasks you must learn to do with Gopher. The most important software client functions you'll need to learn for any Gopher you use are as follows:

» *Saving bookmarks of remote menus and items*

» *Using bookmarks to fetch (connect to) remote servers*

» *Organizing and editing your bookmarks*

» *Saving a file to disk*

» *Printing a file*

» *Viewing a text file or graphic*

» *Discovering where you are in Gopherspace*

» *Searching Gopherspace with Veronica and Jughead*

» *Connecting directly to a remote Gopher server*

When you install and begin to learn about any new Gopher client software program, these tasks are the most essential to learn.

Gopher is also very efficient in its use of Net resources. Instead of holding an FTP or Telnet port on the host server from "log-in" to "bye," even though no data is being received or sent (which is what typical Telnet or FTP programs do), Gopher dynamically connects to the remote site, transfers your needed data, and immediately closes the connection all in one fell swoop. Your use of the remote server is quick, and allows others to share the site also.

The Future of Gopher

Many Internet gurus say that the World Wide Web is better than Gopher, and will eventually replace Gopher—and they're probably right. The best Web browsers (such as Mosaic and Netscape) can do more than a UNIX Gopher, and Gopher can't handle imbedded hypertext links or inline images like a Web browser. But Web browsers have the disadvantage that they are designed with the assumption that users will have very fast Internet connections, fast micro-processor speeds, and at least VGA graphics. Many Internet users simply do not have this kind of computer "muscle power." Furthermore, not all gopher resources are (yet) to be mapped to the World Wide Web.

The original Gopher protocol, on the other hand, was designed to work with slow modem speeds, monochrome graphics, straight ASCII, and slow processor speeds. So, Gopher will serve as the "Table of Contents" for the Internet for several years to come, until all users are ready for the computational demands of the World Wide Web.

Gopher Client Software

The Windows-compatible Gopher client program we demonstrate in this chapter is called WSGopher. This software program has the most advanced, user-friendly bookmark editing on the market (we'll discuss the importance of bookmarks and editing them in the next section). Figure 12-1 shows the WSGopher main screen.

Tip

Here's the address for you to FTP, a free copy of the WSGopher program, and the FAQ:

Host FTP Server	*Subdirectory*	*Exact filename*
`devey.tis.inel.gov`	`/pub/wsgopherwsg-12.zip`	`WSGopher.FAQ`

WSGopher requires you to use a Windows-compatible TCP/IP stack such as Trumpet Winsock, unless you are using Windows '95, which comes with its own TCP/IP software. And because some researchers are using UNIX shell accounts but cannot use SLIP/PPP to use the TCP/IP protocol all the way to their personal computer, we will review the basic functions of the most popular UNIX Gopher client at the end of the chapter.

WSGopher is Windows-Compatible

WSGopher was written by Dave Brooks (gopher@tis.inel.gov) of the Idaho National Engineering Laboratory. He should be proud of this fine Gopher software client. I wish that Netscape and Mosaic had the same kind of flexible, powerful categorical bookmark editing, because bookmarks are the way I record much of my Internet research. And bookmark handling is only one of WSGopher's strong suits.

For instance, cutting and pasting from the Windows Clipboard and from program to program is a breeze. If you use a Windows-compatible e-mail reading program, this allows you to quickly check out a new Gopher item or Gopher menu after reading e-mail about an exciting new resource. You just copy the new Gopher address into the Windows Clipboard from your e-mail reading program by highlighting the address with the mouse and pressing Ctrl+c or

Figure 12-1.
WSGopher has great navigation and bookmark tools now available

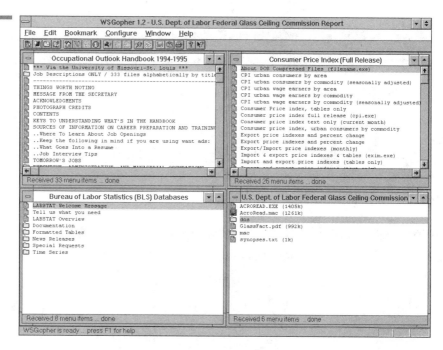

Ctrl+Insert, then open (or maximize) WSGopher and open the File menu to New Gopher Item, paste in the new address, and *voilà!* Table 12-1 gives a handy summary of all the *hot keys* used by WSGopher.

Table 12-1.
WSGopher Hot Keys

Function Key	Drop-down	Menu Operation
F1	Help	Contextual Help
Ctrl+n	File	New Gopher Item
Ctrl+h	File	Home Gopher
Ctrl+i	File	Info on Item
F5	File	Reload/Resubmit Search
Ctrl+s	File	Save Item
Ctrl+p	File	Print
Alt+F4	File	Exit
Ctrl+c	Edit	Copy
Ctrl+Insert		Copy
Ctrl+v		Paste
Shift+Insert		Paste
Ctrl+f	Edit	Find
F3	EditFind	Again
Ctrl+Esc	Control Menu*	Switch to

*As in all Windows applications, the hot key for accessing the Control Menu is Alt+Spacebar

WSGopher Toolbar Buttons

All of the most-used features of WSGopher are conveniently available as buttons on the toolbar. With very little practice you can pick up the meaning of the buttons, and soon hardly ever use the menus. Here are the meanings of the WSGopher toolbar buttons, from left to right:

- » Fetch Bookmark Menu
- » Adding Item Bookmarks
- » Adding Directory Bookmarks
- » Using Bookmark Editor
- » Visiting your Home Gopher
- » Go to the top of the Gopher outline
- » Backtrack one item
- » Find information on a Gopher item
- » Fetch a Gopher item or menu
- » Cancel the current transaction
- » Cancel all transactions
- » Finding text in a Gopher Window
- » Finding text again
- » Saving the current item or selection to disk
- » Copying the current item or selection to the Clipboard
- » Printing the current item or selection
- » About WSGopher, version number, copyright, and contact
- » Get contextual help

WSGopher's Advanced Navigational Tools

As you see, WSGopher allows you to cancel an online operation, which is very helpful when Net-lags are taking too long, or when another priority comes up.

It also allows you to backtrack one menu (choice) at a time, or to jump to the top of the current Gopher host's menu. This is very convenient, because when you discover a new source of valuable research data far down in a menu system, it is often very useful to see the whole panorama of topics available from that Gopher server. Even Netscape and Mosaic have not yet implemented this kind of simple contextual navigation tool. Once again, WSGopher leads the way! Figure 12-2 is from the WSGopher help screen that defines the toolbar buttons.

Figure 12-2.
WSGopher's toolbar buttons are explained in the online help file

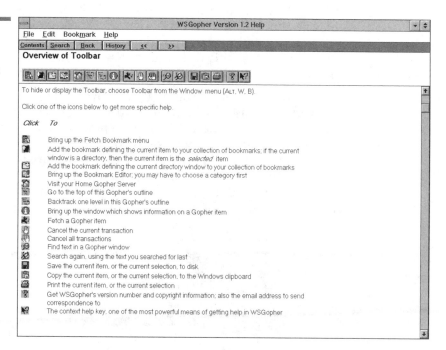

Gopher Bookmarks

Gopher bookmarks are a wonderful time-saver. They work just like a physical bookmark—they allow you to quickly and easily return to wherever in cyberspace you paused before. Just as Hansel and Gretel left a trail of bread crumbs when they ventured out into the forest, you can leave *bookmarks* along your path in cyberspace to trace when you need to come back the same way.

Once my Gopher bookmarks were maliciously erased, just as Hansel and Gretel's bread crumbs were eaten by a wicked crow, and I was lost for weeks! But today, my Gopher WSGopher bookmarks are organized by my own interesting topic names so I can always remember the right topic area to look in. And I back-up my bookmarks file (wsgopher.ini) regularly!

Another good thing about WSGopher is that it comes with a built-in set of bookmarks already loaded. As soon as you've installed it and started the program you can begin your research. Figure 12-3 shows the WSGopher Bookmark editor so that you can see the many categories of bookmarks displayed in a drop-down box for category selection.

WSGopher allows you to save two different types of bookmarks—item and menu—to any bookmark category you have already established, or to create a new category of bookmarks on the fly. You can also set a default bookmark category, and all new bookmarks will be stored in that category until further notice. However, this will require that sometime later you use the Bookmark menu to Edit Bookmarks and sort them into the proper categories.

Although it is quicker and easier to save each new bookmark into a "default" category (such as, New Bookmarks or China Research), I find it impossible to stay on only one topic as I move into new areas of Gopherspace. So I have no default bookmark category defined, and I therefore categorize each new bookmark as soon as I press the toolbar bookmark button. This also makes it slightly easier for me to store a single bookmark into *two* categories, which I occasionally find necessary. Figure 12-4 shows the bookmark category selection/creation tool that always pops up when I make a new bookmark.

Figure 12-3.
WSGopher's advanced design makes bookmarks easy to use.

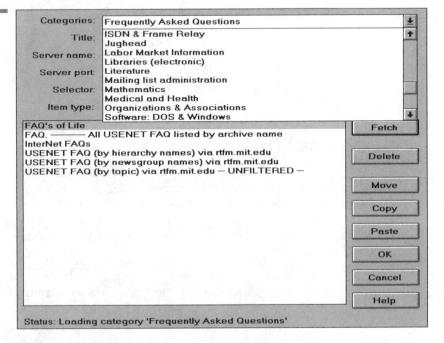

Figure 12-4.
WSGopher's bookmark
category selection tool is
easy to use and
customize.

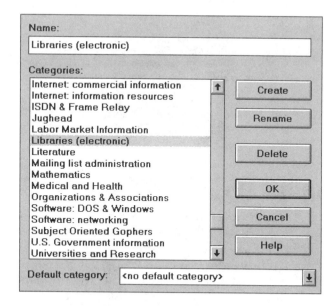

Navigation From Text in the Windows Clipboard

Incredibly, WSGopher has even more impressive bookmark features. It can find a Gopher bookmark *inside text* in the Windows Clipboard! It just looks through all the text you saved to the Clipboard (from your e-mail reader, for instance), and finds the needed information to connect to that new Gopher server. So, if you use a Windows-compatible e-mail reader or Usenet newsreader you just highlight the new Gopher information on the screen and then press Ctrl+c (or Ctrl+Insert) to save the new Gopher address (and all the text around it) into the Clipboard.

Next, when you open the WSGopher File menu, and click on New Gopher Item, a "Fetch this Gopher Item" box appears. Because WSGopher knows that you have already added the Gopher address information to the Windows Clipboard, the top right Paste button will be available, and when you press the Paste button WSGopher parses the information you placed into the Clipboard and puts each data element onto the correct line of the "Fetch this Gopher Item" box for you. Now this is what automation is supposed to be!

Once the information has been pasted into the "Fetch this Gopher Item" box, you're ready to click on the OK button and actually connect to the remote Gopher server to see what your e-mail correspondent liked about this new Gopher address. If you like the site, save it as a bookmark! Figure 12-5 shows the "Fetch this Gopher Item" box after WSGopher automatically fills-in the blanks from the Windows Clipboard.

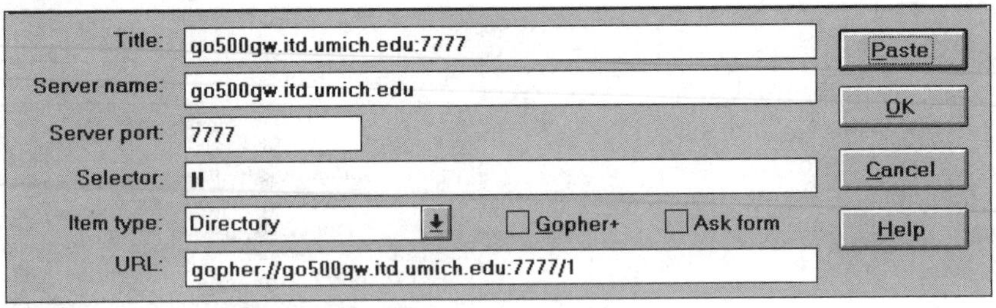

Figure 12-5.
WSGopher's Clipboard
parser fills-in the Fetch
box for you!

Title:	go500gw.itd.umich.edu:7777
Server name:	go500gw.itd.umich.edu
Server port:	7777
Selector:	II
Item type:	Directory ▼ ☐ Gopher+ ☐ Ask form
URL:	gopher://go500gw.itd.umich.edu:7777/1

Buttons: Paste, OK, Cancel, Help

Saving and Printing Files with Gopher

As shown in Table 12-1, WSGopher makes it especially easy to save items and/or print them using Windows hot-keys or from the File menu. The hot key for saving an item from Gopher to a disk drive is Ctrl+s, and the hot-key for printing an item from Gopher is Ctrl+p. Of course, you will have to double-click on the item first to fetch it before you can print it or save it. Figure 12-6 gives a detailed look at the WSGopher File menu.

Gathering Information on a Gopher Item

Sometimes you don't want to save or print an item—you just want to record where you found it for further study later, or to recommend it to someone else. You can always make a bookmark of the item, and place it in a bookmark category that you will understand and recall. But if you want to know exactly where the item is actually stored, on which remote Gopher server, you can get

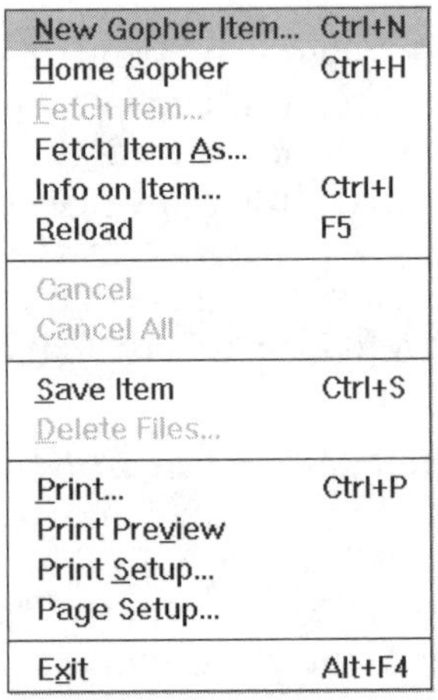

Figure 12-6.
WSGopher's File menu
also allows you to Save,
Print, Cancel, and gather
Info on an item.

New Gopher Item...	Ctrl+N
Home Gopher	Ctrl+H
Fetch Item...	
Fetch Item As...	
Info on Item...	Ctrl+I
Reload	F5
Cancel	
Cancel All	
Save Item	Ctrl+S
Delete Files...	
Print...	Ctrl+P
Print Preview	
Print Setup...	
Page Setup...	
Exit	Alt+F4

this data by using the File menu to gather Info on an item, as was shown in Figure 12-6. This is very handy if you are telling others about a Gopher item's location so they can visit also.

A Beginning Inventory of Gopher Bookmarks

Here are some well-constructed Gopher servers that can lead you to other resources, including many other Gopher servers. Each Gopher server listed has a broad range of subject matter bookmarks, and each one has a reputation for keeping its links up to date. Because the Net changes so quickly, it takes a lot of work to keep a Gopher server at the cutting edge, and the Internet community is indebted to the Gopher-masters at these sites.

Each listing contains both a UNIX Gopher address and an address suitable for WSGopher and Web browsers such as Netscape, Cello, and Mosaic. The URL can be used to connect to each of these Gophers with a Web browser or you can also use this information to connect to remote Gophers using WSGopher. Simply type the second address line into any Windows-compatible word or text processor (the Windows Notepad application, for example), highlight the line with the mouse, then press Ctrl+c (or Ctrl+Insert) to save the new Gopher address (and the text around it) into the Windows Clipboard.

Then open (or maximize) WSGopher, pull down the File menu, and click on New Gopher Item and a Fetch this Gopher Item box will appear. Because WSGopher knows that you have already added information to the Windows Clipboard, the top-right Paste button will be available, and when you press the Paste button WSGopher adds the Clipboard information to the correct lines of the "Fetch this Gopher Item" box. Now just click on the OK button and connect to the remote Gopher server.

Tip   *The Virtual Reference Desk*

The University of California at Irvine operates a "Virtual Reference Desk" containing amazing amounts of library reference materials. It has calendars, dictionaries, a thesaurus, the CIA World Factbook, government and congressional directories, ZIP codes of U.S. cities, a geographical name server, consumer information, plus over 20 other groups of Gopher servers organized by language used, major topics, and geographical location!

```
peg.cwis.uci.edu 7000

gopher://peg.cwis.uci.edu:7000/11%2Fgopher%2Ewelcome%2Fpeg%2F
       VIRTUAL%20REFERENCE%20DESK
```

International Gopher Sites

Europe
Subject Tree

Swedish University Computer Network—SUNET

```
gopher.sunet.se
gopher://gopher.sunet.se:70/11/Subject%20Tree
```

Subject Tree BUBL

Bath University Bulletin Board for Libraries, United Kingdom

```
ukoln.bath.ac.uk 7070
gopher://ukoln.bath.ac.uk:7070/11/L ink/Tree
```

Infosysteme in Deutschland

Technische Universitaet Clausthal

```
solaris.rz.tu-clausthal.de
gopher://solaris.rz.tu-clausthal.de:70/11/Gopher-de
```

North America
The World

Software Tool and Die

```
world.std.com
gopher://world.std.com:70/1
```

NYSERnet Gopher

New York State Education and Research Network

```
empire.nysernet.org 2347
gopher://empire.nysernet.org:2347/1%2Dt1%20%2Dm200%20%09nysernet
```

Finding Information and Resources (Internet Searching Tools)

Yale University

```
yaleinfo.yale.edu
gopher://yaleinfo.yale.edu:7700/11%2FInternet%2DSearchingTools
```

Global Electronic Library (by Subject)

United States Library of Congress

```
marvel.loc.gov
gopher://marvel.loc.gov/11%2Fglobal%09%2Bapplication%2Fgopher
        %2B%2Dmenu%20En%5FUS
```

Subject Menu

AMI MountainNet, West Virginia

```
gopher.mountain.net
gopher://gopher.mountain.net:70/1
```

Information by Subject Area

Rice University, Houston, Texas

```
chico.rice.edu
gopher://chico.rice.edu/11/Subject
```

Browse Information by Subject Area

Texas Agricultural and Mechanical University

```
gopher.tamu.edu
gopher://gopher.tamu.edu:70/11/.dir/subject.dir
```

Internet Resources by Subject

Michigan State University

```
burrow.cl.msu.edu
gopher://burrow.cl.msu.edu/11%2Finternet%2Fsubject
```

Clearinghouse of Subject-Oriented Internet Resource Guides

University of Michigan

```
una.hh.lib.umich.edu
gopher://una.hh.lib.umich.edu/11/in etdirs
```

The WELL

Whole Earth 'Lectronic Link

```
gopher.well.com
gopher://gopher.well.com:70/1
```

Resources by Subject

University of California at Santa Barbara

```
summit.ece.ucsb.edu
gopher://summit.ece.ucsb.edu/11/Resources
```

Gopher Jewels: Gophers by Subject Matter

University of Southern California, Los Angeles, California

```
cwis.usc.edu
gopher://cwis.usc.edu:70/11/Other_Gophers_and_Information_Re
      sources/Gophers_by_Subject/Gopher_Jewels/
```

Gopher Jewels are also mirrored in Australia at Monash University, in the United Kingdom at Warwick University, in Israel at Technion University, and in Turkey at Bilkent University. The site given above provides links to the mirrors. Use the one closest to you if you visit regularly.

PEG—Peripatetic Eclectic Gopher*

University of California at Irvine

```
peg.cwis.uci.edu 7000
gopher://peg.cwis.uci.edu:7000/
```

   * If you need to confine yourself to a single Gopher, this is probably the most complete "research" Gopher in the world.

Australia

Resources Classified by Subject

Australian National University

```
info.anu.edu.au
gopher://info.anu.edu.au:70/11/elibr ary/lc
```

Gopher Searches with Veronica

Veronica is the main search mechanism for Gopher. Veronica searches take into account the "recent" menus of over 5,000 Gopher servers throughout the world. Jughead, discussed in the next section, is a more limited tool that searches *portions* of Gopherspace rather than all of Gopherspace, as Veronica does.

Note

Some Veronica servers, like Jughead, are assigned to only search a defined part of Gopherspace, such as all Australian Gophers, or all Japanese Gophers. This allows us to make the best use of the Internet's precious intercontinental links, only using them when necessary. These geographically limited Veronica servers usually say what part of Gopherspace they search right on the last menu item before you fill in the search word(s). If it says (Australian Gopherspace) or (Japanese Gopherspace), for instance, you'll get only Australian or Japanese items on the search results!

Veronica is a software program that is accessed through a Gopher server. You choose a Veronica search from a menu of a Gopher server, and enter a search word or a set of search words. When the search is finished, the *results* are shown to you in menu form, but these menu items all fit only your search! You can browse the search results just as you do any Gopher menu.

Several Veronica servers are available throughout the world. When you access Veronica, you may be offered an opportunity to choose which server to use. But, because the servers don't all update at the same time, there will likely be some differences in their results. Also, some servers will answer faster than others, depending on their load, the time of day at the host site, and network traffic.

Tip

Dave Brooks, the author of the WSGopher software, shared one of his favorite WSGopher tricks with us, and you might like it, too!

When you're submitting Veronica searches, you can easily resubmit a failed search by just pressing the F5 key. As you'll quickly discover, the Veronica servers of the world are very busy, and sometimes they will reject your query, asking you to send it again "soon." WSGopher lets you send it again, very soon, by pressing the F5 key!

Other Veronica-access menus offer a single Veronica server entry rather than a list of several Veronica servers, and some others try to prioritize the various Veronica servers based on their recent responsiveness. The Gopher at

Washington and Lee University (WLU) is one that prioritizes Veronica servers on its menu based on recent response times.

Veronica Search of Gopher Menus

Washington and Lee University

```
liberty.uc.wlu.edu
gopher://liberty.uc.wlu.edu:70/11/gophers/veronica
```

A new, Simplified Veronica is also available from the University of Nevada, where Veronica was invented. It will try six servers in turn *for you,* so that you don't need to resubmit a search that failed because an individual server was too busy. Simplified Veronica may try three or four servers before one accepts your query, but you'll be able to just wait for it to do the work for you, instead of resubmitting your query over and over. If you don't care which server answers (you just want an answer!), then try Simplified Veronica. Figure 12-7 shows a Simplified Veronica query (for research in food safety) in progress. Two Veronica servers were too busy to accept the query (look at the top of Figure 12-7), and the third server answered. At the bottom of the screen are the search words used. If you don't get a reply from Simplified Veronica within one minute, try again right away. If it's unresponsive for several minutes, just wait an hour or so and try again.

The address to Gopher to in order to submit a Simplified Veronica query is:

Simplified Veronica: Find *All* Gopher Types

University of Nevada

```
info3.scs.unr.edu 8117
gopher://info3.scs.unr.edu:8117/
```

Some Veronica servers commonly allow you to specify whether you want to look for your search topic in:

- » Filenames
- » Directory names
- » Index entries
- » CSO phonebook servers
- » Telnet/TN3270 sites
- » All of the above

Figure 12-7.
Simplified Veronica is easy to use; just wait, it does the work

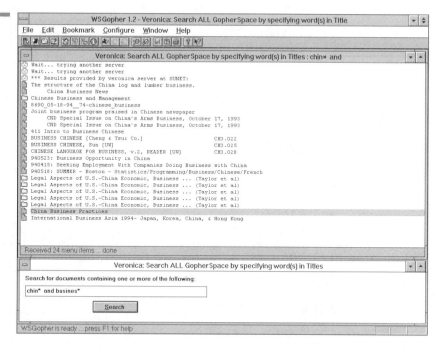

You can use this menu feature to limit your search to the kind of answers you would be most interested in. If you would not be interested in telephone directory entries as answers to your question, you can avoid looking at phone directories in the first place. If you're willing to pick through all kinds of wrong answers, you can use the "All" option, which looks everywhere in Gopherspace for your research words.

Caution

Veronica does not search the text of documents on Gopher servers. Veronica only searches the menu item titles for the documents and files on the servers.

Please note that Veronica does *not* do full-text searches of the contents of all the Gopher items on all Gophers in the world. Veronica, instead, finds resources by searching for your chosen words in titles of all the Gopher items in the world. Veronica finds resources whose titles contain your specified research word(s). The "title" that Veronica compares your research word(s) to is the title of the item or menu as it appears on the menu of its home Gopher server.

You can improve the quality and number of matches that Veronica will display for you by following the Veronica search rules. Steven Foster, who is one of Veronica's inventors, prepared a set of how-to instructions. Here is the URL:

```
gopher://veronica.scs.unr.edu:70/00/veronica/
         how-to-query-veronica
```

Improving Your Veronica Searches

Veronica can match many words from one search item. If you type in the following search pattern:

```
allerg*
```

Veronica will find all these words to match your pattern:

```
allergen
allergenic
allergic
allergist
allergy
```

So, ending your search pattern with an asterisk after the root word is a good idea, *if* you are interested in *broadening* your search scope. If you want to tighten your search, on the other hand, one of the simplest ways is to add a "not" statement. If you were interested in allergies, but wanted to avoid any information about asthma, your search would look like this:

```
allerg* not asthm*
```

Veronica can accept even more complicated searches, and you should study Steven Foster's "Veronica How-To" mentioned above to become a real Veronica guru. Almost all Veronica search menus include the bookmark for this document.

For instance, one of the easiest ways to improve your searches is to carefully use additional words. One-word searches are fine as far as they go, but they often can result in too many "hits" of low quality. You can tighten the focus on a search by adding more specific words.

For example, if you want to find more information about computers in cars, the following Veronica search:

```
comput* (automobile or car)
```

This search returned only one hit, while any of these three words individually returns hundreds of hits.

Gopher Searches with Jughead

Jughead is a newer, more bounded search tool than Veronica. Jughead often searches just one local Gopher server (or a local group of Gopher servers), rather than searching all the Gophers in the world. Jughead can be configured to search *parts of* several Gophers, so that a single college, corporation, or university campus can establish a Jughead for its own internal purposes to provide quicker searches of their own part of Gopherspace.

The Jughead server software comes from the University of Utah, where Rhett "Jonzy" Jones (jonzy@cc.utah.edu) developed this tool. It is usually faster than Veronica, because it only has to search a small part of Gopherspace. And Jughead usually has fewer "near-misses" that match your search word but aren't quite what you were after (because Jughead only searches a small number of Gopher menus, compared to Veronica).

The University of Utah maintains a menu of over 70 Jughead servers around the world for your convenience. By searching Veronica for the word *jughead,* I discovered that there are over 1,400 Jughead servers operating!

Caution   *Jughead reserves some special characters for itself, so you can't search for any of the following characters:*

! " # $ % & `  (  )  +  ,  -  .  /  :  ;  <  =  ?  @  [  \  ]  ^  _  ` { | } ~

If Jughead encounters any of these characters it pretends that character is a blank.

Search Menu Titles Using Jughead

University of Utah

`gopher.utah.edu`

UNIX Gopher Client Instructions

UNIX Gopher clients usually follow this rule: the most relevant actions at any time or cyberspace location are shown at the bottom of the screen. Figure 12-8 shows a typical UNIX Gopher screen, with the possible action options across the bottom.

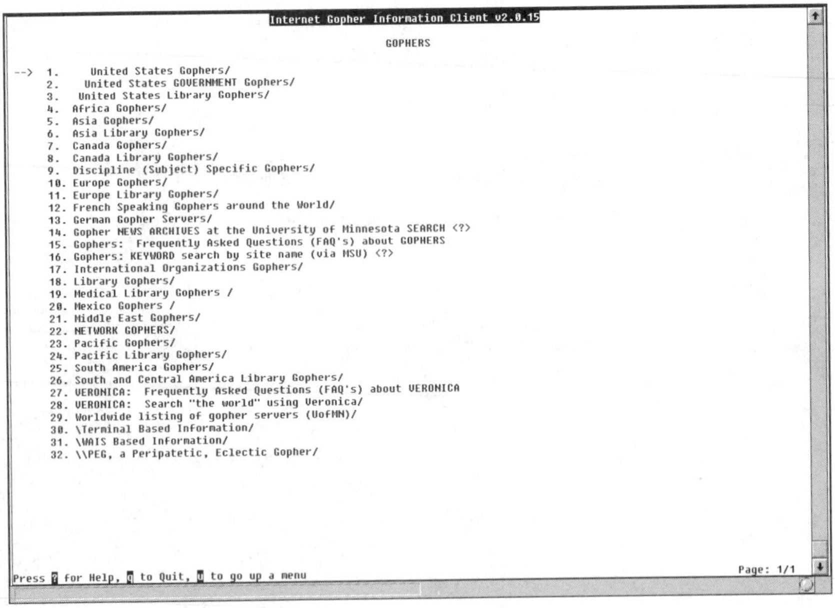

Figure 12-8.
This UNIX Gopher always displays your options at the bottom of the screen.

```
┌──────────────────────────────────────────────────────────────────────────┐
│                  Internet Gopher Information Client v2.0.15              ↑ │
│                                  GOPHERS                                   │
│   --> 1.    United States Gophers/                                        │
│       2.    United States GOVERNMENT Gophers/                             │
│       3.    United States Library Gophers/                                │
│       4.  Africa Gophers/                                                 │
│       5.  Asia Gophers/                                                   │
│       6.  Asia Library Gophers/                                           │
│       7.  Canada Gophers/                                                 │
│       8.  Canada Library Gophers/                                         │
│       9.  Discipline (Subject) Specific Gophers/                          │
│      10.  Europe Gophers/                                                 │
│      11.  Europe Library Gophers/                                         │
│      12.  French Speaking Gophers around the World/                       │
│      13.  German Gopher Servers/                                          │
│      14.  Gopher NEWS ARCHIVES at the University of Minnesota SEARCH <?>   │
│      15.  Gophers: Frequently Asked Questions (FAQ's) about GOPHERS       │
│      16.  Gophers: KEYWORD search by site name (via MSU) <?>              │
│      17.  International Organizations Gophers/                            │
│      18.  Library Gophers/                                                │
│      19.  Medical Library Gophers /                                       │
│      20.  Mexico Gophers /                                                │
│      21.  Middle East Gophers/                                            │
│      22.  NETWORK GOPHERS/                                                │
│      23.  Pacific Gophers/                                                │
│      24.  Pacific Library Gophers/                                        │
│      25.  South America Gophers/                                          │
│      26.  South and Central America Library Gophers/                      │
│      27.  VERONICA: Frequently Asked Questions (FAQ's) about VERONICA     │
│      28.  VERONICA:  Search "the world" using Veronica/                   │
│      29.  Worldwide listing of gopher servers (UofMN)/                    │
│      30.  \Terminal Based Information/                                    │
│      31.  \WAIS Based Information/                                        │
│      32.  \\PEG, a Peripatetic, Eclectic Gopher/                         │
│                                                                           │
│                                                                           │
│  Press ? for Help, q to Quit, u to go up a menu              Page: 1/1  ↓ │
└──────────────────────────────────────────────────────────────────────────┘
```

UNIX Gophers are also sometimes referred to as ASCII Gophers. (ASCII means American Standard Code for Information Interchange, and is the most common computer code that, for instance, all word processors can understand and accept.) The point is that almost anyone—using almost any computer and keyboard—can use these Gophers, because they are controlled by simple keystrokes that can be produced by almost any keyboard. Table 12-2 lists UNIX Gopher single keystroke commands.

Table 12-2.
UNIX Gopher single keystroke commands

General Information	Keystroke Result
?	Get a help summary
=	Display the technical address of the current item
q	Leave or quit Gopher
Q	Leave Gopher immediately
O	See and/or change the options of your UNIX Gopher
^G	Cancel
Enter	Accept

Table 12-2.

UNIX Gopher single
keystroke commands
(*continued*)

File Processing	Keystroke Result
m	Mail the current item to yourself (or someone else)
s	Save the current item to a file
p	Print the current item (if a printer is available)
D	Download the current item to a file
Bookmarks	**Keystroke Result**
a	Adds an item to your bookmark list
A	Adds the current menu or search to your bookmark list
v	View your bookmark list
d	Delete a bookmark
Searching Text	**Keystroke Result**
/word	Search for a word or phrase in a large menu
n	Find the next instance of the word you searched for
Movement in Gopherspace	**Keystroke Result**
Up Arrow	Moves you to the previous line
Down Arrow	Moves you to the next line
Left Arrow	Moves you up one menu level to the previous menu
Right Arrow	Selects or displays (more of) the current item
Space	Moves to the next page of the current menu
m	Jump back to the main menu
b	Moves you back to the previous page of the current menu
number	Jumps to, and selects, the menu item with that number
Alternate Cursor Movement Keystrokes*	**Keystroke Result**
Return	Selects or displays (more of) the current item
u	Move up one menu level to the previous menu
j	Move down one item

Table 12-2.
UNIX Gopher single
keystroke commands
(*continued*)

Ctrl+n	Move down one item (next item)
Ctrl+p	Move up one item (previous item)
k	Move up one item
>	Move to the next page of the current menu
+	Move to the next page of the current menu
<	Move to the previous page of the current menu
-	Move to the previous page of the current menu
*These alternative keystrokes may or may not work on some systems.	

UNIX Gopher Line-end Codes

The UNIX Gopher is textual rather than graphical like WSGopher, so it cannot use pictures and icons to communicate. Instead of menu icons indicating the nature of each item on each Gopher menu, the UNIX Gopher displays indicator codes at the *end* of each menu entry. If a Gopher menu item ends with a period, it is a text document. If a line ends with a forward slash (/) or virgule, it means the menu entry is a pointer to another menu. If it ends with a ?, it is a searchable index, and so on. Here are some common meanings for UNIX Gopher line-ends:

Code

.	Text file
/	Directory/Menu
Tel	Telnet session
3270	IBM 3270 emulation Telnet session
?	Searchable index
hqx	Macintosh compressed file
CSO	Sound file
MIME	Multipurpose Internet Mail Extensions file
HTML	Hypertext Markup Language file
Bin	Binary file
PC	BinDOS binary file
??	Ask form

Knowing what the item represents can help you avoid dead ends.

Public Access UNIX Gopher Clients

These sites allow public access to their Gopher client program. You can Telnet to any of these sites and use their Gopher as if it was on your personal computer, or at least as if it was in your UNIX shell account. The only disadvantages that most of these sites impose on you is that you will be unable to download, print, or save a file while using these Gophers. You'll need to mail the item to your e-mail address, and then you can download, print, or save the file. As of this writing, all of the Gopher addresses in Table 12-3 are working.

Caution

Although—or perhaps because—Gopher originated in Minnesota, the public-access Gopher client in Minnesota is unable to deal with the workload assigned to it. I have not been able to connect to it in over 12 months, and always receive an error message about it being out of working memory. In exploring the situation by e-mail I was repeatedly assured that the server does work, but it just can't handle many folks at one time. If you want to try it, here is the address:

Host Server Address	Log-in ID	Location
`consultant.micro.umn.edu`	`gopher`	`Minnesota`

I wish they could distribute the load among all the servers, as they do with the Simplified Veronica searches mentioned above.

Table 12-3.
Public-Access Gopher Servers

Host Server Address	Log-in ID	Location
Europe		
`gopher.torun.edu`	plgopher	Poland
`nfo.brad.ac.uk`	info	University of Bradford (United Kingdom)
`gopher.th-darmstadt.de`	gopher	Technische Hochschule Darmstadt (Germany)
`gopher.uv.es`	gopher	Universidad de Valencia (Spain)
`gopher.sunet.se`	gopher	Sweden
`hugin.ub2.lu.se`	gopher	Sweden

Table 12-3.
Public-Access Gopher
Servers (*continued*)

Host Server Address	Log-in ID	Location
North America		
`infoslug.ucsc.edu`	infoslug	University of California, Santa Clara
`nicol.jvnc.net`	nicol	Global Enterprise Services, Inc. Princeton, New Jersey
`ux1.cso.uiuc.edu`	gopher	University of Illinois, Urbana-Champaign
`gopher.msu.edu`	gopher	Michigan State University
`ecosys.drdr.virginia.edu`	gopher	University of Virginia
`gopher.virginia.edu`	gwis	University of Virginia
South America		
`gopher.puc.cl`	gopher	Pontificia Universidad Catolica de Chile
`ecnet.ec`	gopher	EcuaNet Corporacion Equatoriana de Informacion (Ecuador)
Australia/Asia		
`info.anu.edu.au`	info	Australian National University
`gopher.ncc.go.jp`	gopher	National Cancer Center, Tokyo

Tip

Although these three public "Gopher" servers listed below do work, and can be used to perform Gopher-like work, they are not using the same UNIX Gopher client as that being used at the many sites listed in Table 12-3. This means that the Gopher commands detailed in Table 12-2 probably will not apply, and if you decide to use these public servers you'll likely need to learn a unique new set of commands. The up-side is that each server has extra resources and services available that should make them worth the extra learning effort.

Host Server Address	Log-in ID	Location
`panda.uiowa.edu`		University of Iowa
`gopher.ohiolink.edu`	ohiolink	Ohio Library and Information Network
`pubinfo.ucsd.edu`	*infopath*	*University of California, San Diego*

More Gopher Information

If you want to find out more about Gopher, here are some leads to more detailed information. The easiest thing to do is to read the hypertext Windows help file that comes with WSGopher. It's well written, clear, and informative. It explains many parts of Gopher. And it's always a good idea to understand the full power of your research tools, in case you ever need one of those advanced features. There is also a WSGopher FAQ, written by WSGopher author Dave Brooks, that should come with WSGopher. If you need the FAQ, it can be obtained from the FTP server where you can also get the WSGopher program, described in a Tip at the beginning of this chapter.

Or you can read and study the online Gopher course by Patrick Douglas Crispen (pcrispe1@ua1vm.ua.edu) called "Let's Go Gophering!" This course had an enrollment of many thousands, and was run entirely on the Internet using the versatile LISTSERV mailing list management software. The archived readings, assignments, and other Gopher details from the course are available at many Net repositories. One way to get them is to Gopher to the following URL:

`gopher://wings.buffalo.edu:70/11/internet/info/gophern`

Also, to keep up with new and changing Gophers, you can subscribe to the LISTSERV mailing list newnir-l by sending an e-mail message to:

`LISTSERV%itocsivm.bitnet@icineca.cineca.it`

Your message should say:

`subscribe newnir-l Your Name`

where you fill in your own name, of course.

This mailing list is called newnir-l, because it is about new public NIR (Network Information Retrieval) and OPAC (Online Public Access Catalogs) services. The mailing list *owner* is Fabio Metitieri (metitier@itocsivm.csi.it).

Also, you can visit and/or join these Usenet newsgroups:

`alt.gopher`
`bit.listserv.gophern`
`comp.infosystems.gopher`

The current version of the Veronica FAQ by Steven Foster can be retrieved through Gopher or a Web browser at the following URL:

`gopher://veronica.scs.unr.edu/00/veronica/veronica-faq`

Or, lastly, you can retrieve and study the Gopher FAQ that is stored at the RTFM FAQ site. Here are two anonymous FTP addresses—the filename is gopher-faq, but the names could easily have been changed (to confuse the innocent):

FTP Server	Directory
`ftp.uni-giessen.de`	`/pub/doc/faq/`
`rtfm.mit.edu`	`/pub/usenet-by-hierarchy/comp/answers/`

From Here

The next step after studying Gopher is to try it out. You can put some of these ideas to work by doing a simple personal research project, like searching for some hobby or family topics. After you see the results, you'll probably want to study the Veronica search rules in more detail, in order to hone in on just the data you want, rather than having the good data mixed in with less valuable data.

Another logical step after studying Gopher is to move on to studying the World Wide Web (WWW or *the Web*). As we said early in this chapter, WWW will probably eventually replace Gopher, but not until *almost everyone* has faster and more powerful computers, with graphics acceleration and color monitors.

If you already have these advantages, now is the time to learn about the Web by turning to Chapter 13. The two biggest advantages that the Web has over Gopher are that the Web can display inline graphics—so you can see pictures on the screen with the text, and it uses a more powerful, more pervasive implementation of the hypertext concept.

13

Researching on the World Wide Web

This chapter gets you started into the world of Web research. As we demonstrated in Chapter 12 about Gophers, index *search tools* and resources organized *by subject matter* sites are two of the most powerful and productive ways to find what you need on the Internet. We'll use those same handles again to get a grasp on the World Wide Web.

We'll then move on to a brief overview of the capabilities of Web browsers, and then plunge directly into a discussion of index searching on the Web. In addition, we'll show you some prominent collections of resources that are organized by subject. Subject organization saves you the time of doing your own index searching to find many items on that subject, and in many cases it helps you identify the better, or best, sites that might show up in a comprehensive search.

It's also time to remind you that the Internet can change very quickly. The World Wide Web has been changing even faster than Gopher, and because of these changes there are growth pains and other discomforts. You may click on a hyperlink, expecting to be immediately transported to the site of your immediate dreams, and discover that nothing happens at all. Or you may get an error message that makes little sense and does not help you get to where you want to go.

The truth is that some World Wide Web hyperlinks fail, either temporarily or permanently. Or they may have moved. Sometimes they leave a forwarding address, and sometimes they don't. To the Internet researcher this means you should not be too dismayed when you discover one of these dead-ends. And, you'll need methods and procedures to circumvent and overcome the larger "box canyons" on the World Wide Web in the future.

Note   *Every link in this book was working when we wrote this, but we know they will not all work when you try them. We apologize. But we just don't know which ones are going to change! Our solution to this problem is to show you the principles behind research methods on the Internet, so that you can handle these inconveniences yourself, and we provide you with additional redundant examples of each kind of research tool (if possible) so that if one fails at the moment you try it, there will probably be another that is working when you try it next.*

The Web is Easy to Use

One of the best properties of the World Wide Web is that there are several graphical, rather than text-based, Web clients available for browsing. Because Macintosh users and Windows users both have easy access to high quality freeware and shareware they can take advantage of all their computer's graphical abilities. The Web is growing rapidly. Newbies and experienced Internauts alike rely increasingly on hypertext, or at least hypertext markup language (HTML), to accomplish their research and information design and display purposes.

More sounds and movies are being built into Web sites, because more Web *users* have the equipment and software to take advantage of audio and video augmentation of the text and graphics available on Web pages. As Web destinations and venues become more interesting and attractive, more people visit and use the best sites. This kind of growth spiral is rapidly expanding in mid-1995 as we write this chapter, and no one knows how much longer the Web can or will sustain such expansive growth. Everyone wants to get on the Internet, and the Web is the easiest part of the Net to use.

Both Macintosh and Windows computers are characterized by their easy-to-use graphical user interface. Even adults can learn to point and click a mouse fairly quickly if trained properly and shown where to click and when. Because clicks are immediately reinforced with sounds and changes in the visual display on the screen, learning a new software program on a graphical user interface is smoother, quicker, and easier—it even seems more *intuitive*.

Web Browsers Do Everything

Most Web browsers will support several Internet protocols, such as Gopher, FTP, Telnet, and World Wide Web—some browsers even accept substitutes (or proxies); if you would prefer to use your own Gopher client instead of your Web browser's version of Gopher, for instance.

Back Up Your Bookmarks

Your research experience is stored in your bookmarks. Your bookmarks become your assets, because they are tools to help you get your research job done. So protect your assets, and regularly make backup copies of your bookmark files.

BrowserBookmark Filename

```
Lynx      lynx_bookmarks.html
Cello     cello.bmk
Mosaic    mosaic.ini
Netscape  bookmark.htm
```

Because Cello doesn't yet handle forms, Cello will not be much use for most of the search engines in this chapter. It will probably be able to do just fine with the information organized by subject, however. Some of the search sites, such as CUSI below, also make special accommodations for Lynx users, offering a special method to use their site even without full forms compatibility.

Caution   *Don't risk editing your Netscape bookmarks until you are an expert at hypertext markup language! Some text editors and HTML editors destroy important features of code in the Netscape bookmark file, so be sure to make a backup copy of your bookmarks before you try to edit them with anything other than Netscape itself.*

What to Do About Dead WWW Links

One of the first things we do when we run into a bookmark or URL reference that once worked but no longer does, is to use the WWW search tools in our bookmark lists to search for the URL's new manifestation. Usually you'll have a name or a URL to work with, so search for those items one at a time and see if the new link turns up.

To search for a URL, try removing the last (right-most) segment of the address, to find all references to the host server that the link used to be on. You can also try to connect to the truncated URL; it often will lead you to fascinating places. The highest likelihood is that the resource is still on that same host server, or at least in that vicinity. Remove one segment at a time from *right to left* until you find a page that may lead back down to the resource you wanted. For example, if the URL for the Harvest search form, http://www.town.hall.org/brokers/www-home-pages/query.html suddenly began to fail, you would try to search for, or connect to, this URL:

`http://www.town.hall.org/brokers/www-home-pages/`

And if that one didn't work, you'd move on to try to connect to:

`http://www.town.hall.org/brokers/`

and so on.

Often, a nonconnecting or dead link is only temporarily out of service, so you shouldn't need to go into search mode unless the link has been bad for over a week. If it stays out of service over a week, and you've tried the Web search tools in this chapter without finding the new link, that old resource may have gone offline.

You can still write e-mail to the postmaster or root account at the node involved, but it's a long shot. Using the same example, the e-mail query to the postmaster or root would be e-mailed to postmaster@town.hall.org or root@town.hall.org.

Searching Indexes on the Web

A number of searching tools are available to assist in the location of information on the Internet. These tools search indexes built from a variety of sources, some from the titles of documents found on the Internet, some from the documents themselves, some from other indexes or directories.

Searching Tools

» Lycos (Carnegie Mellon)

» World Wide Web Worm (McBryan at U. of Colorado)

» WebCrawler

» ALIWEB (NEXOR, UK)

» NIKOS (New Internet Knowledge System)

» JumpStation II

» W3 Search engines (University of Geneva)

» CUI W3 catalog (University of Geneva)

» WWW Home Pages Broker (Using Harvest)

» The Internet Sleuth

» Archie.au request form (Australian FTP repository)

» Additional Resources

» InterNIC Directory of Directories

» Scout report from InterNIC

» All the Gopher Servers in the World

» EFF's Extended Guide to the Internet

» Zen and the Art of the Internet

» Running a WWW service

» Listserv Guides

» Ozlists: a list of Australian electronic mailing lists

» Listserv Home Page

» List of Listserv

The best indexes actually seek out new information and then integrate it with the previously known information and make it all available for searching. Good indexes also go back and check the sites they've already listed, to see if they are still there, and to see if they have changed significantly. If a search site keeps giving you a significant number of search "hits" that do not work, let them know!

Note

Group Search Site Feeding

Most of the Web search engines also allow users to feed them new URLs, to seed the engine's searches. There is even a service that allows you to feed several of the search engines as a group! The name of the service is Submit It! and here is their URL:

`http://www.cen.uiuc.edu/~banister/submit-it/`

Some search sites allow you to search multiple indexes, so you can get more "hits" as a result of the same amount of work. The first four of the following search sites have links to multiple other search sites, and Savvy Search actually submits your request to multiple search engines for you. Savvy Search works a little like the Simplified Veronica demonstrated in Chapter 12, except that Savvy Search gives you the results from each of the searches, rather than just finding the first search engine willing to accept your inquiry.

A couple of Usenet newsgroups to read, if you want to follow the development of these advanced search tools, are comp.infosystems.announce and comp.infosystems.www.announce.

All-In-One

This site gathers URLs for all kinds of other World Wide Web and Internet search sites. Some of them are preloaded, so that you can fill in your query just once and it will be submitted by the All-In-One server to the search site you select. Figure 13-1 is the first screen at the All-In-One search site.

Here is the URL for the All-In-One search site:

`http://www.albany.net/~wcross/all1srch.html`

CUSI

Nexor sponsors this search site that incorporates searches of several other sites, including the CUI W3 Catalog, their own ALIWEB index, the Yahoo subject tree, the GNA Meta-Library, CityScape's Global Online Directory, and the DA-CLOD database of URLs. Figure 13-2 is the first screen at the Nexor CUSI search site.

The URL for the CUSI search site is:

`http://pubweb.nexor.co.uk/public/cusi/cusi.html`

Figure 13-1.
The All-In-One search site has over 20 links to WWW search sites.

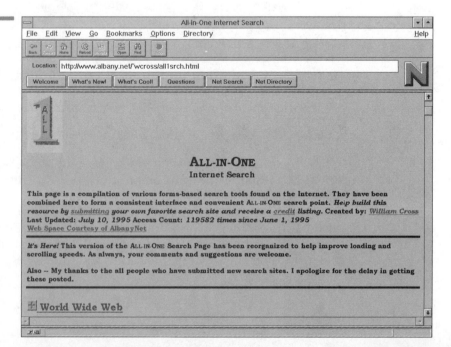

Figure 13-2.
The CUSI search site has several links to other WWW search sites.

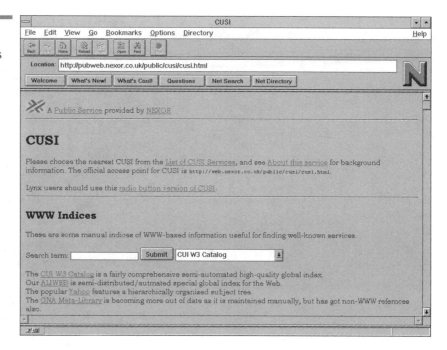

Savvy Search

As previously mentioned, Savvy Search actually submits your request to several search sites (the current maximum is five) and compiles and reports the results for you. Figure 13-3 is the first screen at the Savvy Search site.

The Savvy Search site is at this URL:

```
http://www.cs.colostate.edu/~dreiling/smartform.html
```

Wizard

This service is brought to you by Spry, and is remarkably similar (as in identical) in part of its coverage to the CUSI search engine described earlier. It also offers access to additional information such as the Whole Internet Catalog, Archieplex, Netfind, Internet RFCs, and even a dictionary. (But Wizard does not offer access to the ALIWEB search engine that CUSI searches do offer.) Figure 13-4 is the first screen at the Wizard search site.

The Wizard search site is at this URL:

```
http://www.spry.com/wizard/index.html
```

Figure 13-3.
The Savvy Search site uses links to other WWW search sites to improve your search results.

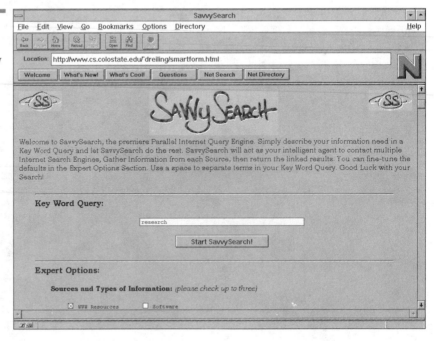

Figure 13-4.
The Wizard search site gathers information from other WWW search sites and resources for you.

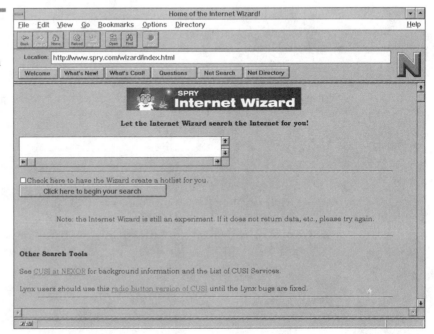

Harvest Broker

The Harvest system involves many computers contributing to and cooperating with a complex system of information gathering and organizing. Several data sources are used, and the range of information indexed is wide. Figure 13-5 shows the first screen at the Harvest system site.

The Harvest search site is at this URL:

`http://www.town.hall.org/brokers/www-home-pages/query.html`

JumpStation II

The JumpStation II robot collects a database of titles, headers, and subjects of WWW documents. JumpStation II is based in England, so you can improve your European and British coverage by using the JumpStation for research. Figure 13-6 shows the document search form at the JumpStation II site.

The JumpStation II document search site is at this URL:

`http://js.stir.ac.uk/jsbin/jsii`

Figure 13-5.
The Harvest system site gathers information from other WWW search sites for you.

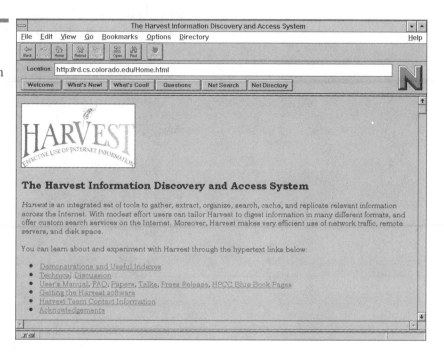

Figure 13-6.
The JumpStation II site gathers information from the Web and brings it back to England for you to search.

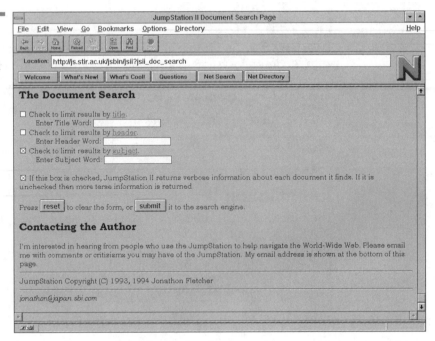

Lycos

Microsoft has recently chosen Lycos as a partner for its Internet offering, but that should only improve the Lycos products by infusing new funding into an already well-developed set of research tools. Lycos will remain at Carnegie-Mellon University and keep indexing and searching as always, only probably better. Figure 13-7 shows the Lycos home page.

The Lycos home page is at this URL:

`http://lycos.cs.cmu.edu/`

NIKOS

Rockwell Telecommunications offers the NIKOS search engine. It searches the World Wide Web with a robot, collecting information for the NIKOS database. Figure 13-8 shows the NIKOS search page.

The NIKOS search page is at this URL:

`http://www.rns.com/cgi-bin/nikos`

Figure 13-7.
Lycos offers you a large catalog or a small catalog to search.

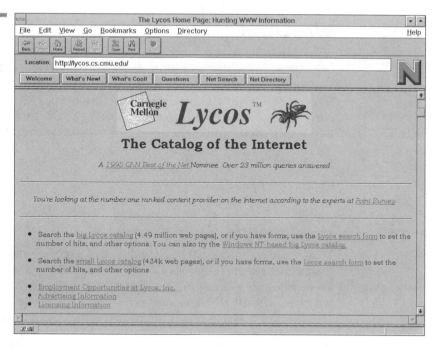

Figure 13-8.
The NIKOS search page prompts your search with examples.

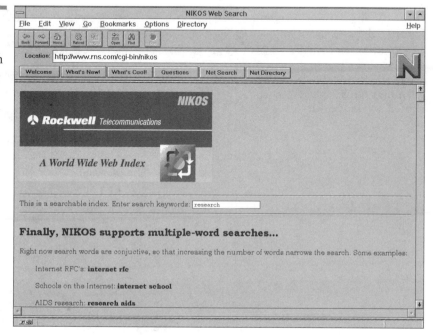

WebCrawler

America Online has recently bought this indexing and searching engine. They now have a way, by providing this ongoing service, of *giving back to the Net*. Previously, America Online had been harshly criticized for taking from the Internet but never give anything back (other than flocks of impudent newbies). Now they have a service they provide 24 hours a day, 365 days a year to the whole Net community! Figure 13-9 shows the WebCrawler search page.

The WebCrawler search page is at this URL:

`http://webcrawler.com/`

World Wide Web Worm

This award-winning search site has four searchable databases, and three search techniques for each database. The World Wide Web Worm collects links from Web pages, so when you find something with the WWWW it tells you about two sites—the site that matches your search and the site where WWWW found the link. Figure 13-10 shows the search form at the World Wide Web Worm search site.

The World Wide Web Worm search page is at this URL:

`http://www.cs.colorado.edu/home/mcbryan/WWWW.html`

Figure 13-9.
The WebCrawler search page also links you to their top 25 sites and to seemingly random pages chosen by WebCrawler.

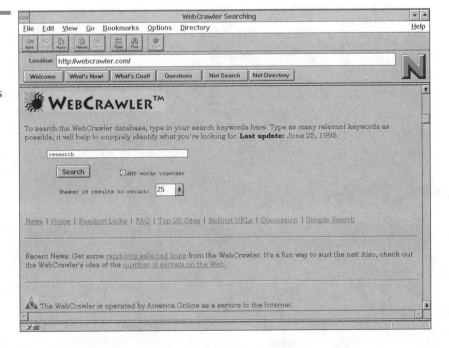

Figure 13-10.
The World Wide Web
Worm search site has hot
links to instructions and
examples.

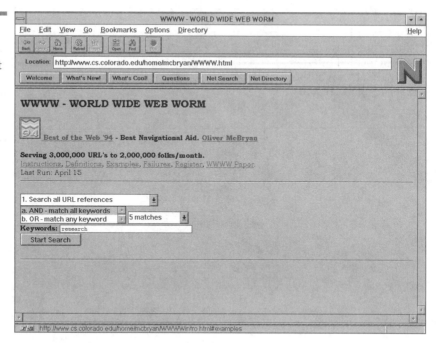

Web Resources Organized by Subject

Many of collections of URLs fill the World Wide Web. Some rise above the others by being hierarchically organized and useful for searching *by subject*. Here we will give you four examples of the largest and best sites for subject searching. There are many more, which you can find for yourself by searching the indexes above for the words *subject* and *by subject* and *subject guide*. Here is a URL for a site that collects URLs for sites that have Web resources organized by subject:

```
http://www.w3.org/hypertext/DataSources/bySubject/Virtual_lib
     raries/Overview.html
```

Michigan Clearinghouse for Subject-Oriented Internet Resource Guides

This in-depth Internet resource is sponsored by the University of Michigan's University Library and School of Information and Library Studies. It also exists as a Gopher and an FTP resource. Louis Rosenfeld (i-guides@umich.edu) is the contact person, if you want to contribute a subject-oriented resource to the collection. At this writing there are over 100 subject-based resource collections at this site; the first few are shown in Figure 13-11.

Figure 13-11.
The Clearinghouse for Subject-Oriented Internet Resource Guides is at the University of Michigan.

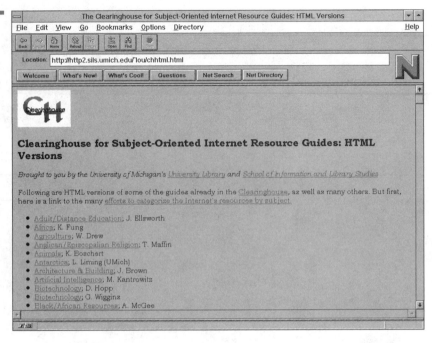

The URL for this site is:

`http://http2.sils.umich.edu/~lou/chhtml.html`

The WWW Virtual Library

This distributed site holds around 100 links to other resources organized by subject. It has indications of which material is new, which is most popular, offers statistics about the site, and has a link to the same resources organized by the Internet tool (or service) used to access them. Figure 13-12 shows the top of the subject tree.

The URL for the WWW Virtual Library is:

`http://www.w3.org/hypertext/DataSources/bySubject/Overview.html`

Yahoo

Yahoo is named for a race of brutes that have the form and vices of men (from Jonathan Swift's satire, *Gulliver's Travels*, about a man who voyages to imaginary lands inhabited by other races). Yahoo recently has begun to categorize entries a little more. Yahoo has begun placing a asterisk (*) next to items they think have good presentation and content for the topic area they reside in. Usually, you should check sites with asterisks first. Figure 13-13 shows you the top of the Yahoo subject tree.

Figure 13-12.
The WWW Virtual Library also has a hierarchical categorical subject subtree.

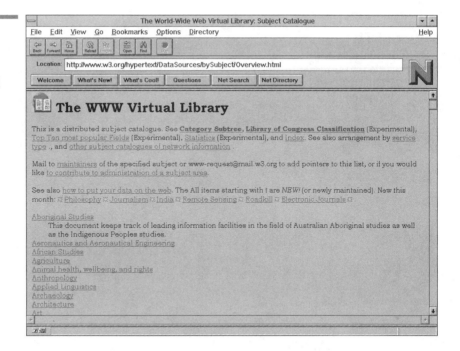

Yahoo also offers random hot links, the 50 most popular categories, new links, links to several search engines, and a form for searching the Yahoo listings themselves. The URL for Yahoo is:

`http://www.yahoo.com/`

Yanoff's Special Internet Connections

Scott Yanoff's Special Internet Connections site contains around 40 top-level subject categories, with many more lower-level categories as you work your way towards more and more specific topics. Figure 13-14 shows the top of the Yanoff subject tree.

The URL for Yanoff's Special Internet Connections is:

`http://www.uwm.edu/Mirror/inet.services.html`

From Here

One of the best learning exercises you can do for yourself as an Internet researcher is to repeat the research that went into writing this chapter. Use the many index searches that are available to you and search for other, newer index searches, and for resources organized by subject. Once every few months you should repeat this background research to be sure that your research tools, *and your bookmarks*, are sharp and up to date.

Figure 13-13.
The Yahoo *by subject* listings are one of the largest on the Net.

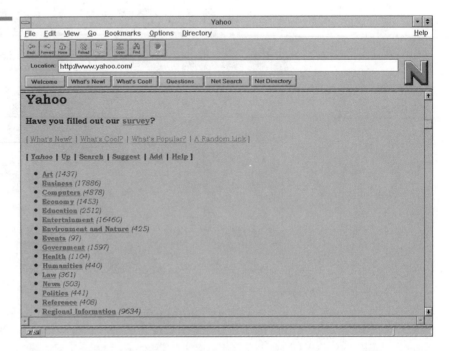

Figure 13-14.
Scott Yanoff's Special Internet Connections is so large it's delivered in three parts!

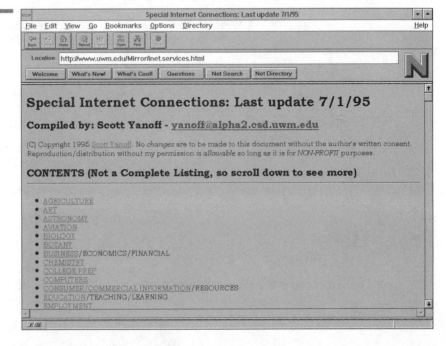

14

Government Resources on the Net

This chapter provides the Internet researcher with many leads to government information on the Internet, including U.S. federal and state, Canadian federal and provincial, and foreign government resources.

The U.S. Federal Government

The United States Congress has made some Congressional information available on the Net. There is Net access to Capitol Hill via both Gopher and World Wide Web.

House of Representatives

The United States House of Representatives has Gopher and Web servers at these URLs:

```
gopher://gopher.house.gov
http://www.house.gov
```

Senate

The United States Senate has a Gopher server at this URL:

`gopher://gopher.senate.gov`

The Library of Congress

In Chapter 9 we discussed the U.S. Library of Congress. Here is the URL for the U.S. Library of Congress:

`http://lcweb.loc.gov/homepage/lchp.html`

Whitehouse—President of the United States

The Executive Branch of the United States government is represented by a World Wide Web site. President Bill Clinton used Internet e-mail addresses and mailing lists in his political campaign to become President, so it would be expected that his Web site was soon available. Here is the White House URL:

`http://www.whitehouse.gov/`

The White House Web pages have links to the Executive Branch agencies, and to the other branches of the U.S. government, including the U.S. Supreme Court, as you can see in Figure 14-1.

The Fedworld Information Network

National Technical Information Service (NTIS) operates the Fedworld site that lists other Web servers, FTP, Gopher, and Telnet sites operated by the federal government. Fedworld also allows you to search the abstracts of recent government reports, studies, and other information products.

The Fedworld site has more than 10,000 files available for FTP access, including information on business, health, and the environment. Fedworld offers Telnet access to detailed information from over 50 agencies and includes access to online ordering services, federal job opportunities, and dial-up access to other Government information systems. Figure 14-2 shows the Fedworld Web home page.

The URL for Fedworld is:

`http://www.fedworld.gov/`

Figure 14-1.
The White House links you to cabinet agencies, independent commissions, and to the other branches of the U.S. federal government.

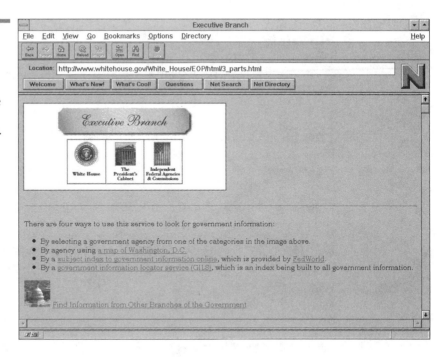

Figure 14-2.
The Fedworld logo graphic takes a long time to load, and is not shown.

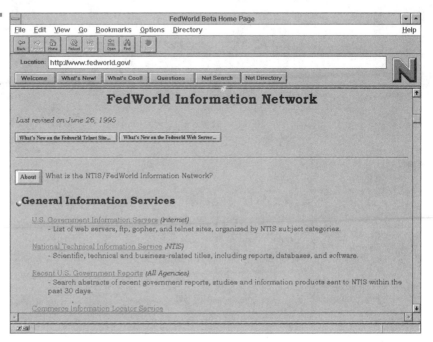

Government Accounting Office (GAO)

To access Government Accounting Office (GAO) reports as full text ASCII electronic files from the Government Printing Office (GPO) via a WAIS database, follow these steps:

Telnet

1. Telnet to: `swais.access.gpo.gov`

2. Log in as *gao*

3. Perform a search for document(s)

4. Use the "m" command to e-mail the file to yourself

For example, in a keyword search on a subject such as *"Welfare Reform,"* or a search on a report number such as reportnum=*"HEHS-95-58"*, you must use quotes in the searches. Document questions may be directed to the GAO at documents@gao.gov. Any questions on using the GPO system should be referred to the GPO at: help@eids05.eids.gpo.gov or by telephone at 202-512-1530.

GovAccess Mailing List

The GovAccess mailing list at majordomo@well.com distributes federal, state, and/or local government access information, action-alerts, and advocacy to improve the effectiveness of citizen participation in the process of our own governance. Archives are available by FTP and Web at:

`ftp://ftp.cpsr.org/cpsr/states/california/govaccess`
`http://www.cpsr.org/cpsr/states/california/govaccess`

To subscribe to the GovAccess mailing list, send e-mail to majordomo@well.com that says *subscribe GovAccess <YourEmailAddress>*. To get further information about the mailing list, send e-mail to majordomo@well.com with the message *info GovAccess*, or send e-mail to the mailing list owner Jim Warren at jwarren@well.com.

Purdue University

Purdue University makes the Federal Register, Congressional Record, and other Government Printing Office records available on the Web. Figure 14-3 shows the Purdue University federal documents home page. The URL is:

`http://thorplus.lib.purdue.edu/gpo/`

Figure 14-3.
Federal information
brought to you by
Purdue University

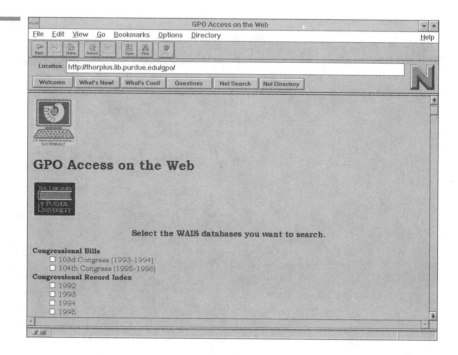

U.S. State Government on the Net

Figure 14-4 shows the home page the State Government on the Net site. Its URL is:

```
http://garnet.msen.com:70/0h/vendor/maven/inet1/nnews/states.
    html
```

Figure 14-5 shows another way to access state government links to the Internet from the U.S. Library of Congress. The URLs for the Library of Congress links, leading to state and local government information, are:

```
http://www.loc.gov/global/state/stategov.html
gopher://marvel.loc.gov:70/11/federal/state.local/
```

Canada

Canada was an early partner in the Internet. Canadian universities and military defense contractors were among the first connections. The country's Internet

Figure 14-4.
This site has links to state government sites on the Net.

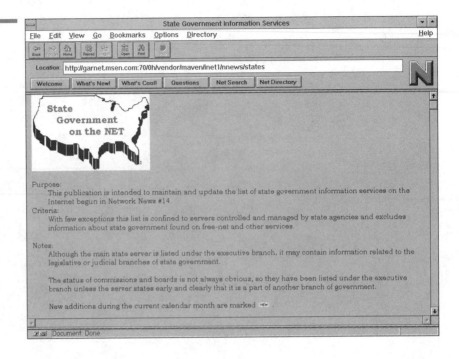

Figure 14-5.
The Library of Congress has links to state government Net resources.

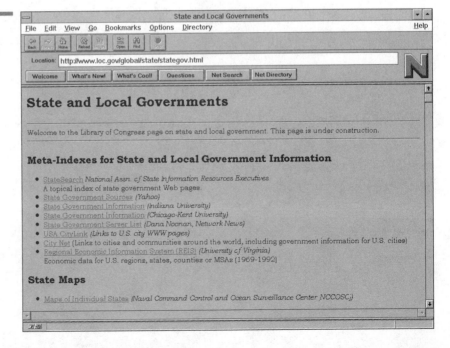

backbone was often slower than the main Internet lines in the United States and many connections were north-south through the U.S. rather than across Canada.

In July, 1995, CAnet, Canada's nonprofit Internet backbone, announced a deal with Bell Advanced Communications to both privatize and upgrade the network. CAnet and Bell Canada say the upgrade will bring the Net connections up to U.S. standards and increase speed by six to ten times to 10 megabits a second, with a capacity of 100 megabits a second if needed. It was expected that the network would be running by September 30, 1995.

Canadian Federal Resources on the Internet

Canada's federal government has been quick to enter the Internet era. Ottawa-based CANARIE, the Canadian Network for the Advancement of Research, is a joint public and private group that is building the country's new information infrastructure.

General Sources

If anyone wants a copy of one of the best online guides to government in Canada they can contact Anita Cannon first at York University and then at Wilfred Laurier. She can be contacted at Government Information listing acannon@mach1.wlu.ca.

Major Gopher and WWW Sites for the Federal Government of Canada

Federal Information (by subject):

1. General Information
2. Archives/History
3. Astronomy
4. Census and Statistics
5. Economics
6. Emergency
7. Environment
8. Geography and Geology
9. Health
10. Industry
11. Law and Legislation
12. Meteorology
13. Science

14. Telecommunications

A complete copy of the guide can be obtained from the Clearinghouse for Subject-Oriented Internet Resource Guides at:

```
gopher://una.hh.lib.umich.edu/inetdirsstacks/
        Clearinghouse.../Guides on the Social Sciences/
        Canadian Government
http://www.lib.umich.edu/chhome.html
ftp://una.hh.lib.umich.edu/inetdirsstacks/canada:cannon
```

Canada's parliament is found at Parliamentary Internet Parlementaire:

http://www.parl.gc.ca, or on Gopher at gopher.parl.gc.ca. It's being developed by the Information Technologies Directorate of the House of Commons, in partnership with the Library of Parliament and the Senate (for more information check http://www.parl.gc.ca/eproject.html).

Another Parliamentary page is found at http://www.cisti.nrc.ca/pio/intro.html, and at the Cable Parliamentary Channel Online:

```
http://www.screen.com/CPAC
```

The Open Government project is a gateway to many Canadian government sources. It can be found at Industry Canada's debra site:

Gopher: `gopher//debra.dgbt.doc.ca/open government project`
WWW: `http://debra.dgbt.doc.ca/opengov`
FTP: `todebra.dgbt.doc.ca:/pub/`

The National Library of Canada Gopher, which we mentioned in Chapter 9, also has federal and provincial government information. It can be found at gopher://gopher.nlc-bnc.ca.

The University of Saskatchewan has a large collection of government information including some census data. It's at http://www.usask.ca/Canadiana.

The University of Saskatchewan also has a government information mailing list, GOVINFO, a discussion forum for Canadian government information at all levels of government. To subscribe, send this message: *subscribe GOVINFO YOUR NAME* to mailserv@sask.usask.ca. To post messages to GOVINFO, address them to GOVINFO@SASK.USASK.CA.

The Canada Communication Group, the publisher for the federal government, posts press releases and other government data on the National Capital Freenet. Telnet to: freenet.carleton.ca/government centre/federal government/CCGP. The log-in is guest.

Select Canadian Federal Agencies and Departments

Agriculture Canada

Canadian Soil Information System

```
http://res.agr.ca/PUB/CANSIS/_overview.html
```

Archives

National Archives Catalogue of Computer Files

```
telnet://freenet.carleton.ca/Government Centre/federal
         government/National Archives of Canada
log-in:  guest
gopher://gopher.nlc-bnc.ca/departments & agencies/
```

Astronomy

Dominion Astrophysical Observatory (DAO)

```
http://dao.nrc.ca
```

Dominion Radio Astrophysical Observatory (DRAO)

```
http://www.drao.nrc.ca
ftp://ftp.drao.nrc.ca
```

Auditor General

Auditor General's Report

```
gopher://gopher.phoenix.ca:70
```

Select the item "Auditor General of Canada/Verificateur general du Canada."

Canadian Heritage

```
http://indy.chin.doc.ca./DCH/flyer-e.html
```

Canadian Heritage Information Network

From the Department of Canadian Heritage comes this server, showcasing the products developed by CHIN or in partnership with such heritage institutions as the National Film Board of Canada and the Canadian Museum of Civilization.

```
http://www.chin.doc.ca/
```

Canadian Information Highway Advisory Council

A mailing list aims at improving communication among individuals regarding the development of the information highway.

Send e-mail to: `listprocessor@cunews.carleton.ca`
`subscribe Pac-Hiway Your-Name [end code]`

Postings to the list should be addressed to:

`Pac-Hiway@cunews.carleton.ca`

CRTC Information Highway Report

`http://www.crtc.gc.ca/eng/highway/hwy9505e.htm`

Emergency Preparedness Canada

`telnet://freenet.carleton.ca/government centre /federal`
`        government of Canada/`
`log-in: guest`

Public Works Canada

`http://www.pwc-tpc.ca`

Consumer Price Index

The Consumer Price Index is also available at the University of Waterloo.

`gopher://provost-admin.uwaterloo.ca/operations`

Supreme Court of Canada

`http://debra.dgbt.doc,ca/open.government`
`        project/supereme.court.rulings`

The Environment Canada Green Lane Web page for Atlantic Canada

`http://www.ns.doe.ca/how.html`

This includes the latest regional weather forecasts, satellite photos, maps and radar images, a FAQ for Atlantic Canadians, and lists of phone numbers and publications.

Canadian Foreign Affairs

Canada's foreign affairs department provides an e-mail information mailing list. Send an e-mail message to listserv@fait.gc.ca with word *"help"* in the body only.

You will then get a description of the services provided by the listserver and how to access them. There's also an FTP e-mail service; send an e-mail message to"ftpmail@fait.gc.ca" with word*"help"* in body only.

The Canadian Embassy in the U.S.
The Canadian embassy in Washington has a Web site at http://www.nstn.ca/wshdc. As well as information on U.S. Canadian relations , there are links from the site to other resources on the Internet such as Industry Canada's Open Government Pilot Project and the World Bank's World Wide Web site.

Municipal

Vancouver

`http://www.city.vancouver.bc.ca`

Victoria

`telnet://freenet.victoria.bc.ca/governmentcentre/municipal`
`        government`
`log-in: guest`
`http://freenet.victoria.bc.ca/vifa.html`

Ottawa

City and Regional Municipality

`telnet://freenet.carleton.ca/government centre/`

Quebec

Montreal Urban Community

`http://www.cum.qc.ca`

International Government Sources

European Union

`http://www.echo.lu`

GATT

Gopher: `cyfer.esusda.gov`

Path: `Americans Communicating Electronically=9B`
`    National Policy Issues`

United Nations

`http://www.undcp.or.at/unlinks.html`

Countries

France

French Embassy Washington

Gopher: `iep.univ-lyon2.fr 70`
Path: `1/amb-wash.fr`

Great Britain

Her Majesty's Government Online

`http://www.open.gov.uk/`

Treasury Internet Service

FTP: `ftp.hm-treasury.gov.uk`
WWW: `http://www.hm-treasury.gov.uk`

Italy

`http://www.mi.cnr.it/IGST`

Japan

Ministry of Posts and Telecommunications, Japan

`http://www.mpt.go.jp/`

Malaysia

`http://www.mimos.my`

Vietnam

`http://www.internic.net/~hot/`

15

The Net for Everyone

The Internet and Scholars

There is a growing problem of a noise-to-signal ratio on the Internet—the difference between junk and valuable information. As more people come on the Net, some of the scholars who were once its mainstay say they are leaving at least the more crowded parts of the Internet. The *Wall Street Journal* has reported that some Net veterans are abandoning Usenet because it's too open. Mitchell Golden, a professor of physics at Harvard, told the *Journal* that physics newsgroups are filled with endless flame wars over the special relativity theory. Many researchers are ignoring Usenet altogether and opting for moderated or private mailing lists.

People are frequently becoming overwhelmed even by the relatively small bits of Net information coming in. If you subscribe to just a few key mailing lists and add your personal mail, you could be receiving between 100 and 500 e-mail messages a day.

There's a debate. Many veteran Net users are complaining about too many students, too many new users, and too many newbies from the commercial services, all flooding the newsgroups and public mailing lists with flame wars, inaccurate information, and silly questions. Others welcome the democratization of the Internet and say the detractors are elitist.

On the other hand, researchers will remain a key element in the Internet from now on. In 1993, the *New York Times* estimated there were four million scientists using the Internet on a regular basis. The *Times* reported that 48 percent of all Internet users were online for research, including commercial research. The key advantage of the Net has always been, and still is, its ability to link researchers cheaply and efficiently. Speed is crucial. Scientific and other research moves much faster in the 1990s than it ever has before.

A strong, but controversial, movement is afoot to put scientific and other academic journals on the Internet. There are at least 40,000 scientific print journals that publish millions of articles each year. Add in journals in other academic disciplines and newsletters and the result equals overwhelming information overload. The very volume of journals means high costs for universities and other institutions who subscribe. With budget cutbacks around the planet, institutions and libraries are dropping their subscriptions to many journals.

The Los Alamos National Laboratory in the United States has been the pioneer in creating electronic journals in physics and genetics. Genbank collects information on the Human Genome Project on computer. The *New York Times* reported that putting the genetic information on computer dropped the publication time from 13 months to 48 hours. "We've gone from being the Wells Fargo of data collection to Federal Express," Dr. Paul Gilna, of Genbank, told the *Times*. There is a backlash to these developments. In June of 1995, the prestigious—and conservative—*New England Journal of Medicine* turned thumbs down on a suggestion that medical studies be posted on the Net. The journal's editors, Dr. Jerome Kassirer and Dr. Marcia Angell, said in an editorial that unreviewed medical information on the Net "might lead some people to use the wrong medication or stop taking needed ones on the basis of inadequate information."

Doctors Kassirer and Angell say that the traditional system of peer review "cannot be replaced by multiple unspecified users of the Internet. When a scientific study is assessed by majority rule, the result is likely to be highly unreliable. Such a process could also invite manipulation, and even fraud.... At present the Internet seems to promote medical rumors more than dispassionate scholarship. Much information about health issues on the Internet, such as the risks of medications and the effects of various foods on health, is of uncertain parentage."

There is a core of truth to the *New England Journal's* position. We have always said throughout this book that *all* information on the Internet must be checked and double-checked. On the other hand, many scientists have complained that many journals are themselves biased and that peer review is often more about academic politics than scientific or academic inquiry. They would argue that opening up discussion on the Internet would allow revolutionary work to get a fair hearing.

The *New England Journal*, for example, has a poor record in fast reaction to medical emergencies. One reason is its rule that no one who has a prospective paper published in the journal may talk to the media during the long peer review and publication process. The *New England Journal*, by the way, does have an Internet e-mail address:

`letters+edit@nejm.org`

In April of 1981, when Dr. Michael Gottlieb of UCLA identified cases of *pneumocytis carnii* pneumonia and cytomegalovirus in gay men, one of the first warning signs of the coming AIDS epidemic, he approached the *New England Journal*. He was told by the editors that peer review would take three months, then there would be a further delay before publication. Gottlieb eventually called the Centers for Disease Control's *Morbidity and Mortality Weekly Report,* which has a much faster turnaround time, and the now famous article using information from Gottlieb and other physicians appeared in the MMWR on Friday, June 5, 1981. It took six months for the *New England Journal* to publish Gottlieb's complete paper on *pneumocytis carnii* longer than even their fastest estimated turnaround time.

The following year, when Dr. Ayre Rubenstein at the Albert Einstein College of Medicine found what is now known as AIDS in babies in New York City, the *New England Journal* rejected his paper in July 1982, again after six months. The journal's reviewers came to the conclusion that AIDS was confined to homosexual men. In 1984, the *New England Journal* did publish one of the first studies that suggested that AIDS could be transmitted through the blood supply, but it also published a letter from blood industry spokesman Dr. Joseph Bove, assuring the public the blood supply was safe. (At that time, in January 1984, the human immuno-deficiency virus had not yet been definitively identified).

The *New England Journal's* position also ignores the growing movement for patients' rights, which began with the AIDS epidemic, then was adopted by the breast cancer movement, and is now spreading to people with other medical conditions.

As the AIDS epidemic has shown, people will turn, often in desperation, to unproven information and rumor, especially if the doctors are unable—or unwilling—to provide support.

The Internet, of course, does have the answer to the dilemma. It already exists in private, moderated mailing lists. This list could, perhaps, have two listservs. One would be private, serving certain members of the medical or some other scientific community. It could act as a system of urgent peer review. The second list could be moderated, but semi-public, available to the profession, the media, and other interested parties.

Finding Electronic Journals Online

The Directory of Electronic Journals and Newsletters from the Association of Research Libraries can be found via Gopher at arl.cni.org/11/scomm/edir/. It's a good source of information for quality academic resources on the Internet. For information e-mail osap@cni.org.

There's also the E-Zine-List by John Labovitz:

FTP: `etext.archive.umich.edu: pub/Zines/e-zine-list`
Gopher: `etext.archive.umich.edu:Zines/e-zine-list`
WWW: `http//www.ora.com:8080/johnl/e-zine-list/`

To get a list of Electronic Journals by e-mail, send a message to:

`listserv@acadvml.uotttawa.ca`

with "get ejournl1directry" and "get ejournl 2directry."

There are also Web pages dedicated to finding academic and other online journals and magazines. At Carnegie-Mellon University is the Online Journal page, found at:

`http://www.cs.cmu.edu/Web/Library/journals.html`

It concentrates on journals for computer scientists. Included are pointers to online repositories (for journals of all types), journal indexes, and a few direct pointers to journal archives themselves. Another Online Journal Web page:

`http://www.physics.iastate.edu/outsidelinks/journals.html`

has a list of selected journals and audio services, concentrating on physics, science, and the Internet. A third Web page:

`http://www.scs.unr.edu/homepage/kristina/journals.html`

lists electronic journals and scholarly conferences in linguistics, communication, computers, and related topics.

The Business of the Internet

The greatest change on the Internet will be the move from a subsidized academic and government communications system to a commercial system. So far, no one really knows how this will affect the future of the Internet. Since its raw beginning in 1969, the Net has evolved into a community of virtual communities. Many Internet users are afraid that business will sabotage the Net community. Business, especially in the 1980s and 1990s, has often found economic and ideological reasons to ignore the needs of communities in the real world. Bean-counting executives, MBAs, lawyers, and accountants with little understanding of the creative process have often damaged the television, motion picture, radio, and recording industries. Some users believe that the consolidation of the computer industry in the face of competition from Microsoft and takeover fever has decreased customer service and response. There are complaints that buggy software is released far too early in the development process.

The question really is, can the often anarchic Internet be forced to conform to someone's spreadsheet? On the other hand, business involvement has improved the Internet in many ways. It has helped improve the reliability and speed of data transmission. Hundreds of small Internet Service Providers have sprung up in the past few years, bringing easy access to hundreds of thousands of users. Dynamic new software companies have created useful tools like Netscape and Agent/Free Agent.

Business is getting involved in the Net for research as well as to provide information. In June of 1995, the Yankee Group (international consultants) reported that business users now represent 48 percent of the Internet. Of 200 companies surveyed by the Yankee Group, 21 percent of employees with desktop computers had Net connections. The main uses are electronic mail, corporate image building on the World Wide Web, research and trading advice, and information among professionals in the same fields.

The two competing forces of the Net—anarchy and business—will collide in the next few years. The small Information Service Providers are fearful of Microsoft and its plans for the Microsoft Network. There are proposals that people pay not by the time they spend online but by the byte. This could decrease the traffic (including congestion) on the Net and the spontaneity that makes it so attractive to people. A similar proposal is usage-based pricing, where low priority ASCII traffic (most e-mail) would cost less than higher priority business traffic sending binary files over the Net.

The trouble with adding research charges to the Internet is that the Net has, so far, found ways around challenges to its culture. Attempts to charge, for example, for a World Wide Web search engine, are already increasing the number of competing no-cost search engines. However, search engines and other World Wide Web pages are beginning to carry advertising as a way around having to charge users.

Gopher and the World Wide Web are both relatively young. Timothy Berners-Lee conceived the Web during the 1980s, began developing it in 1989 and put in a formal proposal for funding in October, 1990. The Web was first installed at CERN, the European Laboratory for Particle Physics in 1991. Two years later, in 1993, the first graphical Web browser was developed at the U.S.

National Center for Supercomputing Applications. Netscape first became available in the fall of 1994; its first full release came in the spring of 1995. Netscape made exploring the World Wide Web easy. With easier access, more Web pages were created, which drew more new users of Netscape, more Web pages, and so on.

The Net is at the same stage now as the airplane—and air travel—was in the years after the Wright Brothers, with flimsy aircraft making their first exploration of the air. Now we have 747s, 767s, and 777s. Air travel is today's common means of transportation. Air travel and the development of the airplane are, even today, a partnership between government and private industry. The Net is similar and, perhaps, the rumors of the total privatization of the Internet are greatly exaggerated. Ten years from now, 20 years from now, the Net will be as different from today as today's Net is from the early ARPANET.

It's likely that today's research bottlenecks will be solved, that there will be new and better ways of verifying information. There will be more moderated mailing lists. New and better mail clients will use innovative ways to filter, sort and store e-mail and other Internet data. Software agents are beginning to come online as research robots, servants of the Net researcher.

Software Agents

Until now serendipity has been a key factor in research. But what if software could duplicate serendipity? A solution for this is the software agent, also called the interface agent or intelligent assistant. Agents have been described as robots and sometimes even as benign viruses. Mobile agents, according to their designers, have the potential to travel the Net, doing the work programmed by their human manager, whether that's researching the human genome or making an airline reservation.

The idea of the software agent is not new. It was first proposed in the 1950s by John McCarthy and Oliver Selfridge, two early experts in artificial intelligence. Now dozens of companies and institutions are working to develop software agents. Among the leaders are MIT's Media Lab and the Silicon valley company General Magic, which is pioneering the use of "intelligent assistants" with AT&T.

To use such agents, a user would type a series of commands and dispatch them onto the Internet (see Figure 15-1). The agent would seek out the information the user wants and then work with software on the host computer. Another idea is that an agent would act as a superfilter for your e-mail and perhaps Usenet groups, searching incoming data and sorting it into priorities.

General Magic has a system it calls Telescript, described in *Science* in August, 1994, and in its Web pages at http://www.genmagic.com. General Magic and

Figure 15-1.
AT&T's Intelligent
Assistants Web Page

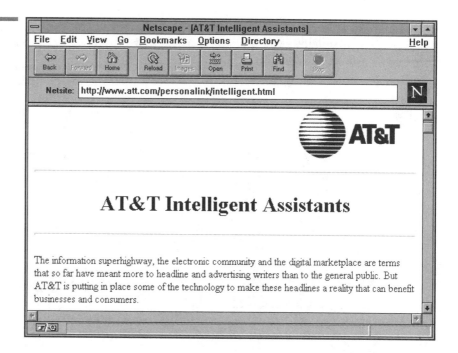

AT&T say "assistants are software programs attached to electronic messages that users will send into AT&T PersonaLink Service's enhanced network service. They can search out and obtain information, program the network to respond to a subscriber's individual wants and needs, filter out some messages and forward others, [and] help arrange transactions."

The developers say intelligent assistants will perform many of the "time-consuming tasks that have discouraged more consumers from taking advantage of online services and the emerging electronic marketplace."

Users can send "smart messages," using the intelligent assistant that works with a network that would "otherwise . . . require timely human intervention and constant attention." Examples used by AT&T include automatically forwarding an e-mail message if it is not picked up by a certain time, instructing electronic mailboxes to forward urgent messages to a personal digital assistant, or forwarding long messages to an off-site fax machine.

At MIT, researchers believe that the agents can go further, learning from users. If, for example, you usually read things in a certain order, no matter how you design the original filter, the program could, in theory, learn from your daily activity and adjust your incoming data. MIT calls this "improving the precision rate" for the software agent. As it learns, the agent would download more relevant articles and discard ones the user regards as irrelevant.

MIT also says it wants agents to have a "recall rate," a method of improving accuracy of new material the agent finds by comparing it with the choices its user makes.

MIT believes that the agent can learn and even evolve from user feedback. "Occasionally new agents are created using a genetic algorithm, which allows the set of agents to broaden the personalized news selection and discover new areas the user might be interested in."

The researchers say that, so far, the real-world demands of the algorithms needed to make agents properly are slowing the development of the agents, so don't expect to turn on your Net 'bot, go to the beach, surf the ocean, and find an answer waiting for you when you get home . . . at least for the next couple of years. You're still going to need the skills in this book to find what you want.

The research we do on the Net was once the stuff of science fiction; now it is part of our working day. However, you have to judge and evaluate the material you find on the Internet just as with every other research source. The library is still there, and you will still need to use it, but you will probably log in to that library's online catalog before leaving home. So pick your research goal, find, download, and learn the correct tools, and embark on your electronic journey into the Web.

Index

A

Access
    checklist, 39–42
    computer research, 180, 181
    direct Internet, 27–31
    Holocaust Research Institute, 172–175
    indirect Internet, 28–31, 142–148
    in-house, 32, 33
    literature, 162–172
    medical information, 176, 177
    news, 66, 177, 178
    problems, 36–44
    restrictions, 42
    scientific information, 178–180
Addresses (*see* sites)
Agents, software, 374–376
Agriculture Canada site, 365
All-In-One, 346
America Online, 31
Archie, 4, 41, 57, 86–90
ARL, 249
ASCII, 100, 101, 107, 108
    Gophers, 334
Assistants, software, 374–376
Association of Research Libraries, 259

Asynchronous communications, 294
Australia, National Library, 250, 251

B

Backup, 8, 38, 343
Bailer, 256
Belgian Academic Network, 255, 256
Belnet, 255, 256
Binary, 107, 108, 135
BITFTP, 144
Bitnet, 2
Bookmarks, 321–323, 343
Boolean
    operators, 61
    searches, 61–63
Britain, government sites, 368
British Library, 248–250
Browsers, Web, 84–86, 232–235, 343

C

Call waiting, 37
Canada
    Communication Group, site, 364, 365

National Library, 246–248, 364
Canadian
    Auditor General's Report, site, 365
    Embassy in the U.S., site, 367
    federal government sites, 363–367
    Foreign Affairs, site, 367
    Heritage Information Network, site, 366
    Information Highway Advisory Council, site, 366
    National Archives Catalogue of Computer
        Files, site, 365
    sites, 361–367
Carr-1, 101
CDV, 213
Cello, 84–86, 233, 234
Censorship, 284–286, 289
CERN What's New, 102
Chameleon, 14, 74, 62, 63, 75, 232
Changing directories, 127
    with FTP command line, 116–122
Checklist, access, 39–42
CIGA Indiana University, FTP sites, 136, 137
Citations, 272
Citizenship, Internet, 196–199
Clearinghouse, Michigan, 238–244, 353, 354
Clients
    definition, 26, 27
    e-mail, 74–76
    instructions, UNIX Gopher, 333–339
    software, Gopher, 318–324
Cocooning, 305, 306
Columbia University, Project Bartleby, 256, 257
Comma-separated outlines, 212–216
Command lines, FTP, 110–122
Commands, FTP, 124, 125
Commercial online services, 31, 32
Communication
    skills, 191, 192, 199–201
    lines, 8, 9
Communications software, 10, 11
Compression FAQ, 100, 109, 110
CompuServe, 31
Computer, 6, 7
    research, 180, 181
Concept analysis, 64
Consumer Price Index (Canada), site, 366
Convenience, 42
Copyright law, 266–273
    plagiarism, 272, 273
    quoting, 271, 272

    reference sites, 289
    reproduction, 271, 272
    sharing, 270, 271
Costs, checklist, 41
Crosstalk, 10
CRTC Information Highway Report, site, 366
CSV, 213
CUSI, 346

D
Data
    evaluating, 66–72
    capable circuit, 9
Databank, 31, 32
    choosing, 50–53
    creating, 56
Defamation, 276, 277
Delphi, 31, 312, 313
Direct access, 27–31
Directories, changing, 116–122, 127,
Disclaimers, 282
Dominion Astrophysical Observatory, site, 365
DOS, FTP sites, 135

E
E-mail, 3, 40, 73–77
    academic, 312, 313
    addressing, 77
    asking questions, 297, 298, 308, 309
    benefits, 293, 295, 304–306, 311
    clarity, 191, 192, 199–201
    filters, 218, 219
    folders, 216–218
    follow-up, 310, 311
    grammar, 192, 200
    interview, 293–313
    mailing lists, 101, 102
    networking, 299–304
    pre-interview, 306, 307
    preparation, 295–298
    privacy rights, 187, 188
    questionnaire, 308–310
    rules and regulations, 188–207
    software clients, 74–76
    tips, 202–204
Edupage, 101
EINet Galaxy, 102
Electronic Information Service, 257
Elm, 74, 75

Emoticons, 190
English literature, FTP sites, 130, 131
Environment Canada Green Lane, site, 366, 367
Ethernet, 27
Ethics (*see* Netiquette)
Etiquette (*see* netiquette)
Eudora, 12, 15, 74, 76, 232
Eudora Pro, 76
European Union, site, 367
Evaluating data, 66–72
Expanding, 89

F

Failed sites, FTP, 105, 106
Fair dealing, 269, 270
Fair use, 269, 270
Falsifying, identity, 282–284
FAQ, definition, 100
Fedworld Information Network, site, 358, 359
File Transfer Protocol (*see* FTP)
Filenames, 150–152
Files
    renaming with FTP command line, 114, 115
    retrieving with FTP command line, 112–122
    transfer and storage, 40
Filters, e-mail, 218, 219
Finger, 14, 15
Flame wars, 193
Folders, e-mail, 216–218
Forté Free Agent, 83
Free Agent, 230–232
Freeware, 15, 16
French Embassy, Washington, D.C., site, 368
FTP, 86, 87
    basics, 103–110
    command lines, 110–122
    commands, 124, 125
    compression and decoding software, 108–110
    definition, 4
    failed sites, 105, 106
    FAQ, 100
    passwords, 105–107, 109
    sites, 130–142
    using, 99–155
FTPMail, 142–144

G

GAO site, 360
Garbo Software Mirrors, FTP sites, 137, 138
Gateway, 2
GATT, site, 367
GEnie, 31
Gigabyte, definition, 7
GNN Whole Internet Catalog, 102
Gopher, 4, 41, 83, 84, 315–340
    basics, 316–318
    client software, 318–324
    Jewels, 101
    Jughead searches, 333
    learning about, 339, 340
    servers, 325–329
    sites, 4, 102, 103
    UNIX, client instructions, 333–339
    Veronica searches, 329–333
Gopherspace, 316
GovAccess Mailing List site, 360
Government sites, 357–368
Government Accounting Office, site, 360
Graphical user interface (*see* GUI)
GUI, definition of, 3
Gutenberg, Project, 162–172
    locating files, 169–172
    mirror sites, 171, 172

H

Hard drive, organization, 220
Hardware, 5–9
    checklist, 39, 40
    Internet, 33–35
    problems, 37, 38
Harvest Broker, 349
HeadsUp, 93–95
Health care information, FTP sites, 131, 132
Holocaust Research Institute, 172–175
Hot keys, WSGopher, 320
House of Representatives, sites, 357
HTML, 342
HTMLcon, 234, 235
Hypertext, 4, 56, 57
Hytelnet, 90–92

I

IAPs, 25

Identity, falsifying, 282–284
In-house, access, 32, 33
Indirect Internet access, 27–31, 142–148
Info-Mac, FTP sites, 140, 141
Infoban Litter Crew, 206
InfoMagnet, 79
Information, saving, 235, 236
InfoSurf Library Gopher, 257
Integrated Service Digital Network (*see* ISDN)
International
      business, FTP sites, 132, 133
      governmental sites, 367, 368
Internet
      access problems, 36–44, 369–371
      beginnings, 157–162
      censorship, 284–286
      charges, 372–374
      citizenship, 196–199
      copyright law, 266–273
      definition, 1–3
      evaluating, 95–97
      FTP help file, 153–155
      hardware, 33–35
      information and tools, FTP sites, 133, 134
      legal issues, 261–291
            disclaimers, 282
            future of the law, 287, 288
            libel cases, 277–281
            jurisdiction, 263–277
            reference sites, 289–291
            venue, 281, 282
      libraries, 237–260
      overview, 157–183, 369–376
      phobia, conquering, 16–24
      research tools, 3, 4, 73–97
      resources, 42–44
      rules (*see* netiquette)
      service providers, 25–44
      software, 33–35
Internet Access Providers, 25–44
Internet Account Providers, 25–44
Internet in a Box, 14
Internet Information and Standards, FTP sites, 138
Internet Messenger, 12, 13
Internet Relay Chat, 41, 93
Internet Resource Directory, 239
Interview, e-mail, 293–313
IRC, 4, 93

ISDN, 9
ISPs, 25–44
      local dial-up, 34
      overloads, 36
      pricing, 32
      reliability, 39
Italy, government site, 368

J

Japan, government site, 368
Journals, online, 372
Jughead, 4, 57, 83, 84, 316, 333
JumpStation II, 57, 349, 350

K

Keystroke commands, UNIX Gopher, 334–336
Keyword, 57
Keyword-search software, 56

L

Labeling, using outlines, 215, 216
LANs, 27, 34, 35
Law libraries, 258
Legal issues, 204–207, 261–291
      general resource sites, 290, 292
      jurisdiction, 263–277
LIBCAT, 251, 252
Libel
      cases, 277–281
      reference site, 289
Libraries, 237–260
      law, 258
      linking to, 251–260
      mailing lists, 259, 260
      medical, 258, 259
      miscellaneous, 252–257
      national, 244–251
      research organizations, 259
      University of Michigan, 238–244
Library of Congress (*see* U.S. Library of Congress)
Line-end codes, UNIX Gopher, 336
Links, dead, 343, 344
Listproc, 77
LISTSERV, 2, 77–79
      database search, 80, 81
Literature, accessing, 162–172

Local Area Network (*see* LAN)
Login, remote, 90
LWGate, 80
Lycos, 350, 351
    search, 57–61
Lynx, 84, 85

M

Macintosh, FTP sites, 134, 140–142
MacSOUP, 12, 221
Mailing lists, 77–81
    e-mail, 101, 102
    finding, 78–80
    library, 259, 260
    rules, 193, 194
    software instructions, 77, 78
    subscriber control, 76, 77
Majordomo, 77, 78
Malaysia, government site, 368
Massachusetts Institute of Technology (*see* MIT)
Medical
    information, accessing, 176, 177
    libraries, 258, 259
Metamail, 222, 224
Metronet, 251, 252
Michigan Clearinghouse, 238–244, 353, 354
Michigan, University of, library, 238–244
MIME, 74
Mirror, FTP sites, 135–142
MIT, Usenet FAQs, FTP sites, 138, 139, 148–150
Modems, 7, 8
    checklist, 40
    speed, 8
    with WWW, 35
Moral issues, 207, 273, 274
MOREnet, 92
Mosaic, 4, 15, 56, 86, 87
Mouse, in UNIX shell, 28, 29
Multipurpose Internet Mail Extensions (*see* MIME)

N

National libraries, 244–251
National Library of Australia, 250, 251
National Library of Canada, 246–248, 364
NCSA What's New, 103
Neighboring rights, 275

Net-Happenings, 101
Net-Train, 101
Netcom, 31
Netiquette, 72, 185–207
    resources, 194–196
NetNews Filter Service, 57, 83
Netscape, 4, 15, 233
Netscape Navigator, 83, 86, 88
Netscape What's New, 103
Network Terminator box (*see* NTI)
Networking, with e-mail, 299–304
Newbies, 197, 198, 205, 206
Newlist, 102
NewNir, 102
News
    accessing, 177, 178
    readers, 230–232
    scanning services, 93–97
Newsgroups
    access to, 66
    Usenet, 81–83
Newshound, 93, 94
NEWSLTR Digest, 102
Newsreading software, 83
Newt TCP/IP stack, 14
NIKOS, 350, 351
North Carolina State University, library access, 252, 253
NTI, 9
Nuntius, 83

O

Offline
    benefits of, 65, 66
    readers, 12, 13, 220–235
Online
    citations, 272
    commercial services, 31, 322
    journals, 372
Online Public Access Catalogs (*see* OPAC)
OPAC, 237
Open Systems Interconnection (*see* OSI)
Operating systems, 14
Organization skills, 209–236
OSI, 2
Ottawa, Ontario, site, 367
Outlines, 210–219
    comma-separated, 212–216

labeling, 215, 216
Overloads, ISP, 36

P

Packets, 2
PAML, 78
Patent law, 275, 276
PCOutline, 211
Pegasus, 75
Peripatetic Eclectic Gopher, 103
Phobia, Internet, conquering, 16–24
PINE, 74, 75
Ping, 14, 15
PKUnzip, 100
PKZIP, 109, 110
Plagiarism, 272, 273
Pmail, 75
Point to Point Protocol (*see* PPP)
POTS, 8, 9
PPP, 3
Preparation for research, 45–72
Privacy rights, e-mail, 187, 188
Problems, access, 36–44
Procomm, 10
Prodigy, 31
ProfNet, 303, 304
Project Bartleby, 256, 257
Project Gutenberg, 162–172
    locating files, 169–172
    mirror sites, 171, 172
Protocol, 2, 3
    transfer, 10, 11
Providers, service, 25–44
Proximity search, 61, 62
Public data networks, 32
Public Works Canada, site, 366
Purdue University, site, 360

Q

Quebec, Quebec, site, 367
Quoting, 271, 272
QWK SOUP, 12, 13, 221–235

R

Readers
    news, 230–232

offline, 12, 13, 220–235
Relevance feedback, 57
Remote login, 90
Renaming, files with FTP command line, 114, 115
Reproduction, copyright law, 271, 272
Research
    advantages with the Net, 47, 55–68
    database choice, 50–53
    developing technical skills, 53–55
    narrowing your topic, 53–55
    pre-Net history, 45–47
    preparation, 45–72
    problems on the Net, 47, 48
    tools, 73–97
Research Libraries Group, Inc., 259
Resource conservation, 201–204
Retrieving, files with FTP command line, 112–122
Rights
    moral, 273, 274
    neighboring, 275
RLG, 259
Robot addresses, 202
Root directory, 56
RTFM, 138, 148
Rural Internet access, 31, 32
Rutgers University, 258

S

Saving, information, 235, 236
Savvy Search, 347, 348
Scientific information, accessing, 178–180
Scott Yanoff's Internet Services List, 92, 355, 356
Scrolling, how to stop, 122
Search engines, 56–63
Searches
    Jughead, 333
    one-word, 64, 65
    Veronica, 329–333
    WWW, 344–356
Security, 42
Senate, site, 358
Serial Line Internet Protocol (*see* SLIP)
Servers
    definition, 26, 27
    Gopher, 325–329
    UNIX Gopher, 337, 338

Service
    checklist, 41
    providers, 25–44
Shareware, 15, 16
Sharing, copyright law, 270, 271
Shell, 3
SimTel, 122–124
    FTP sites, 139, 140
Sites
    FTP, 130–142
    Gopher, 316–340
    government, 357–368
    robot, 202
    WWW, 341–356
SLIP, 3
SLIP/PPP, 27, 30, 35, 230–232
Software, 5, 9–16
    agents, 374–376
    checklist, 39, 40
    communications, 10, 11
    connecting, 9–12
    FTP compression and decoding, 108–110
    instructions, mailing lists, 77, 78
    Internet, 33–35
    newsreading, 83
    suites, 14
    TCP/IP-based, 14–16
SQL, 63
Stanford University, Info-Mac, FTP sites, 140, 141
Structured query language, 63
Submit It!, 345
Subscriber control, 76, 77
SuperTCP Windows, 14
Support, checklist, 41
Supreme Court of Canada, site, 366
Surf, definition, 4
Systems
    operating, 14
    sample, 5, 6

T

TA, 9
TCP/IP, 2, 27, 28, 35
    software, 14–16
Telephone lines, 8, 9
    problems, 36, 37
Telnet, 4, 27, 40, 90–93

Terminal Adapter (*see* TA)
Terminal emulation, 10
Tilde, 223, 224
Tile, 80
Toolbar buttons, WSGopher, 319–321
Tools, Internet, 3, 4
Trade secrets, 276
Transmission Control Protocol/Internet Protocol
    (*see* TCP/IP)
Tree structure, 56, 57, 65
TRICKLE, 144–148
Trumpet, 83
Trumpet WinSock, 16, 100

U

UART, 6, 7
Uninterruptable Power Supply (*see* UPS)
United Nations, site, 368
Universal Asynchronous Receiver/Transmitter
    (*see* UART)
University of California, Irvine, 325
University of California, Santa Barbara, 257
University of Michigan
    Michigan Clearinghouse, 353, 354
    Macintosh FTP sites, 141, 142
University of North Carolina, Electronic
    Information Service, 257
University of Saskatchewan, site, 364
University of Washington, library access, 252, 253
UNIX
    definition, 2, 3
    Gopher
        client instructions, 333–339
        keystroke commands, 334–336
        line-end codes, 336
        servers, 337, 338
    shell accounts, 28, 19
UPS, 8
U.S. federal government sites, 357–361
U.S. Library of Congress, 244, 245, 358
U.S. state government sites, 361, 362
Usenet, 2, 41
    hierarchies, 82
    newsgroups, 3, 4, 81–83
Usenet FAQs, MIT, FTP sites, 138, 139, 148–150
UUCP, 2
UUDECODE, 75

UUENCODE, 75, 110

V

Vancouver, B.C., site, 367
Venue issues, 281, 282
Veronica, 57, 83, 84, 316
    definition, 4
    restrictions, 62, 63, 65
    searches, 329–333
Victoria, B.C., site, 367
Vietnam, government site, 368
Virtual Reference Desk, 325
VT100, 10
VT102, 10

W

WAIS, 4, 41, 57
Washington & Lee sites, 103
Web browsers, 4, 232–235, 343
WebCrawler, 352
WebExplorer, 14
WebSurfer, 14
Whitehouse, site, 358, 359
Whois, 14, 15
Wide-Area Information System (*see* WAIS)
Win Yarn, 12
WINcode, 100, 110
Wincomm PRO, 10
Windows 95, 35
    FTP sites, 135
Windows Clipboard, 323, 324
WinSock, 100
WinYarn, 222, 228, 229
Wizard, 347, 348
World Wide Web (*see* WWW)

World Wide Web Worm, 352, 353
WSArchie, 88–90
WS_FTP, 100, 125–129
WSGopher, 318–324
    bookmarks, 321–323
    hot keys, 320
    saving and printing files, 324
    toolbar buttons, 319–321
Windows Clipboard, 323, 324
WWW, 4, 41, 341–356
    browsers, 84–86
    dead links, 343, 344
    searching indexes, 344–353
    sites, 102, 103
    subject search engines, 353–356
WWW-Announce, 102
WWW Virtual Library, 354, 355

X

Xmodem, 10

Y

Yahoo, 354–356
Yahoo–What's New, 103
Yale University, library access, 254, 255
YaleInfo, 254, 255
Yanoff's Special Internet Connections, 355, 356
Yarn, 12, 222–229
Yes, 222, 227–229
Ymodem, 10

Z

Zmodem, 10, 11, 29